*BLACK   SEA*

**PONTUS**

**KINGDOM
OF
ARMENIA**

*Halys R.*   Amaseia   Neocaesarea   *Lycus R.*

Ibora

*Iris R.*

ncyra   Sebasteia

**ARMENIA**

*Vyssa*

**APPADOCIA**   Caesarea

Nazianzus   *MTNS.*

Sasima

Samosata

Tyana

**PERSIAN**

Podandus

*TAURUS*   **CILICIA**

Tarsus

**EMPIRE**

Seleucia   Antioch

**SYRIA**

*Euphrates R.*

Jerusalem

**PALESTINE**

*Kingdom of Snow*

# *Kingdom of Snow*

## Roman Rule and Greek Culture in Cappadocia

Raymond Van Dam

**PENN**

University of Pennsylvania Press
Philadelphia

10   9   8   7   6   5   4   3   2   1

*Published by*
*University of Pennsylvania Press*
*Philadelphia, Pennsylvania 19104-4011*

*Library of Congress Cataloging-in-Publication Data*

Van Dam, Raymond.
   Kingdom of snow : Roman rule and Greek culture in Cappadocia /
Raymond Van Dam.
    p. cm.
   ISBN 0-8122-3681-5 (alk. paper)
   Includes bibliographical references (p.  ) and index.
    1. Rome—Provinces—Turkey—Cappadocia—History.   2. Cappadocia (Turkey)—
History.   I. Title.
DS156.C3 V36 2002
939'.35—dc21                                                    2002020334

Endpapers: Asia Minor and the Eastern Mediterranean in the fourth century.

*For Jody*

*"I believe in the love that you gave me"*
*—Bruce Springsteen,* Badlands

# Contents

# Acknowledgments

Although Julian became emperor in Gaul, he always left his heart in the Greek East. On his final trip to the eastern frontier he passed through Cappadocia, where he met Basil and Gregory of Nazianzus and may have invited them to join his enterprise.

The trajectory of my academic research has followed a similar journey from late antique Gaul to late Roman Cappadocia. As companions on this intellectual odyssey the Cappadocian Fathers have patiently traveled with me to various academic institutions. They now join me in thanking again for their support: King's College and Churchill College in Cambridge University, Stanford University, Dumbarton Oaks Center for Byzantine Studies, the University of Texas, the National Humanities Center, and the University of Michigan. At the University of Michigan I am especially grateful to my own department of history, which honored me with selection to the Hudson Research Professorship for a year, and to the Alumni Association, which generously invited me to escort some of its trips to Greece and Turkey. For assistance with the publication of this trilogy of books about Cappadocia I am most grateful to Eric Halpern, Alison Anderson, and the other editors at the University of Pennsylvania Press, and to Kate Toll at the University of California Press.

Years after becoming emperor, Julian cherished memories of his student days and revered his former teachers, in particular those at Athens. Some of the chapters in this book discuss education and classical culture. Thinking about those chapters has made me appreciate all the more my teachers at Cambridge, especially Dick Whittaker, and the extraordinary community of graduate students who gathered from around the world. Cambridge was our Athens. Back then we were all blessed to share in the world of Moses Finley.

# Introduction

The core of the Roman empire was the warm, sunny Mediterranean. Roman rule was most effective in the surrounding cities and lowlands, and in Asia Minor emperors had supported the flourishing of Greek culture especially in coastal regions. Then there was the high plateau of Cappadocia. Central Asia Minor was "the kingdom of snow." Cappadocia in particular and its residents had an unsavory reputation. "Cappadocians are always worthless." The region of Cilicia, on the south coast of Asia Minor, was noted as a lair for bandits, and the island of Crete as a haven for pirates. Cappadocia now joined them in heading the list of "the three most despicable [regions beginning with the letter] kappa." Snooty connoisseurs dismissed Kappa-dokia as a cultural backwater. Cappadocians were "deceitful, impudent, headstrong, craven, jeering, selfish, treacherous, brutish, and scornful." A boorish parvenu like Trimalchio readily recognized a kindred spirit in a slave who had mangled his recitation of epic verse: "I know he is a Cappadocian!" Modern scholars sometimes share this ancient castigation. "That region ... bore a sad name for bleak and rural retardation." Lawless, uncouth, cold, Cappadocia was a distinctly odd region to have become part of a Mediterranean empire.[1]

During the fourth century, however, Cappadocia became vital to imperial interests in the East. Location was the key. Eastern emperors faced pressure on two frontiers, one in the Balkans, where the Goths and other barbarians were a nuisance, the other in the Near East, where the revived Persian empire of the Sasanids was pushing its aggressive claims to wider hegemony. The military conflict with the Persian empire focused on the middle and upper Euphrates River and the kingdom of Armenia, and in addition to ready access Cappadocia contributed horses, armor, clothing, and other supplies from its extensive imperial estates and factories. Cappadocia was also a stopover on the roads between Constantinople, the new capital in Thrace, and Antioch, a convenient staging point in Syria for military campaigns into the Persian empire. As they trekked back and forth across the desolate highlands of central Anatolia, Roman emperors repeatedly visited Cappadocia.

Shortly after becoming sole emperor in 324 Constantine traveled to Antioch and back. These hasty journeys marked his only visits as emperor to central and eastern Asia Minor. During the final years of his reign he resided primarily at his new capital of Constantinople. After Constantine's death his son Constantius assumed responsibility for the eastern empire. Although occasionally he traveled through eastern and central Asia Minor to visit Constantinople, his primary residence was Antioch. For a few years his cousin Gallus replaced him as a junior emperor at Antioch. Constantius finally returned to Cappadocia and eastern Asia Minor only a year before his death. His cousin Julian succeeded him as sole emperor at Constantinople, and during his short reign he passed through Cappadocia on his way to Antioch. After Julian's death in a battle against the Persians, the new emperor Jovian intended to return as quickly as possible to Constantinople. He died en route in Galatia. Valens then became the new emperor for the East. His first trip through Asia Minor ended in Cappadocia, when he heard about the usurpation of Procopius at Constantinople. During the early 370s Valens visited Cappadocia several more times. Antioch became his primary residence, until he returned to the capital through Asia Minor for the last time in 378. Theodosius, his successor, was emperor for the East largely in absentia, because during his entire reign the farthest east he ever traveled was to a town hardly more than a hundred miles beyond Constantinople on the southwestern coast of the Black Sea. Theodosius' failure to visit the eastern provinces, even the nearby regions in Asia Minor, became the new norm. From now on the eastern emperors stayed at Constantinople.

During their journeys through central and eastern Asia Minor these emperors met churchmen. Constantine's patronage for Christianity had finally ended the persecutions of previous emperors, and clerics in particular now benefited. Gregory the Elder, the father of Gregory of Nazianzus, certainly sensed the future. Once Constantine demonstrated his support, Gregory the Elder quickly converted to Christianity and soon became bishop of his hometown of Nazianzus. During his lengthy episcopal tenure he was ensnared in the theological controversies provoked by Constantius, and he confronted Julian directly. Even though he was about the same age as Constantine, he outlived the entire Constantinian dynasty and died during the reign of Valens.

The next generation of Cappadocian churchmen was even more prominent. As a junior cleric Basil attended a council at Constantinople in 360 convened by Constantius. As a priest Gregory of Nazianzus supported his father in defying Julian in Cappadocia. During his own priesthood and episcopacy Basil confronted Valens and his powerful prefect Modestus, and a vicar sent Gregory of Nyssa into exile from his episcopal see. Both Gregory of Nazianzus and Gregory of Nyssa attended the ecumenical council at Constantinople in 381 convened by Theodosius, and Gregory of Nazianzus served briefly as bishop of the eastern capital. The Cappadocian Fathers defined the contours of their service as priests and bishops in part through their interactions with a pagan emperor, heterodox emperors, and an orthodox emperor.

*    *    *

Roman rule in Asia Minor has long been a rewarding area for inspired scholarship, and the best historians of Roman Asia Minor have been some of the best Roman and early Byzantine historians of the past century, including W. M. Ramsay, Louis Robert, T. R. S. Broughton, A. H. M. Jones, David Magie, Ronald Syme, Gilbert Dagron, and now Clive Foss and Stephen Mitchell. In these modern studies, just as in the political geography of the ancient world, Cappadocia has nevertheless remained somewhat marginal. For other regions of Roman Asia Minor modern scholars have more inscriptions to study, better editions of those inscriptions, and more extensive archaeological investigations and field surveys. Under the early empire the literary texts likewise typically described society in cities in western and southern Asia Minor that could claim a much longer association with Greek culture.

For the fourth century, however, Cappadocia is the best documented region in Asia Minor. Emperors and imperial magistrates may have finally acknowledged the military and political importance of the region, but it is the writings of the three Cappadocian Fathers that have ensured its lasting historical significance. Their writings were impressively comprehensive and included many sermons, treatises, letters, and poems. In addition, their contemporaries often mentioned Cappadocia and Cappadocians. Some were other natives of Cappadocia, such as Amphilochius, bishop of Iconium, Eunomius, sometime bishop of Cyzicus, and the historian Philostorgius. Others were prominent intellectuals elsewhere, including the rhetorician Himerius, who taught at Athens, the rhetorician Libanius, who taught at Antioch, the philosopher Themistius, who was an orator and magistrate at Constantinople, the historian Ammianus, who passed through Asia Minor during his journeys between the eastern and western frontiers, and the emperor Julian, who had actually grown up in Cappadocia.[2] This extensive documentation provides a unique opportunity to investigate many themes and topics in a specific region during a short time period. The result is a trilogy of books: *Families and Friends*, about the family relationships and friendships of the Cappadocian Fathers; *Becoming Christian*, about the impact of Christianity on Cappadocian society; and this one about Roman rule and Greek culture.

The format of each book in this trilogy is a series of interlocking chapters that in turn provide overlapping interpretations of various topics and issues. *Kingdom of Snow: Roman Rule and Greek Culture in Cappadocia* builds on modern research about the impact of Roman rule and Greek culture in Asia Minor by investigating Cappadocia in late antiquity. These investigations attempt to combine close readings of the texts with a sense of the larger historical and cultural rhythms of the region. They also hope to demonstrate the advantageous intersection of ecclesiastical texts with social and political history. Patristics scholars need to demonstrate a greater awareness of the realities of Greek and Roman society, and social and cultural historians need to acquire a deeper familiarity with the potentialities of theological and ecclesiastical texts.

The first section of chapters discusses local notables within Cappadocia and their interactions both with each other and with outside rulers. Cappadocia was rarely an independent region. Long ago the old Persian empire of the Achaemenids had expanded to include central and eastern Asia Minor, then neighboring Hellenistic monarchs had constantly meddled in the region, and finally the Roman empire and its successor Byzantine empire had imposed centuries of sovereignty. Yet despite the intrusion of these outside powers, local aristocrats were remarkably successful at maintaining their standing and prestige. Deference could be more subversive than open resistance. In the later Roman empire Cappadocian notables had enhanced opportunities to serve as bishops and clerics or to hold magistracies in the Roman imperial administration. Gregory of Nazianzus' brother held imperial offices, while the Cappadocian Fathers became bishops. Becoming a bishop was both advantageous and humbling. Bishops were prominent during the fourth century, but also often still quite weak. They had so few tangible resources and so many powerful competitors. In order to vie with their powerful peers, including emperors, imperial administrators, local landowners, municipal magistrates, and rival bishops and clerics, bishops like the Cappadocian Fathers had to rely primarily upon their rhetorical and political skills and drum up popular support. In the end, many provincial notables might well prefer autonomy over service as imperial magistrates, or even as bishops.

The second section of chapters examines the Cappadocian Fathers in their roles as patrons and brokers. As bishops they often negotiated with the provincial governors and tax assessors. Dealing with emperors was a bit more tricky, since one, Julian, was a pagan, and others, Constantius and Valens, supported heterodox forms of Christianity. In contrast, the emperor Theodosius supported orthodox Christianity. Yet when Gregory of Nazianzus served as bishop at Constantinople, he was still suspicious enough of Theodosius' use of coercion to enforce religious policies that he preferred to keep his distance. At a time when many eastern provincials were converging on the new capital and its opportunities for advancement, Gregory finally decided to go home to Cappadocia.

The final section of chapters investigates reactions to classical Greek culture in an increasingly Christian society. Basil, Gregory of Nazianzus, and the future emperor Julian had all studied classical literature in Cappadocia, and they had all been students at about the same time at Athens, still the shining beacon of the excellence of classical culture. But each imagined a different future for Greek culture. Basil thought it could serve as a preliminary step for biblical studies. Julian tried to prevent Christians from using it at all. Gregory of Nazianzus was so indignant at Julian's restrictions that he argued that it was possible to indulge a passion for classical culture while retaining a devotion to Christianity. By insisting upon the possibility of enjoying classical culture and Christianity simultaneously Gregory was contradicting not only Julian's opposition of the two. He was also disputing Basil's notion of a sequence, first one, then the other. This difference in Gregory's and Basil's reactions to the significance of classical culture was a preview of the fate of their own relationship. As students at Athens they had been intimate friends who had shared an appreciation of Greek culture. Once their ideas about culture diverged and they had to interact primarily as churchmen, their friendship was doomed.[3]

\*   \*   \*

Even though the Cappadocian Fathers and their distinguished contemporaries are the main actors, this book is primarily a study of a particular region in the eastern Roman empire at a particular time. The focus is on Cappadocia, not the Cappadocian Fathers. Regional studies reflect an awareness of the vast diversity and pluralism that survived in the Roman world even after centuries of imperial rule. Both geography and earlier historical developments had dictated the differing tempos and consequences of the imposition of Roman rule, the spread of Greek culture, and the expansion of Christianity. Throughout the eastern empire, Romanness, Greekness, and Christianity acquired distinctly regional characteristics. The documentation available in the writings of the Cappadocian Fathers and their peers now provides the opportunity to examine, for an extended but still compact period, the rhythms of Cappadocia and neighboring regions in central and eastern Asia Minor.

This book furthermore intends to insert Cappadocia and Cappadocian society into the mainstream of research on Roman history. Even if in antiquity rugged terrain conspired to marginalize the region by keeping it on the edges of imperial rule and the world of Greek culture, in modern historical studies Cappadocia can become central. Connections are critical. The impact of Roman rule and the influence of Greek culture in Cappadocia reflect similar developments in other provinces in the eastern empire. These developments were slower to appear in Cappadocia, but they were not necessarily structurally different. In an odd reversal of expectations, during the fourth century the hinterland of Cappadocia can serve as a proxy for other, more central regions that are not as well documented during late antiquity.

We also need to locate Roman Cappadocia in a much longer historical context that occasionally looks as far back as the Persian empire of the Achaemenids and as far forward as the Byzantine empire. In the long run, Roman rule, Greek culture, and even Christianity would represent only passing phases. In this longer context the history of Cappadocia can become a miniature version of the larger rhythms of the world of the eastern Mediterranean and the Near East during antiquity.

# Badlands

The highlands of ancient Cappadocia had consistently been a peripheral region, on the geographical edges of the lowlands and coastal regions where great civilizations and cultures flourished, on the political margins of the grand empires. Culturally and politically Cappadocia had the potential of linking up with either the Near East or the Mediterranean world. Under Persian rule it had been a satrapy in an empire whose royal capital was in Iran, over a thousand miles away. Under Roman rule it was a province in an empire whose imperial capital was in Italy, over a thousand miles away in the opposite direction. In late antiquity Cappadocia again became a contested region. In the mid-third century a Persian king boasted of the cities in Cappadocia he had recently captured; from the mid-seventh century Arab forces occasionally threatened the region. Even as a province in the Roman empire Cappadocia had remained a borderland.[1]

Although Cappadocia became a tributary in these large empires, it usually maintained a certain autonomy in the face of encroaching domination. No empire in the ancient world could overcome the obstacles of distance and rugged terrain in order to impose an effective central administration on highlands. Not only did provincial notables retain their local prominence, but royal or imperial magistrates had to rely upon their support to be successful. The relationships between magistrates representing outside powers and Cappadocian notables were consistently personal rather than merely bureaucratic, symmetrical rather than one-sided, and, above all, negotiated rather than simply imposed. Cappadocian notables became ritual friends with their overlords, they received gifts and honors, and they seized the opportunity to enhance their own prestige through service in the imperial administration or army. In return, they only had to appear to be properly deferential and indebted.[2]

Despite these limitations, the impact of Roman rule was evident everywhere. Because many old royal estates and temple estates became imperial estates, the emperors literally owned much of the region. In Cappadocia the Roman administration supervised vast ranches and huge factories that produced clothing and armor. The imposition of Roman rule encouraged important social and cultural transformations, such as the rise of cities, the spread of Greek culture, and the introduction of exotic cults like Christianity. Local notables benefited from all these changes by becoming municipal magistrates, students and teachers, and eventually Christian clerics. The blessings of Roman rule offered new opportunities for notables to consolidate and enhance their local influence. Roman rule in Cappadocia was hence simultaneously extensive and restricted.[3]

Late antique Cappadocia offers an opportunity to examine both the relationship between Roman rule and provincial interests and the interactions within the province among great landowners, municipal magistrates, and bishops. The chapters in this section discuss aspects of the impact of Roman rule within Cappadocia. Even though emperors and imperial magistrates imposed new demands and new policies, Cappadocian notables retained their influence and an eminent city like Caesarea kept its local prominence. Chapter 1 examines how local notables and cities manipulated their links with outside rulers in order to maintain or enhance their own standing and prestige. The better tactic for preserving local authority and minimizing the impact of imperial rule was cooperation, not resistance. Acquiescence paid dividends.

Bishops too might challenge the standing of these local notables. Although bishops were recruited from the same class of local landowners, as representatives of different interests they feuded over prestige and influence. Chapter 2 investigates Basil's attempts to influence Cappadocian notables. Local landowners had strengthened their influence precisely through sometimes rather callous manipulation of such necessary resources as clothing, water, and grain. Since as a churchman Basil could not threaten these landowners with the use of force, and since churches controlled few resources of their own, in times of scarcity he was reduced to confronting them only with his moral authority.

With the support of imperial patronage, churchmen were of course on the rise during the fourth century. Imperial policies also offered unprecedented opportunities to notables from eastern provinces. Emperors increased the size of the imperial administration, and they promoted the new senate at the new imperial capital of Constantinople. Chapter 3 examines the success of Cappadocians at obtaining imperial offices and acquiring senatorial rank. More Cappadocians than before were successful. Then again, so were other provincials, and in comparison with other eastern provinces Cappadocia still produced fewer imperial magistrates and senators.

In the end, Cappadocian aristocrats might prefer local primacy over participation in a large empire. Chapter 4 discusses the legends about one such autonomous grandee. Rather than accepting an appointment from the emperor, he preferred to remain an independent magnate. He was now the Cappadocian Highlander.

*Chapter 1*
# "The Viper Died":
## Local Notables and Imperial Rule

The inhabitants of Cappadocia had a long-standing reputation for their hardiness. "A venomous viper bit a Cappadocian," one epigram began; then ... "the viper died." Geography and climate played major roles in shaping and perpetuating this fanciful opinion. Situated in eastern Asia Minor, not only was the region of Cappadocia remote from the Mediterranean Sea, it was also up on a high plateau. To the south the Taurus Mountains blocked Cappadocia from the plains of Cilicia and the eastern Mediterranean, while to the west the dreary steppe stretched on endlessly. The natural geographical orientation of the plateau was instead toward the north and the east. To the north Cappadocia was linked to the regions of Pontus and eastern Galatia by the great rivers, the Iris, the Lycus, the Cappadox, and especially the Halys, that emptied into the Black Sea. To the east Cappadocia had close connections with the region of Armenia and extended to the upper Euphrates before the river flowed south and east into Mesopotamia. Cappadocia was hence an outpost of the huge Asian landmass, an "isthmus" linking it to the world of the Greeks centered on the Aegean Sea.[1]

Because of its geographical orientation and landlocked seclusion, however, Cappadocia had always remained somewhat marginal, a rickety bridge wedged into the edges of both the Near Eastern and the Greek civilizations. Even after incorporation into the Roman empire, first as a dependent kingdom and then as a province, nominally linked the region with the Mediterranean world, it still remained peripheral, because Roman authorities invariably found it difficult to subdue highlands and mountainous regions, especially those whose previous cultural and institutional development was rudimentary. The influence of classical culture and the emergence of municipal and imperial institutions appeared in Cappadocia, consistently and predictably, centuries later than in neighboring regions. Hellenization, the spread of cities and Greek culture, came to Cappadocia only in the later Hellenistic period and under the early Roman empire. Romanization, participation in the Roman administration, came only under the later Roman empire with the creation of smaller provinces and the promotion of Cappadocians into the imperial bureaucracy. As a result, despite the seductiveness of Greek culture and the might of Roman rule, local notables were often able to dictate the terms of these encounters.[2]

## Snow

The harsh environment of Cappadocia contributed to its tardy development and long-standing isolation. The swarms of beetles during the growing season were bad enough; the winters were worse. Basil once listed some of the common misfortunes that might make men reluctant to follow the apostolic command to give perpetual thanks, among them hunger, torture, imprisonment, the loss of a wife or children, shipwreck, piracy, banditry, and painful wounds. He then added another disaster that would have had little relevance for people living near the sunny Mediterranean: freezing in a snowstorm. Cappadocians were thought to be "reeking of snow." Every year winter sequestered the Cappadocian plateau from the outside world in a "night that lasted six months." "Indescribable snowfalls" closed the mountain passes "even for those bursting with youth," and a severe winter might leave roads impassable until Easter. Winter turned homes into "tombs" and forced people to stay indoors. During one winter there was so much snow that people were buried in their homes for two months. In the chill of Cappadocia any place that had "naturally hot springs" predictably became a therapeutic spa.[3]

Looming above the Cappadocian plateau was Mount Argaeus, a cold mountain whose summit was shrouded with snow even in the middle of summer. In the Mediterranean world poets romanticized snow-covered peaks; in central and eastern Asia Minor the widespread snow and ice were crippling impediments for half of each year. "Cappadocia is reported to have such severe winters that someone unfamiliar with the region can survive only by cunning." The onslaught of winter affected people's thinking as well as their lives. When Basil once complimented a bishop for his theological support, he thanked him for saving him from "a fearsome winter blizzard." It is no surprise that in the highlands of Cappadocia and the neighboring region of Armenia the most powerful images of persecution and martyrdom focused on freezing cold. The legendary Forty Martyrs of

Sebasteia had been offered the opportunity of deliverance if they would merely step into one emblem of the imposition of Roman rule, a warm bathhouse. Instead, they had chosen to die of exposure on a frozen lake.[4]

After this long frigid hibernation the arrival of spring, with its flowers, singing birds, gentle breezes, and warm sunshine, was most welcome. Gregory of Nyssa compared the soothing effect of God's exhortations to "sunbeams that warm our life when it is frozen in ice." Once central and eastern Asia Minor thawed out, it was an attractive region, with "grain fields waving in the valleys, green meadows filled with various flowers, flourishing glens, and mountain peaks shaded with trees." Just outside Amaseia in Pontus was a glade next to the Iris River blanketed with violets, roses, and ivy and shaded by olive and plane trees. This grove was so seductive that it was known as "Passion." Cappadocians always remembered the natural beauty of their native region. Even though he had been buried far away on the sunny Italian island of Lipari, one Cappadocian nevertheless used his epitaph to evoke the "fields covered with flowers" of his homeland.[5]

Cappadocia was also a productive region. Once the new revenues from the region became available upon its annexation as a province in the early first century A.D., the emperor Tiberius was able to halve the sales tax that provided funds for the substantial bonuses paid to soldiers upon discharge. The natural resources of Cappadocia included its precious stones and minerals, such as a translucent marble, crystal alabaster, silver, lead, and iron, and the wood from its forests. A correspondent once asked Gregory of Nyssa for assistance in acquiring enough trees for three hundred rafters. The regional economy was primarily agrarian, with its usable land divided among farms, pastures, and ranches. Cappadocia was noted for its huge flocks and herds, and throughout the region people were certainly far outnumbered by the sheep, goats, cattle, pigs, mules, camels, and horses. Grain was of course the most important food in the ancient world, and Cappadocia produced enough to export some to neighboring regions. The other distinctive components of a Mediterranean diet, olive oil and wine, had to be largely imported. Although there were some scattered local vineyards, Cappadocian merchants purchased wine in Syria and Armenia. In eastern Cappadocia trees with fruits and nuts were common, and people grew vegetables, seasonings, and flowers for perfumes and ointments.[6]

Appearances could be deceiving, however. Like many other regions in the Roman empire Cappadocia too was impoverished and underdeveloped: "we Cappadocians are poor." Most people in the region endured a hardscrabble life that reduced them almost to the level of the animals they tended. They stored their grain and produce in caves, and perhaps already lived in subterranean chambers too. They shared their residences with their livestock, and their animals were particularly valuable as barometers to forecast shifts in the weather. Sheep announced the arrival of winter by eating more; after being confined during the winter, cattle sensed the coming of spring and crowded to the doors of their stables; and by watching the behavior of pet hedgehogs people could anticipate changes in the wind. When the Cappadocian Fathers wanted to make their pastoral teachings comprehensible to ordinary people, they often used analogies from rural life. In one sermon Gregory of Nazianzus compared some Jewish heroes, as they had honed their resolve for martyrdom, to boars sharpening their tusks, and in a poem he compared the virtuous habits taught by distinguished men to "a cheese molded in wicker baskets." When Basil analyzed the first chapter of Genesis before an audience at Caesarea that included peasants who worked as farmers, raised livestock, and lived directly off exploiting the land, in no fewer than five of his nine sermons he discussed plants, fish, birds, animals, and the weather characteristic of each season. However sophisticated their writings, the Cappadocian Fathers were never far from their rural backgrounds.[7]

Local Notables

Despite the intrinsic limitations of this economy some men and their families were nevertheless able to accumulate substantial resources and establish themselves as local leaders and wealthy elites. They might also become rivals to the rulers of large empires, or even become local kings themselves.

Over the centuries these local aristocrats had represented many interests. From the mid-sixth century B.C. the Persian empire of the Achaemenids had included Cappadocia among its satrapies, outlying provinces governed by satraps who were responsible for local administration and the collection of revenues. Although the size and the names of satrapies often changed, in the early Persian empire the upper Halys River was approximately the east-west dividing line between one satrapy that consisted of the northern regions and peoples of Asia Minor, including the "Syrian" Cappadocians, and another that consisted of the southern regions and peoples of central and eastern Asia Minor, including the "Cilician" Cappadocians. The satraps were frequently Persian outsiders imposed by the royal court, sometimes native notables. Whatever their origins, they often became hereditary local dynasts. Occasionally, when various peoples tried to establish their own autonomous kingdoms, these satraps may have struggled to retain control over their large satrapies, but as governors who developed local ties they were also powerful enough to challenge, tacitly or openly, the Great Kings themselves, who were usually far away in Susa or Persepolis. Their remoteness from the Iranian heartland of the empire hence gave these outlying satraps the opportunity of becoming virtually independent rulers. The breakup of the Persian empire further enhanced the importance and standing of local notables.[8]

In the aftermath of the dissolution of the conquests of Alexander the Great, his feuding successors competed to acquire hegemony over central and eastern Asia Minor. In the north, the region sometimes known as "Cappadocia next to Pontus" or "Cappadocia next to the Euxine [the Black Sea]," a Persian nobleman named Mithridates "the Founder" established himself as king of Pontus during the late fourth century B.C. In the south, the region known as "Cappadocia in its restricted sense" or "Cappadocia next to the Taurus [Mountains]" or "Great Cappadocia," a descendant of an earlier deposed satrap named Ariarathes founded a kingdom in the mid-third century. To offset their powerful neighbors the kings of Cappadocia consistently maneuvered to arrange beneficial marriage alliances, to establish reputations as enlightened patrons at a cultural center like Athens, or to send envoys to an increasingly commodious imperial power like Rome. By the early first century B.C. the Pontic king Mithridates Eupator had exterminated the Ariarathid royal dynasty in his attempt to acquire control over the kingdom of Cappadocia.[9] Since his expansion threatened Roman interests, the senate at Rome supported the Cappadocians in their selection of a new king, a local notable named Ariobarzanes. The civil wars among powerful Roman commanders led to more direct meddling, however, and by 36 B.C. the Roman general Marcus Antonius imposed yet another new king, an aristocrat named Archelaus. After Archelaus' death over fifty years later the emperor Tiberius annexed the kingdom of Cappadocia as a Roman province. After over three centuries of nominal independence Cappadocia was again an outlying province in a large empire.[10]

During this century that led up to the establishment of direct Roman rule, local rulers had consistently relied upon several strategies in order to distinguish themselves and their families and to dominate other notables. Some were able to acquire the support of influential patrons from outside the region by being designated as the representatives of a centralizing administration or of other powerful neighbors. After part of western Asia Minor became a formal province in the Roman empire in the later second century B.C., Roman generals began dreaming about great commands further east. In the early first century Sulla became the first Roman commander to appear in Cappadocia with an army. Thereafter, the kings of Cappadocia were subordinate to the dictates of the senate at Rome or of the individual Roman aristocrats who had become their patrons. Most of these kings commended themselves to their overlords through their acquiescence and obedience. Ariobarzanes became king with Roman support, for instance, but when some thirty years later the Roman general Pompey arranged for his abdication in favor of his son, he cheerfully complied. Another successor, his grandson, had to pay off leading Roman aristocrats for their support. King Archelaus had only to look to his ancestors to find models for deferential trimming, since his great-grandfather had served as a general for king Mithridates Eupator and Pompey had appointed his grandfather to a sinecure of the priesthood of Comana in Pontus. In order to define a legitimating characteristic that was independent of outside patronage, some of these kings also advertised the importance of their bloodlines, especially by publicizing descent from or connections to the old Persian royal family. One haughty daughter of king Archelaus, for instance, offended the other women at the court of king Herod in Jerusalem with her scornful claim of an ancestry that included both the kings of Macedonia and the kings of Persia.[11]

The acquisition of patronage, the advertisement of impressive pedigrees, and even the use of violent force were not limited to kings, however. Within Cappadocia other notables used some of the same techniques in order to promote themselves and their families and sometimes to challenge these regional kings. In particular, at Comana the dominance of a cult in honor of the goddess Ma had made its priest the most powerful man in the kingdom after the king. Most of the inhabitants were "sacred slaves" who, "although in general classified as subject to the king, for the most part obeyed the priest." As the "lord of this sanctuary" the priest at Comana controlled thousands of slaves, extensive territories, and significant revenues. At Venasa was a cult in honor of Zeus, whose priest likewise controlled thousands of sacred slaves, productive territories, and a lavish annual income. The priesthoods of extensive religious cults had become yet another means by which some local aristocrats could enhance their own standing, dominate peasants, and exploit their products. These resources obviously made these priests into potentially formidable rivals to the kings. Since the priest at Comana was in addition usually a member of the royal family, he also had the appropriate pedigree to become king himself. In 51 B.C., for instance, Cicero, then the Roman governor of Cilicia, was able to foil a plot against the king of Cappadocia by a priest, probably the priest at Comana. This priest had already gone so far as to recruit his own cavalry and soldiers.[12]

Since Roman generals were looking for clients and personal agents in outlying regions, support for or opposition to Roman intervention now became an additional factor in the rivalries between kings and local aristocrats. The conflicts among Roman commanders, and especially their intrigues during the civil wars of the mid-first century, spilled over to destabilize the influence of both kings and local notables in kingdoms on the edge of Roman rule. Cappadocian notables opposed to king Ariobarzanes, for instance, also fought against the Roman armies that supported him. In 47 B.C. after his victories in the civil wars Julius Caesar carved out a new principality for the brother of the Cappadocian king, and he appointed as priest for the shrine at Comana in Pontus a Bithynian notable who claimed descent from the royal family of Cappadocia and who eventually acquired his own title of king. A few years later Cassius, one of Caesar's assassins, had the Cappadocian king killed in order to confiscate some of his wealth and to install a more loyal ruler. One local notable then tried to usurp the throne of the Cappadocian kingdom, and may even have acquired the support of Marcus Antonius. In order to consolidate his standing in the East during the buildup to his final showdown with the future emperor Augustus, Marcus Antonius soon selected Archelaus as a new king for Cappadocia, perhaps after having first had a romance with his widowed mother. His amorous liaison was not unprecedented in the region, since earlier a Cappadocian notable who was a member of the royal family had shared his wife with a Roman aristocrat in order to solidify their friendship. Such submissive accommodation had a long past and an equally long future. When Basil once discussed the dissimulation of an octopus and its ability to adopt the color of whatever rock it hugged, he quickly compared it to people who insinuated themselves to the ruling magistrates by readily adapting to their values. In Cappadocia, and in other neighboring kingdoms and principalities, local notables clearly tried to take advantage of the feuds among powerful Roman aristocrats to advance their own standing at the expense of their peers and sometimes of the local kings.[13]

Kings responded to these challenges in various ways. One was to use force. One Cappadocian king had even hired a Roman general to defeat his enemies. Another was to form alliances by appointing local notables to administer the districts into which the Cappadocian kingdom was divided, or by granting them favors and titles. One king designated some of these Cappadocian aristocrats as his "first friends." In the neighboring kingdom of Pontus the ancestors of the geographer Strabo had likewise received a governorship, a priesthood, and other honors from the Mithridatic kings. Yet another response was to encourage alliances through marriages. All these tactics, including the deployment of force, acts of generosity, appointment to offices, and advantageous marriages, were aspects of an ongoing, and often unspoken, negotiation between kings and local notables about their relative standing and influence. This implicit diplomacy was also an indication of an underlying uneasiness and fragility in the relationship between royalty and aristocracy. In fact, one of Strabo's grandfathers eventually betrayed king Mithridates Eupator to a Roman general. It is no surprise that both kings and notables hence took the additional precaution of constructing fortified garrisons for themselves.[14]

## Wealth

In Cappadocia and Pontus regional rulers, whether satraps or kings, and wealthy notables had all schemed against each other, in part by taking advantage of ties to the magistrates and generals who represented neighboring empires. Behind all of this maneuvering and politicking, one characteristic of local power remained consistent. As in other agrarian economies, local domination and wealth represented some sort of exploitation, whether overt or disguised. The most important factor that ensured the continuing authority of local elites, both kings and aristocrats, was ownership of or control over land, the people who worked it, and its products.

In the ancient world land was always the most reliable and durable source of wealth and prestige, and local notables, however much wider prominence they acquired, were never far from their rural roots. In Cappadocia the kings were known as "stock breeders," and the potential of the surrounding land as pastures determined their choice of residences. King Archelaus was furthermore familiar enough with farming and ranching to write an influential treatise on agriculture and livestock. The priests of Comana and Venasa likewise controlled many estates and slaves, and local notables too had presumably acquired estates.[15]

After the transformation of Cappadocia into a Roman province, many of these royal farms and ranches became either imperial estates or public properties belonging to the Roman state, and some of the temple lands may have been assigned to cities as part of their rural hinterlands or become private estates. Local notables hence survived under Roman rule, especially as great landowners. Some flaunted their bloodlines, even continuing to claim royal descent, and a few acquired the patronage that allowed them to hold offices in the imperial administration. But into the later Roman empire the fundamental source of these local elites' wealth and power was still ownership of or control over farms and ranches, their produce, and their livestock. In his exegesis of the six days of creation Basil conceded that the benefits of owning land had been a part of the natural order from the moment of creation: "by preparing pasturage for cattle and horses God provided you with wealth and happiness." For wealthy landowners, "grain becomes gold, wine is aged into gold, and wool is spun into gold."[16]

Because wealth was something to display and use, it allowed, and in fact required, local aristocrats to be extravagant. During the fourth century notables still flaunted their wealth in various ways. One was the possession of rural estates and the construction of large villas in the countryside that "glittered with different colored marbles." In some houses the floors sparkled with mosaics, the walls with frescoes, and the ceilings with gold leaf. In others the ceilings had great timber beams with such intricate filigree that "through the skill of the craftsmanship they are considered trees again, blossoming with shoots and leaves and fruit in their carvings." Some aristocrats had their estates equipped with private bathhouses and gymnasiums and decorated with statues in bronze and marble. Others had one house that could be heated during the winter and another that was a cool retreat during the summer. During the winter they covered the floors with flowers, and during the summer young servants cooled them with fans. These villas were deliberately designed to be overwhelmingly impressive. "The owners do not think that the gates and the gateways and the huge space inside the gates are sufficient for boasting, unless there is something that immediately astounds the visitor with the magnificence of the spectacle."[17]

The archaeology of eastern Asia Minor, both excavations and surveys, is regrettably still rudimentary and contributes little to imagining the countryside of Roman Cappadocia and nearby regions. Fortunately the Cappadocian Fathers described some estates and country houses. Their own families were respectable landowners in the region. Basil's family owned at least several estates scattered throughout Pontus and Cappadocia. On one in Pontus Basil founded an ascetic retreat that was located at the foot of a wooded mountain on an isolated but magnificent plain that looked out over the Iris River. Basil may have stressed the seclusion of the setting, but at his refuge he retained much of the lifestyle of a rural grandee. Guests joined him for hunting expeditions, and Gregory of Nazianzus, who shared his company off and on, confessed that he had become a "vintager" and amused himself at gardening during his visits. Gregory's own family owned at least two or three estates in southwestern Cappadocia, on which there were flocks and herds and which were administered or worked, in part at least, by slaves. His cousin Amphilochius owned a nearby estate that was noted for its vegetables and flowers. Despite the predominance of imperial estates in central Cappadocia, there were other private estates, some owned by churchmen, in the region around Caesarea.[18]

Although the families of Basil and Gregory of Nazianzus were prosperous, they were certainly not among the wealthiest in the region. The estates in Cappadocia that belonged to Olympias, a fabulously wealthy heiress at Constantinople, were only some among her extensive possessions scattered throughout Asia Minor, while the widow Seleucia owned a suburban villa near Caesarea, estates, and a fortified house. Gregory of Nyssa once visited a friend at his large country estate that was located between a wooded mountain and the Halys River. The grounds included cultivated fields, vineyards, orchards, gardens, and a pond. The villa itself was part fortress, with a gateway and high towers, and part grand country house, with a colonnade, a pool, and walls decorated with paintings or mosaics. At Rome a mere glimpse of the extravagant mansions of the great aristocrats led to the acclamation of their owners as virtual divinities, "more than mere mortals." Here in Cappadocia the setting and landscape of this estate were likewise so magnificent and graceful that Gregory thought it must be the work of a painter rather than of a gardener: "nature had obeyed so politely." Gregory always retained an acute awareness of the respect he thought was owed him because of his family, his learning, and his episcopal rank, and even as he described the extravagance of his friend's estate and villa, he was trying to project an air of indifference. Yet it was precisely his casual nonchalance that underlined his deference at the sight of this impressive display of lavish wealth. By transforming this rugged site into a charming estate, the owner of this villa had vaunted his ability to dominate and manipulate the natural landscape. Even the fish in the decorative pond were tame, "docile and submissive, just like obedient puppies." By implication, this estate owner had also demonstrated that the local population should respect and obey him.[19]

Another factor that differentiated local aristocrats was horse breeding. The reputation of Cappadocian horses was long-standing, almost legendary. Mount Argaeus was known, very succinctly, as the "father of fleet horses." In the old Persian empire the annual tribute from the region had included 1500 horses; after Alexander's death one of his generals had enlisted Cappadocian horsemen and acquired support through gifts of Cappadocian horses. Roman emperors too were familiar with the sterling reputation of Cappadocian horses and used them both in their foreign diplomacy and to advertise their generosity at Rome. When the emperor Constantius wanted to establish contact with the ruler of southern Arabia, a region long noted for its fine stallions, his gifts included "two hundred of the best-bred horses from Cappadocia in order to prepare a most sumptuous impression and to offer conciliation." For the races at Rome some of the most popular attractions were "Palmatian" racehorses from an imperial ranch in Cappadocia.[20]

Since all of the Cappadocian Fathers liked to use analogies with horses and horse racing, they were certainly familiar with horses and had attended local races. Gregory of Nyssa seems to have grown up with horses. Even though he often traveled by carriage, in his late forties he could still ride a horse for miles over rough mountainous terrain at night. It is unlikely, however, that his family or the family of Gregory of Nazianzus was wealthy enough to raise horses in large numbers; Gregory of Nazianzus did not mention horses in his will. Raising and breeding fine horses was very expensive, and those local aristocrats who could afford to indulge themselves certainly enhanced their prestige and local influence. The usual avenues for upward social mobility included holding imperial and municipal offices, serving in the army, or acquiring a higher education. In Cappadocia successful horse breeders had as much of a reputation as magistrates, generals, and rhetoricians, and one of them might even be considered for selection as the "patron" of the region. Local horse breeders seem to have measured their wealth in horses and were prepared to pay fines in horses. They also reinforced the prestige of their own families by parading "horses with pedigrees distinguished by the nobility of their ancestors, just like men." To demonstrate their successes they raced their thoroughbreds on frozen lakes. And lest the locals fail to remember their eminence, some breeders branded their herds with their own names.[21]

Roman rule, even centuries after its imposition, had hence not much affected the rural lifestyle of these local aristocrats or their ownership of the large estates whose produce and livestock generated their "enormous annual incomes." In fact, if Gregory of Nyssa had not mentioned the shrine

for martyrs under construction beside the entranceway, his friend's grand estate would have been representative of almost any previous era, as timeless as the Blessed Isles, the paradise of classical mythology that Gregory used as a comparison. Wealth derived from control over land and its resources continued to form the basis of power for local notables.[22]

## Urbanization

Roman rule had nevertheless encouraged a new factor in Cappadocian society by bolstering the trend toward urbanization that had long been characteristic of classical Greek civilization. During the mid-second century B.C., one Cappadocian king had been such an enthusiastic patron of Greek culture that he had acquired citizenship at Athens, sponsored one of the city's festivals, patronized drama and philosophy there, and recruited scholars, artists, and athletes to Cappadocia. Since Greeks had so closely linked their classical culture with the urban setting of a *polis*, a city, this king also tried to establish some proper Greek cities in his kingdom.[23]

These intentions were only partially successful, and the Hellenistic kingdom of Cappadocia remained a region dominated by local notables, tribal configurations, and small villages. At the time of its incorporation into the Roman empire there were still only two important cities, Tyana and Mazaca. Tyana was an ancient settlement located in a fertile plain north of the Cilician Gates, the most accessible pass through the Taurus Mountains. Mazaca was located in a rocky plain that, despite its swamps and volcanic firepits, was covered with grassy meadows suitable for pastures and offered stone quarries and timber from nearby Mount Argaeus. Because of these natural resources the Cappadocian kings had selected Mazaca as their primary residence. As one indication of their preference for Greek culture and cults these kings had retitled both cities with the virtuous Greek name of Eusebeia, "Piety."[24]

The arrival of Roman influence motivated these kings again to use the names of cities as a way of publicizing their new allegiances, and in the late first century B.C., Archelaus, the last Cappadocian king, had renamed Mazaca as Caesarea in honor of his friendship with the new emperor Augustus Caesar. Over the centuries other settlements also acquired the rank of a city, some of them already under the kings. Ariaratheia and Nyssa had become cities perhaps already in the second century B.C. King Archelaus may have converted the sanctuary of Comana into a city (sometimes known

as Hierapolis), and he renamed one town Archelais in honor of himself (although later, after Archelais acquired the rank of a Roman colony, it was sometimes known simply as Colonia). After Cappadocia became a province in the Roman empire, Nazianzus (sometimes known with the imperial name of Diocaesarea) became a city in the mid-first century A.D., Melitene during the reign of Trajan, Arca during the reign of Hadrian, Faustinopolis (or Faustiniana) during the reign of Marcus Aurelius, and Parnassus at some time too.[25]

Urbanization was therefore a very gradual process in Cappadocia that always remained incomplete. Some significant early settlements never became formal cities. Hanisa, for instance, had already by the second century B.C. acquired the magistrates, council, and assembly that were the characteristic administrative features of a Greek city, but in the Roman period it did not have the rank of a city. Venasa likewise, even though under the kings it had been one of the influential religious sanctuaries, never became a city. In the later Roman empire the settlement may have been the site of a local Christian festival, but as a clear indication that it had still not acquired the rank of a city, in the ecclesiastical hierarchy Venasa was administered by a priest, not a bishop. In fact, some of its lands seem to have been incorporated into the large estate belonging to Gregory of Nyssa's friend.[26]

For centuries the Roman province of Cappadocia included much of eastern Asia Minor in addition to the specific region of Cappadocia. Because the dominant features of this zone long remained its small villages and the large estates that belonged to local notables or to the emperors, the province did not contain an extensive network of cities with municipal magistrates who could assist imperial administrators. So initially emperors appointed procurators of equestrian rank as the governors of the new province. Since equestrian procurators were typically concerned primarily with the collection and distribution of revenues, in particular from imperial estates, their appointment here suggests that emperors had decided to base the provincial administration on the administration of the imperial estates. Only in the later first century A.D. did the governor of Cappadocia become a legate of senatorial rank with the standing of a former consul. Even then, because the province that included the region of Cappadocia was so large and also included regions, such as Pontus and Lesser Armenia, that likewise contained few cities, its governors could not rely upon the assistance of municipal magistrates. Under the early Roman empire, "Cappadocia . . . was administered through domains and estates, not cities."[27]

Despite the slow pace of urbanization in Cappadocia, these scattered cities nevertheless gave local aristocrats new arenas in which they could compete for prestige and authority. Each city became a beacon of "Greekness" in a vast sea of uncivilized Cappadocians. One standard characteristic of a Greek city was its use of municipal institutions that commonly included an assembly, a council, and magistracies. Since membership on councils and selection as magistrates typically required a minimum qualification of wealth, service was effectively reserved for local notables. In other regions for which there are adequate honorific inscriptions and literary texts, such as the province of Asia in western Asia Minor, wealthy landowners clearly dominated in holding magistracies and becoming decurions, members of the council. Although few inscriptions and literary texts are available for Cappadocia in the early empire, occasional references seem to indicate the same pattern. At Comana, for instance, the council and the people who met in an assembly voted for dedications in honor of various emperors and a provincial governor. In some cases the dedications mentioned the men who had presided over the decisions, who were presumably magistrates or leading members of the council. The participation of these men indicates that local notables had found another way of maintaining their prominence, this time by accumulating "lists of offices." And in fact, when cities commemorated leading local notables, their honorific inscriptions now listed precisely the municipal offices those men had held.[28]

Cities furthermore required various amenities, in particular buildings. The foundation and expansion of cities allowed local notables to demonstrate their generosity and advertise their wealth in a particularly concrete form by financing the construction of walls, porticoes, baths, theaters, stadiums, monuments, and temples. Rather than merely branding their names on their fine racing horses, local aristocrats could now advertise themselves in markets and gymnasia and on walls and aqueducts by "inscribing their names on their monuments." In Pontus the dedicatory poem inscribed on some new baths left no doubt about the donor's generosity: "Who is the most excellent of all leaders?"[29]

Archaeology again has provided little help in imagining the appearance and size of ancient cities in Cappadocia, even of Caesarea, "a great and prosperous city" that under the Roman empire served as a leading city in the region. Fortunately the Cappadocian Fathers mentioned some of the buildings at Caesarea during the fourth century. The ancient city was located on a rise, a low spur on the north side of Mount Argaeus, overlooking some smaller hills and a plain to the north and east. The center of most

Greek cities was the agora, the market place; at Caesarea porticoes lined the agora on two sides. The city had acquired a reputation for its familiarity with classical culture and the availability of education, and it contained various schools and gymnasiums. It also included some temples, one to Zeus in his guise as "the protector of the city," another to Apollo, and another to the city's tutelary Fortune. Houses, some with two or three stories, lined the streets. Apparently just outside the wall was a stadium, in which, when it was being used as an arena, Basil may once have watched panthers being goaded to attack and shred flimsy mannequins. Surrounding the city, but nevertheless partially enclosed within its sprawling wall, were "suburbs," presumably on the lower hills and the plain, as well as gardens, fields, and pastures. All of these monuments, buildings, and amenities would have enhanced the standing of Caesarea as a "metropolis," the capital city of Cappadocia after the region became a province in its own right.[30]

The cities furthermore provided a stage for the public display of the wealth local aristocrats had accumulated from their rural estates. Some arrived in Caesarea with enormous retinues that included their own cooks, bakers, and wine stewards. Some trained horses specifically to carry them "in luxury through the city." By the time these aristocrats had finished equipping their horses with silver bridles and purple blankets, their mounts were ornamented "like bridegrooms." No longer did they have to stage their races on their own farms or on frozen rivers. Instead, during the celebration of municipal festivals breeders could participate in the horse races and chariot races that were run in the stadium located in a valley below the city's wall. Now everyone could watch. Not only might the provincial governor preside at the games, but the entire population "emptied the city" and gathered "in front of the walls" to cheer on these spectacles and the notables who subsidized them.[31]

The rise and flourishing of cities had clearly expanded the opportunities of local notables to acquire influence and prestige and display their wealth. By the fourth century, however, the public role and importance of cities had been diminished, primarily because imperial policies had gradually undermined the financial resources of cities and the standing of their decurions and municipal magistrates. Magistrates whom the imperial government had in earlier centuries appointed only occasionally as special commissioners to regulate municipal finances or handle judicial cases were now permanent, and the holding of these offices became yet another burden imposed on local decurions. Decurions were also expected to hold other offices created to assist the imperial administration in collecting taxes, levying recruits, and administering public posts and imperial properties. When Basil once listed the obligations of service on a municipal council, he was very precise: "collect revenues and provide provisions for [imperial] bureaucrats." These were increasingly onerous obligations. And not only did the imperial court continue to maintain its right to confirm the selection of these magistrates, but the other members of local councils were collectively liable for financial obligations to the state from their own private resources.[32]

At the same time that local aristocrats were expected to assume more of these official administrative and financial responsibilities, imperial policies had made the cities increasingly dependent upon the generosity of these same notables for the funding of municipal activities and services. Emperors, starting already with Constantine, had repeatedly confiscated the cities' revenues from local taxes, tolls, and rents, and perhaps also their lands and endowments. Valens in particular was active in legislating about municipal finances. Soon after they became emperors, he and his brother Valentinian again confiscated the municipal taxes and lands that their predecessor Julian had briefly restored, as well as the lands belonging to temples that cities had administered to maintain their pagan cults. In the early 370s, as he became more involved in affairs in Asia Minor and on the eastern frontier, Valens supported some concessions to cities. To cities on the west coast of Asia Minor he refunded a variable portion of the revenues from rents so that they could repair their walls, and in 374 he and Valentinian agreed to restore to cities one-third of their civic rents and taxes. Even with these restored revenues cities were heavily reliant upon the generosity, whether enforced or voluntary, of local aristocrats to maintain their services and their buildings. But with increasingly demanding expectations about their service as decurions, municipal magistrates, and representatives of the imperial administration, even local aristocrats who wanted to appear to be unselfish benefactors might well complain.[33]

## Dividing the Province

Other decisions would strain local resources still further. Even as Valens was legislating about the revenues of cities, he was concerned about the administration of provinces and imperial estates. The eastern portion of the province of Cappadocia along the Euphrates River had already been split off, perhaps recently, to become the new province of Armenia Secunda.

Valens now announced a plan to partition the remaining province of Cappadocia yet again into two smaller provinces, Cappadocia Prima in the east and Cappadocia Secunda in the west. This announcement preceded or coincided with the census that was to be completed before the beginning of a new tax cycle on September 1, 372, which was perhaps also the moment at which the division would become effective. The new province of Cappadocia Prima would include a lone city, Caesarea, and the many enormous imperial estates and ranches. Valens' decision to consolidate the imperial domains seems to have been an attempt to give priority to the management of the imperial estates over a provincial administration based on cities and their notables. In some respects this latest reorganization now revived the original arrangements for the new province of Cappadocia over 300 years earlier, when an equestrian procurator had administered a province that contained only a few cities. For centuries the imperial administration had projected an attitude of nonchalant helpfulness toward local affairs by promoting urbanization and the foundation of cities and by relying upon the assistance of municipal magistrates and local notables. Now, after increasingly direct intervention by previous emperors in municipal concerns, Valens seems to have decided that in part of Cappadocia he could do largely without any cities at all.

His decision also had significant, although at least initially probably unintended, consequences for the administration of the church in the region. Caesarea would still be the capital for this smaller province of Cappadocia Prima. But since ecclesiastical administration tended to follow the civil administration, Basil, the bishop of Caesarea, would be left as a metropolitan bishop with no subordinate bishops in other cities. All of the other cities would be in the other province of Cappadocia Secunda, which would then require its own capital city and its own metropolitan see. "The division of the fatherland," as Gregory of Nazianzus later explained, "established two mother cities for the small [provinces]."[34]

Initially the court seems to have intended that Podandus would be that new capital. Located in southern Cappadocia, where it held a commanding position on the road from Tyana through the Cilician Gates to the Mediterranean coast, Podandus was apparently a settlement on an imperial estate. Now, in order to become the capital of a new province, it was to be promoted to the rank of a *polis*. Creating new cities for new provinces was a common initiative. Earlier, when the new province of Armenia Secunda had been formed out of the eastern part of Cappadocia, it had included four existing cities and two new cities. If Podandus was now to be a city and also a provincial capital, it needed "an adequate supply of decurions," as another new city had promised to maintain. In order to provide the local aristocrats to serve as members of the council and municipal magistrates, Valens and the court decided to transfer some of the decurions from Caesarea. Transferring decurions was uncommon, but not unprecedented. About a decade earlier Julian had transferred decurions from Nicaea to the new city of Basilinopolis. Valens apparently intended to do the same in Cappadocia: "almost all of the decurions [of Caesarea] have now migrated to Podandus." According to Basil, these transplanted decurions included "most of the best men in the city, who are now being led away like captives." Other residents of Caesarea apparently shared Basil's overwrought assessment, since some decurions had reacted by fleeing, "a portion of our council and that not the most insignificant, preferring endless exile to Podandus." Presumably these decurions, unless they left the province entirely or acquired exemption from curial service, had for now retreated to their estates in the country-side. Still other decurions had stayed in Caesarea, where Basil claimed that they, and the other remaining citizens, were thoroughly demoralized. "Our community has vanished."[35]

Some aspects of this despair are difficult to understand. Even though in his despondency Basil may have characterized Podandus as the "sinkhole of the entire world," the transplanted decurions were not losing their rank, and the remaining decurions now had fewer competitors for prestige in Caesarea. Two other concerns seem to have been more important in generating this sudden hysteria.[36]

One involved finances, both imperial and municipal. Ten years later in a retrospective summation Gregory of Nazianzus was candidly pungent in claiming that the true cause of the subsequent commotion had been Basil's apprehension over "taxes and revenues." In part, Basil would have been concerned about the ability of Caesarea to maintain its public services and buildings through municipal revenues and the contributions of local decurions. A few decades earlier in Phrygia, in fact, the promotion of a new city had reduced the income of its neighboring city. In letters to imperial magistrates, however, Basil had been more ingratiatingly subtle by hinting at a deleterious consequence for imperial revenues when he suggested that the court should reconsider: "if they do not alter their plans quickly, they will have no people to whom they can display their generosity." Since imperial generosity was often associated with taxes, Basil seemed to be implying that the division of the province and the transfer of decurions would somehow affect the payment and collection of imperial revenues. Both municipal funding and imperial revenues would suffer from Valens' decision. In Basil's estimation, dividing the province would have the same lethal result as trying to create two animals by cutting a horse or an ox in half.[37]

Another consideration was as vital for Basil and the other citizens of Caesarea. Under Roman rule, not only had leading aristocrats competed among themselves over status and influence, so had cities. Their rivalries focused on titles, ranks, privileges, and amenities. In Bithynia "the affliction of jealousy and rivalry" had even driven Nicomedia and Nicaea to support rivals for the imperial throne during a civil war in the late second century. Although Nicomedia had remained the provincial capital, during the fourth century Nicaea could pride itself for having hosted Constantine's ecumenical council. In Pamphylia the city of Perge had benefited from its acquisition of laudatory titles and honors during the later third century by eventually being selected as the capital for a new province in the early fourth century. Imperial patronage was obviously decisive in bestowing these honors and distinctions. In Pontus Neocaesarea claimed that it had received its imperial name from "a distinguished emperor" because of his "love and affection for the region." Soon after the emperor Julian had arrived in Syria, envoys from two rival cities asked him to decide which was to rank second after Antioch. Metropolitan rank, imperial names, and other distinctions were hence important markers of imperial favor and support.[38]

Since emperors conferred many of these honors on cities, sometimes they or their magistrates threatened to remove them too. When Julian had been annoyed at the citizens of Caesarea during his journey through Cappadocia, he decided to withdraw its imperial name and its rank as a city. Nazianzus was another "old and illustrious city" that had acquired the imperial name of Diocaesarea. In order to preserve its local standing against encroachments by neighboring bishops or threats by imperial magistrates, one prominent native son was only too ready to publicize its distinguished past. When the new metropolitan bishop of Tyana tried to extend his influence, Gregory of Nazianzus demurred and suggested that the antiquity of Nazianzus might give it priority instead as the true "mother church" in the new province. When a provincial governor thought about stripping its rank as a city, Gregory stressed that Nazianzus had been founded by emperors and had once survived an attack by the Persians. He further argued that the loss of its rank as a city would turn Nazianzus into an uninhabited wasteland indistinguishable from the surrounding mountains and forests.[39]

Basil now claimed that Valens' decision would prompt the same fate for Caesarea, because several of its most charming features, "the meetings, the debates, the gatherings of distinguished men in the market place," would disappear with the departure of these decurions: "lost to us is whatever else previously made our city notable." Rather than retaining its attractive facade, the city was now becoming an "ugly spectacle." While Basil obviously intended with these comments to generate public sympathy for the plight of Caesarea, he was certainly also concerned about maintaining the city's dominant standing in the region. Years later, but perhaps simply repeating comments he had made at the time, Gregory was again more frank in his assessment when he noted that the driving motivation behind Basil's subsequent feud with the new metropolitan bishop of the new provincial capital of Tyana had been, very simply, "the love of primacy."[40]

## Caesarea and Tyana

Since notables in other cities shared this same obsession, they would have reacted differently to the fate of Caesarea. In fact, it is apparent from Basil's comments in his letters that not everyone in the region shared his estimation that the downfall of Caesarea was a catastrophe. Basil conceded that the "eerie solitude" of the city gave "much pleasure and satisfaction to people who had already been anticipating our demise." This hint suggests that, although Basil and other aristocrats at Caesarea were concerned about maintaining the precedence of the city in the region, since their prestige was linked closely with its standing, local elites from other cities, including bishops, may not have minded a demotion in the stature of Caesarea, since its diminishment gave them and their cities an opportunity to enhance their own influence.[41]

Basil's response was to request assistance from influential men who might become patrons. His letters went to three Cappadocians who had served or were holding high offices in the provincial administration or at the imperial court. Not so coincidentally, these magistrates were also all native sons of Caesarea, or at least had very close ties to the city. Because illness prevented Basil from going to the court himself, he attempted to make his case instead through the direct intercession of these brokers, who would all be speaking on behalf of "our city." In his letters Basil begged these men to demonstrate their concern and zeal on behalf of their *patris*. This particular appeal was powerful not only because of his rather histrionic descriptions of the misfortunes that their "fatherland" was now suffering. It was also a subtle recollection of an underlying tension between center and periphery, between a central administration and a remote province, that had existed for centuries.[42]

Outside powers had repeatedly tried to impose their hegemony and acquire control over the resources of the region; local notables had just as consistently tried to preserve their regional standing and independence. Centuries earlier the kings of Cappadocia who had come to their thrones with the assistance of the Roman senate or of Roman generals had wanted to publicize their loyalty, and so they were the first eastern monarchs to adopt the deferential title "Friend of the Romans." Their submission had nevertheless been unable to shield them from extortion and their kingdom from indiscriminate plundering by Roman generals. Even Cicero could only shrug in explaining why the kingdom could not provide him any assistance during his governorship in Cilicia: "Cappadocia is bankrupt." Archelaus, the last king of Cappadocia, had a particular reason to be grateful to Augustus, who had retained him on his throne despite his miscalculated support for the emperor's rival during the civil wars. The king had subsequently demonstrated his appreciation by renaming his capital city as Caesarea.[43]

Yet Archelaus nevertheless tempered his deference by adopting the sobriquets of Founder, Savior, and Philopatris, "Friend of the Fatherland." These titles were perhaps pointed indications of his intention to balance his loyalty and gratitude to emperors with a devotion to the interests of his own kingdom. His domain in fact eventually expanded beyond Cappadocia to include Pontus, Lesser Armenia, and much of Cilicia, and through judicious marriages he also acquired influence in the kingdoms of Judaea and Armenia. The king's extensive predominance made the emperor Tiberius uneasy enough to appoint a "guardian" for his kingdom and to have him summoned to Rome on a charge of sedition. In Cappadocia, however, Archelaus' reign seems to have represented a last attempt at autonomy from outside inference, and the city of Comana had been grateful enough to erect a dedication that publicized the king's titles. By stressing a similar concern for their mutual fatherland, Basil now seems to have implied that his correspondents, fellow Cappadocians, could earn for themselves a similar renown, and similar titles, by opposing Valens' decisions and saving their homeland. They too should now show themselves to be friends of their fatherland, and in particular friends of Caesarea. "If you have any influence," Basil wrote to one, "extend your hand to our city that has slipped to its knees."[44]

Basil's appeals apparently had some impact at the imperial court. Early in January 372 the emperor Valens, his prefect Modestus, and the imperial

court again visited Caesarea. After this visit Podandus did not become a
new provincial capital or even a city, but instead remained a settlement on
an imperial estate. This reconsideration seems to have represented Valens'
concession to Caesarea, since its decurions did not after all have to transfer
to a new city. But the emperor still decided to proceed nevertheless with the
partition of Cappadocia, and the new capital of the new province of Cappadocia Secunda was now to be Tyana, located on the important roads leading to the Cilician Gates. Since Tyana was a long-established city, it already
had municipal institutions and a register of local aristocrats serving as
decurions. And since only a few years earlier, in 365, it had hosted a regional
council of bishops, it already had some ecclesiastical standing too. Yet Tyana
was still only "the foremost city after the most important city" in Cappadocia, and as a clear indication of its subordination, at this earlier council
the bishop of Caesarea had nevertheless presided. So in the early 370s the
decurions and bishop of Tyana may well have been among those who
were not displeased at the diminishment of Caesarea, and the promotion of
their city may have represented their own success at lobbying the imperial
court.[45]

As a new provincial capital, Tyana acquired the rank of metropolis
and hosted its own resident provincial governor and his staff. In some
respects the city and its local aristocrats were now only reviving an earlier
prominence. Tyana had been the hometown of Apollonius, a sage of the first
century A.D. who had been hailed as a holy man after his death. A shrine
in his honor had enhanced the standing of both the city and the local notables who served as its priests. Emperors had honored Apollonius' memorial,
and in the early fourth century even a Christian pilgrim had made a point
of visiting his birthplace. The subsequent expansion of Christianity, however, had not only erased the importance of this pagan shrine, but the
imposition of an ecclesiastical hierarchy had also subordinated the city's
bishop to the metropolitan bishop of Caesarea.[46]

Valens' elevation of Tyana as a provincial capital hence offered an
unexpected opportunity for the city, its municipal notables, and its bishop
to regain their renown. The prefect Modestus may himself have helped fund
some construction at Tyana. The city's decurions, its bishop and its clerics,
and even the other bishops in the new province now quickly distanced
themselves from Caesarea, their former provincial capital and metropolitan
see. Basil soon responded to one perceived slight by writing a letter to the
municipal council at Tyana, in which he firmly lectured its members about

the importance of community and cooperation. Anthimus, the bishop of Tyana and now a metropolitan bishop himself, sparked a spat with Basil, previously his metropolitan, over ecclesiastical prerogatives. Once he and his "gang of bandits" even held up Basil on the road. And the other bishops in the new province of Cappadocia Secunda dismissed their former metropolitan bishop as a "foreigner" and pretended not to know him.[47]

Changes in ecclesiastical jurisdiction exposed hard feelings among ambitious men. Basil still had supporters in this new province, however, in particular at Nazianzus. Eventually bishop Anthimus and some of his suffragan bishops visited Gregory the Elder and Gregory of Nazianzus to discuss ecclesiastical jurisdiction and assert their claim that Tyana was the "new metropolis." Even though Nazianzus was now within his metropolitan authority, this was an uncomfortable visit for Anthimus. Gregory the Elder had so much seniority as a bishop, having by now served for over forty years, that in a catalogue of bishops he was still listed before Anthimus. And only a few years earlier Gregory the Elder had been a major advocate of Basil's selection as the metropolitan bishop of Caesarea. At that time he had openly acknowledged his loyal subordination to his new metropolitan bishop by conceding that a metropolitan city was the center of a circumscribed circle. Bishop Anthimus now tried to convince Gregory the Elder and Gregory of Nazianzus to transfer their loyalty to him. To demonstrate his claim about his new priority to these longtime supporters of Basil, he seems to have drawn an actual map of the new boundaries by "tracing out a circle" that included Nazianzus within the jurisdiction of Tyana.[48]

Bishop Anthimus was not the only boaster of Tyana's eminence. During the 380s the bishop of Caesarea was Helladius and the bishop of Tyana was Theodorus. During the first few years of Helladius' episcopacy Cappadocia had been reunited as a single province, and Helladius was again the only metropolitan bishop. In 381 the emperor Theodosius restored the two smaller provinces and Theodorus became a metropolitan bishop. Helladius reacted with the same dismay Basil had shown almost a decade earlier, and his annoyance matched Basil's earlier resentment. Even though Nazianzus was no longer in his province, Helladius continued to meddle in the affairs of Gregory of Nazianzus, "not because of his canonical scrupulousness, but because of his excessive anger." Gregory even thought that Cappadocians were "fighting a civil war." This feud between Helladius and Theodorus became a legendary example of jealous passion: "they strove with one another about some contemptible claim of right in their parish, and fell into great and long rivalry."[49]

In the early fifth century the metropolitan bishops of Caesarea and Tyana supported opposite sides during the great doctrinal controversies over Christology. At the council of Ephesus in 431, bishop Firmus of Caesarea was a partisan of bishop Cyril of Alexandria and his theology, while bishop Eutherius of Tyana supported bishop Nestorius of Constantinople and his doctrines. After his party's success at this council Firmus went with a posse of supporters to Tyana and tried to replace his rival with a new bishop. The intervention of an imperial magistrate foiled this scheme, and the citizens of Tyana also resisted: "immediately everyone gathered and confronted these [opponents] and the man whom Firmus had consecrated." In the past, cities that had dueled for local primacy had wanted to acquire new imperial names and titles. Now, in the context of these ongoing disputes over articulating the theology of Jesus Christ, Tyana acquired a new name that was perhaps a blatant attempt to trump its rival's imperial name of Caesarea. Tyana would be known as Christoupolis, "Christ's city."[50]

## Rank and Status

These examples demonstrate that the competition over prestige and rank among local aristocrats and among cities certainly survived into the later Roman empire after the spread of Christianity. Cities now contended over the new privileges that came with being designated as provincial capitals and metropolitan sees. Bishops, who were typically recruited from among local aristocrats, transferred their squabbling over influence into clerical service. The disruptive meddling of outside powers also survived. For over a thousand years the native kings, local aristocrats, municipal magistrates, and finally bishops of Cappadocia had had to deal with remote monarchs, intrusive neighboring kings, powerful generals, visiting emperors, and numerous imperial administrators who were suspect outsiders to the region. Often local notables and the cities had themselves invited this intervention, because becoming the representative of an outside authority, a landowner as a satrap or a city as a provincial capital, was a means of acquiring more prestige and influence.

These ongoing negotiations between outsiders and locals, between imperial capital and province, and between central administration and regional autonomy influenced, and were in turn influenced by, the strictly local disputes among cities and among local notables. During the early 370s Basil's reactions to the partition of the province of Cappadocia were another clear indication of the intersection between appeals to imperial magistrates and disputes with local rivals. In fact, the letters that Basil had sent to his powerful friends in the imperial administration also became weapons in his local feuds. In Caesarea, Basil had more than likely published copies of his letters, or at least publicized their posting, in order to demonstrate that he had responded appropriately to the request for his help from the citizens of Caesarea. His letters hence had a local function that complemented their purpose as attempts to acquire assistance at the imperial court, because within Cappadocia they demonstrated again the preeminence of both Caesarea and its bishop. Only Caesarea had such a lineup of influential and prominent native sons, and only the bishop of Caesarea could appeal to such powerful patrons.[51]

Even though Basil may have been unsuccessful in preventing the division of Cappadocia, he was successful in acquiring some additional authority for himself from the emperor Valens. In this case the bishop had furthermore worked to protect the interests of other local notables, decurions and large landowners. Caesarea likewise retained its local prominence in subsequent centuries, and its prosperity. After the Arabs once seized the city in the mid-seventh century, they regretted an agreement that prevented them from plundering its "impressive opulence." Caesarea also kept its standing among the metropolitan sees of the Byzantine empire. Over the next millennium emperors and bishops continued to draw up and revise lists that carefully established a hierarchy among episcopal sees. After the great patriarchal sees of Rome, Constantinople, Alexandria, Antioch, and Jerusalem the lists ranked the metropolitan sees. On these lists Tyana, the rival metropolitan see in Cappadocia, was never among the top ten metropolitan sees. In contrast, at the top of all the lists of metropolitan sees, ranked higher than Ephesus, Ancyra, Nicomedia, Nicaea, and Chalcedon, was Caesarea, "the [most] supremely honored of supremely honored cities and the leader of the entire East." And since, after the seventh century, the surviving fragment of the eastern Roman empire that became the Byzantine empire included only Constantinople of the patriarchal sees, Caesarea was in fact nominally the second city in the empire's ecclesiastical hierarchy.[52]

Over the centuries the region of Cappadocia had maintained its standing, and often its autonomy, against the encroachments of neighboring

empires. Within Cappadocia itself, despite the imposition of outside overlords, despite challenges from neighboring cities and ambitious bishops,
Caesarea, its notables, its people, and its bishops had retained their rank
and status. Attempts to impose a general hegemony over the region or to
downgrade the standing of Caesarea had been ineffective. An epigram that
seemed to belittle Cappadocians was in fact a warning against meddling by
outsiders. "A venomous viper bit a Cappadocian; the viper died."

# Chapter 2

# "The Hook Hidden in the Bait":
# The Rewards of Giving

The development of cities in Cappadocia had offered local aristocrats new opportunities to distinguish themselves. Within cities they could hold offices and priesthoods, subsidize the construction of new buildings or the endowment of festivals, or simply flaunt their wealth through displays of conspicuous extravagance. For centuries after the introduction of Roman rule, notables whose wealth derived from rural estates had dominated cities as municipal magistrates and priests and patrons. In the later Roman empire the relationship between local notables and cities changed. Now, as the imperial administration confiscated the resources of cities, it increasingly pressured landowners in their roles as municipal magistrates and decurions. At the same time bishops and clerics began to emerge as new leaders. Although they may have linked their own institutional structure firmly to cities, they nevertheless had different attitudes about wealth and its use. By encouraging the central importance of cities, their civic magistrates, and their municipal and regional priests, the imposition of Roman rule had at first enhanced the prestige and influence of local notables. In the long run, however, as the assumption of municipal offices and the funding of municipal amenities became increasingly burdensome and as urban society became identified with a single religious cult and its bishops, participation in those cities seemed only to pose challenges to the standing of landowning notables.

During the fourth century local aristocrats faced pressure from two directions, from an imperial administration that compelled them to undertake expensive service as decurions, and from bishops and other churchmen who took over some of their civic functions and usurped their prestige. The oddity of these challenges is that all the participants, local landowning aristocrats, bishops and clerics, and imperial provincial administrators, came from essentially the same backgrounds. Both bishops and imperial magistrates were recruited from local landowners, men with curial rank.

Once they entered the ecclesiastical hierarchy or the imperial administration, however, they became representatives of other interests. Then, even though these men often still exchanged letters and favors, they might also become rivals and sometimes antagonists.

One essential focal point of their rivalries was the distribution of regional resources. The central administration and the Roman army on the eastern frontier required huge amounts of supplies. With its imperial estates and ranches, its imperial factories, and, of course, its taxes, Cappadocia was an important source of rations and provisions. Despite this diversion of regional resources to the imperial administration and army, large landowners were still wealthy and still prepared to use their wealth in their hometowns and native region. In Cappadocia, as elsewhere in the Roman empire, local aristocrats had certainly long promoted an image of themselves that stressed their generosity and the beneficent use of their wealth. They were the guardians of that wealth, prepared to distribute it fairly and generously to the citizens of their cities who would in turn shower them with praise and honors, hailing each of them as a "nourisher" or "benefactor." The reality behind that flattering ideology, however, was control, sometimes violent control, over the use and distribution of resources and commodities, in particular the produce from the countryside. In addition to owning great estates, local aristocrats were not above intimidating and coercing their neighbors. Within cities these notables could launder the wealth and resources acquired through threats and confiscation into gifts of magnificent generosity. Outside cities these benefactors remained rural ruffians.

In a region that was dependent on an agrarian economy and often very chilly, warmth and food were obsessive concerns. Among the resources that local elites in Cappadocia might dominate and manipulate to their own advantage were clothing, water, and grain.

## Clothing and Water

In the valleys and low plains around the Mediterranean, heat and dryness were the prevailing characteristics of the climate; in the high plateau and mountains of Cappadocia, coolness and sometimes frigidness were the dominant features during much of the year. When the Cappadocian Fathers mentioned clothing, they emphasized cloaks and outer garments. Cloaks and capes were typically sewed together from animal hides or woven from wool or other fibers. With its enormous flocks and herds Cappadocia was predictably renowned for its production of clothing. During the fourth century the imperial administration established a weaving mill in Caesarea, whose clothes presumably went to soldiers and imperial magistrates on the eastern frontier and to officials at the imperial court. Locals worked in this mill, including the women who processed the silk threads brought in by merchants from the East. These workers were numerous enough to form an imposing mob. During one confrontation with an imperial magistrate, Basil's supporters included weavers from the imperial mill, among them women prepared to used their spindles as makeshift spears.[1]

Despite the presence of these extensive production facilities, in his sermons Basil was concerned that ordinary people in Cappadocia nevertheless often risked being inadequately clothed. Basil repeatedly insisted that the poor included many "naked" people, and that the failure to clothe a naked man was similar to the outright theft of a garment. "The cloak that you guard in your cabinet belongs to the naked man, the sandal that rots in your possession belongs to the barefoot man." "One of your chests of clothes," Basil once complained about the wealthy, "could clothe the entire population." To make his point more forcefully, he added a detail that was especially appropriate for Cappadocia, claiming that these unclothed people were freezing. Basil also insisted that one cloak was adequate, and he even went so far as to try to dictate the proper length for a cloak, since the wealthy apparently paraded their standing by having long trailing mantles. Some of them also went out of their way to acquire silk garments, clothing embroidered with gold threads, and even clothes dyed with the imperial colors of purple and scarlet. Clothing was clearly a precious component among the possessions of the wealthy. Macrina may have given away many of her clothes, but Gregory of Nyssa was able to provide a linen robe to dress his sister's body for her funeral. In his will Gregory of Nazianzus made a point of apportioning articles of clothing along with his estates and flocks and gold coins. He still had some of the luxurious silk, linen, and wool clothes that had once belonged to his brother, and in addition he now dispersed some of his own clothing, three wool robes, five tunics, five cloaks, and one plain garment.[2]

Among poor people, however, heavy cloaks, warm outer clothing, and sometimes just adequate ordinary clothes were often so scarce that some had to stitch together tunics from rags. People were so desperate that at the lavish funeral of a wealthy notable they complained that "the most expensive clothing was going to rot with the corpse," and at one festival some men tried to steal even the "cheap clothing [collected] for beggars." Basil knew about ragged clothes. When he once worried about the fragile state of ecclesiastical harmony, he compared it to "an old cloak that is easily ripped"—and then apologized for using such a "vivid but shabby analogy." Throughout the empire Cappadocia had a reputation for the quality and beauty of the clothes it exported, including cloaks made from soft rabbit pelts. Within Cappadocia, however, even though the region was overrun with flocks and herds, the ostentatious pretensions of local aristocrats combined with the incessant needs of the imperial administration and the frontier army to limit the availability of adequate clothing for ordinary people. Poor people had great need but small possessions. In Cappadocia they were sometimes reduced to a threadbare existence, wearing clothes made by weaving bark and thorns into "a fabric like haircloth."[3]

A second resource that local aristocrats could manipulate to their advantage was water. The development of cities was contingent upon supplies of water, and even cities situated next to rivers had to worry about the availability of water suitable for drinking or for filling their municipal baths. Amaseia, for instance, may have been located along the Iris River, but because the river's water was unreliable, an aqueduct that brought water from mountain sources was cut into the face of the cliff along the river valley. At Tyana the most impressive surviving monuments are the arches of an aqueduct that joined with a canal to bring water from springs almost three miles away. At Caesarea there was apparently an aqueduct and a large bathhouse. In many cities the construction and restoration of aqueducts, fountains, and baths provided yet another means for notables to demonstrate their generosity and enhance their local standing: "men are extolled for constructing aqueducts."[4]

The availability of water was also an important consideration for both farming and grazing in eastern Asia Minor. Sometimes there was too much. Just as at the beginning of the process of creation when water covered the earth, "even still now excessive wetness is for the land an obstacle to productiveness." Heavy snowfall during winter led to the flooding of rivers during the spring thaw, which in turn inundated neighboring farmlands and pastures. A river swollen with runoff was dangerous as it swept down timbers and boulders. Gregory Thaumaturgus had once demonstrated his miraculous power by controlling the Lycus River, the rampaging "Wolf" River whose destructive flooding had consistently left people "shipwrecked in their own homes." On the Euphrates River an unexpected landslide had led first to flooding upstream and then, after the blockage broke, to flooding downstream. Later in the growing season sudden cloudbursts and hail-storms might ruin the ripening crops. A sophist once claimed that Zeus would sometimes offhandedly decide to have a thousand bushels of hail dumped on Cappadocia.[5]

More common, however, was the lack of water, a consequence of in-adequate snowfall during the winter or of drought during the summer. The impact could be catastrophic: "during droughts the fields spontaneously produced thistles." Some men could make a livelihood by prospecting for water; Basil once illustrated an exegetical point in a public sermon by refer-ring to the activities of well-diggers. Access to rivers, streams, lakes, springs, and wells was hence an invaluable privilege. Because Gregory of Nazianzus had once studied at Alexandria and most likely witnessed the benefits of the annual inundation of the Nile River, his list of seductive temptations included, along with gold and silver, "a large fertile domain rippling like the fields of Egypt." In Cappadocia people built huge cisterns to store the runoff, carved out underground tunnels and channels, and constructed elaborate irrigation systems "for a great river to spread over the fertile land through thousands of ditches." In one instance two brothers even raised small "armies" from their dependents in order to settle their competing claims to a marshy lake.[6]

In these conflicts over the availability of adequate clothing and water bishops and clerics were at a distinct disadvantage. Local aristocrats actually owned estates that produced clothing and the material for clothing, and with their retainers they were prepared to fight for the rights to water. The churches in Cappadocia by now had most likely acquired some properties, but they had not yet become great landowners. As a result, even though churchmen were concerned about the welfare of ordinary people, the most they seem to have been able to do was express their outrage and indig-nation. This apparent imbalance in power and resources was perhaps most obvious in crises over the availability of grain.

## Food Shortages

All cities in the Greek world worried about an adequate inventory of pro-visions in their markets. In addition to the practical requirements, the supply of food was an indicator of a city's status and influence. "The avail-ability of goods for sale in the market defines the prosperity of a city." Grain was such a staple in the ancient diet that its absence was a true gauge of poverty: poor people instead had to eat "cabbage pickled in vinegar." Even Basil's frugal meals included bread. Since the supply of grain was a special concern, municipal magistrates were expected to regulate both its availability and its price. In the Roman period Cappadocia typically produced enough grain that it could export some to neighboring regions. But when cities in the region did have to cope with shortages, they faced an awkward handicap. High up on the central Anatolian plateau they could not readily import a heavy product like grain. Gregory of Nazianzus acknowledged this difficulty when he mentioned a food shortage in Cappadocia. "Regions on the coast endure such shortages without difficulty, since they send their produce away and accept produce by way of the sea. But for us in the interior a surplus [of produce] is useless and a shortage is unimaginable, because we are unable to distribute what we have or to acquire what we lack." Instead, people had to rely upon the generosity and resources of local aristocrats. This dependence offered local notables another opportunity to enhance their influence.[7]

Local aristocrats manipulated the availability of grain in different ways. One was hoarding. The returns of agriculture generally provided landowners with a reliable, but still unspectacular, income. In order to derive huge profits they had to take advantage of the increased demand and high prices resulting from shortages. Some agricultural writers had even recommended that large landowners stockpile nonperishable products not simply for their own security, but also for sale later at an opportunistic moment. In Cappadocia too local aristocrats apparently indulged in stockpiling and profiteering. Sometimes they preferred to let the water in their cisterns go foul rather than releasing it. Hoarding grain was easier, especially in cool, dry caves. It was also more profitable: "you let grain rot rather than feed the poor." In times of shortage they could gouge the local population by raising their prices. "Your granaries are always full, and you sell at times of misfortune. You close your granaries, and then you cleverly open them in accordance with changing circumstances." As a result, some people resorted to theft. Others would become debtors to large landowners, presumably contracting their labor in exchange for food. Some would actually contemplate selling their children into slavery.[8]

Another way that large landowners extended their domination in the countryside was through the use of forcible coercion. While the truly impoverished had to resort to begging, the less poor were oppressed by usury, and then might become destitute themselves. During periods of duress lenders would encumber peasants with loans and subsequently confiscate their property: "then the lender extends his hand with money, just as the fishing line extends the hook hidden in the bait." Large landowners did not always respect the boundaries of others' fields and resorted to the use of violent force: "excessive wickedness becomes a means of increasing their power." "I see you first as a lender, then straightaway as a collector [threatening] tortures and imprisonment." Wealthy men would seize teams of oxen, or plow, sow, and harvest in "fields that were not theirs." Those who resisted were threatened with beatings, accusations, expulsion, and imprisonment: "no one withstands the violence of a rich man."[9]

Hunger was a potent weapon for maintaining power and influence. In Gregory of Nyssa's estimation, only the dunning of a relentless tax collector imposed a burden more oppressive than a stomach's demand for food. During the later 360s the harvests in Cappadocia failed, apparently as a result of drought during the winter and excessive heat and insufficient rainfall during the spring. According to Basil, the sky had become cloudless and "watertight." Farmers were so distressed that they knelt in grief in their barren fields, caressing the parched stalks of their crops and wailing as if they had lost young sons. The result was not a famine, a catastrophic lack of food leading to a dramatic rise in mortality rates in the face of which people were completely helpless, but rather an unexpected and severe food shortage.[10]

Basil had resumed his service as a priest at Caesarea a few years earlier, and he now delivered some sermons about aspects of this food shortage. In one sermon he stressed that God was not responsible for the appearance of misfortunes, in another that the wealthy should share their resources, and in another that people must repent for the sins that had upset the natural order and caused this drought. Basil claimed that adequate grain was in fact available, but only in the granaries of wealthy landowners: "although granaries are filled with an abundance of supplies, we do not have pity on a man in distress." The problem Basil faced was therefore not the complete lack of grain, but rather its hoarding by local notables and merchants intent upon profiteering during a time of diminished resources: "you have, but you did not give." Hoarding, and not simply bad weather, was responsible for this food shortage. Basil's goal was to convince these men to release their grain either for sale in the local markets or as outright gifts to the people.[11]

As a churchman, Basil's instinctive first reaction was to interpret this crisis in terms of Christian teachings. In one of his sermons he linked this food shortage with the consequences of Adam's original sin. That first sin had also involved food, or rather the wrong food that Adam had been tempted to eat because of his pride. In Basil's estimation, the current crisis offered people an opportunity to compensate for that initial gluttony: "absolve the original sin by a donation of food. Just as Adam transmitted the sin by eating incorrectly, so we can wipe out [the consequences of] the treacherous food by alleviating the need and hunger of a brother." In another sermon Basil stressed personal responsibility. One common spontaneous reaction to this crisis was to accuse God of being responsible, because supposedly everything happened according to His wish. Since some might then question God's compassion, they could also rationalize their own oppression of other people. "If there is no one watching, if there is no one who rewards each person according to the value of his life, what is there to prevent us from oppressing the poor, murdering orphans, killing widows and strangers, and undertaking any evil act?" Basil's response was to argue for the significance of individual free will: "the source and root of sin is the free will in us." In this perspective, even though God sent disasters to punish and instruct, people were responsible for their own reactions. In terms of both theology and Christian morality, people could alleviate this crisis only by choosing repentance and demonstrating their generosity.[12]

The people who needed persuading were of course local notables, the wealthy landowners with grain in their granaries. To convince them, however, some time-tested tactics were unavailable to Basil. One was the employment of coercive force. Emperors and imperial magistrates had sometimes used such coercion with success. Antioch, for instance, had faced recent food shortages. In 354 the emperor Gallus had menaced the leading decurions who had objected to his insistence upon lowering the price of grain, and he had finally made a scapegoat of the provincial governor, who was then lynched by a mob. Upon the emperor Julian's arrival at Antioch in the summer of 362, the residents complained that prices for grain were too high. Although drought was apparently the primarily culprit for this food shortage, the presence of the imperial court and the troops that Julian was massing for his campaigns against the Persians had exacerbated the crisis. Julian first tried to convince the leading decurions to forego their profiteering. When this request failed, he imported grain from nearby cities and from Egypt and imposed price controls. These measures were ineffective too, because without the restrictions of rationing speculators purchased much of this cheap grain and resold it at a profit while continuing to hoard their own stocks. After Julian's departure the provincial governors and the counts of the East directly supervised the supply of food for Antioch, in particular by regulating merchants and shopkeepers. One count even ordered bakers who had charged excessively high prices to be flogged in public.[13]

As a priest Basil obviously was unable to employ force against local aristocrats, or even to threaten its use. Nor did he choose to appeal for the assistance of Valens and his court, perhaps because the emperor supported a heterodox version of Christian theology, or of the provincial governor. Instead, he relied entirely on his rhetorical persuasiveness. Long ago a provincial governor in Cilicia had convinced local notables to make available their hoarded grain simply through the authority of his eloquence, "not by any force or legal proceeding or bluster, but by influence and exhortation." For local aristocrats in Cappadocia the dry weather had presented an opportunity for profiteering by taking advantage of a food shortage. For Basil, this disaster offered an opportunity to enhance his standing in the city and in the entire region. By confronting the wealthy and criticizing their behavior Basil could present himself as the champion for the poor, the needy, the naked, and the hungry. But without resources of his own that could alleviate this shortage, without the threat of physical intimidation to back up his criticism, all he could do was recast this crisis into a context that gave him the moral high ground.[14]

In his sermons Basil employed several different tactics simultaneously. One was to argue that the charity of the wealthy would earn more than just the same honors they had received previously for their other acts of public generosity. Basil suggested that wealthy notables consider the accolades earned by their peers who had funded theatrical performances, wrestling matches, mimes, and wild beast hunts. Although these benefactors had earned "the shouts and the applause of the people," their honors had lasted "only a short time." The rewards for the typical municipal benefactions were transient. In contrast, those aristocrats who helped the needy directly would still certainly be hailed with "all the titles of generosity," as "nourisher" and "benefactor." In addition, they would receive "eternal honor" in the kingdom of heaven where God and the angels would sing their praises. Generosity to the needy hence offered the eternal rewards and ceaseless acclamations that ordinary euergetism could not match.[15]

A second tactic was to appeal to aristocrats' sense of decency by trying to shame them into helping the poor. The wealthy preferred to spend their wealth on themselves and often tried to ignore the needy who clustered outside their doors. Some notables thought it was enough to have scenes of Christ's miracles, such as the feeding of the multitude, embroidered on their clothes. Their bishop simply sneered at their refusal to act: "do not depict the baskets of leftovers; instead, feed the hungry." Basil was likewise indignant at such a myopic outlook: "the poor man is starving, the naked man is freezing, the debtor is being strangled, and you postpone your generosity until tomorrow?"[16]

Basil's argument that generosity would generate even more honors, eternal honors, had been an attempt at extending the traditional system of values by redefining it into a Christian context. His attempt at shaming local wealthy elites, however, marked a significant challenge to their traditional expectations. The wealthy had always justified their accumulation of wealth by claiming that they were looking after their families and their conventional standing. Increasing their wealth had been simply good economic practice, benefiting themselves, their families, and their cities. Now, by outright accusing the wealthy of being miserly, Basil had located their behavior in a different system of ethics. From his moral perspective he could criticize their accumulation of wealth as plain stinginess. Not only was it morally wrong; in addition, wealth such as theirs was symptomatic of a spiritual illness, an alienation from the Christian community. For such moral and spiritual estrangement, open generosity would be a therapy leading to social reintegration and redemptive wholeness. In the old perspective the wealthy had hoarded resources in order to ensure their self-sufficiency, and the purpose of their acts of beneficence had been the enhancement of their own influence and prestige. In the new Christian perspective that Basil now proposed the purpose of charity was a straightforward concern for other people. Assistance for others was the primary motivation, and any honor and praise that resulted for the benefactors were supposed to be incidental consequences. Hoarding had become a sign of miserliness, not power. Basil claimed that in their concern for food, drink, and enjoyment the wealthy hoarded "what a privy receives." This was less a salacious comment about these men than an observation that such constipation hurt their own standing in the community. According to an interpreter of dreams, a wealthy man's defecation was a sign of his imminent generosity.[17]

By stressing the public honors, the moral approval, and the spiritual health that local aristocrats could earn through demonstrating their concern for the hungry and needy, Basil was essentially offering a face-saving means for them to give way and make their grain available. In Pontus one tombstone complimented a notable for his piety, which had consisted specifically of his hospitality to everyone, his protection for his family, his respect for his friends, and his assistance for the poor. In his sermons Basil was trying to convince these great landowners to behave in life as they were praised in death.[18]

Failing that, another tactic he used was less subtle. Local aristocrats had extended their influence over peasants through the use of forcible intimidation, and emperors and imperial magistrates sometimes used overt coercion to bend large landowners. Because Basil was unable to employ the same tactics, he instead presented them with threats about their fate on Judgment Day. Then they would face accusations not of simple theft, but of a failure to have participated in the community by sharing their possessions. At this final hearing they would be unable to use their resources to manipulate the judicial system as they were accustomed. Not only could they not bribe the judge, but they would be unable to rely upon a hired orator to act as their advocate, the presence of their friends and supporters to influence the hearing, or the impact of their prestige to serve as a character reference. Their penalty would be a "bitter eternity of distress" in the "unquenchable fire" of hell. At the end of one sermon Basil made sure that these wealthy people understood what awaited them. "Do not think that I am frightening you with false horror stories, as some mothers and nurses are accustomed to do with young children. These are not myths, but words proclaimed in a truthful voice." In another sermon he again was blunt with his message: "if these horrors do not terrify you. . . , we are speaking to a heart of stone."[19]

Redefining the traditional system of honors to include Christian values, belittling conventional aristocratic values, and posing threats about the final judgment in heaven were all components of Basil's rhetorical strategy in dealing with local aristocrats. Gregory of Nazianzus would later praise his friend's success at ending this food shortage. In his retelling, Basil had been successful in "opening the granaries of landowners" simply "through his oratory and his exhortations," and he had become the community's "grain-giver."[20]

Gregory's evaluation was in fact an upbeat, and hence somewhat misleading, retrospective assessment. At the time, Basil's appeals had been perhaps not all that successful. Public preaching about theology and morality had its limitations. Gregory himself once noted that people skipped attending even the Easter festival in order to care for "their own field, a recently acquired team of oxen, a new bride." During this grain shortage, most people simply continued on with their business. Few joined their priest in prayers, and those who did could hardly wait for the conclusion to the biblical readings and for their own release from the church, "as if from a prison." Only young boys were keen to assist Basil, perhaps because their help gave them a holiday from their schoolwork. Since he could not enforce it with creditable force or set an example with his own resources, Basil's rhetoric had had only a modest impact.[21]

Even in his later panegyric Gregory implicitly conceded Basil's fundamental haplessness. Gregory readily compared Basil to the Old Testament hero Joseph, who had managed the pharaoh's grain supply and saved Egypt from famine. But he pointedly declined to compare Basil with miracle workers like Moses, who had successfully prayed for food to fall from heaven, or the prophet Elijah, who had made small jars of food last many days, or Jesus, who had fed a multitude with a few loaves. In the mid-fifth century a drought would again cause a food shortage in Cappadocia and surrounding regions. Then relief would come from "the providence that saves everyone" and that finally provided that "sustenance from the sky known as manna, just as for the Israelites." Manna was "bread that was ready to eat," that required "no cultivation and no plowing," whose availability was immune to the vagaries of weather and the greed of local notables. Divine providence clearly had its own unlimited resources. Basil did not. All he could do was to try to influence the distribution of others' grain. With his limited resources even he could not work miracles.[22]

## Gifts

If Basil was going to confront and compete with local notables and landowners with any prospect of success, he needed more prestige and tangible resources. Like Joseph, he had to be able to store grain for later distribution. A year or so after this grain shortage Basil improved his local standing by becoming bishop of Caesarea. He then followed the lead of other bishops by sponsoring building projects. At Nazianzus Gregory the Elder had started construction of a new church that his son Gregory of Nazianzus eventually completed. Basil wanted to send martyrs' relics to another bishop who had recently built a new church. Gregory of Nyssa constructed a martyrs' shrine for which he supplied some of the materials, and he hoped that bishop Amphilochius of Iconium would send some workmen. Basil himself presided over the construction of a large complex just outside Caesarea that included a magnificent church, a residence for the bishop and clerics, hostels for travelers, hospitals for the ill, a poorhouse, and other buildings.[23]

These construction projects were expensive. As Gregory of Nyssa fretted over the wages for the workmen, he apologized for his meticulous haggling by pleading poverty. These churches and shrines were also an investment that paid returns, because once constructed, they began to acquire donations, estates, and resources that would benefit all the locals.

Their possessions were considered to be communal resources. At one city the shrine of St. Julitta protected a spring of fresh water. Through her open generosity this saint was hailed as "mother"; most important, her "milk," this sweet water, was "available to everyone." At Amaseia an imperial accountant was funding a poorhouse "with the resources the Lord has given you." Gregory of Nazianzus left much of his property to the church in his home town "for the provision of the poor who are dependent upon the aforementioned church." One poorhouse in Cappadocia hoped that its "small property" would be exempt from imperial taxes; another depended upon the revenues of two estates that had been gifts from a local notable. Gregory requested exemption from taxes for these estates, and Basil once requested relief for "an estate belonging to the poor." Basil's new complex outside Caesarea also acquired endowments. Basil may have donated some of his own possessions. He encouraged others to contribute. When he spoke to one young man about the virtues of adopting a life of poverty, he urged him to sell his excess clothes. He then added that the presence of a poorhouse made it easy for contributors like this young man to distribute their wealth. "It is imperative not to assume one's own distribution of wealth, but to entrust it to the administrator of the poor." Basil's poorhouse would act as a clearinghouse for donations. In the past local notables and their prominent families had distributed gifts in their own names. Basil now encouraged them to contribute their wealth to his new ecclesiastical foundation, which would become "a common storehouse for the wealthy."[24]

Other gifts came from an unlikely benefactor. Emperors, of course, had reputations as the greatest benefactors of all. In Cappadocia poor people might even use the example of imperial generosity to embarrass local notables. Some beggars carried icons of the emperor when they requested alms, "so that they might shame those who ignored them with the ruler's image." Even a heterodox emperor could take the hint. After Basil had repeatedly stood up to Valens and his court officials, the emperor was so impressed that he donated some "beautiful estates that he owned there." These gifts were most likely some of the imperial estates in Cappadocia, and Valens now presented them specifically "to the poor in Basil's care." Even though Basil had not requested assistance from the emperor, Valens had nevertheless contributed land to the church.[25]

Basil and other bishops presented themselves as the champions of ordinary people. But to be effective champions, they needed more than powerful oratory or appeals to an outraged morality. They also needed control over the tangible resources, land and its produce, which would finally allow them to compete effectively with other local notables and landowners. Such ambitions of course made them vulnerable to criticism, and not just from their rivals. Other Christians were concerned that the acquisition of wealth, however laudable its usefulness, threatened fundamental biblical recommendations about the virtues of poverty and warnings about the distractions of wealth. At Sebasteia one priest who was in charge of the local poorhouse finally rebelled by claiming that his bishop was interested only in "the accumulation of wealth and the acquisition of everything." This priest instead stressed his complete renunciation of possessions. True to his convictions, he and his supporters wandered off into the countryside, "dusted with snow, taking refuge in the forests, camping outdoors under rocks."[26]

To compete with local landowners and to care for their congregations, churchmen could not indulge in such scruples. In such a combative context successful bishops could not afford to be shy or rigidly principled. Kings and emperors had set the standard by founding or refounding cities and giving them their names. Within cities local aristocrats had advertised themselves by displaying their names on the civic monuments and buildings they funded. In the process, they had turned the residents of the cities into extensions of their own families, so that they would each be hailed as the "father of a thousand children." Basil now looked outside that civic order to the people who were often kept on the margins, the poor and destitute. He furthermore became the protector of the "poor" in an extended sense, all the people who were dependent on the patronage of the great notables. For them Basil founded an upside-down reflection of the classical city, a "new city" that castigated miserly notables and elevated outcasts, subordinates, and the humble. Within this new community Basil nevertheless enhanced his prominence, in time-honored fashion, by publicizing his own name. This new complex next to Caesarea was now known as Basilias, "Basil's place." To be successful as patrons, bishops had to acquire control over resources like grain, water, and clothing, and they too had to turn their names into brand names.[27]

*Chapter 3*
# "The Singing of the Sirens": Service in the Imperial Administration

In the ancient world rivers commonly defined nominal frontiers between states. The Halys River had long served as a political boundary in central Asia Minor, first between the kingdom of Lydia and the old Persian empire, then between satrapies within the Persian empire, finally (more or less) between the kingdom of Pontus and the kingdom of Cappadocia. In the Roman empire, however, the Halys River no longer marked a frontier. The original province of Cappadocia had corresponded approximately to the kingdom of Cappadocia. In the later first century A.D. the emperor Vespasian had combined this province with neighboring regions to form a huge province that included most of central and eastern Asia Minor and stretched to the Euphrates River. After the breakup of this large province late in the reign of Trajan, the province of Cappadocia included the regions of Pontus and Lesser Armenia as well as the region of Cappadocia. The eastern frontier of this new province was still the upper Euphrates, the "king" of rivers, but the Halys River was now just another interior river. The disappearance of its role as a political border was a clear symbol of the imposition of Roman rule over all of central and eastern Asia Minor. In the succinct summation of a governor of Cappadocia during the 130s, "long ago the Halys River was the boundary between the kingdom of Croesus and the Persian empire; now it flows under Roman dominion." Once the interior of Asia Minor had been pacified, old political frontiers became irrelevant.[1]

Initially the emperors and the imperial administration seem to have thought of Cappadocia largely in terms of its fiscal and military significance. The primary responsibility of the equestrian procurators who governed the province was to divert to the Roman treasury the revenues and resources that had previously gone to the Cappadocian kings. These revenues were so considerable that the emperor Tiberius was able to cut in half a sales tax that he had declined to reduce only a few years earlier. In the mid-first century, when the emperor Nero waged war against the Parthian kingdom for

control of the kingdom of Armenia, Cappadocia became an important staging point for his campaigns. The Roman commander Corbulo used troops
that were already wintering in Cappadocia, and he later drafted more recruits from Galatia and Cappadocia. He finally installed a descendant of the
old Cappadocian royal family as the king of Armenia. Vespasian stationed
legions permanently on the Euphrates frontier. These troops maintained
their links with the rest of the eastern frontier and the interior of Asia Minor
through an extensive system of roads. Men from central and eastern Asia
Minor continued to be recruited into the Roman army, and some even
served far away from the eastern frontier. If the rivers oriented eastern Asia
Minor toward the Black Sea and the Near East, then the roads connected it
to the Mediterranean world of the Roman empire.[2]

Despite its location on the distant northeastern edge of the empire,
Cappadocia was an important enough province that senatorial legates with
consular rank replaced equestrian procurators as its governors. The governorship of Cappadocia became an attractive position in the careers of
Roman senators. To become the governor of Cappadocia, according to a
satirist, a Roman senator would visit sixty households every morning and
bestow a thousand kisses. But Cappadocians themselves, including local
aristocrats, seem not to have received the same regard. In the early Roman
empire few Cappadocians held imperial offices or acquired high ranks.[3]

In other provinces in Asia Minor the usual sequence had been the promotion first of descendants of veterans and of families that had immigrated
from Italy, then of descendants of the old native royal families, and finally
of men from the leading local families whose members already dominated
municipal offices and priesthoods. In Cappadocia there were apparently no
Italian immigrants (or at least none who became prominent), and apparently few veterans settled there after service on the eastern frontier. At
Comana funerary dedications mentioned two men who were quite likely
descendants of the Ariarathid royal family and of king Archelaus. Although
the format of their names suggests that these two men had somehow
acquired Roman citizenship, no known descendants of the royal families
in Cappadocia acquired senatorial rank. Some men from Cappadocia may
have acquired equestrian rank already in the late first and early second
century, perhaps as a result of their service in the Roman army. Men with
senatorial rank appeared still later. In the later second century Tiberius
Claudius Gordianus, a native of Tyana, held various posts in the imperial
administration and finally received a suffect consulship. He was the first
Cappadocian to hold a consulship. Since Gordianus (or Gordius) was a

common name in Cappadocia, it is possible that the family of Marcus Antonius Gordianus, the proconsul of Africa who became emperor for less than a month in 238, had ties to Cappadocia. A dedication at Comana honored Aurelius Claudius Hermodorus and called him a senator.[4]

This small roster of examples indicates clearly that in comparison with other provinces in Asia Minor, Cappadocia lagged far behind in producing equestrians and senators. Before the fourth century about seventy-five families whose members acquired senatorial rank are known from the province of Asia (which included most of western Asia Minor), more than twenty families from the province of Lycia and Pamphylia (in southwestern Asia Minor), more than fifteen from the province of Galatia (in central Asia Minor), and about ten from the province of Bithynia and Pontus (in northern Asia Minor). From the province of Cappadocia only two or three families that produced senators are known. The only province in Asia Minor that Cappadocia surpassed was Cilicia on the south coast. Even this was a dubious distinction. Because of the rugged mountains, parts of Cilicia were so incorrigible and difficult to administer that eventually Roman troops tried to contain its so-called bandits by imposing a virtual blockade. In the early empire Cappadocian notables likewise rarely advanced beyond their local prominence.[5]

## New Opportunities

In the later Roman empire local aristocrats from Cappadocia, as well as from other eastern provinces, finally had the chance to participate more fully in the imperial administration. These opportunities were the consequences of new policies introduced by Diocletian, Constantine, and their fellow emperors during the late third and early fourth centuries. One was an increase in the size of the imperial administration and the army. By subdividing many of the existing provinces emperors approximately doubled the number of provinces, and therefore of provincial governors. They also added additional layers to the imperial administration by appointing vicars or, for some of the eastern regions, counts of the East to supervise clusters of provinces, as well as praetorian prefects to oversee still larger regions. All of these provincial and regional magistrates of course had many bureaucrats to assist them, with up to one hundred lesser administrators serving on the staff of each provincial governor and up to one thousand on the staff of each prefect. Emperors also enlarged the ministries attached directly to their courts, thus making available thousands of jobs in various financial, legal, and secretarial departments. By enlarging the size of the army emperors in addition increased the number of officers needed to command its units. Provincial elites hence had many more opportunities to serve in the imperial administration, the palatine ministries, or the military command.[6]

Another new policy was an increase in the number of imperial courts. During the mid-third century countless usurpers had appeared, often to defend peripheral sectors such as northern Gaul or regions in the East that the Roman emperors seemed to be ignoring because of their preoccupation with campaigning on other frontiers. Diocletian had finally resolved the problem of multiple illegitimate emperors by sanctioning multiple legitimate emperors. Thereafter, with few exceptions there were usually two or more emperors reigning concurrently during the fourth century. As the newly revived Persian empire of the Sasanids boldly asserted its claims in the Near East and the eastern Mediterranean, and as the Goths emerged in the Balkans, one of the Roman emperors was often campaigning on the eastern frontier or the Danube frontier, or was resident in a nearby city such as Antioch or Sirmium. Local elites in the eastern provinces, and in particular those in the provinces of central and eastern Asia Minor along the great highways connecting the eastern frontier with the Balkan frontier, hence had more opportunities to make contacts with the powerful officials at an imperial court who might act as patrons for appointment to provincial or palatine offices.

The most consequential imperial innovation, however, was Constantine's foundation of Constantinople as the new capital for the eastern empire. In 248 the emperors had celebrated the millennium of the foundation of Rome with a series of magnificent games and public hunts. The slaughter of so many exotic animals was yet another conspicuous display of the emperors' willingness to exploit the provinces to the advantage of a capital. Less than a century later, in order to match Rome's splendor, amenities, and size as quickly as possible, "Second Rome" began to siphon away the resources of the eastern Mediterranean. "Constantinople was dedicated by stripping bare almost all other cities," as one chronicler wryly observed. These resources included grain and other foodstuffs, building supplies, historical artifacts and statues, and even important biblical relics, such as, it was claimed, the ax Noah had used to build the ark and some of the crumbs from Jesus' miraculous feeding of the multitude. Although these two relics nicely symbolized two of the most important concerns for a city with an expanding population, nonstop construction and the supply of food, leftovers alone would obviously not satisfy the demands of this new capital. "Constantine exhausted nearly all the imperial resources on Constantinople." In particular, the new senate at Constantinople attracted local elites from the eastern provinces, almost demanded them as a form of taxation. Many provincial notables left their hometowns for the new capital, where they now had the opportunity to acquire senatorial rank. Constantine inaugurated the new capital in 330; by the late 350s its senate included about three hundred members, by the 380s two thousand members.[7]

An increase in the size of the imperial administration and army, enhanced accessibility to imperial courts, and the parasitic impact of the growth of Constantinople all multiplied the opportunities for local aristocrats in the East to acquire offices and high ranks. During the fourth century notables from Cappadocia and neighboring provinces became senators at the capital, magistrates in the provincial administration, lesser administrators and secretaries in the imperial bureaucracy, or officers in the army. One contemporary immediately recognized the importance of these administrative changes for the rise of provincials from central and eastern Asia Minor. "Look at the ministries of the two courts, that of the East and that of the West, and you will find there as many men from Pontus, Paphlagonia, Cappadocia, and Galatia as in other cities and provinces."[8]

Within Cappadocia itself some Cappadocians served as *officiales* or *cohortales* in the *officium*, the bureau of secretaries assisting the provincial governors. Others served as clerks and administrative assistants on the staffs attached to other great magistrates or in the palatine ministries. These lesser administrators included Anthimus, on whose behalf Gregory of Nazianzus once requested assistance. Another was Briso, whose death bureaucrats and men of the highest ranks alike mourned. Cledonius, "once upon a time glorying in his renown at the court of an earthly ruler," had apparently served in a palatine bureau before returning to become a monk in Cappadocia. Maxentius was a member of a distinguished family who likewise served at an imperial court before adopting an austere Christian lifestyle. Firminus was also presumably serving in a palatine ministry when Basil suggested that he return to his native region. Helladius was a "member of the prefect's household" before he became a tax assessor in "our homeland." Nicobulus the Elder was the husband of one of Gregory of Nazianzus' nieces. He was from a wealthy and distinguished family, and he had served as a soldier in campaigns against the Persians. After his military career he had returned to Cappadocia and served on the staff of the governors. Nicobulus then sent some of his sons to Tyana to learn shorthand, which would have qualified them to serve as clerks or lesser bureaucrats in the provincial administration or in an imperial ministry.[9]

Since it is likely that in Cappadocia, as in other regions of the empire, most of the clerks in the governors' bureau were recruited locally and served for long, perhaps almost lifetime, tenures, probably many more Cappadocians also served on the provincial staff. The governors, in contrast, were outsiders. Although one or two of the known governors during the fourth century may have owned land in Cappadocia, no native Cappadocian served as governor there. This was a predictable exclusion, since a long-standing interdiction forbade the appointment of natives as governors of their home provinces. In 380 the emperor Theodosius issued an edict that reaffirmed this prohibition.[10]

Only a very few Cappadocians are known to have served as provincial governors anywhere in the empire during the fourth century. Two Cappadocians served as prefects of Egypt during the first half of the century when the prefect of Egypt was still simply the governor of the province of Aegyptus and not, as later, also the equivalent of a vicar for all the provinces in Egypt. Magnilianus was prefect in 330, and Philagrius served as prefect twice between 335 and 340. Philagrius supported the heterodox opponents of Athanasius, the contentious bishop of Alexandria, and in 339 after a council had deposed Athanasius, he assisted in the installation of Gregorius as his replacement. Gregorius was himself a native Cappadocian, and Philagrius now suppressed the resistance to the new bishop by plundering and burning a church. In the later 340s Philagrius served as vicar of Pontica, the diocese that included Cappadocia and other provinces in eastern Asia Minor. During his tenure as vicar he seems to have resided some of the time in Cappadocia. Decades later, Gregory of Nazianzus knew just enough about Philagrius to associate him with Athanasius' episcopacy in Egypt, but not enough to straighten out the chronology or to realize that Philagrius and Athanasius had been enemies.[11]

Another Cappadocian started his career by administering provinces in the western empire. Martinianus served as governor of Sicily and then in 358 as vicar of Africa. It is not obvious how a Cappadocian ended up as a high-level magistrate in the West; one possibility is that he received these offices as rewards for having somehow supported the emperor Constantius against the usurper Magnentius during the early 350s. In 378 Martinianus would serve again in the imperial administration, this time as the prefect of the city of Rome. Despite these connections with the West, after holding each of these offices Martinianus may well have retired to his homeland of

Cappadocia, since Basil knew him well enough to ask for his assistance in the early 370s in appealing to the emperor Valens' court, and Gregory of Nazianzus would compose a series of laudatory epitaphs that warned grave robbers away from his tomb.[12]

These few Cappadocians who served as a governor or a vicar in the provincial administration were apparently exceptional, since many, perhaps most, of the Cappadocians who advanced beyond offices in provincial bureaus served in palatine ministries or on the staffs of vicars or prefects. Evagrius was apparently another Cappadocian who had advanced under Constantius and eventually served as a *comes rei privatae*, a count who administered the emperor's private revenues, until being sent into exile in late 361 by the supporters of the new emperor Julian. Another Cappadocian who became a *comes rei privatae* was Arcadius, who served under the emperor Valens in the mid-360s. Caesarius, the brother of Gregory of Nazianzus, served at the courts of Constantius and then Julian before becoming a treasurer responsible for imperial revenues in Bithynia.[13]

During the later 360s and the 370s the most prominent Cappadocians in the imperial administration were Sophronius and Aburgius. Both were friends of Basil and Gregory of Nazianzus. In 365 Sophronius was already a clerk in an imperial bureau when he reported the news of a usurpation to the emperor Valens at Caesarea. A few years later, at about the same time that Modestus became prefect of the East, Sophronius became *magister officiorum*, the chief of staff in charge of coordinating the various departments at Valens' court. He remained as *magister* for five and perhaps almost ten years. Later, perhaps in 382, he was prefect of Constantinople, and he continued to retain some influence at the capital even after he retired to Cappadocia. In several letters Basil requested Sophronius' assistance; in other letters, sometimes with regard to the same concerns, he requested Aburgius' assistance. These letters seemed to imply that Aburgius too was serving or had influence at the imperial court during the early 370s. Another possibility is that Aburgius was, or subsequently became, the count of the East (the equivalent of a vicar) stationed at Antioch, where Valens and the imperial court resided during most of the 370s. Aburgius may eventually have become prefect of the East in 378, as the successor to Modestus, and after his retirement he seems to have retained some influence at Constantinople still a decade later. Both Sophronius and Aburgius were hence apparently among the protégés of the powerful prefect Modestus.[14]

No doubt other Cappadocians also acquired offices in the imperial administration during the fourth century. When Caesarius, Gregory of

Nazianzus' brother, had first visited Constantinople during the 350s, he had been dazzled with offers of public honors, marriage into a distinguished family, and membership in the senate at the capital. Adelphius, another educated Cappadocian, would receive similar offers of assistance and honors. "Many of the aristocrats in your vicinity approach, and many of those with great prestige are offering wealth, family connections, friends, authority in cities, and influence at the palaces." For provincial aristocrats these were seductive enticements, and it was difficult to decline them. Although Gregory patiently tried to convince his brother to stay in Cappadocia, Caesarius repeatedly drifted back to the court. Gregory argued that the overtures Adelphius was considering were only "faddish toys," but Adelphius seems eventually to have become governor of Galatia. During the fourth century service in the imperial administration provided another means for local notables from Cappadocia to maintain and improve their standing. Basil's description of a prosperous man reflected the impact of these trends. People admired "a distinguished man" for his wealth, the crowd of supporters who surrounded him, and the entourage of relatives and servants who accompanied him. "Add to his wealth some municipal office or honors from the emperors or the administration of regions or the command of armies or a herald loudly announcing his arrival or lictors [walking] on both sides and striking a deep fear into his subjects with [threats of] beatings, confiscations, exiles, and imprisonment. The fear among his subjects grows to become unbearable."[15]

Although the rise of Cappadocians into the imperial administration was an impressive and significant trend, it was not uncontested. Cappadocians certainly had more opportunities now than in the early empire to serve in the imperial bureaucracy or to acquire higher offices, but they also had to compete for those positions with local notables from other eastern provinces. Although there were more Cappadocians who served in the imperial administration during the fourth century than under the early empire, the same was no doubt true of notables from other provinces. Since the lists of magistrates for the later empire are so fragmentary, one indirect way to gauge the relative impact of Cappadocians is to assess their presence as students.

The acquisition of higher offices in the imperial administration generally presupposed an education in classical culture. Many young men from the eastern provinces went to study with the great sophist Libanius, who taught at Antioch from 354 until the early 390s. Libanius once boasted about the diverse backgrounds of the "children" who came for his instruction.

According to him, these students came from almost all the regions in the great swath of territory between Thrace and Arabia, including most of Asia Minor. Of Libanius' 196 attested students, the origins of 167 are known. One large group came, predictably, from Antioch and Syria (22 percent). Another large group came from nearby provinces such as Phoenice and Palestine to the south, Cilicia to the northwest, and Euphratensis to the east (26 percent in all). From central and eastern Asia Minor twenty students came from Armenia, sixteen from Galatia, and twelve from Cappadocia (29 percent in all, 7 percent from Cappadocia). A few students from Constantinople studied with Libanius, but hardly any from Egypt or Greece. Within Libanius' primary sphere of influence, which stretched from central Asia Minor to Palestine, students from Cappadocia were not very prominent. In his survey of students Libanius had already conceded as much about Cappadocians: "not many students come to me from there." In addition, teachers at other illustrious cities, such as Alexandria in Egypt, Ephesus and Nicomedia in western Asia Minor, Athens in Greece, and of course Constantinople, were transforming more young provincials into candidates with the credentials for service as imperial administrators, and sometimes notables from western provinces arrived with new emperors to hold offices in the eastern empire.[16]

Even allowing for all the uncertainties about the interpretation of this data and the correlation between education and office-holding, it is likely that Cappadocians were still not a large percentage of the higher magistrates in the imperial administration during the fourth century. There were simply too many competitors from other regions.

## The Ecclesiastical Hierarchy

Notables from Cappadocia, as well as other provincial aristocrats, could also choose other options for maintaining and enhancing their prestige and authority. Ownership of land and control over its resources obviously still conferred great influence, and men could still serve as municipal magistrates or decurions in their native cities. They also had increasingly more opportunities to serve in the ecclesiastical hierarchy. In the later Roman empire the ecclesiastical hierarchy expanded in size probably even more rapidly than did the imperial administration. Gregory of Nazianzus had already noted a correlation, and he deplored the lowering of standards that it implied: "wise generals and noble bishops pop up suddenly like mushrooms, although they have no previous experience for sharing in the honor." During the fourth century the province, and later two provinces, of Cappadocia included about ten cities. The clerical staff that the bishop of each of these cities supervised was probably about the same size as the bureau of clerks that assisted each provincial governor. As metropolitan bishop of Caesarea, Basil alone presided over fifty "rural bishops," as well as other clerics. Even though the imperial administration was expanding, the ecclesiastical hierarchy became larger.[17]

At least two of the Cappadocians who had studied with Libanius eventually became bishops. Amphilochius, a cousin of Gregory of Nazianzus, had started a career as an orator and advocate, probably at Constantinople, before returning to Cappadocia and then becoming bishop of Iconium, a metropolitan capital in Lycaonia. Optimus became bishop of Agdamia, a small city in Phrygia, and then transferred to the episcopacy of Antioch, a metropolitan capital in Pisidia. Libanius was impressed enough to compliment Optimus on his transfer, even as he congratulated him for maintaining "the purity of the Greek language." For local landowners and educated provincials, service in the clergy had become an option that might be more attractive than service in the imperial administration. Even Caesarius, Gregory's brother, had decided before his sudden death to exchange his office in the provincial administration for service at another "court."[18]

Two small examples hint at the growing prestige of becoming a cleric or, better, a bishop. During the fifth century one of the bishops of Caesarea was Archelaus. Descendants of the old royal family of Archelaus, the last king of Cappadocia, seem not to have prospered in the early Roman empire, and centuries later it is most unlikely that this bishop Archelaus could claim to have any royal blood. But it is telling that a man whose royal name might have led him toward service in the imperial administration instead became a cleric. Also in the fifth century, Helladius served as governor of Cappadocia or as some other imperial magistrate in the region. This Helladius was apparently a native of Cappadocia, and he may well have been a descendant, perhaps a grandson, of the Helladius who had succeeded Basil as bishop of Caesarea. Archelaus would become a bishop despite his royal name, and the family of Helladius would produce both a bishop in one generation and an imperial magistrate in another. Service as a cleric was as viable an option for local aristocrats as service in the imperial administration. During the fourth century and thereafter, even though local notables from Cappadocia acquired increased access to service in the imperial administration, they could also choose to serve as clerics in the church.[19]

## A Cappadocian Emperor

Basil had once prided himself on having resisted "the singing of the Sirens" by sailing past Constantinople. After the sophist Libanius returned to his hometown of Antioch, he too sometimes railed against the increasing prominence of the upstart capital. Because Constantinople vacuumed away so many resources, Libanius described it as "that city that lives in luxury on the sweat of other cities." Few of their peers were as ascetic as a Cappadocian Father or as disdainful as an opinionated teacher. Many local notables were unable to resist the honors and offices that were now available through the founding of a new eastern capital, the increase in the size of the imperial administration, and the proximity of imperial courts. Caesarius, Gregory of Nazianzus' brother, was certainly not the only provincial, or even the only Cappadocian, who now became a "shining morning star at the imperial court." Even if they represented only a small percentage of the eastern provincials who acquired offices, during the fourth century more Cappadocians than before served at the court and in the imperial administration.[20]

In the early Roman empire the rise of provincials to higher offices and ranks had previewed the appearance of provincial emperors. First emperors from the western European provinces had replaced Italian emperors, then emperors from North Africa and the Balkan regions had become prominent. Even though the rise of Cappadocian notables was comparatively so much more tardy than the rise of other provincials, eventually there was an emperor from Cappadocia too. Maurice was a native of Arabissus, a city in eastern Cappadocia that during the fourth century had been reassigned to the new province of Armenia Secunda. Like so many other aspiring provincials, Maurice started his career as a clerk at an imperial court. Eventually he became the chief military commander on the eastern frontier. His local contacts were helpful, since he was able to recruit troops from his homeland and neighboring regions. In 582 he succeeded to the throne, and the Roman empire had a Cappadocian emperor.[21]

Maurice had the misfortune to become emperor in difficult times. Even as he had to impose financial stringency, he was supporting military campaigns against the Persians on the eastern frontier, the Slavs and the Avars in the Balkans, and the Lombards in Italy. At the same time he was trying to appease ecclesiastical controversies with the bishops of Rome and doctrinal disputes with Monophysite Christians throughout the eastern provinces. He eventually lost the imperial throne in a military coup.

An epigram had once warned of the dire consequences if Cappadocians acquired imperial offices: "throughout their tenures they will be as
bad as bad can be." Despite its evident sarcasm, this epigram was seemingly
prescient, because in the early seventh century the eastern frontier began to
crumble from attacks first by the Persians, then by the Arabs. This epigram
had foreseen a future in which Cappadocians were to blame for the decline
and fall of the Roman empire. "The world will disintegrate once it has been
'Cappadocianized.'"[22]

# Chapter 4

# *The Highlander*

Long before the spread of Greek culture and then the imposition of Roman rule had drawn Cappadocia into the Mediterranean world, the region had had political and cultural links to the Near East and the Middle East. "Cappadocia" was supposed to have been a Persian name meaning "the land of the beautiful horses." One legend associated its consolidation as a geographical region with a magnificent gift of land from a Persian king to a huntsman who had saved him from a lion.[1]

Hints of these oriental connections lingered throughout the Roman period. Families with Persian affiliations and cults with Iranian origins still appeared in the later Roman empire. Gregory of Nazianzus once compared the emperor Valens to Xerxes, the Persian king who had long ago unsuccessfully invaded the Greek world. Basil explained the presence of "Magusaeans," members of a religious cult, by describing them as the descendants of "colonists from Babylon who had been imported to our region a long time ago." Gregory of Nyssa discovered that a friend was growing some sort of "Persian fruit," perhaps nectarines, that reminded him of almonds, walnuts, and peaches. He also once mentioned the distinctive iridescence of the Halys River, which "shimmered like gold trim on a long purple robe." Although Gregory attributed this coloration to silt in the water, the orator Himerius had a more elaborate explanation. He claimed that the god Dionysus had long ago settled people from India in the mountains of Cappadocia alongside the river, and that as they bathed in the river's currents, its clear waters turned dark. As a greeting Cappadocians commonly said "I bow before you." Even though he conceded that it was one of "the customs of the region," the pedantic Libanius still thought that this excessively deferential salutation was too reminiscent of the old Persian custom of subjects' paying rulers "a reverence worthy of gods."[2]

Just as oriental customs and legends survived under Roman rule, the power and influence of local notables proved to be remarkably durable. Ownership of or control over land, whether farms or pastures, provided resources that large landowners could use to enhance their own local standing. The imposition of imperial administrators and the increasing prominence of Christian bishops and other churchmen may have modified and sometimes challenged their authority, but these rivals could not eliminate the power of large landowners. Outsiders and newcomers usually allied with local landowning notables, typically through marriages or by coopting them into service in the imperial administration or the ecclesiastical hierarchy. Sometimes they confronted each other.

From the Roman well into the Byzantine period, even emperors might feel threatened by large landowners from central and eastern Asia Minor. In the early third century the emperor Elagabalus became suspicious of Valerianus Paetus, whose family owned land on the border between the regions of Lycaonia and Isauria. Valerianus Paetus had had his image stamped on gold medallions that he intended to use as gifts for his many mistresses. But Elagabalus surmised that he intended to start a rebellion in Cappadocia, and had him executed. In the mid-third century a Cappadocian horsebreeder named Palmatius was so wealthy that his house was larger than an imperial palace, and he began posing as the equivalent of an emperor. The emperor Valerian finally confiscated his estates. In the late tenth century the emperor Basil II traveled back to the capital through Asia Minor after his campaigns against the Fatimid caliphate. In Cappadocia the great landowner Eustathius Maleinus provided for the emperor and his entire army from his own enormous land holdings. His family's estates stretched out for over seventy miles. Basil was so intimidated that he invited Eustathius to Constantinople, and then kept him in custody, "like a wild animal in a cage." After Eustathius died, the emperor confiscated his estates. Control over the resources of Cappadocia could transform powerful local aristocrats into rivals of emperors, and both Roman emperors and Byzantine emperors struggled to maintain their authority over the region.[3]

## Samson and the Lion

In the later Byzantine empire poets celebrated the legendary deeds of Digenes Akrites. Digenes Akrites was reputed to have been a heroic warrior in the frontier zones facing the Arabs. Although these epic legends were patched together from oral traditions, his exploits seem to have looked back, through a lens tinged with romanticism, as far as the ninth century. His name acknowledged both his pedigree and his background. Since his father had been an Arab emir and his mother the daughter of a distinguished Roman family, "Digenes" was a "half-breed," a man of "double descent." Often the legends called him a Cappadocian, "the sweet flowering offshoot of the Cappadocians." Since these legends located him and his activities in eastern Asia Minor, the region around the upper Euphrates River and the Taurus Mountains, "Akrites" was a man of the mountain peaks, a "Highlander." In many respects Digenes' life was predictably traditional, remarkably similar to the aristocratic lifestyle of the Roman empire. He and his family owned estates and raised horses. He built an enormous house in the middle of lovely gardens, and he wore expensive clothing. He spent much of his time hunting wild animals and raiding his neighbors. He and his wife were eventually buried on a mountain ridge in a tomb carved from purple marble, and notables from throughout the region attended his funeral. There they hailed him as "the bloom of the Romans."[4]

The Highlander had been a landowner, a warrior, and a hunter. The Cappadocian Fathers would have readily recognized his kind. Missing from his life, however, were two institutions that had influenced the local landowning aristocracy in the later Roman empire. One was the imperial administration. One of the legends described a meeting between Digenes and an emperor. Digenes welcomed the emperor with a bow and complimented him for having received his imperial rule from God. After an exchange of flatteries the emperor asked what Digenes would like from the empire. Under the rule of Achaemenid Persian kings, Cappadocian and Pontic kings, and Roman emperors, Cappadocian notables had always been ready to serve as clients or to assume magistracies. Digenes now confounded expectations by declining all favors. Instead, he merely reminded the emperor to look after his own subjects. Even though the emperor then did confer upon him a high rank and the "authority to administer the frontier highlands," Digenes continued to live autonomously, "less ... an imperial agent ... and more ... a marcher lord."[5]

To make his independent authority perfectly clear, Digenes had abruptly interrupted his conversation with the emperor to strangle a menacing lion. Gregory of Nyssa's friend had kept tame fish at his rural villa as a reminder of his local domination. Digenes now impressed an emperor by killing a lion, the "emperor among wild animals." The reaction was predictable: "everyone was astounded and afraid." Long ago, when a huntsman had once saved the Persian king from a lion, he had received all Cappadocia as his reward. Digenes now seemed to think that he should have similar autonomy. The emperor could issue writs of authority, but in the world of

Digenes, the frontier zones of Cappadocia and Armenia, he had little effective influence.[6]

It was not coincidental that the legends identified this emperor as "Basil
the fortunate, the great, the trophy holder." The emperor and the Highlander were essentially political twins, men of equal standing with the same
name. This particular ballad about their meeting began with the naming
of the emperor as "Basileios." At its conclusion the ballad identified the
Highlander as "Basileios," as if he had somehow usurped the emperor's
name. By the end of their meeting it was also apparent that the Highlander
had effectively appropriated more than the imperial name. His autonomous
power had made it clear that now local notables would maintain their
standing in their home regions without subordinating themselves to outside rulers. Digenes Akrites could now be "Basileios," an "imperial ruler,"
on his own terms.[7]

The second conspicuous omission from Digenes' career was the church.
None of the legends included a meeting between Digenes and a bishop,
either similar to the tense confrontations between bishop Gregory the Elder
and the emperor Julian or bishop Basil and the emperor Valens, or reminiscent of the more supportive encounters between bishop Gregory of
Nazianzus and the emperor Theodosius at Constantinople. Digenes was
certainly aware of biblical stories. In the expansive dining rooms of his new
house he included mosaic decorations of episodes from Greek mythology
and the legends of Alexander the Great. Mixed in were scenes from the Old
Testament, the marvels of Moses, the conquests of Joshua, the battles of
Samson, the victory of David over the giant Goliath. Digenes furthermore
knew about saints. In one courtyard of his house he constructed a shrine in
honor of the military martyr St. Theodorus, and he attributed his success
during battle to St. Georgius and St. Demetrius.[8]

Despite this Christian aura, the legends about Digenes included little
hint of bishops and the ecclesiastical hierarchy. Churchmen were civilians,
and the prominence of bishops in Cappadocia during the fourth century
had presupposed a period of relative peace, a New Testament world of
ecclesiastical expansion and consolidation when people were willing to listen to bishops' moral messages. Once Cappadocia became a military zone
again, warriors dominated. The Highlander lived in an Old Testament
world, an era of battles and combat. He did not concern himself with bishops and churchmen. His rivals now were all local toughs, such as neighboring emirs, bandits, and even an Amazon warrior princess. In this violent
society an appropriate model for notables in central and eastern Asia Minor

was the strongman Samson. He too had once killed a lion with his bare hands. Perhaps more significantly, Samson had been neither a monarch nor a cleric.[9]

Over the centuries one ruler after another had tried to incorporate Cappadocia into a larger kingdom or empire. Christianity too had been an imported religion, its spread a consequence of the inclusion of the region in the Roman empire. Local notables had patiently endured these outside impositions, sometimes benefiting from service as magistrates or clerics, sometimes contesting the authority of emperors and bishops. By the time of Digenes Akrites, both Roman rule and Christian dominance were in decline, and local strongmen had reasserted their influence. In the outback of central and eastern Asia Minor ownership of land, personal patronage, and a reputation for physical prowess were more influential than imperial power and ecclesiastical authority. Neither emperors nor bishops could survive in the world of the Cappadocian Highlander.

# Empire and Province

"Man of steel." The emperor Constantius had earned his reputation for his exceptional vigor and stamina the hard way. In early 342 he had dashed from Antioch to Constantinople and back in order to deal with unrest at the capital while still continuing his military preparations on the eastern frontier. Crossing the Taurus Mountains and the rugged terrain of central Asia Minor in the dead of winter, rapidly and twice, was an impressive accomplishment, and back at Antioch the panegyrist Libanius was amazed that Constantius had been able to survive "the hard winter, the heavy snowfalls, and the continual storms." Libanius knew firsthand the difficulties of this journey, because when he had once made the same journey at the beginning of a winter, he had become deathly ill. Decades later the rigors of this overland trip between Constantinople and Antioch claimed Libanius' beloved son, who died from an injury to his foot after he fell out of his wagon in Cilicia. The harshness of central and eastern Asia Minor certainly tested the mettle of travelers, including wealthy aristocrats and even emperors.[1]

Another liability of the region was the apparent lack of culture. Cappadocia in particular had a reputation as a cultural wasteland. One man who figured he was on his way up after holding provincial governorships in Phrygia and Galatia balked at assuming supervision of the imperial estates in Cappadocia. In part he worried whether his son could receive a proper education. Libanius reassured him that by now Greek culture had indeed taken hold. "In Cappadocia the affairs of Hermes [the patron deity of eloquence] are notable, and rhetoric is widespread." Libanius furthermore hoped to sweeten these arguments by trying to convince Philippus, a rhetorician and poet in Cappadocia, that this new magistrate would be a suitable topic for some laudatory odes.[2]

Despite these inhospitable handicaps, during the fourth century Cappadocia became vital to the affairs of the eastern empire. Its prominence was in part an unexpected consequence of the flourishing of Constantinople and Antioch. Ecclesiastical disputes and a concern over military readiness had enhanced the importance of both cities. Since the episcopal sees at both cities were seemingly always in dispute, since both cities hosted important councils to discuss doctrinal disagreements, bishops and church-men repeatedly passed through central and eastern Asia Minor. So did emperors and their entourages, as they struggled to keep watch on the Goths along the Balkan frontier and the Persians along the eastern frontier. Cappadocia was suddenly central to ecclesiastical and imperial interests in the East. Now teachers from Cappadocia might think about more than lauding the accomplishments of just another provincial magistrate. One won appointment as a rhetorician at Constantinople on the basis of a single impressive oration. Others became court biographers. Bemarchius was a sophist from Caesarea who taught at Constantinople and recorded the deeds of the emperor Constantine in ten books. Eustochius, another Cappadocian sophist, wrote a life of one of Constantine's sons. Now it was no longer an embarrassment to be a Cappadocian. Eustochius was apparently proud enough of his regional heritage that he also wrote an encyclopedia of the antiquities of Cappadocia.[3]

The careers of the Cappadocian Fathers conveniently coincided with this new esteem for Cappadocia, and they too had to deal with emperors and the imperial administration. The local imperial magistrates included the provincial governors, of course, as well as the various officials who determined the assessments for taxes. In their capacity as priests or bishops the Cappadocian Fathers often negotiated with these magistrates, request-ing favors and assistance and dispensing praise and encouragement in return. Local patrons like the Cappadocian Fathers and provincial magis-trates like governors and tax assessors shuffled along in a mutual embrace, each needing the other to help sustain their influence and authority.

Chapter 5 discusses these relationships with governors and tax asses-sors; the next three chapters discuss emperors and their courts. Although the relationships of the Cappadocian Fathers with emperors and powerful court officials such as the prefects seemed to resemble those with provin-cial magistrates, the overwhelming power of emperors threatened to tilt the interactions out of balance. Even as they conceded the need to work together, they were all wary.

Three very different emperors helped define the adult careers of the Cappadocian Fathers. Julian was the last survivor of Constantine's dynasty who nevertheless might have preferred to become a learned sophist. Valens was a professional soldier who seemed underqualified to become emperor. Theodosius was a native of Spain who had never been farther east than the middle Danube River before being selected as emperor of the entire eastern Mediterranean. An intellectual, a low-ranking army officer, a Westerner:

none of these three seemed an obvious choice to become emperor for the Greek East. These emperors also had distinctly different religious preferences, since Julian supported paganism, Valens a heterodox Christianity, and Theodosius orthodox Nicene Christianity. It is hence not surprising that orthodox Cappadocian bishops confronted Julian and Valens. But it is surprising that Gregory was likewise so circumspect about the intentions and methods of Theodosius. During his tenure as leader of the Nicene community in Constantinople he was unexpectedly reluctant to request Theodosius' assistance.

The imperial administration at all levels tended to be sluggish, more inclined to react than to initiate. Even though during the fourth century emperors were seemingly more aggressive and ambitious in their policies, many of their imperial edicts were still responses to requests and complaints, either from imperial magistrates or from cities and private citizens. Petitions and edicts represented the two sides of an ongoing conversation between administrators and provincials, and emperors and other imperial magistrates anticipated the flow of incoming requests as reassurance that they were not just talking to themselves. In one letter Gregory teased a provincial magistrate about his need for petitions. "What is this, you perhaps ask? Gregory [writing] again to me? Letters again? Requests again?" Gregory already knew the answer to these playful questions. Not only was he indeed submitting yet another request, but he was certain that the magistrate would be glad to hear from him. For the imperial administration to function properly, emperors and administrators relied upon petitions from local notables. Gregory was doing a favor by providing this magistrate with another opportunity to show his generosity.[4]

# Chapter 5

# *"Surpass Me with Your Generosity":*
# *Provincial Governors and*
# *Tax Assessors*

The kingdom of Cappadocia had been formally annexed as a province of the Roman empire in A.D. 18. In the later first century this large province was combined with the equally large province of Galatia to its west and north and the former kingdom of Lesser Armenia to its northeast to become a single huge province that included most of central and eastern Asia Minor. Even after Galatia again became a separate province in the early second century, the remaining province of Cappadocia was still enormous, since it then included the eastern part of the region of Pontus along the Black Sea as well as Lesser Armenia (and, for a few years, Greater Armenia, that is, the kingdom of Armenia).[1]

In the later Roman empire, however, emperors preferred to divide rather than to join regions. By the later third century Pontus had become a separate province. Under the emperor Diocletian at the end of the third century both Pontus and Cappadocia, like many other provinces, were "chopped into bits," becoming the new provinces of Diospontus (later Helenopontus) and Pontus Polemoniacus along the Black Sea, Armenia (Minor) along the upper Euphrates River, and Cappadocia in the interior. During the fourth century the eastern portion of Cappadocia became the province of Armenia Secunda (and Armenia Minor became Armenia Prima). The emperor Valens reassigned cities from Pisidia, Galatia, and Isauria to create the new province of Lycaonia, contiguous to the southwestern border of Cappadocia. In 371 Valens decided to partition Cappadocia yet again into two smaller provinces, Cappadocia Prima, still with Caesarea as its capital city, and Cappadocia Secunda, with Tyana as its new capital city. Excepting a few years between probably 379 and late 382 during which Cappadocia was reunited as a single province, these two smaller provinces survived into the early Byzantine empire.[2]

## Magistrates

One objective behind Diocletian's and subsequent emperors' decisions to partition provinces was to enhance administrative and fiscal control by increasing the number of provincial governors and lesser magistrates. Emperors had also enlarged the imperial administration by clustering provinces into dioceses, larger administrative regions under the jurisdiction of vicars and their staffs. Cappadocia Prima and Cappadocia Secunda, as well as Helenopontus, Pontus Polemoniacus, Armenia Prima, and Armenia Secunda, were all in the diocese of Pontica, an immense region that stretched from Bithynia across northern, central, and eastern Asia Minor to the frontier on the upper Euphrates River and that included almost a dozen provinces. A vicar was nominally responsible for the supervision of the provincial governors in each diocese. But since the principal residence for the vicar of Pontica was Ancyra in the province of Galatia, he in fact seems to have appeared in the northern and eastern provinces of his diocese only infrequently, primarily when he accompanied the imperial court during its journeys across Asia Minor or when he came to enforce specific imperial decisions. For the provinces in Cappadocia, Pontus, and Armenia, the vicar of Pontica was hence more of a court magistrate than a regional administrator, and Basil and Gregory of Nazianzus wrote letters to or about a vicar usually only after he had meddled in local provincial affairs.[3]

As in almost all of the other one hundred or so provinces in the empire, the most prominent imperial magistrate in Cappadocia, and then in Cappadocia Prima and Cappadocia Secunda, was the provincial governor. Each governor was responsible for acting as a local judge, administering the public post, supervising public works, overseeing cities, and maintaining law and order in his province. Assisting him was an *officium*, a staff of lesser bureaucrats and civil servants who served more or less permanently in the province. Governors and their staffs also participated in the collection of imperial revenues, including the rents from the imperial estates and the various taxes. Over the centuries Roman rule in Cappadocia, again as in other provinces, had promoted the roles of cities, whose territories included sometimes huge tracts of rural hinterland. But from the time of its incorporation into the Roman empire, and well into the period of the Byzantine empire, there were also in Cappadocia many imperial estates and ranches known collectively as the *domus divina*, the "sacred household." These properties were under the supervision of the *comes domorum*. This "count of the estates" was himself under the jurisdiction of the *comes rei privatae*, the "count of the [imperial] private property," who was in turn a high-ranking member of an emperor's court. After Valens' partition of the province all of the cities except Caesarea were in Cappadocia Secunda, and most likely all of the imperial estates were in Cappadocia Prima. As a result, Valens apparently now delegated to the governor of Cappadocia Prima the responsibility for collecting rents from the tenants on these estates.[4]

Of the many taxes imposed by the imperial government those paid in gold and silver were owed to a department under the jurisdiction of the *comes sacrarum largitionum*, the "count of the sacred revenues," although governors and their staffs actually collected many of them. Other taxes, often in the form of levies in kind or forced labor, were paid to departments headed by the prefect of the East, who was nominally, and usually in fact, the most powerful member of an eastern emperor's court. For Cappadocia these levies included grain and other foodstuffs, livestock (especially horses), and probably metallic ores from the mines in the Taurus Mountains for use in local arms factories. Although governors and their staffs provided fiscal information, assisted in the collection of many of these levies, tried to collect arrears, and supervised the transportation of commodities, the main responsibility for determining assessments was assigned to various lesser magistrates appointed by the imperial administration, including *censitores*, "registrars," and *peraequatores*, "equalizers," and the primary responsibility for collecting levies fell upon prominent decurions, the municipal councilors who were also local landowners. The lives of the Cappadocian Fathers hence coincided with repeated administrative reforms as emperors and their courts struggled to improve control over the provinces in the interior that supplied much of the revenues and supplies needed to maintain the armies on the frontiers.[5]

In some respects provincial and diocesan boundaries were irrelevant, since the Cappadocian Fathers also exchanged letters with governors and other imperial magistrates outside Cappadocia. Their families' interests, their ecclesiastical careers, and their own journeys linked them with neighboring provinces, not only those in the diocese of Pontica but also some in the contiguous dioceses of Asiana (which corresponded to western Asia Minor and included the province of Lycaonia) and Oriens (which was centered on Syria but also incorporated a small part of southeastern Asia Minor south of the Taurus Mountains that included the provinces of Isauria, Cilicia, and Euphratensis). As clerics and bishops, however, in their concern for daily affairs Basil, Gregory of Nazianzus, and Gregory of Nyssa interacted most often with the provincial governors, the members of their staffs, and the various tax assessors who served in the larger province of Cappadocia or in the smaller provinces of Cappadocia Prima and Cappadocia Secunda.

## Provincial Governors

In their letters to governors the Cappadocian Fathers often acted as brokers introducing the petitions of others, or as patrons protecting the interests of their communities and members of their congregations. Sometimes they appealed on behalf of individuals with private grievances about the theft of grain or threats against a house, while at other times they submitted petitions on behalf of a city or its decurions. Basil's summary of the functions of a good governor emphasized his role as a judge, "a true guardian of justice, accessible to victims, terrifying to lawbreakers, and evenhanded to poor and rich." Yet the Cappadocian Fathers, like other notables and aristocrats, did not distinguish notions of justice from considerations of status and rank. Even though they occasionally alluded to Roman laws, the justice that they considered most appropriate was not the strict and blind application of laws and ordinances, as rather the proportionate distribution of favors and benefactions. In another letter Basil conceded that a governor's primary concern was to "indulge justice," but he then added another obligation that seemed to be an elaboration of the first, "to benefit friends and look out for those who flee to your patronage." Gregory of Nazianzus once reminded a governor that he should respect his petitioner's old age and ill health and show solicitude for the people he represented, because the "Judge" in heaven would someday evaluate this governor in a similar fashion.[6]

Since the Cappadocian Fathers were seeking partisan favors rather than impartial justice, they were less concerned about arguing the absolute merits and legal technicalities of their petitions and more interested in establishing personal relationships with their correspondents. The importance or even the rightness of the actual favors they requested in their letters was not necessarily the most consequential aspect of their petitions, because the success of these requests depended heavily upon their form and the manner of their presentation. In particular, Gregory and Basil often represented both themselves and their correspondents as devotees of Greek classical culture. Such an identification had advantages for both writers and recipients. It first of all made it possible to establish an instant intimacy and a sudden friendship. Basil served as a priest and then bishop at Caesarea for over fifteen years, and Gregory had likewise been a priest for over a decade before serving sporadically as acting bishop at Nazianzus. Both were also local notables who were long familiar with people and circumstances in the region. In contrast, provincial governors typically served only one or two years before assuming another magistracy or returning to a leisured retirement. Because they were furthermore not natives of the provinces they governed, governors who were not sufficiently wary could easily become pawns in local animosities. In the province of Armenia Prima, for instance, a hostile military commander manipulated the governor to use his authority against Gregory of Nyssa, who had just been selected as bishop of Sebasteia.[7]

In dealing with provincial governors Basil and Gregory of Nazianzus hence had to allow for short tenures, rapid turnover, and limited awareness of local issues. Familiarity with classical culture became a substitute for personal familiarity, because even though governors and bishops barely had time to get to know each other personally, they could still claim to know the kind of men that education implied learned men to be. "Birds of a feather flock together": by citing this Greek proverb Gregory had no hesitation in introducing himself to a new magistrate, and he went on to claim that one "Attic gentleman" likewise enjoyed the company of another. Basil similarly once introduced himself to a governor by citing a line from Euripides: "even if I never see him with my eyes, I consider the wise man to be a friend." Having established their intimacy through a quotation that described the importance of a classical education and that only a man with such a classical education could decipher, Basil then asked to be included on this governor's "catalogue of friends." In a letter to another governor Basil only alluded to a proverb; in his reply the governor was able to demonstrate his familiarity with obscure erudition by actually citing the proverb. In this case Basil had tested this governor's worthiness to be a friend, the governor had demonstrated his virtuous character by catching the allusion, and sharing a classical proverb had created their immediate rapport. Obviously the governors too were interested in establishing these friendships as quickly as possible, since they might someday need assistance. Basil, for instance, eventually appealed to court officials on behalf of two former governors who had lost their offices through misfortunes or slander. More than any other factor, familiarity with classical culture created the networks of patronage, friendship, and influence that extended throughout the Roman empire among aristocrats, including imperial magistrates, local notables, and bishops. Gregory's short letter to Themistius, the noted orator and high-ranking senator at Constantinople, neatly summarized this conflation of interests, since λόγοι was the first word, καὶ φίλους the last: "culture and friends."[8]

Familiarity with classical culture was also a means for allowing petitioners to request favors and governors to grant them in a polite context that seemed to imply no overtones of groveling or haughtiness. When Gregory wrote to one governor, he cited the poet Hesiod to support his claim that educated men enjoyed a friendly rivalry in performing favors for each other. Basil likewise observed that a governor could no more easily ignore his obligation to provide "assistance for the needy" than he could escape his own shadow. Even though Basil and Gregory were, in their own letters of course, consistently the petitioners, in fact the governors were in a much more precarious situation. Sometimes they might threaten or intimidate people in their province. "Mix a little terror with your gentleness," one epigram for a magistrate stated; "only a whip can drive a headstrong horse in a straight line." As Gregory the Elder once conceded to an angry governor of Cappadocia, "it is all too easy for you, if you wish, to use some force." But in most cases the structure of the imperial administration left provincial governors vulnerable. Not only did they serve at the pleasure of the emperor; they could also not be certain of the support of the imperial court during their governorships. Gregory of Nazianzus once even had to remind a magistrate that fear of his superiors should not prevent him from showing compassion or gentleness.[9]

Uncertainty about the reactions of a remote court was one concern for provincial governors; another was anxiety about the reactions of their subjects. Governors were typically men who were close to the beginning of their service in the imperial administration, and who were hence comparatively low on the lists of official ranks. Among the nominal subjects in their provinces, however, there were often local notables who had acquired higher rank and standing, either by having held some great office or by having been admitted into the rapidly expanding senate at Constantinople. The ecclesiastical hierarchy was also enhancing its prominence, and in some cases governors arrived in their provinces to discover that emperors or court officials had already delegated special powers to bishops. Basil once explained to a new governor that the emperor Valens had allowed him to administer the churches directly, without having to consult with the governor. He furthermore defended the construction of a new church, a new episcopal residence, and new hostels at Caesarea by claiming that the buildings enhanced the reputations of both the city and the governor. Basil could then conclude that, rather than competing with the governor, he was doing him a favor, even honoring him, because these new buildings were "a source of pride for our governor." And if anxieties about both imperial support and provincial reactions were not worrisome enough for governors, they were also aware that emperors and provincial subjects sometimes communicated directly. Although governors certainly sent dispatches and requests for advice to the imperial court and received instructions about the decisions of emperors or prefects, emperors were still curious enough about provincial magistrates to encourage local communities to evaluate their governors with public acclamations, and to send copies of their acclamations directly to the court.[10]

Governors were therefore suspended precariously between their uneasiness about the imperial court and their concern to acquire both the approval of the people they governed and the support of local notables like bishops. In the letters of Basil and Gregory of Nazianzus that support consistently came with a price, even though it was never openly stated as such. Few of their letters were as explicit as one from Gregory to a magistrate that began and ended with the same exhortation: "be a benefactor." Instead, by appealing to traditional virtues and examples from classical mythology and ancient history (or, when appropriate, from biblical stories) they implicitly reminded these governors how good magistrates were expected to behave toward their subjects. Gregory considerately flattered one magistrate by calling him "an ally of virtue and an opponent of evil," and others by addressing them as the personification of various virtues, "your Perfection" or "your Goodness"; Basil likewise addressed magistrates as "your Nobleness" or "your Perfection." Both Gregory and Basil reminded governors of examples of generosity and kindness from ancient history that were still relevant paradigms. In particular, they recalled the behavior of earlier rulers in Asia Minor such as the Lydian king Croesus, the Persian king Cyrus, and the prototypical conqueror, Alexander the Great. When Basil mentioned "the excellence of your rule" to a governor, his compliment was the equivalent of an acclamation. And just as public acclamations put enormous pressure on magistrates and even emperors to respond favorably, so these compliments virtually compelled the governors to support Basil's and Gregory's requests. In a letter to one governor Basil neatly combined his commendatory greeting with his request. "Let my salutation of your magnanimity fulfill the first purpose of my letter; after my prayer, receive also my petition." Such laudatory compliments were furthermore previews of the dedicatory inscriptions that governors hoped to earn upon their departure, voted and funded in their honor by grateful communities. Gregory tellingly praised one governor for leaving with "your renown and your name inscribed in all our hearts, which are monuments that cannot be overturned."[11]

These compliments were hence neither mindless flattery nor hollow formalism, but rather hints and reminders of how good governors were expected to behave. As a result, the predictable conventions of the literary genre of epistolography made it possible for strangers to submit requests and petitions even to new, unfamiliar governors, and the shared conventions of civilized behavior among educated elites made it possible for governors and petitioners to bestow and to receive benefits with uncommon grace. "No one was compromised by political transactions that took place in the name of friendship."[12]

On the basis of his extant letters, Basil seems to have corresponded with governors exclusively during his tenure as bishop. As an important leader in Caesarea he often acted as a broker presenting petitions on behalf of individuals or as a patron for the entire community. Often his letters to governors were short and pointed, sometimes even a bit overwrought in their presentation. Emotionally they were consistently a bit cool and remote; only rarely did he make requests about his own personal affairs or his own relatives.

Gregory of Nazianzus also wrote to governors while he was acting bishop of Nazianzus for a year during 382–383, and he subsequently served as a patron on behalf of the community. But his extant letters also indicate that Gregory developed close friendships with some of these governors and hence was much more willing to request their assistance on behalf of his relatives, both while acting as bishop and while living as a landowner on his estates. Two provincial governors who became friends were Olympius and Nemesius, the first despite his apparent lack of familiarity with classical culture, the second despite not being a Christian.

## Christian Governor and Pagan Governor

Olympius was governor of the reunified province of Cappadocia when Gregory returned from Constantinople in the summer of 381. Gregory had not lived in Cappadocia for six years, ever since he had abandoned his first stint as acting bishop of Nazianzus in order to retreat to seclusion in Isauria, and he was now returning to his homeland after his failure in presiding over the great ecumenical council at the capital. Once back in Cappadocia, however, he resumed his standing as a prominent local notable. Not only was he a landowner and the scion of a prominent family, but he was a former bishop of Constantinople, he corresponded with a wide range of imperial magistrates, and he still received an invitation to attend a council directly from the emperor Theodosius. However much Gregory may have fussed about his old age and his ill health, Olympius certainly recognized that he was someone to respect and cultivate.[13]

Gregory sent requests to Olympius about several concerns. In some letters he asked for assistance on behalf of various people in distress, including some relatives. In others he appealed on behalf of Nazianzus and its citizens. He complained that the consecration of a bishop had been improper. He also worried over the city's standing, since at one point it appeared that Nazianzus might be stripped of its rank as a city. The circumstances of this threat are not clear, although it seems to have been proposed as the penalty for overturning some statues. Gregory wrote immediately to Olympius to plead on behalf of Nazianzus. He suggested that the governor should discipline only those "few young men" who had disobeyed his edict, and he encouraged him to take pity on the other citizens, magistrates, and aristocrats who would all suffer from such an indiscriminate penalty. He may in addition have been silently concerned about the ecclesiastical standing of the city, since the loss of its rank as a city would also entail the loss of its standing as an independent bishopric.[14]

Gregory tried to convince Olympius to grant these requests by appealing to two considerations. One was the governor's inherent virtues, which included his generosity, his courage, his wisdom, and, not least, his tenderness. According to Gregory, Olympius had previously distinguished himself for "the immensity of his gentleness." Since all these characteristics were the necessary qualifications for his office, in Gregory's estimation Olympius already "possessed all the virtues of a magistrate." A second consideration was imitation of God's behavior. Gregory suggested that Olympius should copy God's qualities of arbitration and correction, and he noted that God would repay him in kind for his favors to Gregory.[15]

Noticeably missing from these appeals was any reference to classical literature, or any of the customary flattery of his correspondent's knowledge of classical culture. Even though he appealed on behalf of his hometown of Nazianzus, Gregory did not use any extended comparisons with ancient history or classical mythology. He mentioned only that the city was old, that it had been founded by kings, and that it had once been spared by the Persians. Rather than alluding to classical culture, Gregory emphasized Olympius' Christian beliefs and his innate virtues, and he concluded that this was enough to establish a relationship: "accept my advice as if from a friend."[16]

This proposal to demote the rank of Nazianzus was perhaps a reflection of further organizational changes in Cappadocia, because in 382 the imperial court was tinkering again with the administration of the province. This time the modification affected Gregory's friendship with Olympius. A few years previously, perhaps in 379 when Theodosius became emperor in the East, Cappadocia had been reunited as a single province. Now, apparently with the beginning of a new indiction, a new tax cycle, in September 382, it was to be partitioned again into two provinces. Olympius would then no longer be the governor of the province that included Nazianzus. Gregory's dismay at losing Olympius as his governor was a poignant indication of the friendship they had developed in just the year since Gregory's return to Cappadocia. "The great Olympius is no longer with us; no longer does he steer our rudder. We are dead; we have been abandoned." Once Gregory had begun to serve again as bishop of Nazianzus in mid-382, Olympius had frequently deferred to his episcopal judgment. Because Gregory had probably counted upon Olympius' support during his acting episcopacy, he was all the more dismayed at his friend's departure as governor for his province. Perhaps it was not coincidence that within a year Gregory ceased his episcopal service.[17]

At least this time Gregory remained in Cappadocia, living again on his estates and continuing to send petitions to governors. During the mid- or late 380s Nemesius served as governor of Cappadocia Secunda, the restored smaller province that again included Nazianzus and Gregory's estates. Since Gregory was no longer acting bishop at Nazianzus, his appeals to Nemesius were strictly on behalf of individuals. Gregory seems to have been most pleased that these letters provided him with opportunities to share with Nemesius a "fellowship of culture." In his letters to Olympius, Gregory had not included any literary allusions, which suggests that Olympius did not have an extensive classical education or that as a Christian he preferred biblical citations. With Nemesius, Gregory now sprinkled his letters with allusions, stories, and quotations from classical literature.[18]

Nemesius had acquired a reputation for his legal and rhetorical skills before becoming governor. During his governorship Gregory claimed to be so impressed with his decisions that he paid him the ultimate compliment for an educated man who had entered the imperial administration:

although a magistrate, Nemesius had still acted like a philosopher. In addition to his learned letters, Gregory responded with a long poem. Although he described this poem as a substitute for the hymns, portraits, and statues that others might offer, it was more than a panegyric. Nemesius was not a Christian. When writing to another non-Christian, Gregory of Nyssa had been so respectful of his correspondent's "devotion to external culture" that he declined to quote any biblical passages. Nemesius was not so strict, however, since he had already promised to discuss Christianity with Gregory of Nazianzus. Now, since familiarity with classical culture had established a bond between them as friends, Gregory would use it to introduce Nemesius to Christianity. In his poem he politely, and at length, argued in favor of Christian beliefs and against pagan deities. He also provided a new context for understanding the classical poets whom both he and Nemesius so admired by suggesting that whatever truth their poems contained, they had appropriated from the Bible.[19]

The sharing of classical culture with Nemesius had created a friendship and an intimacy that overshadowed religious differences. So Gregory now took the additional step of trying to use that classical culture to guide Nemesius to what he considered to be the true culture of Christianity. With Olympius, Gregory shared Christianity and respected his correspondent's aversion to classical culture. With Nemesius, he shared classical culture and decided to use it as an introduction to Christianity.

## Tax Assessors

The assessment and collection of taxes were onerous responsibilities for magistrates. When Gregory of Nazianzus once reminded himself that he had in fact not suffered the most in his life, the people whom he listed to console himself as having endured even greater afflictions were the ill, the dead ... and tax collectors. Since both he and Basil often interceded with imperial magistrates about the "many-headed Hydra" of imperial taxes, levies, and rents, they too shared the headaches.[20]

They rarely wrote to provincial governors about taxes. Occasionally they may have complained to or about governors concerning the collection of taxes that they or others considered to be unfair or oppressive, and Basil once complimented a governor for "providing for many soldiers," presumably through his participation in the collection of imperial revenues and levies. But wise provincial governors kept a low profile with regard to taxes.

Prefects, other court officials, and their subordinate staffs calculated the rates and amounts of taxes and rents and distributed the funds and food-stuffs, lesser magistrates such as equalizers and registrars determined the specific assessments, and decurions actually collected the local levies. Governors could hence shelter themselves from criticism and blame by claiming that they were only applying the orders of superior magistrates or by simply allowing their subordinates and local decurions to get on with their jobs. Perhaps it was precisely because governors could marginalize themselves in the process of imposing and collecting imperial taxes that they and local notables such as Basil and Gregory could so readily establish friendships.[21]

When Basil and Gregory tried to influence the assessment of taxes and levies or took exception to their collection, they usually wrote either to powerful magistrates at the court or, more commonly, to local officials. When Basil was on speaking terms with the prefect Modestus, for instance, some of his letters to him were about the assessment of taxes and levies. Basil also wrote about exemptions for a poorhouse to *numerarii*, accountants in the dioceses who were responsible to the prefect, and to a *tractator*, an accountant in the province. Once he wrote directly to the count who administered imperial properties about an improper levy of mares.[22] At the local level Basil also wrote directly to registrars, equalizers, and tax collectors, usually about others' concerns but sometimes on behalf of his own properties too.[23] Provincial governors had seemingly little impact. In fact, in order to influence these other magistrates Gregory occasionally requested the assistance not of governors, but of his own prominent friends. Once he wrote to his cousin Amphilochius, then working as an advocate, to try to acquire an exemption for a deacon; at another time he wrote to Nectarius, bishop of Constantinople, for assistance in obtaining generosity for a man facing "many losses." With regard to taxes, Basil and Gregory wrote to almost everyone except provincial governors.[24]

In their letters to local magistrates Basil and Gregory softened their petitions and complaints with the customary flattery and formality. Their relationships with equalizers and registrars hence followed the same pattern as with provincial governors, but with one important difference. Governors were unknown outsiders, while the men appointed as tax assessors were typically local aristocrats who had previously acquired higher ranks. Many of them were already longtime friends of Basil and Gregory.

One such friend was Hellenius, who served as tax assessor at Nazianzus during the census preceding the beginning of a new indiction in September

372. Gregory noted that he and Hellenius had been friends for a long time, and that Basil had introduced them. Since Hellenius was a native of Armenia, he may well have been among those Armenians whom Basil's father had taught in Pontus and who later were students with Gregory and Basil at Athens. In presenting a request to his friend, Gregory followed the same strategy that he and Basil used with provincial governors of trying to shape behavior by recalling past benefactions and imagining future honors. He first thanked Hellenius for giving tax relief to ten monks, and then noted that the citizens of Nazianzus would praise his name and erect an honorific dedication if his assessments were equitable. The assessment of taxes must have been a thankless task that generated criticism whatever the decisions. Through these reminders of past magnanimity and previews of future accolades, however, Gregory reassured Hellenius of the support of the local citizens and made it easier for him to fulfill this request.[25]

Another friend was Julianus, who had also been a fellow student with Gregory and who was serving as an assessor during 374 or early 375 at Nazianzus, when Gregory was continuing to serve as bishop there after his father's death. Initially Gregory wrote letters to Julianus and requested that he show generosity to the poor and provide immunity for clerics by removing them from the tax register. In order to convince him of these requests Gregory used several arguments. One was to remind Julianus of their mutual interest in classical culture, which was the foundation of their friendship. Another was to insist that he himself had no personal interest in the decision. Even though Nicobulus, Gregory's nephew, was also disputing with Julianus, Gregory maintained that he was as much concerned about that quarrel as about "events in India." In the past Gregory had appealed to imperial magistrates on his nephew's behalf, but this time he would not allow family affairs to clutter up his petition: "there is no reason for disagreement, nor will there be." Another argument was to appeal to precedent by noting that clerics in other cities were already immune. And yet another argument was to remind Julianus that his decision had consequences not only for his reputation, but also for the "salvation of his soul." Gregory hinted that Julianus should remember what he had learned from his Christian parents: "you would of course do what you know to be advantageous for yourself, even if I had not written."[26]

By mentioning friendship, classical culture, precedent, Julianus' parents, and his own impartiality, Gregory had given this tax assessor every possible opportunity for a graceful display of generosity. Julianus' response, however, was an invitation for Gregory to visit and help him directly with the assessments. This reply was perhaps unexpected, primarily because it upset the delicately balanced protocol between magistrate and petitioner. As the petitioner Gregory was only supposed to provide a justification for Julianus' revised assessments and not become directly involved in his decisions. By inviting Gregory's direct participation Julianus was clearly trying to insulate himself from criticism; but from Gregory's perspective, acceptance of this invitation would have ruined his standing as a seemingly impartial broker. So Gregory pleaded illness as an excuse not to visit. Instead he resorted to a different tactic of stepping outside the courtesies of private letters in order to negotiate publicly with Julianus at a local festival. Julianus eventually visited Nazianzus, in part presumably to conduct his investigations on the spot, but also to participate in the celebration of a festival of martyrs. Gregory not only seized the opportunity to raise his concerns about a "just and generous enrollment" openly before an audience. He also put pressure on the magistrate to grant his requests.[27]

In his oration Gregory cited some biblical examples. In particular, he stressed that because Jesus Christ had been born at the time of an imperial census, Julianus, the current assessor, had a special obligation to imitate Christ's compassion. Gregory also reminded Julianus that another "Registrar" was keeping his own books in heaven, and that that divine assessment would be based on Julianus' assessment of others: "help yourself in that enrollment by being generous and helpful to us." Both imitation of the biblical past and concern for his ultimate fate in heaven should therefore have disposed Julianus to display the generosity that Gregory had already requested in his letter.[28]

To reinforce this moral pressure Gregory relied upon his personal friendship with Julianus and their mutual interests. In a letter, Gregory had mentioned their camaraderie and their shared interest in Greek culture. In his oration, he alluded to Julianus' distinguished ancestry and his pious homeland (probably Cappadocia, perhaps even Nazianzus itself), and mentioned their school days together. Although in public speeches orators were expected to mention the family and pedigree of an imperial magistrate, they were also supposed to include only some brief comments. They were then expected to use most of their oration to praise the magistrate's wisdom, justice, temperance, and courage in rather bland and generic terms. In his oration to Julianus, however, Gregory had alluded to some very personal experiences. "What do you say to this, you who are the best of my friends and the best of my comrades, you who shared my teachers and my studies?" This personalized address put Julianus on the spot. By mentioning, even in these vague terms, their friendship and their common experiences as students, Gregory was now pressuring Julianus to comply with his requests. The polite compliments and exquisite courtesies of private letters would not be sufficient, for Julianus now had to live up to the expectations of an intimate friendship that Gregory had decided to make public. "Surpass me with your generosity," as Gregory once invited a magistrate in another oration.[29]

Finally, Gregory could now also use the presence of an audience to create more pressure on Julianus. After his father's death Gregory would have preferred to retreat again into a life of contemplation, "secluded in Christ." But because of unhappiness with the assessment of taxes, people at Nazianzus had requested assistance from Gregory, who they thought had inherited his father's responsibility for what even he now called "my flock." For the people in his audience all Gregory could offer as immediate solace was an exhortation to contentment and obedience by suggesting that flocks were not to stray from their pastures. But Gregory also made it plain that he now represented these people before Julianus, and that he had their support. His request was not just personal, but collective. As a magistrate Julianus would have realized that he too was playing to the same audience. He had been sent to resolve these people's complaints over assessments, and to be successful he needed their goodwill. Now he was facing them in person, in public, without a bishop or any local aristocrats acting as mediators or even providing any overt support. In addition, as a fellow Christian he would have been expected to demonstrate his own virtues. The monks and clerics on whose behalf Gregory petitioned had once sacrificed all their possessions to God; Gregory now provided Julianus with a face-saving solution by noting that, without depriving himself of anything, he could be equally generous by removing them from the register. Knowing that everyone in the audience would be interested in the response, at the end of his oration Gregory put Julianus openly on the spot: "what are you writing [in your register]?" Another oration to a magistrate made plain the importance of winning popular support through a public gesture of generosity: "O most excellent of rulers, and, if it might be added, most gentle?" The conditional hesitation in Gregory's skeptical salutation was significant, for although this magistrate had already shown his "excellence," his "gentleness" was still open to demonstration and evaluation.[30]

Julianus was obviously astute enough to understand all of Gregory's hints. Whether at this festival or later, he apparently did concede Gregory's request, since in another letter Gregory thanked him for his gift. He also offered Julianus additional compensation by pointing out that his reward included more than the gratitude of these people at Nazianzus. In Gregory's estimation, Julianus could eventually cash in on his generosity with "the Grand Remitter of debts."[31]

Provincial magistrates and local aristocrats, including bishops, were therefore always implicitly, and often explicitly, negotiating with each other, whether privately in letters and conversations or publicly at festivals and assemblies. All the participants were just powerful enough to influence each other's decisions, and just insecure enough to need each other's support. Although governors and other magistrates may have represented the might of an emperor, they were unsure both about the backing of a remote court and about their support among the locals. Bishops certainly needed the assistance of magistrates in modifying the impact of detrimental imperial decisions, but since they had the support of their congregations, if not of all the local citizens, they could challenge magistrates to earn their reputations for sympathetic governance. Bishops were aware that their requests had to be reasonable and performable, and their letters hence reflected a preassessment of magistrates' willingness and ability to grant these favors. But when presented with reasonable petitions, governors and tax assessors could hardly refuse.

Deference had its rewards. Professing weakness and dependence put bishops into an advantageous position, since any reluctance to assist them and the people they represented would appear to be an unwarranted neglect of the helpless. Gregory may once have modestly admitted to his friend Olympius that he "worried about draining away your generosity," but in fact he, and Basil too, knew that the recipients of their letters appreciated the requests. Governors and tax assessors needed opportunities to demonstrate their generosity, over and over again.[32]

## Hands

Facilitating this incessant diplomacy was an awareness of the expected courtesies and the appropriate protocol that made each encounter between magistrate and petitioner a formalized ritual. Since a petition always carried the possibility of refusal, people could manage their uncertainties by following correct form. Perhaps the most significant aspects of these rituals were the physical gestures, as patrons pushed petitioners forward with their hands, as petitioners offered their requests with their hands, and as magistrates likewise indicated their responses with their hands: "I place this man beneath your hands, and through your hands beneath the governor's hands." Such overt gestures expedited the exchange of petitions and responses by serving as public indications of deference and acceptance.[33]

In the absence of face-to-face meetings, however, letters had to substitute for these gestures. In their letters Basil and Gregory often tried to conjure up a representation of an actual meeting. When Nazianzus faced the loss of its rank as a city, Gregory asked the governor Olympius to imagine the city kneeling "as if in a theatrical drama" and pleading with him to "give me your hand." In other cases the exchange of the letters itself became a replacement for the formalized presentation of petitioners and the reception of petitions. The genre of epistolography had its own literary conventions that defined the necessary characteristics of attractive letters. Each letter was therefore a ritualistic object, signed by hand, passed from hand to hand among couriers to acquire its own increasingly prestigious lineage, then finally received and opened in the hands of the recipient. Unlike modern gifts, which often seem to lose value if they are transferred on to become hand-me-downs, ancient gifts, including letters, increased in value as they were passed from hand to hand.[34]

To sustain the relationship each letter then required a reply. It is hence not surprising that when Basil and Gregory were unable to visit in person, they sent letters that asked governors to accept petitioners by extending their hands, to show the same stylized gesture of soothing support and potential munificence frozen for eternity in countless portraits and statues of emperors and imperial magistrates. In their letters this request had a double significance, however, because they expected the governors to use their hands both to accept and grant the petition and to write a letter in reply. Just as receiving a letter entailed replying, so accepting a petition implied granting it. "Accept this letter as the equivalent of the hand of friendship." Each exchange of letters was the equivalent of a modern handshake, simultaneously a greeting and an indication of a willingness to listen and be generous.[35]

A shared familiarity with classical culture, the stylized conventions of exchanging letters, and the protocol of personal friendships hence conjured up bonds that could transcend even religious differences. With governors and other magistrates who shared their version of theological orthodoxy, Basil and Gregory could in addition appeal to biblical and Christian virtues. But during the mid- and late fourth century, when the displacement of paganism by Christianity and arguments over the proper definition of orthodox theology generated rancorous disputes, they could not always look forward to dealing with governors and other magistrates who endorsed their religious preferences. In these cases, because provincial magistrates served usually for only short tenures, bishops could at least anticipate a replacement in a year or so.

In contrast, emperors served for life; and of the emperors who reigned in the East during most of Basil's and Gregory's adult years, Constantius and Valens were not sympathetic to their notion of Christian orthodoxy and Julian opposed Christianity entirely. Nor did Basil and Gregory share their comprehensive education in classical literature with most emperors, who had instead worked their way up through the military ranks; while Julian, the one emperor who knew and loved classical Greek culture, had a different vision for its future. With such emperors appeals to examples from classical culture or reminders about doctrinal orthodoxy could not be expected to have much impact. The easiest way to deal with uncongenial emperors was by maintaining some distance. For bishops in the highlands of central and eastern Asia Minor, seclusion should seemingly have been easy to achieve. But for various reasons, during the middle and later fourth century emperors and their entourages repeatedly came to them.

# Chapter 6

# *"Men in an Oven":*
# *Emperors in Cappadocia*

Provincial governors, tax assessors, and the counts in charge of the imperial estates were, of course, resident in Cappadocia during their tenures in office, while emperors, prefects, and officials serving at the imperial court visited only occasionally. Even though their presence was sporadic, emperors nevertheless appeared in Cappadocia much more frequently than in other provinces that were likewise not directly on the frontiers. Only rarely did emperors visit the provinces in Britain and southern Gaul, or even the important cities of western Asia Minor. After the reigns of the Tetrarchs and Constantine they never again during the fourth century visited the provinces in Spain, southern Greece, Palestine, Egypt, or North Africa, despite the undeniable significance of the latter two regions in particular for their supplies of grain. The entire southern portion of the empire, from the Pyrenees through Spain and North Africa to Egypt and Palestine, now had little direct contact with emperors, who instead spent almost all of their time somewhere in the great arc that stretched from Trier in northern Gaul along the Rhine and Danube Rivers through central and eastern Asia Minor to Antioch in Syria, residing either directly on the northern and eastern frontiers or in cities such as Milan, Thessalonica, Constantinople, and Antioch that gave ready access to those frontiers. Cappadocia was not, strictly speaking, a frontier region. But because it was near the upper Euphrates River, and because it was on a main route between Constantinople and Antioch, emperors and their entourages often passed through. As a result, during the fourth century emperors made more visits to Caesarea than to Rome.[1]

These visits by the emperor and his imperial court were a mixed blessing. Many people considered the presence of an emperor to be desirable, an event of such longing and expectation that Athanasius, the bishop of Alexandria who was often at odds with emperors, nevertheless compared the joyous incarnation of Jesus Christ to an imperial arrival. Yet the presence of an emperor and his entourage was also a thoroughly unsettling and even disruptive occasion. At Rome emperors would be properly deferential to the resident senatorial aristocracy and the huge crowds of citizens. The monumental setting alone was overwhelming. When Constantius finally visited Rome in 357, fully twenty years after becoming a senior emperor, he had gawked like any tourist at the lavish temples, the immense baths, the huge public squares, and the trophies and statues of his imperial predecessors. Caesarea did not, of course, have such extravagant sights or so many amenities. Instead, its environs offered an opportunity to relax. The imperial estates belonging to the "sacred household" in Cappadocia provided emperors with a rustic retreat on which to rest, to hunt, perhaps also to receive a beleaguered bishop or a neighboring king, before trekking on to the hot, dusty plain of Cilicia or the bustle of Constantinople. During one journey through Asia Minor, for instance, Constantius stopped in Cappadocia to hunt wild animals, most likely in the controlled environment of a game park.[2]

During their visits emperors and their court officials also met Cappadocian notables, including landowners, municipal magistrates, and bishops. Even though these local grandees lacked the impressive pedigrees and ancestral traditions of the senators at Rome, they were still men accustomed to dominating their own cities and countryside. Because emperors and prefects were equally accustomed to having their own ways, it is not surprising that during the ecclesiastical careers of the Cappadocian Fathers almost every visit to Cappadocia by the emperors Constantius, Julian, and Valens and the powerful prefect Modestus led to disarray in local affairs and often outright confrontation.

## Constantius

In 360 the emperor Constantius traveled through Asia Minor to Cappadocia. Although he had not visited Asia Minor for a decade, the journey was not unfamiliar, because during the late 330s and the 340s he had often passed through the region while traveling between Constantinople and the eastern frontier. As teenagers studying at Caesarea, Basil and Gregory of Nazianzus would certainly have seen him and his entourage. Since 350, however, Constantius' primary concern had been the Rhine and Danube frontiers, and initially he left the eastern frontier to Gallus, his cousin whom he appointed as junior emperor in 351 and sent to Antioch. After he had had Gallus executed for insubordination, he had appointed Julian, another cousin, as junior emperor in late 355 and sent him to Gaul; he had himself then spent most of his time in northern Italy or even closer to the Danube frontier at Sirmium. But after hearing about the capture of Amida by the Persians, Constantius returned to Constantinople for the winter before finally setting out again for Syria in the late winter or spring of 360. While he was resting at the "comfortable and distinguished city" of Caesarea, messengers arrived with the disturbing news that the legions in Gaul had proclaimed Julian as a senior emperor.[3]

A few years after Constantius' death, Gregory of Nazianzus would praise him as the "most divine emperor, the emperor whom Christ loved most," who had always been concerned with enhancing the standing of Christians. By then, of course, Gregory had seen the future, and Constantius seemed more acceptable in comparison to his successor. In this retrospective evaluation Gregory's most severe criticism of Constantius focused only on the misguided "simplicity" that had led the emperor to acknowledge Julian as his successor. Gregory's lingering bitterness about Julian's policies had distorted his memories, however, because in fact Constantius too had consistently meddled in ecclesiastical affairs and tried to impose doctrinal standards. Most recently, in January 360, a council at Constantinople under the emperor's supervision had promulgated a creed that diluted the doctrines of the venerated Nicene Creed. Constantius had enforced that new orthodoxy by sending many recalcitrant bishops into exile, including some from central and eastern Asia Minor. The emperor's presence in the region would have agitated an already volatile situation among the churches. Added to these ecclesiastical tensions was now Constantius' rage at hearing about Julian's usurpation: "the emperor's fury burned beyond the bounds of anger."[4]

After long deliberations Constantius decided to continue with his capaign against the Persians. He first sent for the king of Armenia and reaffirmed their alliance. He then traveled on east from Cappadocia to Melitene on the upper Euphrates River before heading south to view the ruins of Amida. Constantius was never to return to Cappadocia alive. After wintering in Antioch he campaigned against the Persians during the summer of 361. He then returned to Antioch and prepared to march back west in order confront Julian. On this journey Constantius died in Cilicia before crossing the Taurus Mountains. Only his funeral cortege returned through Cappadocia.[5]

## Julian

Upon becoming sole emperor Julian inherited Constantius' concern over the Persians. He spent the winter and early spring in Constantinople. Already during his stay in the capital he had begun looking forward to moving to Antioch, to whose embassies he had responded with a generous remission of arrears of taxes. During the late spring of 362 he set out through Asia Minor, where reactions to his presence were consistently extreme, either extravagantly favorable or outlandishly hostile. The bishop of Chalcedon publicly cursed him as an atheist and apostate. Julian himself worshipped at pagan shrines and tried to promote the standing of pagan priests. He next went to Caesarea.[6]

Julian's journey through Cappadocia was a bittersweet homecoming. After Constantine's death in 337, only his three sons had eventually succeeded as co-emperors. One of them, Constantius, had engineered a massacre of all potential rivals in the imperial family. One of the murdered men had been Hannibalianus, a nephew of Constantine, who had once been designated as a candidate for the throne of the kingdom of Armenia and then sent to Caesarea to await his opportunity. Another of the murdered men had been Constantine's half-brother, Julius Constantius; the only survivors were his two sons, the child Julian and his older half-brother, Gallus. Like their cousin Hannibalianus earlier, both boys were eventually sent to Cappadocia, this time as a form of detention.[7]

From 342 until 348 they lived at Macellum, "The Market," a settlement on "an imperial estate that was near Mount Argaeus not far from Caesarea, and that had a magnificent palace, pools, gardens, and perpetual fountains." Julian had been raised as a Christian, and his education continued in Cappadocia under the supervision of imperial eunuchs. In particular, he was able to borrow books, including texts of classical literature and philosophy, from the extensive library of Georgius, a Cappadocian who later became bishop of Alexandria. Julian furthermore apparently attended church services, served as a reader, and may have been baptized, and he and Gallus also attempted to construct a shrine in honor of St. Mamas. As he himself later conceded, throughout his teenage years he had traveled on "the way" of Christianity. Julian was about the same age as Basil and Gregory of Nazianzus, who were now both studying at Caesarea, and it is quite likely that these three bright teenagers knew of each other's reputations. Eventually Constantius allowed Julian to leave Cappadocia. Like Basil and Gregory at about the same time, Julian began to visit famous teachers in some of the important towns of the old Greek world around the Aegean. His journeys took him to Constantinople, Nicomedia, Pergamum, Ephesus, and eventually Athens. In many respects, with his Christian education, his participation in the affairs of the local church at Caesarea, and his fascination with classical culture, the young Julian was a mirror image of the young Basil and the young Gregory.[8]

Yet Julian did not grow up to become another Cappadocian Father, because within a few years he had openly broken from his family's religion and was actively promoting a revival of paganism. His hostile rejection of his Christian heritage seems, in addition, to have colored his interpretation of his earlier years in seclusion in Cappadocia. In his memories Macellum had become just "some farm," "an alien estate," "a Persian garrison" in which he had been spied upon and isolated from companions of his own age. When he heard about the death of Georgius the Cappadocian, who had been lynched by a mob at Alexandria in December 361, Julian actually agreed that that "enemy of the pagan gods" had deserved his bloody fate. His primary concern was to confiscate Georgius' library and destroy the Christian books in it.[9]

As he traveled through Asia Minor in mid-362 Julian probably did not have any pleasant memories of Cappadocia. Recent events there would certainly not have improved his disposition. For some months already he had been angry at the region, because during the previous winter the Christians in Caesarea had defied his renovation of paganism by destroying a local temple dedicated to Tyche, the tutelary "Fortune" of the city. This defiance may have been a reaction to a visit by Julianus, Julian's uncle, whom the emperor had sent on ahead as count of the East and whom he had requested to take the lead in restoring pagan shrines at Antioch. As he had passed through central Asia Minor, count Julianus may well have begun to anticipate his mission in Antioch by promoting pagan shrines, such as the temple dedicated to Tyche at Caesarea, and the local Christians may have reacted to his presence by destroying the shrine. The emperor now retaliated, perhaps already before his arrival, by removing both Caesarea's rank as a city and its imperial name, confiscating three hundred pounds of gold that belonged to the church, enrolling its clergy in the local *officium*, the roster of bureaucrats who assisted the provincial governors, and imposing additional taxes on all Christians.[10]

Because of his anger Julian also became entangled in a local controversy over the manner in which Eusebius had been selected as the new bishop of Caesarea earlier that spring. During the emperor's journey through central

Asia Minor people had lined the road to present him with petitions and accuse their local rivals of treason. Usually Julian had been patient and indulgent. At Caesarea, however, he was presumably, and perhaps unwittingly, following the lead of the governor of the province, who had previously disagreed with Eusebius and who now apparently tried to manipulate the opportunity provided by an emperor's presence to settle an old score. In the name of the emperor this provincial governor wrote to the bishops who had consecrated Eusebius and threatened them. One of his opponents was Gregory the Elder, the bishop of Nazianzus, who refused to back down and instead boldly replied that his own "Emperor" had supported this consecration. Julian was so impressed by Gregory the Elder's defiant reply that he stopped his intimidation of Caesarea.[11]

The Christian congregation of Caesarea and this elderly bishop were not the only opponents the emperor met during his visit to Cappadocia. Julian had once spent a few months in 355 studying at Athens, and although Basil had apparently already departed, Gregory of Nazianzus had noticed him as a fellow student. Years later Gregory claimed that already then he had seen a preview of Julian's erratic behavior in his "fickle character and his extreme excitement." At that time, Julian's spastic movements, his twitching neck, his swaying shoulders, his rolling eyes, his convulsive laughter, his incoherent comments, all suggested that he would never became a proper cultured gentleman, much less the emperor. By the time of Julian's visit in 362 Gregory had become a priest at Nazianzus in order to assist his father, and Basil had become a priest at Caesarea. Both had strong reasons to dislike the emperor. Gregory certainly shared his father's disdain for an emperor whom he considered "the incarnation of evil," and Basil, as a cleric at Caesarea, might have been liable for conscription into the governor's office of clerks if Julian had been able to carry out his threats. Gregory was outraged in particular that Julian, supposedly an educated, cultured man like himself, was now so intolerant toward others who did not share his religious beliefs. Not only was there no precedent for this retaliation, but previous Christian emperors, he claimed, had in fact been lenient toward pagans.[12]

So Gregory attempted to trump Julian by transforming the emperor's threats into a positive opportunity for local Christians to imitate earlier martyrs. In his perspective Julian was comparable to Antiochus Epiphanes, the Seleucid king of Syria who had long ago desecrated the Temple at Jerusalem and persecuted the Jews. Since Julian was now proposing the rebuilding of the Temple at Jerusalem as part of his strategy to undermine

Christianity, he would certainly have appreciated the subtle, and ironic, undertones of this comparison. The leaders of the opposition to Antiochus had been the family of the Maccabees and other dissenters, whom Gregory commemorated in a sermon shortly after Julian's visit. According to Gregory, one of these conscientious objectors had pointedly informed king Antiochus that "God was the only King." It was certainly no coincidence that in Gregory's telling this defiant response was remarkably similar to Gregory the Elder's bold reply to Julian.[13]

This fierce opposition in Cappadocia may well have intimidated Julian. Before leaving, he described Basil and Gregory as the "rivals and opponents to my enterprise," and he tried to convince others to label them as such. He also tried to save face by insisting that, like the Cyclops who had spared Odysseus for his last supper, he was now simply being hospitable by reserving them for his final persecution! Julian furthermore defended his quick departure by offhandedly maligning Cappadocians in general. His endorsement of what he called "Hellenism" had implied that familiarity with classical culture was a credential that could help promote provincials into service in the imperial administration. In his perspective, a classical education could civilize anyone, even Cappadocians who were consistently censured for their congenital uncouthness. As one example of such a refined Cappadocian Julian might have thought of Caesarius, Gregory's brother, who had in fact served briefly at his court. While in Cappadocia Julian seems to have hinted that Basil and Gregory might eventually join him too, since Gregory later claimed that he and Basil had indignantly rejected the emperor's offer to join "your abyss." Not surprisingly, Julian's reaction was to dismiss all Cappadocians as unworthy of his attention. To Aristoxenus, a philosopher and friend whom he had invited to meet him at Tyana on the road out of Cappadocia, Julian now claimed that he had found no true "Hellenes" among the Cappadocians. Since Julian used the label "Hellene" to indicate both adherence to pagan cults and familiarity with classical culture, his remark was both a concession about and an insult to Cappadocia. Even as he admitted that there were few pagans in the region, he also implied that there were no genuinely cultured gentlemen.[14]

In Cappadocia Julian had therefore discovered not only two former students at Athens who had recently become clerics, but also a city that ignored his religious preferences and bishops who challenged his authority. Once before as a young man, and now again as emperor, Julian left Cappadocia with relief and with a parting taunt. Despite his sputtering indignation at these slights, he had more pressing concerns on the eastern frontier.

Once he passed through the Taurus Mountains he met Celsus, the governor of Cilicia. Celsus had also been a student at Athens where he had known both Basil and Julian. But not only was Celsus a friend and a learned gentleman, he was also a pagan. He and Julian performed a sacrifice together at the altar of some pagan gods, and he then welcomed the emperor with a formal panegyric. Celsus was clearly a more congenial companion, and the governor now accompanied the emperor to Tarsus.[15]

Julian too was never to return alive to Cappadocia, because in June 363 he was killed while fighting the Persians. Julian had already planned to spend the winter at Tarsus after his campaigns. His stay in Antioch had been acrimonious, with the citizens mocking his small stature, his pinched shoulders, and his bushy beard. The region of Cilicia in contrast seemed to offer more sympathetic religious and personal associations. In an earlier treatise Julian had linked himself with Hercules, the helper of the gods who had extended his assistance to mankind; Tarsus claimed Hercules as a founder. In an overview of his predecessors Julian had particularly admired the emperor Trajan for his leniency and his military successes, especially on the eastern frontier; Trajan had died in Cilicia. And Julian had relatives in Cilicia. After his final campaign Julian did indeed return to Tarsus, but only to be buried outside the city. Gregory of Nazianzus could not let his spite for Julian die so easily, however. According to his relentless retellings of the emperor's funeral, comic actors and musicians had frolicked about the imperial cortege and taunted the emperor for his apostasy and his loss to the Persians. The shrine to the emperor consisted of "an accursed tomb and a detestable temple, not worthy of being seen by pious eyes." The ground itself had tried to reject the tomb through an earthquake.[16]

Because of his support for pagan cults, because of his own lingering resentment about his earlier detention there, Julian's presence had been deeply disruptive in Cappadocia, and it had certainly brought out the worst in Gregory. In contrast, Jovian, the new emperor, did not share Gregory's disdain for his predecessor. He had become emperor in difficult circumstances. The Roman army was demoralized, his selection as emperor had been contested, and he already had a reputation as a feeble and flaccid officer. Jovian hence wanted to emphasize his links to the previous imperial dynasty and gloss over any personal or religious fractures within that dynasty. He openly supported Christianity, and he adopted Constantius as his model. On his journey from Antioch to Constantinople he also made a point of visiting Julian's tomb at Tarsus. Even if he was not a member of the Constantinian imperial dynasty, he would nevertheless pay his respects to both of his immediate predecessors. Jovian then crossed the mountains into Cappadocia, where he stopped at Tyana to hear reports from various envoys. From there he went on to Galatia, where he died early in 364.[17]

## Valens and Procopius

As his imperial colleague the new emperor Valentinian selected his brother Valens, who assumed responsibility for governing the eastern empire and, despite the treaty previously patched together by Jovian, for defending the eastern frontier against the Persians. In the summer of 365 Valens set out from Constantinople for Syria. During his journey through Asia Minor he lingered in Cappadocia at Caesarea while waiting for the sweltering heat in the Cilician plains to break. His mere proximity was enough to disrupt the Christian community at Caesarea. Valens was a Christian, but he supported heterodox doctrines. During his visit to Cappadocia his presence apparently intimidated bishop Eusebius of Caesarea. In 362 Gregory the Elder, one of Eusebius' suffragan bishops, had taken the initiative in replying to Julian's threats. This time Basil, although only a priest, returned from his self-imposed exile to assist his metropolitan bishop, and in the process to take over the leadership of the church at Caesarea.[18]

This menace from Valens soon passed, in part because he learned that in his absence Procopius had emerged as a usurping emperor at the capital. Procopius was a native of Cilicia and a relative of Julian, and he had made a career as a tribune and a notary in the secretariat attached to the imperial court of Constantius. In 363 Julian had left him in command of a large reserve force in Mesopotamia. He had also, according to a rumor, suggested that his relative assume the throne if he died. After Julian's death Procopius had had the honor of burying his body at Tarsus. Accompanying an imperial funerary cortege conferred great distinction. When Jovian had escorted Constantius' body to Constantinople a few years earlier, the enthusiasm of the crowds that greeted him had portended his subsequent succession to the throne. Even though Procopius now renounced his claim to the throne and retired to his estate near Caesarea in Cappadocia, the new emperors still considered him a threat. So he became a fugitive, until in September 365 he acquired the support of military units at Constantinople and was proclaimed emperor as the true heir to "the family of the highest distinction," the dynasty of Constantine, Constantius, and Julian.[19]

The transition to new emperors was always an unsettling process, and the initiation of an entirely new dynasty was even more awkward. Valentinian and Valens faced several handicaps at the outset of their regime. One was the suspicion resulting from not being related to the previous dynasty of Constantine, Constantius, and Julian. Valentinian's oldest son, Gratian, would eventually marry Constantius' daughter, but not until about a decade after his father had assumed the throne. Another liability was the scramble to acquire supporters. In particular, the new emperors had limited contacts in the Greek East. They were from Pannonia, and many of the men whom they promoted early in their reigns were likewise from regions near the Danube River and in the Balkans. Soon after his accession Valentinian had left for northern Italy and the Rhine frontier, where he already had additional connections because of his earlier extensive military service. Valens, however, had had limited military service, and he now effectively distanced himself from his base of local supporters by soon leaving for the eastern frontiers. In the eastern empire the new emperor was isolated, with no direct links to the previous imperial dynasty and few prior connections to eastern notables, magistrates, and military commanders.[20]

Procopius hence tried to highlight Valens' weaknesses in the East. Once he emerged as a usurping emperor at Constantinople, he pointedly emphasized his links to the previous imperial dynasty. He appeared with Constantius' widow and infant daughter, and he acquired the support of some of the Gallic aristocrats who had followed Julian to Constantinople and of some former magistrates who had served under Julian. By stressing his relationship to Constantius and Julian, he was furthermore able to recall earlier treaties with various barbarian groups, including some of the Goths along the Danube frontier, and acquire their military assistance.[21]

To top off his newly minted imperial image Procopius defined Valens as a strictly "western" emperor by denouncing him as a "Pannonian impostor." The incongruities here, of course, are that the Constantinian dynasty that Procopius claimed to be reviving was itself originally from a region in the Balkans near Pannonia, and that both Constantine and Julian had started out as usurpers in the West. But Constantine had reinvented himself by founding his new capital at Constantinople, and Julian, who had in fact been born at Constantinople, had highlighted his Greekness through his promotion of Greek culture. Even when commanding troops on the Rhine frontier, Julian had remained true to a classical Mediterranean lifestyle, and he had once dismissed the beer of northern Gaul for being too reminiscent of "goat's breath"! In the Mediterranean world the consumption of wine was an important criterion for distinguishing civilization from barbarism.

It is hence not surprising that at Constantinople Valens was now "insulted with lampoons" that were perhaps similar to those used at the neighboring city of Chalcedon, where he was derided as an outsider to the classical world by being mocked as a "beer drinker." By publicizing his connections to Julian, by claiming membership in the imperial dynasty of Constantine and Constantius, and by presenting himself as an eastern "Greek" emperor Procopius was trying to bolster his position at the capital. His propaganda seems to have had some effect more widely in the Greek East too, since at Antioch the prominent sophist Libanius, who had earlier effusively praised Julian, would later have to explain away an accusation of having written a panegyric in honor of Procopius.[22]

Cappadocia was an awkward place for Valens to hear this news about Procopius' usurpation. Not only did he now seem to be trapped between Julian's relative in Constantinople and Julian's tomb in Cilicia, but he was in the middle of Procopius' own home region. Since Procopius was a native of Cilicia and a landowner in Cappadocia, he already had some local support in central and eastern Asia Minor. Hyperechius, a prominent aristocrat from Ancyra in Galatia, eventually commanded Procopius' troops in Bithynia. Araxius, who served as prefect of the East, may have been a native of Pontus or Cappadocia. Another of Procopius' supporters was Eunomius, a Cappadocian who had served briefly as bishop of Cyzicus and who had acquired a reputation as a theologian, especially at Constantinople.[23]

Because a challenge to his emperorship had also become a regional threat, Valens now looked to shore up his standing in central and eastern Asia Minor by appointing local notables to offices in the imperial administration. Some of these new appointees were natives of Cappadocia or Pontus. The emperor received the news of Procopius' successes from Sophronius, already a clerk presumably in one of the imperial ministries. Sophronius was a Cappadocian and a friend of both Basil and Gregory of Nazianzus, and he duly received his reward by later becoming *magister officiorum*. Arcadius, a native of Caesarea, now became probably the *comes rei privatae* in the East. Zeno was a member of a wealthy family in Pontus who entered the civil service as a courier under Valens. Primus the Younger, whom an epitaph at Amaseia in the province of Helenopontus honored for having been "pleasing to the emperors," may now have acquired an office under Valens. Primus may have benefited from a family connection with Arinthaeus, who was perhaps another native of Pontus. Arinthaeus had started his military career under Constantius, and then served as a commander under Julian. He was one of Valens' commanders against Procopius, and in 366 he became the commander of all infantry units in the eastern field army. Antonius Tatianus was another of Julian's appointees who transferred his allegiance to Valens. As governor of Caria he carefully erased Julian's name from one dedication, and then set up another in honor of Valens.[24]

Not only was Valens promoting, and sometimes rehabilitating, men who had once served under Julian, but he also tried to recruit men who had previously fallen out with Julian. Caesarius, the younger brother of Gregory of Nazianzus, had once quarreled with Julian and returned to Cappadocia. He was now made to feel welcome again at Valens' court, and was soon appointed to a financial magistracy in Bithynia. The jolting news that Valens received while in Cappadocia hence compelled him to begin firming up his connections with prominent local aristocrats.[25]

## The Prefect Modestus

Valens soon left Cappadocia for Galatia, where he organized the final defeat and death of Procopius. After reasserting himself on the throne he campaigned for the next few years on the Danube frontier. These campaigns not only allowed him to defend Constantinople and the Balkans from Goths, they also kept him closer to the regions in which he had prior local support. At the conclusion of these hostilities he turned again to deal with the Persians on the eastern frontier. In the spring of 370 he and his entourage set out for Antioch and passed through Caesarea on the way. After campaigns against the Persians the imperial court returned to Constantinople during the autumn, probably by way of Cappadocia. During the summer of 371 Valens again traveled to Antioch. This journey included visits certainly to Ancyra in Galatia and probably to Caesarea, since it was on the road from Ancyra to the eastern frontier. During the winter he and his entourage left Antioch to return briefly to Cappadocia, where he celebrated Epiphany at Caesarea on January 6, 372. Thereafter Valens remained in or near Antioch for several years, until in the spring of 378 he returned to Constantinople.[26]

In the early 370s Valens and his court hence visited Caesarea three or, more likely, four times in less than two years, and most of their visits involved an intriguing mixture of confrontation and accommodation. By now the court included Modestus, the new prefect of the East who became both an antagonist and a confidant of Basil. Despite the rapid transition from Constantius to Julian and then to Valens, Modestus had flourished by holding important imperial offices under all three emperors. Under

Constantius he had become count of the East (the equivalent of a vicar) in 358. At his headquarters in Antioch he initiated the construction of a colonnade, and during his tenure he traveled widely in his diocese that stretched from Cilicia in the north to Mesopotamia in the east and Egypt in the south. Since at the beginning of his term Constantius was still campaigning along the Danube frontier, Modestus had organized the supply of the army and led the defense against Persian attacks. He also acquired a dubious enough reputation for Constantius to conclude that he was sufficiently ruthless to preside over trials in Palestine involving accusations of treason. Modestus remained as count after Constantius' death. Once Julian arrived at Antioch in 362, he decided to send Modestus back to Constantinople to serve as prefect of the city for a year. During his tenure as prefect Modestus began construction on a cistern for the capital. Valens and Valentinian, soon after they became emperors, gave Modestus an estate, and he built a house opposite one of the forums in Constantinople. During the coup by Procopius at the capital, Modestus remained loyal to Valens. In 369 Valens appointed him as his powerful prefect of the East. The career of Modestus is hence one telling example of how new emperors often had to rely upon prominent magistrates of earlier regimes, especially in regions in which they had limited personal connections.[27]

By spending the early years of his reign on the Danube frontier Valens had at least been close to his home region of Pannonia, and he (and his brother Valentinian) had recruited men from the Balkans into the imperial administration. Most of these Pannonians had then served in the Balkan provinces or in western provinces. In the later 360s, after finally concluding his Gothic wars, Valens was again planning to move to the eastern frontier. This move compelled him to look again for support from men with eastern connections.[28]

Finding them was not easy. One obvious handicap he faced was language, because as a native of a Latin-speaking region he was not proficient in Greek. He also already had an example of the baneful consequences of a Pannonian holding office in the Greek East. In 365, when he had initially set out for the eastern frontier, Valens had sent on ahead Petronius, his father-in-law. Petronius had a reputation for harshness and cruel greediness, and his savage behavior had been counterproductive because it had made provincials even more receptive to the usurper Procopius. Inexperience and ignorance were liabilities. The esteemed orator Libanius had pointedly dismissed one governor Valens appointed for Syria as a "fraud," because he did not know Greek. Because Valens did not want to repeat this mistake, he needed all the more the advice of influential Greek aristocrats like Modestus, who had experience of warfare on the eastern frontier and who still had wide contacts at Antioch and throughout the eastern provinces.[29]

Eastern aristocrats who most likely had prior connections to Modestus now appeared holding high offices in the imperial administration in the East. Olympius Palladius was in his hometown of Samosata in the early 360s, when Modestus was traveling throughout his eastern diocese. Palladius served as governor of Isauria, and in 370 became prefect of Egypt. His successor as prefect of Egypt was Aelius Palladius, a native of Palestine. Clearchus made a reputation at Constantinople, where Modestus served as prefect, and in 363 he was an ambassador from the capital's senate to the new emperor Jovian at Antioch. As vicar in western Asia Minor he supported Valens against Procopius. In 372 he became prefect of Constantinople, and like Modestus he improved the city's water supply by constructing an aqueduct. Vindaonius Magnus was at Beirut in the early 360s. In 373 he became the count responsible for the imperial revenues in Egypt, and in 375 prefect of Constantinople, where he likewise benefited the city's water supply by dedicating a public bath. Fortunatianus, a philosopher, rhetorician, and poet primarily at Antioch, was certainly a protégé of Modestus, whom he had known at least since Modestus' term as count of the East. Shortly after Modestus became prefect, at least by early 370, Fortunatianus was serving as *comes rei privatae* responsible for imperial properties. He held this office for an extraordinarily long tenure, at least until mid-377, as long as Modestus' own tenure as prefect.[30]

Like Modestus, many of these men had served under previous emperors, and they all now returned to serve under Valens. Modestus was the key patron. In fact, one general who set up a dedicatory inscription in the early 370s carefully associated himself with the prefect. During the 370s many of the high office holders in the administration of the eastern empire were less Valens' associates and more Modestus' cronies.[31]

By demonstrating that his only firm allegiance was to the advancement of his own career, Modestus had also been able to survive reversals in imperial religious preferences. Julian was initially suspicious of him, but apparently changed his mind upon meeting him at Antioch. Soon Modestus was openly worshipping the pagan gods. Upon becoming Valens' prefect, Modestus accepted Christianity and was baptized by the heterodox bishops whom Valens supported. Others of Valens' imperial magistrates had been equally flexible about their religious beliefs, in their own heavy-handed ways. During Julian's reign Vindaonius Magnus had burned a church at

Beirut. Under Valens, however, he went to Egypt to impose the new bishop for Alexandria whom the emperor supported. Having become a Christian, Modestus too began to meddle in the disputes over Christian theology. He had the heresiarch Eunomius exiled to an island, although in this case he was probably most concerned to punish him for his support of Procopius. Modestus furthermore demonstrated his support for the emperor's theological preferences when it was rumored that he had put eighty opposing clerics on a ship and set it on fire. In a period when each new emperor had his own preferences in religion, Modestus and others had benefited from their adaptability, "venerating [an emperor's] purple robes rather than a particular god."[32]

Once Valens and Modestus began to travel between Constantinople and Antioch, however, they encountered more formidable opposition from Basil. In the early 370s all three men were at the height of their careers. Valens had eliminated the usurper Procopius a few years earlier, and now he was "elated by his recent successes" over the Goths and felt that "no one should oppose his intentions." Just before leaving Constantinople in April 370 he had furthermore presided over the dedication of the Church of the Holy Apostles. Modestus had revived his career by recently becoming prefect, and he would become a consul in 372. And by autumn 370 Basil had finally taken over the see of Caesarea and become the metropolitan bishop for the province. Although Valens had perhaps met Basil during his earlier visit to Caesarea in 365, Modestus was probably now meeting him for the first time. Among such powerful men, an emperor, a prefect, and a metropolitan bishop, each encounter became a careful ballet of uneasy posturing and mannered antagonism.[33]

## Military and Diplomatic Strategies

In the spring of 370 Modestus confronted Basil about his support for the Nicene Creed, first by threatening him with confiscation, exile, and tortures, then, in a complete reversal of behavior, by quietly asking for the elimination from the creed of the doctrinal formulation that God the Son was "identical in essence" with God the Father. Although Modestus called his suggestion a "small favor," Basil ignored the threats and rejected the request. During a subsequent visit Valens tried to challenge Basil again, first through Demosthenes, a prominent functionary on his domestic staff, and then for a second time through Modestus, who again threatened Basil and tried to intimidate him by conducting a mock trial before court attendants. Apparently during this second confrontation, Basil neatly defused most of Modestus' threats by calmly pointing out their irrelevance. When asked why he refused to observe "the emperor's religion," Basil replied that his own "Emperor" was opposed. When asked whether he feared the prefect's power, he pointed out that he owned virtually nothing worth confiscating and that death would only "send him to God more quickly." Since by the time of this second confrontation Basil had most likely already assumed the episcopacy of Caesarea, Modestus tried to belittle him by deliberately not addressing him as "bishop." Between such self-important men intimidation and bluster were seemingly the preferred modes of communication. During one meeting the prefect even threatened to cut out Basil's liver! Basil just "scoffed at this unsophisticated threat."[34]

At the end of their conversations, however, both prefect and emperor seemed ready to admire the bishop's stubborn candor. Valens and Modestus soon realized that they needed to work with Basil. Their plans for campaigns against the Persians took priority over the imposition of their religious preferences, and for several reasons Cappadocia was vital to their military and diplomatic strategies.

Their first concern was the kingdom of Armenia, which had long been a point of contention between the Roman empire and the Persian empire. In these ongoing struggles Cappadocia was a critical strategic link with Armenia. Families from Armenia owned land in Cappadocia and settled there. The region was an important staging area for diplomacy and military campaigns. The emperor Constantine had once parked one of his nephews at Caesarea with the hope of making him king of Armenia, and during a meeting at Caesarea the emperor Constantius had confirmed an alliance with king Arsak. Cappadocia also had strong religious ties with the kingdom of Armenia. Gregory the Illuminator was venerated as the founder of Christianity in Armenia. He himself had accepted Christianity while in exile in Cappadocia, and early in the fourth century he had returned and converted the king of Armenia. Gregory the Illuminator then became the primate of Christianity in the kingdom. Because a council of bishops at Caesarea had consecrated him as primate, the metropolitan bishops of Cappadocia subsequently enjoyed great influence in Armenia in accordance with "ancient custom." A later Armenian history referred to the bishop of Caesarea as the "primate of primates," and Basil himself may already have known Nerses, the current primate, who was reputed to have been educated at Caesarea.[35]

Valens now hoped to use that ecclesiastical connection between Cappadocia and the kingdom of Armenia. Since the later 360s the Persian king had been bickering over regional influence in Armenia and conniving to oust pro-Roman kings. King Pap of Armenia had stayed in exile at Neocaesarea in Pontus before Valens restored him with the support of Roman troops. One of the Roman generals who assisted king Pap was Arinthaeus, who was already familiar with the region because he was probably a native of Pontus. In 371 the Persian monarch launched more military attacks that ended inconclusively. At Antioch Valens and Modestus then contemplated new initiatives for the kingdom of Armenia. In order to take advantage of the religious ties between Cappadocia and the kingdom, they had to talk with Basil, now the metropolitan bishop of Caesarea.[36]

A second, related concern was horses and armor. Among the troops that the Persian king had used in 371 were heavily armored soldiers riding armored horses. The Roman army already included similar armed cavalry. Julian had once taken them on a march through the forests of Gaul, and the retinue escorting Constantius when he entered Rome in 357 had included "armored horsemen whom they call *clibanarii*." Because horsemen wearing mail and an iron helmet sweltered, these *clibanarii* were, literally, "men in an oven," and their appearance reminded onlookers of "shiny statues." The Persians had nevertheless been able to incorporate them successfully into their attacks. Their "iron cavalry" had participated in the capture of Amida, and horsemen wearing plate armor had harassed Julian as his army retreated from Mesopotamia. To confront these armored horsemen Roman troops needed armor and horses of their own, and Cappadocia was an important supply base for both.[37]

At Caesarea there was a factory producing heavy cavalry armor. As an indication of the importance of this factory in Cappadocia now, at about the time that Modestus became prefect Sophronius became *magister officiorum*, the court official who had perhaps already assumed supervision of all the armor factories in the eastern empire. Sophronius was a native of Cappadocia and would have been familiar with the imperial factories in the region. Cappadocia furthermore had a high reputation for its large but swift horses. Valens himself was very knowledgeable about horses. Before becoming emperor he had served as *tribunus stabuli*, the tribune of the stables. Because this officer supervised the supply of horses to the army, he was also concerned about breeding. One such supply officer would be especially interested in horses sired by Cappadocian stallions. As emperor Valens continued his interest in horses and their supply. Already in 367 he had changed the procedures for requisitioning horses from imperial estates, and at Antioch he would visit the stables at dusk to look after his favorite mount. Since much of Cappadocia consisted of imperial estates and ranches, he could now examine their herds directly during his visits to the region. Valens' military plans hence continued the standard policies of earlier emperors who had decided to respond to Persian military tactics by using their own armored horsemen. At least one emperor was so fixated on this plan that he could hardly think of anything else. When Constantius had visited Rome, he had marveled at the huge equestrian statue of Trajan, and then suggested that as his own contribution to the city's grandeur he would set up a copy of . . . only the bronze horse! With its immense herds of horses and its manufacture of heavy armor, Cappadocia could supply many metal-clad horses for the Roman armies on the eastern frontier.[38]

A final concern of Valens and Modestus was the funding of their expanded military campaigns. Not only had the emperor not raised the rates for imperial taxes during the first three years of his reign, but during the fourth year, most likely with the beginning of the next five-year cycle of the tax indiction in September 367, he had even lowered rates. In order to maintain imperial revenues Valens instead resorted to other sources and methods. One was to encroach on municipal revenues by confiscating a considerable portion of the income from the lands and endowments belonging to cities. Another was to improve the collection of imperial taxes by shifting the responsibility for their exaction from municipal decurions to imperial officials and by imposing a check on the purity of the gold coins received in payment by having them melted into ingots before shipment to the court. Yet another was to make provincial governors responsible for the collection of rents from imperial properties. Valens hence redirected some revenues and modified responsibilities within the imperial bureaucracy.[39]

He also decided, perhaps as a consequence of his journeys through central Asia Minor, to reorganize the provincial administration by creating the new province of Lycaonia and by dividing the province of Cappadocia into two smaller provinces. The division of Cappadocia was due to come into effect most likely in September 372, at the conclusion of a new census and the beginning of the first five-year cycle of a new indiction. More provinces produced more magistrates for collecting taxes and levies. And since one of the new provinces in Cappadocia would include probably all of the imperial estates but only one city, its governor and his staff would be better able to assist the count in charge of the imperial farms and ranches.[40]

As Valens and Modestus moved with the court to the eastern frontier, they fretted about strategy over the kingdom of Armenia, military tactics against the Persian armored cavalry, and the funding for their campaigns. During the later 360s Auxonius, the prefect of the East, had contributed to the success of Valens' campaigns against the Goths in the Balkans through his efficient supply of the troops. At the same time he had earned a reputation for not burdening taxpayers "beyond what was proper and necessary." Modestus, the successor to Auxonius as prefect, now apparently hoped to be as successful and efficient during the campaigns against the Persians on the eastern frontier. The primary concern of Valens and Modestus was to improve administrative and fiscal control in the provinces, including those in central and eastern Asia Minor, in order to support their proposed campaigns against the Persians.[41]

## Dealing with a Bishop

People in the provinces, however, had a different reaction, especially to the changes in provincial administration. As bishop of Caesarea, Basil quickly recognized that he would lose his metropolitan authority over the bishops of the cities that would be transferred into another province. He would also have to deal with a new metropolitan bishop in that new province. In addition, decurions at Caesarea were upset that the original proposal for dividing Cappadocia had announced the transfer of some of them to membership in the municipal council of the new capital of the new province. In 371, apparently after Valens and his entourage had passed through Caesarea during that summer, Basil wrote to some eminent Cappadocians who might be able to present these local concerns at the imperial court. One of these correspondents was Sophronius, now the *magister officiorum* at Valens' court. In this letter Basil used an analogy that would have been chillingly effective for anyone familiar with the seismic shocks in the region: no city had ever been buried as quickly as Caesarea, "our city swallowed up by this new administrative arrangement."[42]

Emperors were especially vulnerable to appeals about natural disasters. The illustrious sophist Aristides had once reduced Marcus Aurelius to tears after informing him about the destruction an earthquake had caused at Smyrna. The emperor was so moved that he agreed to support the reconstruction of the city. Other emperors likewise had recently assisted cities devastated by earthquakes. Julian had wept when he viewed the ruined walls of Nicomedia, and he was particularly upset when he saw the city's decurions "in squalor." After a journey through western Asia Minor, Valens himself had donated funds for the rebuilding of Ephesus. Basil was apparently successful in convincing the court that Caesarea too was now the victim of a natural disaster, because late in 371 Valens, Modestus, and the imperial entourage traveled to Cappadocia.[43]

Traveling into the Anatolian highlands during winter was dangerous. When the emperor Maximinus had marched his army through Asia Minor early in 313 "during an especially savage winter," the snow and mud and cold had killed his pack animals and demoralized his troops. Jovian had left Antioch during the winter soon after becoming emperor, presumably to stake his claim at Constantinople, and had pushed on through Galatia despite a hard storm. He had died en route. In Cappadocia and Galatia even ascetic monks had enough sense to live in cities or villages because of "the severity of the winters that were always a natural characteristic of the region." The journey of Valens and Modestus to Cappadocia in the dead of winter was presumably an indication of the importance they attached to the affairs of eastern Asia Minor.[44]

Even though Valens and Modestus were concerned about military and administrative issues, leaving Antioch now was a surprise. Admittedly the emperor and his court had not endeared themselves to the city. Their arrival had initiated a series of hysterical accusations about conspiracy, treason, and fortune-telling as imperial magistrates and local notables jockeyed for position. As prefect, Modestus supervised the judicial proceedings, and he was only too ready to resort to the sort of tortures he had already threatened against Basil, whips, chains, lashes, and summary executions: "it resembled the slaughter of cattle." Yet Modestus was also scheduled to become consul in 372, and his departure meant that he would miss the high honor of assuming the office during the new-year celebrations of the Kalends of January at Antioch. Greeks thought that "Romans" in particular were keen on celebrating the Kalends of January "according to some ancestral regulation." Those celebrations would have spotlighted Modestus' inauguration with a public procession, acclamations, panegyrics, and festive games, and they would have given him an opportunity to improve his reputation at Antioch. Instead, Valens, Modestus, and their entourage left for Cappadocia.[45]

One reason for this trip was most likely a desire to meet with Arinthaeus, the general who was already commanding military actions along the upper Euphrates against the Persians in support of king Pap of Armenia. Arinthaeus was scheduled to become the other consul for 372 with his colleague Modestus. Since he would be unable to attend the festivities in

Antioch, the emperor had gone to him. Valens and the imperial court would have been able to celebrate the inauguration of both new consuls at a party with the troops. Soldiers had a reputation for celebrating the Kalends with gambling and cross-dressing, and Valens might have preferred their raucous company to the tense atmosphere at Antioch. And by honoring Arinthaeus with a difficult trip during winter in order to be present at his installation as consul, Valens could also indicate the seriousness of his commitment to supporting the king of Armenia, especially since he knew that the Persians were mustering their own troops in anticipation of the return of warmer weather.[46]

Another motive for this trip was to ensure the support of local decurions, who were still responsible for the collection of some taxes and who were upset by the emperor's proposed creation of new provinces. Whatever his reassurances in Cappadocia, immediately upon his return to Antioch Valens issued another imperial constitution about the correct procedures for the payment of taxes. The trip of Valens and Modestus to Cappadocia hence gave them the opportunity to plan strategy for the kingdom of Armenia with the regional commander and to guarantee the goodwill of the local decurions.[47]

These imperial concerns overlapped with Basil's obsessions. At Caesarea Valens celebrated Epiphany on January 6, and already during the liturgy the bishop and the emperor began jousting over their public images. During imperial ceremonies emperors were expected to demonstrate their mastery of a divinelike impassiveness by standing motionless. Most famously, during his arrival at Rome in 357 Constantius had never flinched at the deafening shouts, had never turned his head, and had never wiped his nose. During this ecclesiastical service, however, in a reversal of expectations, Basil was unmoving as he waited to receive the emperor, while the thunderous chanting of the Psalms made Valens tremble as he approached the altar. In this public phase of their negotiations Basil had acquired an advantage.[48]

During a subsequent conversation, however, they seem, in a roundabout way, to have agreed to assist each other. Valens now conceded that Basil's episcopal authority was independent of the supervision of the provincial governor, and he donated some imperial estates to the church at Caesarea. The emperor's generosity was presumably his response to Basil's request for assistance after the "earthquake" of the imperial decision to partition the province and relocate some of the city's decurions. Basil agreed to help select properly qualified bishops for Armenia, that is, the kingdom of Armenia. This concession acknowledged the historical role of the metropolitan of Cappadocia in selecting bishops for the kingdom of Armenia. In return, these new bishops would presumably help Valens consolidate Roman interests in the kingdom. Even though the emperor then issued an edict to codify, and publicize, Basil's prominent role, all along his primary objective had been to shore up Roman influence in the kingdom of Armenia. Despite disagreements over Christian theology, fiscal solvency and military security took priority.[49]

### Exchanging Favors

During the 360s and early 370s visits by emperors to Cappadocia had been consistently disruptive and unsettling. They were themselves "men in an oven," sweating even before they entered a region in which they could not be sure about their authority. Emperors showed up rigidly intent upon imposing their plans, or they became enraged on receiving bad news. Bishops and clerics took the lead in confronting emperors, sometimes over religious concerns, sometimes on behalf of cities and locals. In the end, they often compromised and worked together. Once they all removed the heavy armor of their pride and insecurity, they could get down to business. Bluster became bargaining, and confrontation turned into compromise. Julian backed away from his threats against Caesarea, and perhaps invited Basil and Gregory of Nazianzus to join him. Valens and Modestus toned down their threats against Basil and cut a deal about the supply of bishops for the kingdom of Armenia.

This meeting between Valens and Basil was the climax of this process, and also the last for a long time. Despite their earlier differences, and despite their ongoing disagreements over Christian doctrines, emperor and bishop were now prepared to work together on fiscal and military concerns, and they seem to have established a relationship of mutual assistance and even respect. Valens declined to sign an edict decreeing exile for Basil. Modestus, who had once threatened Basil, now requested the bishop's assistance when he became ill. After the imperial court returned to Antioch, Basil wrote some letters soliciting favors directly from Modestus. In one he asked that the new census preserve immunity from taxation for members of the clergy. In another he requested a reduction in the "levy of iron ore" that the miners in the Taurus Mountains had to supply, presumably to the armor factory at Caesarea. In another letter he requested an exemption for a man from having to serve as an "equalizer" of taxes. In each of these letters Basil was asking for specific favors about imperial taxes that were presumably beyond the authority of the provincial governors, who assisted only in the collection of some taxes, or of the lesser magistrates in charge of tax assessments. In other cases he applied discrete pressure merely by remembering his friendship with the prefect. For a friend in distress Basil wrote a vague letter to Modestus that appealed directly to the prefect's "benevolence." To another correspondent he hinted suggestively that the prefect would certainly support this request, if he were to find out about it.[50]

Even though Basil seemed to sense that he had to take immediate advantage of this recent thaw in his relationships with emperor and prefect, he was still exceptionally careful. Requests about relief from taxation were particularly awkward at this time, since the court was now concerned about raising revenues for its military campaigns. So Basil tried to make it easy for Modestus to grant these favors by suggesting an exchange for something he knew was dear to the prefect's heart: the clerics to whom he granted immunity would then be free to "pray on behalf of the imperial estates."[51]

In his letters to the prefect Basil had implicitly, and rather presumptuously, defined their relationship in terms of mutual advantage and parity. A recognition of such interdependence had in fact been the outcome of most contacts between local notables and the emperors and court magistrates who visited, no matter how much swaggering there might have been initially. The earlier confrontations between Modestus and Basil had been simply the unavoidable consequences of a courting ritual that had finally led them to a cautious embrace of mutual assistance. Modestus was to be his "patron" who would also look after Basil's clients. In return, Basil considered himself to be a "benefactor" for Modestus, since he provided the prefect with opportunities to demonstrate his goodness. Even in situations in which Basil was clearly the suppliant it was to his advantage to define his requests in terms of mutual opportunity and an exchange between peers. The petitioner had become the benefactor of his potential patron.[52]

# Chapter 7

# "Birds Cowering Before an Eagle": Basil and Valens' Court at Antioch

During the mid-fourth century emperors and their entourages frequently visited Cappadocia and its imperial estates; yet almost every visit turned into a moment of crisis, often for both the imperial court and local inhabitants. The arrival of an imperial entourage was an intimidating sight, "chariots and horses and mules and a crowd of escorts." Imperial expeditions might include a large retinue of court officials and servants, detachments of soldiers, and an enormous baggage-train stretching for miles that carried equipment and provisions on hundreds of wagons and pack animals. Some cities profited from the presence of these imperial entourages, since from miles around merchants came to service the soldiers and envoys to beseech the emperors. Others complained, not least because of the sudden inflation in local prices. In Cappadocia the resources of the imperial estates may have spared the local population from having to provide the lodging, provisions, draft animals, fodder, and escorts that communities elsewhere were expected to supply for imperial journeys. Even with these imperial resources the passage of soldiers and magistrates could be a burden. In the early fifth century bishop Firmus of Caesarea would complain to an imperial magistrate that Cappadocia was "devastated by a shortage of food": "relieve the expense of [supporting] soldiers that is now an encumbrance, and give an order that no army pass through our region."[1]

The passage of an imperial court was hence disruptive in many ways. Churchmen in Cappadocia who were not sympathetic to the emperor's religious preferences would feel particularly uneasy. In some instances the presence of an imperial court exacerbated ongoing local disputes between a governor and a bishop or arguments among churchmen over religious doctrines, because now the disputants could appeal to new, more powerful arbitrators. In other instances an emperor or a prefect initiated new conflicts by trying to intimidate local bishops. During one early conversation with Basil, even the prefect Modestus' offer of friendship had been a veiled threat: "Is it not important to you to be on my side?"[2]

During most of Basil's episcopal tenure Valens' imperial court was in or near Antioch, almost two hundred miles from Caesarea on the other side of the Taurus Mountains. Bishop and emperor were nevertheless interested in the other's neighborhood. Basil was involved in the controversy over the episcopacy of Antioch, and Valens and Modestus hoped for the assistance of Cappadocian bishops in advancing their plans for the kingdom of Armenia. Because of these overlapping concerns, the relationship between Basil and the court remained tense and uneasy.

## Brokers

Initially the emperor Valens seems to have preferred to approach Basil indirectly through Modestus or other court officials, until they finally met during the celebration of Epiphany in 372. Emperors had to be wary when they decided to meet bishops in their churches. At Tomi the bishop had first defended himself from Valens' haranguing, and then simply removed the congregation to another church. Valens was left standing alone with his entourage, steamed at this slight. In his own episcopal city Basil too was prepared to confront the emperor directly with his "forthright candor" by transforming the meeting into an encounter of biblical significance: "John [the Baptist] spoke candidly to [king] Herod, and Basil to Valens." In his own church a bishop could make even an emperor flinch.[3]

Outside his church a bishop had to be more careful. Although Valens donated some estates and negotiated an arrangement for supplying bishops to the kingdom of Armenia, subsequently Basil seems to have been hesitant to deal directly with the emperor. Even after meeting and receiving favors from the emperor, Basil did not write to him directly. One possible reason for Basil's hesitation was his respect for protocol. "Differences in rank define the [amount of] respect for magistrates," Gregory of Nyssa once explained. "Subjects do not approach emperors and lesser magistrates with exactly the same demeanor." Another reason was the absence of a shared interest. The noted orator Themistius had already tried to cope with this problem of establishing a relationship with an emperor who did not share the cultural expectations of learned Greeks. Valens' proficiency in Greek was limited. Themistius' reaction had been to transform the emperor's ignorance into a virtue by noting that even though Valens did not "share the language of my culture," he still "looks for the hidden sense and, once a small starting point is provided, he hardly needs an interpreter." Another handicap was the emperor's lack of familiarity with classical culture and ancient history. As a professional soldier he had not received a proper education in classical culture. Themistius' response this time had been to insist that Valens was now allowing culture to smooth out his rough edges. He even suggested, perhaps rather wistfully, that the emperor honored the Muses, the goddesses of culture, no less than Enyo, the goddess of war, and that he "was attentive to culture no less than to the sound of the military trumpet." In this case Valens may well have sensed the need to learn more about the history of the empire he now ruled, since he commissioned two of his magistrates to write short summations of Roman history, in Latin.[4]

For Basil an additional obstacle was that Valens did not share his definition of orthodox Christianity. With provincial governors and tax assessors Basil and Gregory of Nazianzus had been able to appeal to a common familiarity with ancient history and classical culture, a shared notion of Christian beliefs, or both. With Valens, not only could Basil not refer to historical precedents or literary allusions or mutual religious convictions, but his letters in Greek would be incomprehensible.

To present his requests to the imperial court Basil hence used brokers and mediators. Some were fellow Cappadocians who were now serving at the imperial court or had access to the court. These Cappadocian brokers included the *magister officiorum* Sophronius, Aburgius, who was most likely the count of the East or another court official, and Martinianus, a retired notable who had earlier held imperial offices. Basil had already written to these men about Valens' decision to divide Cappadocia into smaller provinces, and he continued to appeal for their assistance afterwards. With all three he could share the usual allusions to culture and history. In a letter to Aburgius he mentioned the writings of Homer and the tribulations of Odysseus, and he filled a letter to Martinianus with references to poetry and tragedy and history. If his familiarity with Greek culture made him attractive to Basil's entreaties, Martinianus had another asset that was useful for approaching Valens' court. During the later 350s Martinianus had served as the governor of Sicily and the vicar of Africa. During his tenure as vicar he had received some edicts from the emperor Constantius. Holding these offices in the western empire and receiving these edicts suggest that Martinianus knew Latin. From Basil's perspective, Martinianus was therefore a perfect broker to Valens. As a native of Cappadocia Martinianus would be committed to the welfare of their common homeland, Basil could approach him as a learned Greek, and Martinianus could then communicate directly with Valens in Latin.[5]

Another broker was the prefect Modestus. A prefect was a dauntingly powerful magistrate, "an emperor without the purple." Following their meetings in Cappadocia, Basil and Modestus had reached a begrudging accommodation, and Basil now wrote directly to the prefect. Despite their history of confrontations, and despite their differences of opinion over theological doctrines, at the very least they could share a familiarity with classical culture. Modestus was a long-standing correspondent of the sophist Libanius, and already back in the late 350s, when Modestus had served as count of the East, Libanius had tried to mitigate his conduct as judge by appealing to his noble character and by addressing him as the "nursling of Justice." Yet Basil was always aware of the delicacy of his relationship with the prefect, and his concern about correct protocol was evident in several ways.[6]

First, Basil made sure that he did not embarrass Modestus with either trivial or excessive requests. Instead, he insisted that his requests were both important enough for a prefect's attention and capable of fulfillment by a prefect's powers: "I know how to evaluate myself and how to measure your powers." In his discussion of the prayers that Christians might offer to God, Gregory of Nyssa likewise stressed the importance of matching the petitions to the patrons: if an emperor intended to distribute offices, it was quite improper for a poor peasant to request mere clay pots and fail to "elevate himself to the heights of the benefactor." Gregory of Nazianzus also emphasized the need "to match the request with the person being requested." "It is equally odd to seek a considerable favor from an inconsiderable man, and an insignificant favor from a significant man. One is annoying, the other is petty." Basil hence wrote to Modestus only about administrative concerns. With regard to his strictly "private matters," he instead wrote to a member of the prefect's administrative staff who could then use his "freedom of speech" to approach Modestus. Second, Basil subordinated his specific requests to his praise for Modestus by claiming that he was honored just to be able to write to such a powerful magistrate as the prefect, who was also consul in 372: "I am delighted to converse with such a man." Since Basil had already defined his own success in terms of simple interaction with the prefect and not on the basis of the outcome of his petitions, Modestus would be able to grant the bishop's requests without feeling pressured. Finally, Basil consistently used flattery to remind Modestus how he should behave. Sometimes he mentioned the attitudes that should accompany his benefactions, in particular "the gentleness of your character." Sometimes he addressed Modestus as if he were the personification of various virtues, "your Magnanimity," "your admirable Generosity." And once Basil conjured up the traditional ritual of homage and compassion by suggesting that Modestus should stretch out his hand to a Cappadocia that was on its knees. In his letters to Modestus Basil carefully highlighted his propriety and deference, even as he pushed his requests.[7]

Although Basil wanted to be scrupulously correct as he wrote to a prefect who was hostile to his version of Christianity, he was certainly not unique in using such fulsome language in his letters. It is hence thoroughly misleading to interpret his (and others') letters simply as examples of either indifferent formalism or meaningless flattery. The inflated vocabulary, the deferential tone, the careful exchange of letters, were all components in the shaping of the behavior of the prefect and, through him, of the emperor. Basil and the other Cappadocian Fathers had of course used the same tactics when appealing to governors and tax assessors. Yet one unique considera-tion distinguished those letters from these letters to Modestus. Governors and tax assessors were lesser administrators in the imperial hierarchy, sub-ordinate to the directives of emperors and higher magistrates. Emperors were thoroughly unconstrained. When writing to the court, Basil's overrid-ing worry was the emperor's awesome power, or rather its fickle and some-times seemingly irrational application. During the fourth century almost all emperors acquired reputations for their ferocity and cruelty.[8]

## Temper Tantrums

One contributing factor was a flaw characteristic of the principate since its foundation centuries earlier. Augustus, the first emperor, had certainly wanted to accommodate himself to the expectations of the old Roman republic by gradually assuming traditional offices and powers and by trying to work with ancestral institutions such as the senate at Rome, but in fact the foundation for his authority had been his personal prestige and his manip-ulation of networks of supporters. From the beginning there had been no constitutional structure for the principate, and therefore no legal restric-tions on the power of emperors. Outrageous behavior by emperors, then and during subsequent centuries, was a reflection of this absence of structural constraints. In the early first century, when the emperor Gaius had heard of a frightened relative who was trying to build up his resistance to the poisons that were the favored means of assassination at the court, he was quick to mock him for his true fear: "An antidote against the emperor?" In the fourth century violence was endemic and common at all levels of society. Basil once offhandedly argued that there was no more sense to criticizing God for having created dangerous animals that threatened people than to complaining about a teacher who disciplined a rowdy student "with blows and a whip." Emperors and their prefects often seem to have resorted too readily to threats and intimidation in place of listening and arbitrating. Gregory of Nyssa would summarize the impact of Valens in Cappadocia as a sequence of "banishments, confiscations, exiles, threats, fines, dangers, arrests, imprisonments, whippings." Sometimes the nominal guardians of the law were its greatest offenders. According to a succinct evaluation precisely of Valens and his actions, an emperor "carried death at the tip of his tongue."[9]

The personality of an emperor was another factor contributing to this fear of imperial power. Valens was perhaps especially susceptible to such outbursts of violence. Anger and a violent temper were characteristic traits in his family. His brother Valentinian would become so angry while listening to some barbarian envoys as they justified their hostile behavior that he would curse them and then die from a stroke. Valens too had an uncontrollable temper, and "his anger was always implacable especially when it was disgraceful for him to be angry at all."[10]

In the early 370s Valens seemed especially out of control, since his arrival at Antioch had touched off another round of accusations of treason. Years earlier the emperor Constantius had decided it was time, after an absence of over a decade, to return to Antioch in preparation for new campaigns against the Persians. In anticipation of his arrival, members of the imperial court had apparently tried to ensure the loyalty of the region by fabricating accusations against retired imperial officials and local aristocrats, especially at Antioch and Alexandria. These charges had led to a series of trials for treason in 359 at Scythopolis in Palestine. After concluding that his prefect of the East was too lenient, Constantius had instead appointed Modestus, then count of the East, to assist in presiding over these trials. A decade later Modestus returned with the imperial court. In 370, for the first time in his reign, Valens had finally visited Antioch and the eastern frontier for a few months, before returning again in the summer of 371. This time accusations against and by members of the court led to a sequence of confessions and revelations about conspiracy that eventually marked out for torture and execution "many men from widely separated regions who were noted for their honors and their high birth."[11]

The accusations and trials in 359 and again during the early 370s were hence indicative not of a special fascination with magic, divination, and conspiracy at Antioch, nor of wanton terrorizing by the emperor and his agents, but rather of the antagonisms that appeared as local aristocrats suddenly had to jockey with the presence, or impending presence, of powerful court officials who perhaps had different religious and cultural sensibilities. Members of the court, including the emperor himself, likewise had to come to terms with the notables in their new host city. Valens perhaps initially found this integration difficult. He was more accustomed to living with troops rather than with civilians, and in tents rather than in cities where the local notables expected respect for decorum and a strict code of deportment. As a military man who did not have the grooming of aristocratic civility and who was not fluent in Greek, Valens reacted with "an unnatural ferocity that spread widely like a blazing fire."[12]

The trials at Antioch were a consequence of the lack of restraints on emperors' behavior, the mixing of an emperor and his court with a municipal population that included local notables and retired magistrates from earlier regimes, and Valens' own untamed behavior. The atmosphere was so terrifying that one eyewitness compared the emperor to "a wild animal in the amphitheater." Few options were available to help victims survive these outbursts of imperial ferocity. They might appeal to an emperor's pity and remind him how he was supposed to behave, usually by invoking classical precedents. Gallus, a junior emperor under Constantius, had also once bullied the people at Antioch. One adviser had then tried to make Gallus' decisions "more gentle" by "describing ancient myths and stories from poetry and history." Gallus at least had had an education in classical culture before becoming emperor; but for an uneducated emperor historical precedents and literary allusions had no effect. One spectator at Antioch during these trials lamented that "wise men" had been so ineffective: "if only it had been possible for Valens to learn . . . that it is characteristic of a good ruler to temper his power and resist implacable anger."[13]

Others tried to sidestep the handicaps of language and culture in different ways. The illustrious monk Aphrahat shared the emperor's lack of familiarity with classical Greek culture. In addition, since he had been raised in Persia and then took up residence in Edessa, his primary language was Syriac, and he barely knew enough Greek to preach at Antioch. So when he once confronted Valens over his persecution of the Nicene community at Antioch, he made his point by telling a simple tale about the responsibilities of a young girl charged with looking after her father's house. In contrast, when the prefect Modestus tried to advise Valens, he had to ignore not just his own education in Greek culture, but all pretense of cultural standards. Valens was known for his coarse speech; Modestus now flattered the emperor by claiming that his "crude and uncouth words" were in fact "blossoms of Cicero." In the one case, a Syriac-speaking monk was reduced to telling a simple morality story presumably in pidgin Greek to a Latin-speaking emperor. In the other case, a powerful magistrate who was educated in Greek culture had to compliment the emperor's rough Latin by comparing it to the rhetoric of the great Cicero. Foul-mouthed, uneducated, ill-disciplined, liable to temper tantrums: from the perspective of many bishops, monks, and even imperial magistrates, Valens might have been a petulant adolescent ruling the eastern empire.[14]

Appealing to an emperor like Valens was risky. Even Modestus had to be careful. When Valens once discovered that Modestus had failed to enforce an edict, the emperor cursed his prefect and punched him on the jaw. With all these perils Basil kept his distance from the emperor, and preferred to send his appeals to other magistrates, including the prefect, who could then act as his brokers. Using these mediators had an additional advantage, since the process was never closed. An unfavorable response from an emperor himself allowed no further appeals. A disappointing response from a lesser magistrate implied only that a petitioner might try again, this time by using another mediator.[15]

Through correspondence and conversations with imperial magistrates and letters to sympathetic churchmen in the area, Basil kept himself informed about the attitudes and actions of the imperial court at Antioch. The court meanwhile likewise kept track of Basil and his actions.

## The Court at Antioch

After their visit to Cappadocia Valens and Modestus had returned to Antioch by spring 372. During the next six years their primary concerns were the defense of the eastern frontier and their military campaigns against the Persians. Valens also left his mark on life in the city, funding the construction of a new forum, a basilica, a market place, an arena for staged hunts of wild animals, and a public bath. This display of his generosity was welcome to offset the noxious atmosphere resulting from the trials for treason that persisted and even expanded to include accusations about the use of magic and divination. Valens also continued to force into exile various eastern bishops who rejected his heterodox Christian doctrines. In early 372 Meletius, the Nicene bishop of Antioch, had gone into exile, presumably about the time when Valens and the court returned to the city. Since Meletius' partisans refused to accept the heterodox bishops Valens supported, they were expelled from the city's churches and had to suffer both persecution and the indignity of holding their services outdoors.[16]

Meletius and Basil had begun to correspond soon after Basil became a bishop, and Meletius had presumably also become an important informant about events at the imperial court in Antioch. Basil received letters about affairs in Antioch, and he quickly started trying to mediate between Meletius' supporters and a rival faction led by Paulinus, another supporter of Nicene Christianity who had himself been consecrated bishop of Antioch almost a decade earlier. To resolve this dispute Basil hoped to enlist outside intervention. "The good order of the church at Antioch clearly depends upon your piety," he wrote to Athanasius, the esteemed bishop of Alexandria. He also appealed for the support of Damasus, bishop of Rome, and other bishops in the West, and he even gently flattered Epiphanius, a bishop on Cyprus who had become a relentless pursuer of heresies. More than any other factor, Basil's involvement in the religious feuds at Antioch gave him wider contacts throughout the Mediterranean world and transformed him and his ideas into "common talk everywhere on land and over the sea."[17]

His concern over the episcopacy of Antioch also kept him intensely interested in the attitudes of the court. Meletius, upon leaving his see, had retired to his family's estate apparently near Nicopolis in Armenia Prima, a province between eastern Pontus and the kingdom of Armenia along the upper Euphrates River. Since Basil had been entrusted by the emperor to select new bishops for the kingdom of Armenia, he could now also visit Meletius when he consulted with the nearby bishops who were to assist him. Meletius certainly maintained his familiarity with events at his old see, since at one point Basil asked him for advice in dealing with accusations about himself, apparently at the court. Basil explained that the courier would inform him "about what is being brewed or has been contrived about me at Antioch," unless Meletius had already received his own report. Since other bishops and clerics in central and eastern Asia Minor were also ostentatiously trying to acquire imperial support, Basil once wrote to Meletius that complaints at Sebasteia about his theology were linked to appeals to the court. Meletius may well have suggested that Basil too should appeal his case directly to the emperor at Antioch.[18]

Basil furthermore remained in touch with events in Syria and with the activities of the imperial court through other sources. Churchmen from the area were effective informants. Initially, his primary contact was Eusebius, bishop of Samosata, a city on the Euphrates River about 150 miles northeast of Antioch. Basil had begun to correspond with Eusebius in the later 360s, and Eusebius had traveled to Caesarea in 370 to support his selection as bishop. Basil returned the favor by visiting Samosata during the late summer of 372. During the next year, as he consulted with Eusebius about ecclesiastical controversies, he also received news about the emperor's affairs. Valens and the court had toured a section of the Euphrates frontier during the summer, and Basil noted that the presence of "a man who threatens you from nearby" had compelled Eusebius and others to seek cover, "just like birds cowering before an eagle." The metaphor is telling, in a two-fold sense. Not only was Basil alluding to the menace of the emperor's presence; he also seems to have hinted at some intimidation through the use of troops, whose military standards included the famous legionary eagles. Basil invited Eusebius to visit again. In 374 Eusebius did travel to Caesarea, but only as a stop on his journey to Thrace. He too was now on his way into exile.[19]

Basil was also in touch with other bishops and clerics in the region, especially after Eusebius' exile,[20] and with priests at Antioch.[21] He furthermore corresponded with magistrates at the imperial court, other magistrates in or near Antioch, and some of Valens' generals and magistrates along the eastern frontier. He exchanged letters with high-ranking military officers, such as Terentius, Traianus, and Arinthaeus, all generals campaigning in the kingdom of Armenia during the early 370s, with Victor, another general in the eastern provinces, and with other imperial magistrates in provinces close to the frontier, such as Andronicus, who was governor probably of the province of Armenia Prima. Basil most likely found some at least of these influential magistrates and military officers sympathetic to his theological preferences. The general Terentius, for instance, outright annoyed the emperor by requesting the use of a church for Nicene Christians. The general Traianus made no attempt to disguise his opposition to heterodox doctrines when he once supported a Nicene monk, and a few years later he was joined by the generals Arinthaeus and Victor in blaming Valens' losses to the Goths on the emperor's persecution of the Nicene communities. Basil's correspondents at Antioch included Sophronius, his friend from Cappadocia who was now serving at the court, and Aburgius, another

Cappadocian serving probably in the eastern administration. These letters indicate that, although he may once have complained to Sophronius about the "servile flatterers" spreading lies at the court, Basil was certainly not above trying to enlist his own supporters among the "drones that buzzed around the hives."[22]

Even though he had no direct contact with the emperor Valens and sent only a few small requests primarily about administrative concerns to the prefect Modestus, Basil tried to keep himself informed about the activities of the court at Antioch through correspondence with bishops and clerics in and near Syria, generals and magistrates in nearby provinces, and imperial magistrates at the court. By passing on his petitions these magistrates would at the same time have passed on information about Basil to Modestus, and probably also to Valens. Both emperor and prefect were certainly interested in Basil's activities, because during their visit in January 372 they had agreed to his assistance in providing bishops for the kingdom of Armenia. This plan soon collapsed. Already later in that year, after Terentius, one of Valens' generals in the kingdom of Armenia, had written apparently to remind him of his commitment, Basil had to admit that he would be unable to supply these bishops. New circumstances had recently weakened his authority.[23]

Because of a disagreement over another theological issue, Basil was unable to secure the assistance of bishops in the two Armenian provinces that were directly on the upper Euphrates River next to the kingdom of Armenia. In addition, Basil's standing in Cappadocia had been compromised. Because Cappadocia had been recently divided into two smaller provinces, Anthimus of Tyana was now a rival metropolitan bishop. Anthimus took advantage of Basil's weakness to consecrate a primate for the kingdom of Armenia on his own authority. Although Anthimus was not a supporter of the emperor's heterodox theology, his new standing as a metropolitan gave the imperial court another way of tapping into the long-standing link between Cappadocia and bishops in the kingdom of Armenia. Concerns over their strategic interest in the kingdom of Armenia had earlier compelled Valens and Modestus to overlook their theological differences with Basil in the interest of mutual cooperation. Now, however, perhaps because it had become obvious that Basil would be unable to help their plans, they no longer had any incentive to humor his theological opposition. Valens soon extended his overt hostility to Cappadocia. As Basil put it, previously "smoke from neighboring districts" had moved the region to tears, but now the "fire spreading over most of the East" burned in Cappadocia too.[24]

Significantly, Valens and Modestus tried to impose their own theological preferences not through letters or an edict, but directly through an imperial magistrate. Equally significantly, the magistrate they used was not one of the provincial governors, who were perhaps too compromised through their close dependence upon the good will of local bishops. Instead, they selected the vicar of Pontica, who, although nominally stationed in his diocese, would have appeared in Cappadocia as an outsider, a representative of the court.

## "An Angel of Satan"

Soon after becoming vicar Demosthenes stopped at Caesarea, probably in early 375. After his departure Basil expected the vicar to summon him for a hearing. Instead, Demosthenes instructed his officials to detain Gregory of Nyssa, apparently on some charges about the misuse of ecclesiastical funds and irregularities regarding his selection as bishop. Gregory, pleading illness, soon slipped away into seclusion. In a letter Basil hinted that a vicar had no jurisdiction to examine ecclesiastical affairs, and he also begged Demosthenes to hold his hearing in the "fatherland," that is, presumably in Cappadocia.[25] Demosthenes instead convened a council in Galatia, apparently at Ancyra, during which at least one bishop was banished; he also ordered Gregory of Nyssa to be removed from his see. He then visited the imperial court, presumably at Antioch. Upon his return Demosthenes seems to have tried to weaken Basil's standing in both the Cappadocian and the Armenian provinces. At Caesarea he enrolled clerics in the municipal council and compelled them to assume the responsibilities of decurions, and he did the same to Basil's supporters at Sebasteia. He also promoted some of Basil's opponents, in particular the partisans of Eustathius, bishop of Sebasteia. At Nyssa, most likely in spring of 376, Demosthenes convened a council of bishops from the region who replaced Gregory as bishop. They then moved on to Sebasteia in order to impose their own candidate at Nicopolis, where the bishop had recently died. Even after he had heard a rumor that they might convene another council and invite him to attend, Basil was still duly dismayed.[26]

Although Demosthenes' decisions were hostile to Basil and openly favorable to his theological opponents, ongoing feuds over doctrines do not provide the best interpretive context. The vicar's activities were instead consistent with the policy toward the kingdom of Armenia that Valens had decided upon earlier with Basil. Now, however, because Basil himself had conceded that personal and doctrinal disputes had left him unable to secure the cooperation of key bishops in the Armenian provinces and supply new bishops for the kingdom of Armenia, the imperial court preferred to bypass him and support, or select, more acquiescent bishops in both the Cappadocian and the Armenian provinces. These partisan bishops would then be obligated to select bishops for the kingdom of Armenia, who would in turn enhance Roman hegemony. The emperor, his court, and his high-ranking magistrates and generals were typically more concerned about their military and diplomatic plans than about the imposition of their religious preferences, and their defense of the frontier took priority over their promotion of a particular theology.

Basil acknowledged that he had "enemies at the court," and he responded in various ways. One was to defend himself and argue his interests at the court. In this case, rather than writing directly to Valens or the prefect Modestus, Basil again used intermediaries. His correspondents included Terentius, who had previously been a general in the kingdom of Armenia but who was now living in Antioch, where he was "dealing with the highest magistrates." Basil also wrote to Abram (or Abraham), the bishop of Batnae, after he had finally tracked him down in Antioch where he was staying, not so unexpectedly, at the house of Saturninus, a military officer. As Basil once summarized his own activities, he was "appealing to those in power and writing to those at the court who love us."[27]

When Basil wrote to Terentius, he had urged him to support Meletius rather than Paulinus as the bishop of Antioch. Yet in recent years the situation in Antioch had become much more complicated through the influence of Apollinarius, the bishop of Laodicea. Apollinarius had taught in Antioch for a few years and had consecrated yet another bishop there who represented his distinctive theological views. Since Basil had once been sympathetic to Apollinarius' ideas, his opponents in eastern Asia Minor now revived some old accusations about him. At Antioch Basil's support for Meletius was increasingly ineffective. Evagrius, a priest from Antioch who had been living in the West, stopped at Caesarea to inform Basil that his proposals were not acceptable at Rome. Once back in Antioch, Evagrius even stopped worshipping with the remnants of Meletius' congregation. Evagrius was also now the host for Jerome, who had himself earlier traveled through Cappadocia. During that journey he had not met Basil in person, but at Antioch he presumably heard about him while staying at Evagrius' house. Jerome was young and headstrong, still going through the process of finding himself as a mature scholar. Since he eventually allowed Paulinus to ordain him as a priest, his opinions at the time presumably reflected those of Meletius' opponents at Antioch, who were also opponents of Basil. Strong opinions about Basil were clearly in circulation: even though he was admired for his asceticism and intelligence, he was criticized for having tainted his accomplishments "with his one vice of arrogance."[28]

Despite these complaints about his imperious haughtiness, and despite Demosthenes' personal animosity and the doctrinal opposition of the emperor, the prefect, and various regional bishops, Basil's appeals to his friends at or near Antioch were nevertheless somehow effective at the court. Basil himself was never sent into exile. One of his correspondents once described himself as someone who had "many friends at court who were eager to do favors for him." With this sort of support to offset the schemes of his opponents it is not surprising that Basil noted that the court had once even reversed itself by issuing a "second decision" modifying its "first impulse" that would have surrendered him to his accusers.[29]

Appeals to friends and brokers at the court were one aspect of Basil's tactics; another was to insult and belittle the vicar Demosthenes and other opponents in his letters to nearby correspondents and other supporters. In his blunt estimation, the man who replaced his brother as bishop at Nyssa was "a slave, worth only a few obols," the new bishop at Doara, another town in Cappadocia, was "a household slave who had escaped from his masters," and the new bishop at Nicopolis was "an execration for all of Armenia." In a region like Cappadocia where aristocrats prided themselves on breeding famous horses, perhaps the worst insult of all was to call an opponent a "muleteer"![30]

Demosthenes' impact was particularly apparent, predictably, in the Armenian provinces, which were of greatest importance to the court's plans for the adjacent kingdom of Armenia, and Basil seems to have sensed that he had lost his opportunity to use his influence there. Basil had hoped to transfer another local bishop to Nicopolis. But when members of that bishop's current community objected, Basil warned them not to appeal to the courts or to the "public authority," which seems to have been an attempt to deter them from appealing to Demosthenes. After the installation of a new bishop at Nicopolis, however, his opponents (including some priests with whom Basil corresponded) could no longer use the church and were banished outside the city's walls. Since expulsion was a standard penalty

imposed upon heretics in imperial constitutions, this banishment was perhaps an indication that Demosthenes was now enforcing some imperial
edict on behalf of the new bishop whom he had supported. Basil was clearly
distraught, and in one letter he argued that because Demosthenes had
"pummeled us and strongly defended heresy," he had become "an angel of
Satan." When he wrote to his friend Amphilochius, bishop of Iconium, Basil
almost seemed envious of his brother, whose exile now insulated him from
having to endure the "disturbances of the shameless." In particular, Gregory
of Nyssa did not have to deal with the turmoil at Doara that resulted from
"the meddling of the bloated sea monster."[31]

The malicious tone of these insults raises questions about Basil's tactics, and perhaps about his own character too. Basil seems to have let his
bitterness turn into outright meanness, and even duplicity. When he wrote
to his friends and supporters, he casually maligned his opponents, and
especially the vicar Demosthenes. When he wrote directly to Demosthenes,
however, he complimented him for his Christianity, his honest character,
and his strict enforcement of the law. In this letter Basil even slipped in his
appreciation for Demosthenes' boss, "the emperor, a friend of God." The
apparent discrepancy between these viewpoints was a consequence of the
demands of rhetoric and audience, rather than necessarily of a flaw in Basil's
temperament. Scathingly impolite evaluations of hostile magistrates and
other opponents behind their backs were the predictably inverted reflections
of the unfailingly polite remarks that Basil addressed directly to the magistrates. When presenting petitions Basil often reduced his correspondents to
generic patrons who were expected to feel the pressure of historical precedents or literary allusions. When indicating his scorn, he likewise deper-
sonalized his opponents by refusing to mention them by name. Instead, he
resorted to snobbery and abuse. Praise and flattery created a community of
insiders; insults and derision tried to preserve that community by branding
opponents as outsiders, slaves and monsters who were on the fringes of the
natural order.[32]

A protocol of loathing mimicked an etiquette of friendship. In private
letters to his friends Basil was almost as coarse as the emperor Valens
about his opponents, but when writing to court officials, he was generous
and laudatory. Court officials needed the support of local notables and were
just as complimentary in return. At the imperial court, however, their sen-
timents about Basil were probably more withering and much less flattering.
Both emperor and bishop indulged their anger and frustration with abusive
language and temper tantrums.

## Hunting

After their meeting early in 372, both Basil and Valens remained interested in the same region defined by the kingdom of Armenia to the north, Caesarea in Cappadocia to the west, Antioch in Syria to the south, and the frontier along the middle Euphrates River in Mesopotamia to the east. Through his letters and travels Basil was active in eastern Asia Minor, while Valens and the imperial court resided in Antioch and occasionally visited the middle Euphrates. The connecting point between their spheres of involvement was Samosata, and although there was no direct contact between Basil and Valens, each seemed to be fully aware of the other's activities. Even at a distance bishop and emperor were stalking each other.[33]

Hunting wild animals was one way for notables to demonstrate their mastery over the forces of nature and to enhance their reputations for power and strength. In Cappadocia local grandees lounged about in silk robes embroidered with scenes of war and hunting. In Pontus they wore cloaks decorated with "lions, panthers, bears, bulls, and hunters." The association between hunting and prowess was in fact so pervasive that one imperial magistrate thought the best way to honor the achievements of some martyrs was by decorating their shrine with representations of hunting scenes. Many emperors likewise fancied themselves to be great hunters. A few, like Commodus, had turned their staged hunts into notoriously farcical public entertainments at Rome that were meant to intimidate senators; others, like Constantius when he visited Cappadocia, had used the imperial hunting parks. Despite the good intentions of his father Valentinian, who had scrupulously summoned the best tutors to train him in classical culture, the young emperor Gratian still enjoyed slaughtering wild animals caged in pens. A portrait memorialized the moment when he had killed a lion with only one arrow.[34]

For an emperor, hunting represented more than a mere diversion or relaxation, since it could readily become a metaphor for his entire reign. As Cleopatra had once reminded Marcus Antonius, "your quarry is cities and kingdoms." Success in hunting became a symbol of an emperor's effectiveness in imposing imperial rule. As he had traveled restlessly throughout the entire empire Hadrian had hunted almost everywhere, wild boars in Britain and Italy, bears in Boeotia, lions in Egypt. By demonstrating his mastery over the most ferocious of beasts in each region an emperor was also tacitly stalking the greatest local notables and reminding them of their subordination and his capacity for enforcing his will. And lest his subjects forget these displays of strength and manliness, an emperor might leave behind monuments to his heroism. After killing a bear in Mysia, for instance, Hadrian had founded a town there named Hadrianotherae, "Hadrian's Hunts." In the later Roman empire emperors distributed portraits representing their successes. Some portraits depicted the emperors' crowns of victory or the famous cities that had paid homage, others the great magistrates kneeling before them or the defeated barbarians lying at their feet. Another icon of imperial power was "skill at archery and the slaughter of wild animals."[35]

The conflicts between Basil and the emperor Valens or the prefect Modestus were hence not the consequences simply of religious differences or of arrogant personalities (although these may have been contributing factors). For their power to be acknowledged, great men had to be seen as powerful, and in public they and their audiences constantly measured their prestige and authority against that of other influential men. Emperors and prefects commanded troops and appointed provincial magistrates; large landowners acquired regional support by acting as patrons and benefactors; and bishops, themselves often recruited from locally prominent families, provided spiritual leadership for the members of their congregations. When these powerful men met, confrontation was almost inevitable. Among so many self-promoting political entrepreneurs, power, whether imperial, administrative, patronal, or ecclesiastical, was defined, acquired, and exercised in "a clash of personalities" and "a tournament of wills." Imperial journeys were one means that emperors such as Valens and powerful court officials such as Modestus used to "take symbolic possession of their realm": "the realm was unified ... by a restless searching-out of contact, mostly agonistic, with literally hundreds of lesser centers of power within it."[36]

These confrontations in turn provided local notables with opportunities to assess themselves against eminent rivals. From their perspective, the wildest of beasts they might snare were emperors and high-ranking imperial magistrates. Emperors and ferocious animals were common analogues. Some emperors kept wild animals and even used them as models. The emperor Licinius had kept lions, and Galerius had found some bears that actually resembled himself, "similar in size and ferocity." Not surprisingly, in order to demonstrate their own bravery the Cappadocian Fathers and other churchmen consistently associated antagonistic emperors with wild animals. Gregory of Nazianzus called the emperor Julian "the beast that is now menacing the churches." He then insisted that he could nevertheless confront this terrifying threat: "I do not fear this perfect evil, even if he threatens the use of wild animals." The emperor Valentinian kept two man-eating bears at his side to intimidate petitioners. His brother Valens used the prefect Modestus as his own ferocious enforcer. Modestus apparently groomed himself to resemble a lion, and when he had first confronted Basil he had roared like a lion. But Basil had tamed the prefect by arguing that wild animals were "treats," since they could grant him his spiritual objective of martyrdom. The prefect was stupefied: "until today no one has spoken to me with such boldness." Emperors and prefects stalked local notables and bishops, and bishops hounded them in return. In their meetings they were all hunters.[37]

In the ancient world distance was one great obstacle to effective centralized administration, and relentless traveling was one way of overcoming it. But traveling also compelled powerful men to meet, and therefore often to confront each other. In order to manage those conflicts men relied upon a careful protocol and implicit rules of behavior. Gifts and favors turned confrontations into negotiations. Once Valens and Modestus had stopped shouting and instead offered a donation of estates, they had been able to devise an agreement with Basil. Another factor that eased possible tensions among emperors, magistrates, provincial aristocrats, and bishops was, not so surprisingly, distance itself, because long-distance relationships based upon the exchange of letters were in many respects easier to maintain than direct personal contacts. Even when he was critical in private, Basil was polite and complimentary in his letters to magistrates. By placing such restrictions on the exercise of power and by compressing virtually all power into merely local power, distance was the great equalizer that allowed the court and local elites to accommodate each other. After their meeting Valens and Basil continued to disagree. But then one was in Antioch and the other in Caesarea.

The administration of the Roman empire had always relied more upon personal contacts than upon the strict application of formal procedures and standards of bureaucratic efficiency. Although a series of intermediate magistrates, such as provincial governors, usually insulated people in the provinces from the direct impact of emperors and high-ranking magistrates such as prefects, imperial journeys sometimes brought them into immediate contact. Confrontations with Julian, Valens, and Modestus became defining moments in the careers of some of the bishops in Cappadocia, in part because differences over religious preferences had exacerbated the confrontations. After Valens' death, however, the new emperor in the East was to become a firm supporter of orthodox Nicene Christianity. Would the accession of a sympathetic emperor eliminate or at least reduce the potential for uneasy confrontations?

Chapter 8

# "Everything Yields to Theodosius": Gregory of Nazianzus at Constantinople

In the later 370s Constantinople was a city under siege. In 376 Valens had allowed the settlement of one band of Goths inside the empire; others simply pushed their way across the Danube frontier. These Goths combined forces and joined with deserters from the Roman army to rampage through Thrace "like wild animals who had broken their cages." Initially Valens sent some of his generals and troops from the Armenian and eastern frontiers, and he appealed for assistance from the senior emperor in the West, his nephew Gratian. In the spring of 378, however, Valens finally left Antioch and traveled through Asia Minor one last time on his way back to Constantinople.[1]

By then he was probably eager to leave the eastern frontier. His conflict with the Persian empire over the kingdom of Armenia had sputtered on inconclusively. The Persian king himself conceded that the kingdom of Armenia had become "a continual source of headaches" and was hardly worth the effort. Another important motivation for Valens' departure was the recent loss of Modestus, the most influential of his comrades who had been at his side as the prefect of the East for nine years. During the previous autumn the prefect had abruptly disappeared from office, most likely due to his death. Throughout their stay at Antioch Modestus had been the emperor's most important contact with aristocrats in the Greek East, and after losing his prefect's support Valens may have preferred to move closer to the Balkans and his homeland in the Danubian provinces. Modestus had also been a fearsome champion of Valens' heterodox Christianity. Now, at about the same time as his prefect's departure from office, and perhaps even as a consequence, Valens had allowed the return of bishops banned from their sees for their loyalty to Nicene theology. The coincidence between Modestus' death and the emperor's new toleration suggests that all along Modestus may have been a primary force behind the exile of Nicene bishops. Valens' departure from Antioch was hence a tacit recognition of the failure of his, or perhaps his prefect's, strategy of retribution against Nicene bishops in the East.[2]

Among the bishops who now returned were Basil's friends Eusebius of Samosata and Meletius of Antioch, as well as his brother Gregory of Nyssa. Even a downpour could not prevent Gregory from traveling in triumph along roads lined with well-wishers. Although Basil himself was by now apparently quite ill, he was certainly aware of the retreat of the imperial court. Valens barely lingered at Constantinople before pushing on into Thrace, where he began to organize an expedition against the Goths. The culmination of the emperor's campaign was a disastrous defeat at Adrianople in August, during which he himself was killed. The emperor Gratian had meanwhile traveled to the middle Danube frontier in order to offer assistance. The most important consequence of Gratian's visit was the selection of a new emperor. In January 379 Theodosius officially became the emperor for the East. Once Gratian left for northern Italy, the new emperor soon took up residence in Thessalonica.[3]

At about the time that Theodosius was being considered as emperor, Gregory of Nazianzus went to Constantinople to help the small, floundering community of Christians that had remained loyal to Nicene theology.

## Exile

As in other cities in the Greek East, at Constantinople too several competing Christian communities, and hence several competing bishops, had popped up during the mid-fourth century. The current official bishop was Demophilus, a supporter of Arian Christianity, who had taken over the see in 370 with the intimidating assistance of soldiers sent by the emperor Valens. Demophilus had too many liabilities ever to achieve his goal of ecclesiastical unity. His consecration was already a rowdy occasion, since opponents in the crowd made a mockery of the usual acclamations of support by chanting instead that he was "unworthy." As a preacher Demophilus had a reputation for spewing out his doctrines "in an uncontrolled torrent." Yet another handicap was his own bewilderment about the subtleties of current theology. In one sermon he confused everyone by proclaiming that "the body of the Lord was mixed with the divinity just like a pint of milk poured into the entire sea." Not surprisingly, when he heard about Demophilus' consecration, Basil had been nonplused and dismissed the new bishop's attempts at apparent conciliation as mere "pretense of orthodoxy."[4]

Other varieties of Christians had also continued to thrive in the capital. These splinter groups included supporters of many churchmen, Apollinarius, Eunomius, Macedonius, and Novatian. Among these congregations that each pushed its own version of Christian theology the Nicene community had little influence until the later 370s. Then the convergence of Valens' new toleration for Nicene bishops and the emperor's unexpected death perhaps provided the catalyst toward trying to expand the influence of the Nicene community in Constantinople by inviting Gregory's assistance.

Gregory had spent the last few years in Isauria. After his parents' deaths he had served for about a year as acting bishop of Nazianzus, until in 375 he had once again adopted his occasional lifestyle of philosophical solitude. His departure had hence coincided with the hostility of the vicar Demosthenes in Cappadocia that had led to threats against Basil and the removal of Gregory of Nyssa. Rather than staying to help his friends confront this opposition, Gregory of Nazianzus had disappeared into another of his self-imposed exiles that he justified as contemplative solitude. His deep regard for Basil had already unraveled over his unwanted consecration as bishop of Sasima, and during these years of isolation he seems to have lost contact with his former friend. Yet Basil may well have played a role in convincing Gregory to go to Constantinople. Gregory seems first to have returned to Cappadocia, perhaps in the wake of Valens' final journey through eastern Asia Minor. "One of the good men" then sent him out to Constantinople as an "exile." This reference to banishment suggests that Gregory was now departing again from his home region of Cappadocia; and although Gregory pointedly declined to name this man who had recommended him to the Nicene congregation at Constantinople, he was most likely Basil.[5]

Over twenty years earlier Gregory had refused to follow so many other eastern provincials by resisting attempts to recruit him into membership of the senate at Constantinople. Now he went to the capital to help the Nicene community. At Constantinople Gregory finally had to do what he had been avoiding for years, deal directly with an emperor and the powerful magistrates at his court. His interactions with the court focused on three episodes, a rival's appeal for Theodosius' support in 380, the emperor's arrival at the capital later that year, and his own meeting with the emperor while an ecumenical council was in session at Constantinople in 381.

## Rivalries

Soon after Gregory's arrival at Constantinople he had to cope with both personal opposition and a general panic. The members of his congregation were as terrified as everyone else in the capital at the proximity of the Goths. The only comparable disaster seemed to be the lamentable destruction of Jerusalem centuries earlier: "what is seen and heard now is also terrible, devastated homelands, thousands of victims, the ground covered with blood and ruins, people speaking like barbarians." Despite these worries some in his congregation also complained about their new leader. Even though the Nicene community was small, its members seem to have included various imperial and municipal magistrates. Many of these officials were themselves recent immigrants from cities throughout the Greek world who had acquired their high ranks and new status through imperial patronage, "a nobility that is owed not to pedigree and documents but to favors performed in the dead of night, and to the hands of emperors who are likewise not noble but who create nobility by decree." Some of the members of Gregory's congregation had nevertheless quickly adopted a big-city snobbery, and they now openly worried that their "nobility might be defiled" by the insignificance of the cleric who baptized them. With regard to their new leader, they criticized Gregory's appearance, clothes, native city, and provincial accent.[6]

If uneasiness within his own congregation were not enough, during the celebration of his first Easter in the capital partisans of the rival Arian Christian community threw stones at his congregation. The Arian community was still clearly the dominant Christian group in Constantinople, and since it controlled the city's major churches, Gregory's community was meeting in a private home. Gregory's name for this house church, Anastasia, "Resurrection," may have been a wishful indication of his hopefulness for the eventual success of his community and its theology, but he remained realistic about the situation in the capital. In his estimation the conflicts among Christians at Constantinople were more disturbing than the nearby battles against the Goths. "We have become more inhuman than the barbarians now fighting us."[7]

During his first year as emperor Theodosius was too preoccupied with rebuilding his field army to become involved in theological controversies. Early in 380, however, he issued an imperial constitution that defined "catholic" Christianity in terms of the doctrinal preferences of certain bishops who accepted the creed of the Council of Nicaea. Theodosius addressed this constitution to the people of Constantinople, and once it became apparent that the emperor was prepared to enforce the adoption of Nicene Christianity, a rival appeared to challenge Gregory's leadership of the small Nicene congregation in the capital. Maximus had arrived in Constantinople already in 379. He had style but few scruples. As a native of Alexandria he claimed that under the influence of the great bishop Athanasius he had long since rejected the teachings of secular philosophy. Yet with his rouged face and his flamboyantly long hair that he had had curled and dyed blond, he nevertheless assumed the airs of a traditional philosopher. Gregory, who candidly acknowledged his naive readiness to accept new converts because of the smallness of his community, seems initially to have admired him enough to invite him to share meals and conversation and to deliver an oration in his honor.[8]

Maximus repaid this hospitality by plotting against his host, first by soliciting the support of a prominent priest in Gregory's congregation, later by appropriating the funds that a visiting priest was supposed to have used to purchase marble panels. He also acquired the support of Peter, the current bishop of Alexandria. Since Peter was Athanasius' brother and had a long reputation of opposing Arian theology, Theodosius had named him in his recent imperial constitution as one of the guarantors of orthodox Christianity. Initially Peter had demonstrated his support for the selection of Gregory as leader of the Nicene community at Constantinople by exchanging letters, but now he switched his support to Maximus, perhaps in part because he was a native Egyptian. Peter was able to influence events at Constantinople through the many Egyptians who traveled there. In particular, sailors from the barges that brought Egyptian grain to the capital joined with Maximus' other partisans to try to compel his consecration. Although Maximus' supporters were finally forced to withdraw from the Anastasia, they did proclaim him as bishop. Eventually Maximus decided to appeal directly to Theodosius in the hope of acquiring the episcopal throne at Constantinople "by an imperial edict." The new emperor had quickly acquired a reputation for his openhanded generosity toward petitioners, and in one edict issued from Thessalonica he even chided himself for "granting requests that should not be allowed." Other notables at Constantinople had already benefited from visiting the imperial court. During the previous year, for instance, the eminent orator Themistius had led a delegation of eastern senators to congratulate Theodosius upon his accession. Not unexpectedly, Themistius eventually became the tutor for the emperor's young son Arcadius. But in this case the emperor treated Maximus "like a dog" and outright rejected his petition. When Maximus then returned to Egypt to appeal again for Peter's support, the prefect expelled him.[9]

The overt assistance of an emperor who was sympathetic to their cause was hence no guarantee of harmony within the Nicene community at Constantinople. Instead, imperial patronage had generated rivalries, since now leadership of the Nicene community was a prize worth contending over. Even though Theodosius' rejection of Maximus had clearly benefited him, Gregory was in fact more alarmed at having lost bishop Peter's support than at his rival's attempt to acquire the emperor's backing. Gregory furthermore seems not to have contemplated his own direct approach to Theodosius at Thessalonica. Perhaps he now kept his distance because his previous experiences with emperors had not been encouraging. In one sermon Gregory had already reminded his audience at Constantinople that Constantius had marred his reign with exiles, confiscations, executions, and "clerics arming themselves against clerics," that Julian had died in battle for having persecuted Christians, and that Valens had supported Arian Christians against the "true Christians." In Gregory's recollections, interventions by earlier emperors in ecclesiastical affairs had consistently led to divisive feuds. Gregory was furthermore all too familiar with the consequences of imperial intervention in the conflicts over the sees of Alexandria and Antioch, and presumably he was reluctant to have the same wrangling appear at Constantinople. A schism at this moment, as he later claimed, would lead to the dissolution of the faith.[10]

Gregory instead tried to define and create a religious community that could stand independently of imperial patronage. In particular, he used his rhetorical skills. Decades earlier when a young student at Athens Gregory had become a member of such a community defined by a "madness over sophistry." Back then he and his fellow students had recruited newly arriving students by cheering their own teachers and jeering at their rivals, as if they were spectators shouting at the horse races. These rhetoricians and sophists had often lectured in their own homes, which they decorated with busts of their favorite students. Their houses had become sacred shrines to the Muses, "no different from a holy temple." As he now met with his Christian community in a house in the capital, Gregory was reliving his student days, this time with himself as the teacher. His sermons at Constantinople, and especially his great theological orations, established his reputation as "the Theologian" among both Greek and Latin churchmen. One visiting scholar who listened to his sermons was Jerome, who would eventually claim Gregory as one of his teachers and guides. Rather than worrying about the emperor's support, Gregory had concentrated on his preaching. As he himself was proud to remember, "then Constantinople flowed to my sermons." In this admittedly nostalgic retrospective on his service at the capital Gregory prided himself at length on the success of his preaching. At Constantinople he had become the rhetorician and public orator he had always dreamed of being.[11]

As a telling indication of how he saw himself and his community, he also admitted that he would have preferred to end his account at that point, after having highlighted his role as a pastor. Like a weary farmer on the verge of reaping the rewards of a successful harvest, he must have hoped that he would receive all the credit for having cultivated the Nicene community, rather than having it go to "people who had invested no sweat." Then an unexpected, and perhaps even unwelcome, visit intervened. "Suddenly the emperor arrived."[12]

## The Emperor at the Capital

Even in this productive period of theological reflection and ecclesiastical leadership, Gregory had not been able to escape the influence of the emperor. Theodosius may have been resident at Thessalonica, over three hundred miles away, but news about his nearby campaigns circulated at Constantinople. Already in late 379, and then again in early 380, official dispatches announced the emperor's victories over the Goths. The capital most likely commemorated these successes in the usual fashion by staging races in the hippodrome. These games clearly became a distraction for some members of Gregory's congregation, and they may have unintentionally revealed their true interests in their impatient complaints about the length of one of his sermons. "One of those people who are too attracted to festivals might say, 'Spur your horse to the turning post!'"[13]

The distraction became even more immediate when, in late November 380, Theodosius visited Constantinople. Even though Maximus had been unable to acquire Theodosius' support, his recent appeal had supplied the emperor with firsthand information about the doctrinal confusion and ecclesiastical conflicts in the capital. By autumn several additional factors may have motivated Theodosius to leave Thessalonica.

One was his need to celebrate victories over the Goths. Even though in fact his successes were not all that decisively impressive, the public celebration of a triumph in the capital would enhance his prestige.[14] A second consideration was his recent baptism, which had forced him to face the same ambiguities about his standing in the church that had troubled earlier Christian emperors. Constantine, for instance, had consistently demonstrated his unprecedented authority by disputing with bishops, meddling in ecclesiastical affairs, and even presenting himself as the equivalent of Jesus Christ. After his baptism on his deathbed, however, he seems to have sensed that he had somehow forfeited some of his prerogatives, since he declined to put on his imperial robe again. During the autumn of 380 Theodosius had also been baptized during a serious illness on what he seems to have thought was his deathbed. Then he had recovered. Since at his inauguration as emperor Theodosius had been cloaked with the actual imperial robe of Constantine, he was a direct heir of the first Christian emperor, and his reign would highlight the tensions in the relationship between a baptized emperor and bishops that Constantine's death had conveniently forestalled. The consequences of Theodosius' standing as a baptized emperor would become most apparent a few years later during his celebrated confrontations with bishop Ambrose of Milan. At this moment, however, he may already have foreseen the ambiguities of his relationship with Ascholius, the bishop of Thessalonica who had baptized him. In fact, later traditions would try to preserve the emperor's authority by insisting that he had himself taken the initiative in confirming Ascholius' orthodox credentials at the moment of his baptism. By leaving Thessalonica now, Theodosius could separate himself from the bishop who had become his spiritual patron through having baptized him.[15]

Ascholius was an influential bishop in his own right, in particular because of his close ties to prominent western bishops such as Damasus, bishop of Rome. Early in his reign Theodosius had depended heavily upon the support of Westerners. Those supporters included bishops. In the imperial constitution defining his theological preferences Theodosius had named Damasus as one of the two arbiters of catholic Christianity. Those supporters also included aristocrats. As a native of Spain the emperor had close links with notables from western provinces, and at the beginning of his reign he had promoted members of his family and other notables to high positions in the administration of eastern provinces. In addition, he was still reliant on military support from the western emperor Gratian. All of these restrictions might hamper his success in the East. So yet another consideration influencing Theodosius' decision to leave Thessalonica was his need to free himself from his dependence on Gratian and his western connections.[16]

Aristocrats from Constantinople now offered Theodosius the opportunity of recreating himself as a distinctively eastern emperor. Soon after his accession a delegation from the senate at Constantinople had downplayed the significance of the western emperor by claiming that Gratian had merely announced the selection of the new emperor. This delegation had instead highlighted Theodosius' own attributes, by arguing that he had become emperor through his "preeminent virtue" and "evident strength." By visiting Constantinople Theodosius could hence celebrate a public triumph, bask in the appreciation of the capital's notables, develop links with other eastern aristocrats, distinguish himself from Gratian's authority, and distance himself from the influence of Ascholius and other western bishops. Because of the uncertainty over episcopal leadership in the eastern capital, he also had a timely opportunity to intervene in its ecclesiastical affairs.[17]

Theodosius now appeared in Constantinople much as Valens had arrived in Caesarea over a decade earlier, elated by his victories over the Goths and prepared to assert his own religious preferences, and he immediately transformed the celebration of his military triumph into a demonstration of his own right to interfere in ecclesiastical matters. Upon his arrival he quickly expelled Demophilus, the Arian bishop who defiantly refused to accept the emperor's preferred creed. He also met with Gregory and promised to hand over the Church of the Holy Apostles. Gregory later recorded one of the emperor's comments during their meeting: "Through me God gives this church to you and your labors." With this remark Theodosius revealed himself as one of those people who had not previously worked up a sweat on behalf of the Nicene congregation, but who now pushed Gregory aside in claiming credit for its success. Since many people resisted and an "armed mob" occupied the church, Theodosius, dressed in his imperial regalia, marched through the city with his troops. Gregory, ill and gasping for breath, had to trudge along.[18]

Even though the emperor had again supported him and his Nicene congregation, Gregory seems to have been suspicious of Theodosius' methods, and perhaps his intentions. In December Gregory preached a sermon in the Church of the Holy Apostles before an audience that included Theodosius. In this sermon he described the detrimental effects of "envy," in order to defend himself against accusations that he had come to Constantinople simply to usurp the episcopal throne. One example drew upon his personal memories of the emperor Julian. "Envy motivated the apostate tyrant against us. Even though we avoided the flame, his hot coals still now trouble us." The greatest challenge by an emperor to Gregory's family had

been the confrontation between his father and Julian, and it is most revealing that within a few weeks after Theodosius' triumphant endorsement of
the Nicene community, Gregory was thinking about the possibility of being
scorched again. Theodosius may well have taken the hint, since later traditions credited him with destroying a statue of Julian in Constantinople.[19]

A few years later in a retrospective evaluation Gregory would praise
Theodosius' devotion to Nicene theology, while at the same time still ques-
tioning the emperor's readiness to use overt coercion. In his estimation,
the emperor's fervor was not an appropriate substitute for forethought
and consideration. Gregory insisted that the proper method was instead to
persuade people to change their thinking voluntarily, presumably through
the sort of preaching that he himself was offering, and he was clearly
uncomfortable with the use of force against heretics, even when that coercion enhanced his own standing. Some critics seem to have chided him
for his "gentleness" in passing up the opportunity to retaliate in kind, "to
shove, expel, intimidate, and incite," but Gregory preferred to use modera-
tion, even if not appealing for imperial support made him look weak. "I
allowed others [to knock at] the doors of the powerful." Ten years earlier
Valens had used troops to expel a new Nicene bishop from Constantinople in favor of Demophilus. Now Theodosius had used troops to expel
Demophilus in favor of Gregory. This display of military force set a pattern
for his reign, because Theodosius was consistently ready to impose his policies and religious preferences through coercion and to sanction the use of
local violence. Gregory did not share Theodosius' tendency toward belliger-
ent confrontation. Since he had misgivings about the use of imperial power
on behalf of any version of Christianity, he admitted that his happiness
about the emperor's support was tempered by apprehension. In fact, in his
sermons at Constantinople Gregory seems never to have mentioned, or even
to have hinted at, Theodosius' earlier edict in favor of Nicene Christianity.[20]

Theodosius now took up residence in Constantinople. Gregory, meanwhile, was trying to come to terms with the onerous duties that accompanied his new prominence in the religious life of the city, and he had to
endure complaints about the smallness of his congregation. He also continued to preach to a congregation that now included Theodosius, various
court officials, and senators. In the same way that he had once used a public oration to lobby a magistrate about the taxes at Nazianzus, so Gregory
sometimes pointedly addressed the emperor and these other dignitaries. In
a sermon he preached in December he encouraged senators not to boast of
their pedigrees and court officials to be loyal to God. He also reminded the

emperor that, even though he governed the "entire world," he was nevertheless answerable to God: "the heart of a king is in the hand of God." Gregory
was not the first orator to cite this verse from Proverbs in the presence of
an emperor at Constantinople. In order to praise Valens for his moderate
behavior after defeating the usurper Procopius, the pagan orator Themistius
had once used the same precept (which he coyly called an "Assyrian proverb"). But Gregory now deduced from this biblical citation that Theodosius should concede that his power was dependent upon God, not upon
his wealth or military support. For an emperor who was still flush from his
victories over the Goths, who had recently paraded his soldiers through the
city, and who was probably still receiving the exceptional levies of gold that
accompanied announcements of victories, Gregory's argument was most
likely quite deflating.[21]

For Gregory himself, however, this exhortation seems to have represented an attempt to reclaim his own moral standing by downplaying the
importance of the troops that had seized the very church in which he
was now preaching. In another sermon Gregory transformed an extended
exegesis on the relevance of a passage from the Gospel of Matthew into a
recommendation that the emperor issue an edict to support the Nicene
interpretation of the Trinity. "My oration will not be able to do as much
fighting on behalf of the Trinity as an edict." In this case Theodosius seems
to have responded to Gregory's suggestion by publishing soon thereafter an
edict that reaffirmed Nicene Christianity and strongly prohibited heretics
from meeting inside cities.[22]

## Theodosius' Agenda

Proposing penalties for heretics was not Theodosius' primary concern at
this time, however. Pressure from the Goths was a greater threat. On the day
after he issued the edict against heretics in January 381, he went out from the
capital to receive a notable Gothic chieftain who had fought against Valens
during the late 360s but who was now a refugee. Even though this Gothic
chieftain was a pagan, and even though he had also once persecuted the
Christians in his kingdom, Theodosius now received him with honor. After
this chieftain's death two weeks later, the emperor arranged an official funeral
that deeply impressed the other Goths. The people of Constantinople were
apparently also duly impressed by the emperor's success, and the orator
Themistius complimented him for his generosity toward a former enemy.[23]

Constantinople was clearly a city in which Theodosius wanted to vaunt his prestige, and to commemorate his own achievements he probably now began to prepare plans for the construction of a new forum that would eventually include an equestrian statue of himself, a triumphal arch, and a tall column with spiral reliefs depicting his military successes. The emperor's plans were publicized, and perhaps initiated, fairly quickly, because within a few years Themistius would praise him for having splendidly filled in the city's empty "silhouette" with new monuments. In early May Theodosius presided for the first time at the annual celebration of the anniversary of the dedication of Constantinople. This celebration included chariot races in the hippodrome and a public procession of soldiers escorting a statue of Constantine, the city's founder, that ended at the emperor's box in the hippodrome.[24]

During the first months of 381 Theodosius was hence consolidating his relations with the Goths and promoting his public image in the capital. The sculptured reliefs on the base for the obelisk eventually erected in the hippodrome in 390 provided a succinct summation of the emperor's activities in the capital at this time, depicting him supervising building activities, presiding over the chariot races from the imperial box, and receiving homage from barbarian captives. "Everything yields to Theodosius," as one of the dedicatory inscriptions insisted.[25]

The emperor's move to Constantinople may also have encouraged him to think that Christian communities and their bishops should also yield to his preferences, and the celebrations of his diplomatic and military successes perhaps accelerated his intentions to resolve the disputes over theology among Christians in the eastern empire. At the same time that Theodosius was planning his monuments, hosting the Gothic chieftain, and issuing a constitution about theological orthodoxy, he was making the final preparations for the opening of a large ecclesiastical council at Constantinople. This council started its deliberations in May, probably during or soon after the celebration of the capital's birthday. One leader was Meletius, one of the bishops who had competed for years to be acknowledged as the sole bishop of Antioch. After his return from the exile imposed by Valens he had become the dominant bishop at Antioch, and for months before the opening of the council he had been in Constantinople, presumably lobbying at the imperial court. He already had the emperor's favor, since Theodosius once announced that, in a vision before his selection as emperor, he had seen Meletius offering him an imperial crown. Upon Meletius' arrival at Constantinople, Theodosius had greeted him "like a boy who loves his father." At the opening of the council it was hence no surprise that Meletius had presided, as a conspicuous indication of the emperor's own preference about the proper bishop for Antioch.[26]

One of the council's first actions was the formal installation of Gregory as bishop of Constantinople. After a lifetime of avoiding episcopal service, Gregory's lack of reluctance in this case suggests that he had reconciled himself sufficiently to the presence of the emperor that he was prepared to stay. Meletius' sudden death, however, compelled him, once again, to modify his thinking. The leadership of the council passed to the new bishop of Constantinople. In his new role Gregory proposed a charitable solution to end the conflicts over the episcopacy of Antioch by suggesting that Paulinus, Meletius' surviving competitor who also accepted Nicene theology, simply be acknowledged as the sole bishop. Gregory himself had only recently emerged from a similar situation in which several rivals had competed for recognition as the sole bishop of Constantinople. Because he was perhaps still dismayed that he and his congregation had become dominant only through an intimidating display of imperial troops, his proposal may well have been an attempt to head off the use of soldiers to resolve the situation at Antioch. Gregory's generous suggestion, however, only aroused cries from "a crowd of young men," who then convinced the "distinguished older members" to join them. Gregory did not identify the members of this "flock of crows," nor did he mention the emperor's reaction, although in an imperial edict issued upon the completion of the council Theodosius did not commit himself to supporting any of the contenders at Antioch. An illness then forced Gregory to withdraw from the council.[27]

Once the bishops of Egypt arrived and contested the validity of Gregory's consecration on the grounds that he had already once before been consecrated a bishop elsewhere, Gregory took advantage of their opposition by using it as an excuse to leave the capital. Before he departed, however, he talked with Theodosius. This interview marked the only occasion on which Gregory took the initiative in approaching the emperor. In order to indicate that he was not appearing as a mere petitioner, he went alone, without any friends or magistrates to support his appeal, and he took no gifts. In requesting permission to depart, Gregory stated that he was ill. He furthermore explained his decision to leave by claiming that he had had to yield to "envy," precisely the corrupting sentiment that, according to one of his earlier sermons, had once motivated Julian to threaten his father. Yet Gregory was careful not to attribute any animosity to Theodosius. Instead he argued that the emperor should insist upon harmony at the council. The threat from the Goths was still on his mind too, since he suggested that Theodosius, who had already "repressed the rigid fury of the barbarians," would now be able to erect yet another commemorative monument if he could convince the feuding bishops to disarm.[28]

Gregory's remarks in his conversation with the emperor were an admission of his own inability to generate enough support from other bishops. His comments about barbarians and commemorative monuments were also an implicit concession that supporting Nicene orthodoxy was only one aspect, and perhaps not the most important one, of Theodosius' current ambitions. The other bishops too had to acknowledge both the emperor's plans for enhancing his reputation in Constantinople and his apprehensions about maintaining the frontier against the Goths. Even a general council convened to define the standards of doctrinal orthodoxy had to make concessions to the emperor's other, more compelling concerns.

The opening of the council seems to have been a part of or a sequel to the annual celebrations commemorating the original dedication of the city in 330. Then Constantine had given his new capital the official title of "Second Rome"; now one of the canons endorsed by the council called Constantinople the "new Rome." This canon certainly had significant ecclesiastical implications, because by acknowledging the elevated standing of Constantinople it clearly promoted the city's bishop and made him second only to the bishop of Rome in the episcopal hierarchy. This canon furthermore implicitly endorsed the significance of the emperor's recent plans for making the city the equal of Rome again, and it seems to have hinted at a comparison between Theodosius and Constantine. Other texts were less coy. Within a few years the orator Themistius would describe Theodosius as virtually another founder of Constantinople, comparable to Constantine himself. And by characterizing the emperor as "another sun," the inscription on the base of the equestrian statue of Theodosius in his new forum likewise recalled another comparison with Constantine, whose huge statue on top of a tall porphyry column in his forum still depicted him in the guise of Helios, the sun god. During his first years in Constantinople Theodosius was hence trying to identify himself with, and perhaps surpass, the standing of Constantine.[29]

In addition, even after his move to the capital Theodosius remained concerned about reaching a settlement with the Goths. Another of the canons issued by the council combined both political and religious interests by conceding that "the churches of God among the barbarian peoples must be administered according to the prevailing custom derived from the [church] fathers." Although the council endorsed Nicene Christianity as orthodoxy and rejected Arian and Arianizing doctrines, it nevertheless had to allow space for Theodosius to maneuver in anticipation of a treaty with the Goths, many of whom were already Arian Christians. And in fact, a year later Theodosius negotiated an important treaty whose unprecedented concessions would earn him a reputation as "the friend of the Gothic people."[30]

At the conclusion of the council the bishops fulsomely thanked Theodosius for inviting them to Constantinople and then requested "the most pious emperor" to ratify their decisions. Their letter is a candid admission that all along they had had to temper their decisions about the resolution of doctrinal feuds with consideration of the emperor's concerns over the security of the frontiers and the promotion of his own standing at Constantinople.[31]

## The New Samuel

After his departure from this council Gregory had returned to Cappadocia. Time and distance did not erase his hesitations about Theodosius' motives and methods for supporting Nicene orthodoxy, and he still prided himself upon having kept himself aloof. He had not appealed for the emperor's support in his dispute with his rival Maximus, and he had been dismayed at having to participate in the victory celebration that accompanied the emperor's arrival. Even though Gregory had once urged the emperor to issue an edict against heretics, he still complimented himself for having never been a suppliant at the imperial court. At his birth his mother had dedicated him to a future career in the clergy as a "new Samuel." In his farewell oration to the ecumenical council Gregory had readily compared himself again to Samuel, this time defending his tenure as bishop of Constantinople by recalling the prophet's renown for providing honest guidance to the kings of Israel. "I have kept my priesthood pure and undefiled. If I have loved power or the loftiness of thrones or walking in emperors' halls, may I never acquire any distinction, and if I do, may I be hurled away." At the end of his tenure in Constantinople, Gregory continued to highlight his aloofness from the emperor and his court. According to his farewell oration, he had made his appeals to the emperor and the court officials not as a petitioner in the palace, but as a preacher offering advice in his churches.[32]

Interestingly enough, Gregory's later memories of the churches of Constantinople were another revealing indication of his diminishing estimation of the significance of imperial patronage. After Theodosius' arrival at the capital, Gregory and his congregation had acquired control over the important churches in the city. Gregory preached sermons in the Church of the Holy Apostles, and he once referred to a fresco or mosaic on one of the church's walls in order to make a point. He also preached in the Church of Holy Wisdom. These two churches were both foundations of Constantine's imperial dynasty and had close associations with the court. Yet in his subsequent memories Gregory did not identify his brief episcopacy with either of these prominent churches that he had acquired through the emperor's support.[33]

Instead, the church he remembered most fondly was the Anastasia, the original meeting place that he and his small congregation had used before the emperor's arrival. "I do not have such a painful yearning for those churches as I do for the Anastasia." Gregory once recounted a dream he had had about the Anastasia after his return to Cappadocia. In this vision he had imagined himself again presiding over the clergy and preaching to the people. Once he awoke, the image had slowly faded from his heart. This vision, and its retelling in a poem, were some of the means by which Gregory came to terms with his departure from Constantinople. They also represented an admission that he had not had the temperament to participate in the politicking at the imperial court or in the capital city. In a letter to Nectarius, his successor as bishop of Constantinople, he conceded that "an ornament suitable for the emperor must decorate the imperial city." Nectarius, a former magistrate at Constantinople, a senator who could "instruct" the emperor, was such an ornament. Gregory, who seems always to have been most comfortable in secluded retreats and small towns, was not: "give me the desert, the countryside, and God." When he dreamed up an appropriate comparison for the Anastasia, he thought, not so surprisingly, of a small town: the Anastasia was the "most recent [equivalent of] Bethlehem." Since Gregory had also once compared Nazianzus to Bethlehem, perhaps it is only to be expected that a year after leaving the Anastasia he began to serve again as bishop in his small hometown. Despite his enormous reputation for his rhetorical skills and theological acumen, Gregory always remained a small-town bishop, too unassuming and modest to be comfortable as the bishop of Constantinople.[34]

Back in the capital Theodosius continued to expand on his imitation of his model, the emperor Constantine, by increasingly intervening in ecclesiastical affairs. Already during the council that met in Constantinople in 381, he had published decisions about the legal standing of bishops after a hearing before his high-ranking magistrates, and at the conclusion of the council he had issued an edict that named the bishops who would act as arbiters of orthodoxy. Two years later he instructed bishops representing various Christian sects to submit creeds, on the basis of which he alone determined orthodox theology. His residence in the capital seems to have given Theodosius the opportunity, and perhaps the confidence, to adopt a less deferential attitude toward bishops. As a result he even dared to revive his predecessor Constantine's image of the emperor as a bishop of sorts, because during church services he now separated himself from the rest of the congregation by sitting in the sanctuary among the clergy. He also seems to have appreciated hints that his imperial power came directly from God. In January 383 even the pagan orator Themistius was claiming that God himself, through "the decree from heaven," had directly summoned Theodosius to rule. For all his support for Nicene theology Theodosius still had to ensure his own authority, in particular with regard to bishops. In the process, even as he resolved some issues over definitions of orthodoxy, his predominance and interference continued to exacerbate other concerns. These fundamental ambiguities and uncertainties about the source of the emperor's power, his role in ecclesiastical affairs, and his relationship with bishops and especially with the patriarch of Constantinople, would continue to haunt Byzantine society for centuries.[35]

While the setting of the capital encouraged its residents to accept such grandiose conceptions of imperial authority, people in the outlying provinces were perhaps more reluctant to make these concessions. Gregory's departure from the capital had been yet another instance of his tendency to react to difficult personal situations by resorting to flight. This time, rather than fleeing to seclusion in Pontus or Isauria, he had returned to his hometown in Cappadocia.

Already during his years in Constantinople Gregory had been uneasy about imperial patronage, although then, in part because Theodosius was supporting his preferred theological doctrines, he had been hesitant or compliant in his reactions. In Cappadocia, however, he now openly demonstrated his own lingering mistrust of imperial support, even the patronage of an emperor who supported Nicene orthodoxy, by turning down a summons. Distance allowed Gregory to be bold, almost defiant. Without the pressure to be deferential to an emperor with whom he shared the city, in his native province Gregory could finally imitate the examples of his father, who had once confronted a pagan emperor, and of Basil, who had defied a heterodox emperor and his powerful prefect. When imperial magistrates conveyed an invitation from the emperor Theodosius to attend another council at Constantinople in 382, Gregory declined. As he put it in one of the poems that he now wrote in Cappadocia, not only would he never again "participate in any of the councils where geese and cranes wrangle over disorderly issues," but he was no longer "a companion of the mortal emperor." In the later Roman empire imperial magistrates, generals, and even local aristocrats had consistently prided themselves upon being named members of the "order of imperial companions," since the rank conferred high status and significant privileges. Back in his home province, however, Gregory no longer cared about the emperor's companionship, and he was no longer attracted to the seductions of the capital and the court.[36]

Theodosius may not have minded his absence, because at the same time the frontier along the upper Euphrates seemed to fade in significance for the emperors. Capital and province, Constantinople and Cappadocia, were drifting apart. Gregory never again left the region. And for over two centuries emperors did not visit Cappadocia either.

## Home

Gregory had gone into self-imposed retirement in his homeland. After his many years of education overseas, his long interludes of ascetic seclusion in Pontus and Isauria, and his ecclesiastical service at Constantinople, in the end he still thought of himself as a Cappadocian: "this is the account of Gregory, whom the land of Cappadocia nourished." Back in his hometown he remained interested in events at Constantinople. Just as Basil had tried to find out about affairs at the court of Valens in Antioch, so Gregory kept up contact with men who would have been knowledgeable about the court of Theodosius. He corresponded with Nectarius, his successor as bishop of the capital, and perhaps with other clerics. He exchanged letters with various generals whom he had most likely met at Constantinople. He wrote to some high-ranking court officials and the prefect of the city. He kept in touch with various friends at the capital who passed on news and gossip: "through you radiant Constantinople is with me." In these letters Gregory was still trying to promote his own theology and meddle, ever so slightly, in events at the capital. Most of the time he was only nurturing his friendships, perhaps requesting a small favor or two. "Different people have different weaknesses; mine are friendship and friends." After a few years, however, his correspondence with court officials, generals, and churchmen at the capital faded, and he instead exchanged letters primarily with provincial governors, bishops, and teachers in Cappadocia about local matters. He was no longer even trying to keep up with events in Constantinople.[37]

The imperial court likewise seems to have disregarded Cappadocia and other regions on the eastern frontier. In the past emperors had often traveled throughout the eastern provinces, and memories of their presence had inspired souvenirs of their visits. Statues of emperors littered the Greek world. In the early second century the governor of Cappadocia had even found a statue of the emperor Hadrian at Trapezus, on the very edge of the Roman empire at the eastern end of the Black Sea. He was appalled at its crudeness: "because of its workmanship it does not resemble you." During the fourth century there were statues of emperors at Caesarea and Nazianzus, and no doubt at other Cappadocian cities too, perhaps as mementos of visits by the imperial court.[38]

Then emperors began to reclaim some of these statues. In order to decorate the new buildings and the spacious plazas at Constantinople they appropriated statues and other monuments from cities throughout the eastern empire. The decorations for the hippodrome at the capital included statues from cities in central and eastern Asia Minor, such as Caesarea, Tyana, Iconium, and Sebasteia. Emperors also imported holy relics. In the early fifth century relics of the prophet Samuel passed through central Asia Minor on their way from Palestine to Constantinople. These impounded mementos were a form of symbolic imperialism, reminders to the provincials of their subordination to the demands of the capital. One-sided confiscation had replaced the mutual interaction between the imperial court and Cappadocia that had characterized much of the fourth century. Now few Cappadocians went to the capital. Like the "new Samuel," Gregory of Nazianzus, they stayed home. Although there were immigrants from Paphlagonia, Pontus, Galatia, and Pisidia, during this period there are no epitaphs at Constantinople of immigrants from Cappadocia.[39]

While Cappadocians stayed in their homeland, emperors stayed in the capital. Previously, whenever emperors had resided at Antioch, petitioners had been able to approach them in person, "at the gate of the palace." After Valens' return to Constantinople in 378, however, no emperor passed through Cappadocia in order to visit the eastern frontier again during the fourth century. The orator Libanius issued invitations for emperors to return, and the imperial palace at Antioch, "as beautiful and splendid as those at Rome and Constantinople," stood ready, "on the chance that the emperor would visit the region." Then the palace was locked up, and eventually an old ascetic pitched a tattered tent beneath the deserted gateway. Now it was no longer possible to accost emperors face-to-face. The emperors who assumed responsibility for the eastern empire instead spent their time either near the Danube frontier or, increasingly more commonly, in Constantinople. During the next century the closest an emperor came to Cappadocia was to spend summer vacations at Ancyra in Galatia. In the imagination of emperors the region of Cappadocia was now so isolated and remote that they used it as a detention center for opponents. Cappadocia had become an oubliette, a place for exiles to be forgotten, a "fortress of oblivion." No emperor visited Cappadocia again until Heraclius in the early seventh century.[40]

The imperial administration had nevertheless tried to retain its control over distant provinces. Because the court had a special interest in the imperial estates and ranches in Cappadocia, it imposed an elaborate hierarchy of supervisors, overseers, accountants, and collectors. At the beginning of his reign the emperor Justinian tried to reinforce this administration by enhancing the powers of the provincial governor of Cappadocia, and he stationed new garrisons in the region. Since Cappadocia was still an important source of supplies for both the court and the army, with these reforms the emperor hoped to ensure that his wife continued to receive "gold and clothing," and that he could fund his military campaigns throughout the empire. Even as he was proposing these reforms, however, Justinian also had to concede their implausibility. The main obstacles were the great landowners who had been confiscating imperial lands. The emperor "blushed" to admit how many were indulging in "banditry." In the past the empire had prided itself on its power to control its subjects and eliminate lawlessness. One early governor of Cappadocia had left no doubt about some peoples on the Black Sea. "Long ago they became liable for taxes to the Romans, but because of banditry they do not pay their exact taxes. Now, however, with divine support they will pay or we will defeat them!" Four hundred years later, Justinian could only grumble helplessly about the intransigence of local notables in Cappadocia and the loss of imperial revenues. "Almost all the estates belonging to the treasury have become private property. Along with their herds of horses these estates have been ripped apart and appropriated."[41]

These complaints about anarchy in a remote province were reminders of the long consistency, almost reappearing sameness, in the relationship between imperial centers and peripheral provinces. The confrontations between Cappadocian bishops and emperors during the mid- and later fourth century had represented only one brief moment in the ongoing dialectic between centralized imperial rule and local authority. In the sixth century emperors in the capital were still trying to control the resources of the provinces, and local aristocrats were confiscating imperial estates in the provinces. And this process of reciprocal appropriation certainly continued into subsequent centuries.[42]

By now the blessings of Roman rule were in decline, the imperial administration, the network of cities, the veneer of Greek culture, even the ecclesiastical hierarchy. Cappadocia was becoming again what it had been in the beginning, a rural landscape dominated by powerful landowning notables. This transformation in Cappadocia was symptomatic of the eastern empire as it assumed its "Byzantine" contours. Constantinople was the capital, the sprawling metropolis, the residence of the emperors and increasingly the focus of ecclesiastical controversies. Despite the military achievements of Justinian in the sixth century and Heraclius in the early seventh century, from the perspective of the capital Cappadocia had now become just another outlying province. In the Roman empire of the fourth century Cappadocia had been a pacified interior region on the roads between Constantinople and the frontier. During the seventh century the Arabs extended their caliphate as far as the Taurus Mountains, and their victories would only confirm the reemergence of the region as a borderland. By then Cappadocia had become what it would remain for centuries in the Byzantine empire, a true frontier zone once again.[43]

# Culture Wars

When Julian became sole emperor in late 361, he was already an accomplished escape artist. An ancient novel could hardly have crammed more narrow escapes into his first thirty years. By then he had already survived the massacre of his father and other relatives when he was a youngster, years of house arrest in Cappadocia, the suspicions resulting from association with his unstable half-brother and with teachers of ill repute, and the attempts of his cousin, the emperor Constantius, to keep him on a short leash during his tenure as a junior emperor. During their civil war Julian faced almost certain defeat. Then Constantius, still only in his mid-forties, unexpectedly died. Julian had been reluctant to become a junior emperor; now, almost by accident, he was sole emperor.

Julian reigned for less than twenty months. Yet his exuberance, his voluminous writings, his nonstop chattering, all contributed to the enhancement of his reputation, then and now. His policies, and especially his overt support for paganism and his disparagement of Christianity, were as controversial as his personality. Prominent pagans hailed his reign: "To be ruled by such virtue was the most blessed of all events." Christian leaders were aghast, almost apoplectic in their horror. A member of the Christian imperial dynasty of Constantine and Constantius, himself brought up as a Christian, Julian had nevertheless become a patron of paganism.[1]

Because this Christian reaction was so dominant after his death, Julian's subsequent reputation has consistently been tainted with the accusation of religious apostasy. He himself preferred being defined in terms of his passion for classical culture as "a disciple of the teachings of Plato and Aristotle," "a master of philosophy." Julian's capacity for linking his philosophical ideas with his life was boundless, and he often seemed to be living in a fantasy landscape of mythological heroes and historical legends. Julian always remembered how one of his first teachers had reminded him that the realm of classical literature was more realistic than real life. "You have a passion for a horse race? Homer has very skillfully created one. Take his book and study it carefully." Homer's poems became Julian's scriptures, an endless source of examples, proof texts, insights, and consolation, and he always kept the texts with him, as if they were "protective amulets." When Constantius proclaimed him as a junior emperor in late 355, Julian had been both diffident and terrified. As he sat with Constantius in the imperial carriage, he finally accepted his destiny by muttering a verse from Homer: "A purple death has seized me, and so has a powerful fate." When Constantius later removed a trusted advisor, Julian thought of another Homeric moment: "I remembered 'Odysseus was left alone.'" When he once praised Constantius' accomplishments, he also hinted at their latent discord by referring to the simmering animosity between Achilles and king Agamemnon: "the author of these stories says that Agamemnon did not treat his commander with the proper discretion or respect." Julian lived in the world of Odysseus.[2]

He was not the only resident. In the eastern provinces under the Roman empire classical Greek culture had flourished through revivals and imitations. An education in classical literature, rhetoric, and philosophy offered a way for Greek aristocrats to define themselves and their roles in their cities. It also provided the qualifications and the connections that might earn them offices in the imperial administration. In the Roman empire, classical Greek culture had become a proper "cultural system," "an historically transmitted pattern of meanings embodied in symbols . . . by means of which men communicate, perpetuate, and develop their knowledge about and attitudes toward life." Christians, because they subscribed to a different system of sacred symbols, were suspicious. They could see some of the benefits, in particular the rhetoric and the philosophical ideas that would help them articulate their theology. But the alliance between Greek culture and Roman rule was disconcerting, since imperial magistrates and sometimes emperors had in the past condoned persecution. Nor did Greek culture consist only of abstract ideas, philosophical terms, and elegant literature. Educated Christians also had to contend with the myths about the gods, the beautiful temples, and the magnificent religious festivals. Early Christianity had a distinctly ambivalent relationship with classical Greek culture.[3]

Yet Greek culture was just too seductive to abandon entirely. Classical literature was the core of a traditional education, and boys from Christian families who wanted a higher education had virtually no choice but to study classical texts. In 355 three young men were students at Athens, the emblematic citadel of Greek culture. Basil and Gregory of Nazianzus had already been studying there for several years. Soon after Basil left, Julian arrived for a few months. These three young men were remarkably similar. They were about the same age, they had all previously been students in Cappadocia, and after their student days at Athens none of them had a career that his substantial education in classical culture might have implied. They did not return to native cities to become municipal magistrates or decurions, and they did not hold offices in the imperial administration. Instead, their subsequent careers seemed to contradict their educations.

Julian soon became an emperor. In the previous one hundred years most of the emperors had been career soldiers who had not had the luxury of a classical education. One, in fact, had outright belittled classical culture as "slime and a public menace." Since his immediate successors too would be career soldiers, Julian's standing as a learned emperor would have been enough to make him an anomaly during the fourth century. Basil and Gregory returned to Cappadocia where they at first thought about becoming teachers. Instead they became ascetics and clerics. Given the long-standing latent suspicion between Christianity and classical culture, their careers as learned ascetics and learned clerics were also eccentric.[4]

During the 360s all three tried to define the relationship between classical culture and religion, whether paganism or Christianity. In part this was an abstract intellectual enterprise, coming to terms with the classical past. But in part it was also a totally personal quest, coming to terms with their own pasts.

Julian had been raised as a Christian in Cappadocia, and until he was in his late teens he had read and studied Christian texts as well as classical texts. Once he declared himself an open supporter of pagan cults, he identified classical culture exclusively with paganism and insisted that Christians could not use or enjoy classical texts. Such an interpretation forced him effectively to renounce a large part of his own upbringing. When he returned to Cappadocia as emperor in 362, he again had to confront his own Christian adolescence.

Basil had had a similar education. But after he adopted a life of ascetic seclusion and then became a priest, he did not follow Julian's example of disavowing much of his early education. Instead, he defined a traditional education in classical culture as a preliminary step for advanced study of biblical and ecclesiastical writings. Julian saw a disconnection between his early and later years, while Basil found a continuation between the halves of his life.

Gregory of Nazianzus never divided his life according to the phases of his education. He always loved classical culture, and he was always devoted to Christianity. Late in his life he still insisted that already at the great university town of Athens he had studied not only with pagan sophists, but also with clerics "in our sacred buildings." His memories of Athens included both Greek culture and Christianity. Rather than opposing classical culture to Christianity, rather than seeing his classical education merely as a prelude to Christian exegesis, Gregory wanted to find a perspective that allowed him to enjoy both passions together throughout his life.[5]

*Chapter 9*
# "A True Hellene
# Among the Cappadocians":
# Julian in Asia Minor

In November 361, while he was lingering at Naissus, the birth-place of his uncle Constantine, Julian learned about the death of his fellow emperor, his cousin Constantius. As the only survivor of Constantine's imperial dynasty, Julian now became the sole emperor and soon entered Constantinople, his birthplace. Even though he had not resided in the eastern capital for over a decade, the people demonstrated their enthusiasm for his arrival by greeting him with acclamations of "fellow citizen" and "foster son." Julian seems to have enjoyed his homecoming too. On the first day of the new year he attended the ceremonial installation of the two new consuls, whom he greeted with overt affection before escorting them through the gawking crowds to the senate house.[1]

In his oration of gratitude one of these new consuls argued that Julian's reign had restored liberty to the state. Perhaps equally significant was the sense of liberation that his arrival at Constantinople represented for the emperor himself. Until then Julian had almost always been under the sometimes stifling supervision of the minders and mentors that emperors had assigned to look after him. After the massacre of Julian's father and other relatives, Constantius had first sent his young cousin to Nicomedia in Bithynia, and then compelled him to live most of his teenage years on an isolated imperial estate in Cappadocia. Once Julian was allowed to leave, distrust followed him on his grand tour to visit and listen to notable teachers. "Threats from friends and relatives" lurked behind his visit to Constantinople; a warning to avoid the lectures of Libanius overshadowed his return to Nicomedia; and one of his teachers at Pergamon advised him to shun Maximus, a sophist at Ephesus with a suspect reputation for his mystical fervor. True to form, Julian promptly visited Maximus. As Julian traveled among various teachers in the old Greek world, he was accompanied by "a bodyguard and the emperor's suspicions."[2]

When he again returned to Bithynia, he established himself at a family villa and invited philosophers and poets to visit. In order to deflect misgivings that he was forming a conspiracy of learned pagans, he served as a reader in the church at Nicomedia. Yet his own half-brother Gallus, who had by now become a junior emperor stationed at Antioch, was upset enough by the reports he received about Julian's behavior to send the theologian Aetius to interview him. Gallus soon lost Constantius' support and was executed. Since he had recently visited his brother, Julian too was summoned to Milan and kept under house arrest for over half a year. Eventually Constantius again let him leave, this time to study in Greece. Julian clearly enjoyed his few months at Athens, and he seems to have contemplated disobeying the emperor's summons to return to court. "I stretched out my hands to your Acropolis, and I begged Athena to save her suppliant." Even though Constantius then promoted him as a junior emperor and sent him to command military campaigns in Gaul, Julian still had to endure the interference, and sometimes outright hostility, of the prefect, generals, and other imperial magistrates who were all Constantius' appointees. For over twenty years Julian had chafed under the surveillance imposed by Constantius. Once Julian's army proclaimed him as a senior emperor in 360, he then faced a potentially ruinous civil war that ended only with his cousin's death.[3]

## Constantinople

Upon entering Constantinople as sole emperor, Julian was finally free of these restraints. One indication of his immediate relief was his attempt to revive the more pleasant aspects of his earlier years by sending invitations to some of his teachers, friends, and supporters. Saturninius Secundus Salutius had been an elderly advisor for Julian in Gaul until Constantius had forced his removal. Soon after reaching the capital, Julian appointed him a prefect and put him in charge of the commission investigating some of Constantius' supporters. Aetius was a heterodox Christian theologian who, after having been sent to evaluate Julian's behavior in Bithynia, became his friend and tried to convince the emperor Gallus that his brother was indeed a Christian. Eutherius was a eunuch from Armenia who had served the dynasty of Constantine for decades before becoming a high-ranking official in Julian's imperial household. In 360 he had served as Julian's envoy to negotiate with Constantius at Caesarea in Cappadocia. Aetius had been forced into exile after Gallus' execution, and Eutherius had gone into retirement;

Julian now invited both to Constantinople. He also corresponded with some of his earlier teachers. Proaeresius was a distinguished teacher, whose lectures Julian had apparently audited during his months as a student at Athens. Since Proaeresius may now have hinted that he intended to write a history of current events, Julian offered to show him some confidential letters. Priscus had been another reputable philosopher at Athens whom Julian had already tried to get to join him in Gaul, and whom he now summoned to Constantinople. Himerius, another of his teachers from Athens, also went to the capital, and so did the sophist Maximus. If as emperor Julian could not go to Athens, then he would bring Athens' teachers to himself at Constantinople.[4]

Julian could also begin to try to impose his own reforms throughout the empire. Most obviously, he now had no hesitation about publicizing his disdain for Christianity and his support for paganism in all its many manifestations. Almost his first thought upon hearing of Constantius' death had been to proclaim that the motivation for his support of paganism came from divine inspiration. "The gods order me to restore all their affairs to prominence, and they promise to give me in return great rewards for my efforts." Many of the supporters who now joined Julian at the capital were pagans. Upon his arrival Himerius delivered a panegyric in honor of the capital, but only after he had joined the emperor in a celebration of the mysteries of Mithras. Maximus already had a reputation for his ability to manipulate pagan deities, and Julian had in fact first gone to visit him after hearing about his success at making a statue of Hecate smile. When Julian invited Maximus to join him at Constantinople, he admitted that he had already abandoned Christianity and become a supporter of pagan cults. "I openly venerate the gods, and I sacrifice oxen in public." Once free of his escorts and watchmen, Julian dropped his pretense of acting like a Christian and came out as a pagan.[5]

Support for pagan cults was only one component of the reforms that Julian now initiated at the capital. Another was his attempt to reduce the size of the imperial court and diminish the protocol and ritual that had steadily enveloped the emperors. Emperors had become increasingly remote figures, shielded by court officials and barely accessible to ordinary people. Emperors were on display, but usually at a distance. Two years earlier in Gaul, shortly after his proclamation as a senior emperor, some soldiers had been unnerved by a rumor that Julian had been assassinated. Their confidence had returned only when they saw the emperor sitting in his assembly hall, "shining in his imperial robes."[6]

At Constantinople Julian now conspicuously relaxed these formalities.

He "humbled" himself to accompany the new consuls to their inauguration, and in an edict issued from the capital he classified himself as a member of the senatorial order. Previously the senate would occasionally be summoned to the imperial palace and listen to brief pronouncements, but now Julian attended its meetings and participated in its debates. He also began to reduce the staff at the court, including cooks, barbers, wine stewards, waiters, and "more eunuchs than the flies [that swarm] around flocks in he springtime." He expelled the many functionaries who extorted fees and prevented petitions from reaching imperial magistrates. He was skeptical about the notion that his purple robes made him special, and he often thought about not wearing his gold crown. Julian was now going to be a common emperor. When his former teacher Maximus arrived, Julian immediately left a meeting of the senate to greet him with a kiss.[7]

In many respects Julian was now trying to revive the contours of the early Roman empire, when emperors had surrounded themselves with fewer courtiers and had maintained at least the pretense of respecting the senate, when the imperial provincial administration had been smaller, and when pagan cults had been integral to imperial ceremonies, senatorial identity, and municipal rituals. In his edicts Julian liked to point out that he was restoring the practices of "the founders of ancient law." Greek culture had also flourished in the early Roman empire, and by the time he reached Constantinople Julian had already begun to think about its significance.[8]

Julian's notion of "Hellenism" was the key to his reforms and thinking, and also the adhesive holding them together. Hellenism, "Greekness," was "a genuine Greek work for Greek culture" in all its many aspects, language, literature, philosophy, mythology, art, and architecture. Greek culture also presupposed a particular political setting, a *polis* or city, as well as a sense of civic patriotism, and it implied the adoption of a distinctive lifestyle. In the mid-fourth century an affiliation with Hellenism was appealing to an educated emperor with ambitions. Greek culture was widespread, and not just throughout the Mediterranean world. The conquests of Alexander the Great had contributed to its spread throughout the eastern Mediterranean world and parts of the Near East, and the imposition of Roman rule had made it increasingly attractive in the western Mediterranean and in the hinterlands. Even Cappadocia and other regions in the interior of Asia Minor had been receptive to the charms of Greek culture and the benefits of cities. With its potential for universality Hellenism might well reinforce Julian's authority, both inside and outside the empire. Greek culture could be a platform for an extension of Roman political power.[9]

Hellenism was attractive also because it could include more than a cultural and political worldview. In the Roman empire it acquired the additional meaning of "paganism." Pagan intellectuals took the lead in equating the two, in particular by considering the mythology in the classical texts and the philosophical discussions of the ancient gods as religious statements. The next step was to suggest that the literature itself had become sacred texts. Julian claimed that the classical poets, historians, and orators had written under the influence of divine inspiration. "Of course the gods guided Homer, Hesiod, Demosthenes, Herodotus, and Thucydides in all their learning." If Hellenism now included both Greek culture and paganism, then Julian could deduce two consequences for his policies. One was to associate his patronage for pagan cults with his support for the revival of cities and classical culture. The vitality of cities, devotion to pagan cults, respect for classical culture, all presupposed each other: Greek culture and veneration for pagan cults were "brothers." Another consequence was to insist that Christians had no right to use classical literature. Julian had been incensed to discover that Christians, after "sailing to Athens" to study literature and philosophy, then "armed their hateful tongues with rhetorical tricks and turned them against the gods of heaven." Since in his expanded notion of Hellenism classical literary texts were in fact pagan religious texts, it would be disingenuous for Christians to read and appreciate them. An image of Hellenism as both Greek culture and pagan cults provided Julian with a comprehensive foundation for his imperial policies.[10]

Like Constantine and Constantius, his predecessors as emperors in the East, Julian too now contributed to the boom in construction at Constantinople. He was thought to have constructed a pagan shrine and altars in the palace, and he improved a harbor and funded the construction of a new portico leading to the wharf. Significantly, within this portico he included a public library that he endowed with his own books. The books that he donated may have included those that he had received when he first set out for Gaul as a junior emperor, "books of philosophers and the great historians and of many rhetoricians and poets." Since Julian insisted that these very books had been able to transform even barbarian Gaul into "a shrine for the muses of Greekness," he may have thought they could certainly do the same for Constantinople. Since his notion of Hellenism included both paganism and Greek culture, for transforming a capital founded by a Christian emperor into a proper "Greek" capital Julian seems to have decided that a library was as important as a temple or a shrine to a pagan deity. Having acquired sole imperial power, Julian was now rethinking the cultural and religious significance of Constantinople and the roles there of emperor, court, and senate.[11]

Not everyone at the capital appreciated the new emperor's informality. Some criticized his stroll with the consuls as "affected and tawdry," others his dash from the senate to greet a former teacher as "unseemly." Even though Julian was now trying to promote their standing, senators may well have been among his critics. In the later 350s Constantinople had finally evolved into a formal administrative capital, complete with its own senate to match the venerable senate at Rome. Because many of these eastern senators were immigrants from the provinces or parvenus without distinguished ancestors, they were perhaps self-conscious enough about their lack of distinction to be sensitive to breaches in decorum. Themistius, one prominent senator at the capital, offered advice to Julian about ruling as an emperor. Since Themistius had recently visited Rome in 357 in order to participate in the ceremony celebrating a visit by Constantius, he knew how emperors were supposed to behave in a capital city. Constantius had been extravagantly flamboyant during the parade and politely deferential when he addressed the senate. Julian had already demonstrated his deference, but he needed to work on his ostentatiousness. In his letter to the new emperor Themistius hoped that Julian would consider himself the equivalent of Hercules and Dionysus, gods who had ruled on earth.[12]

Julian declined this recommendation. Even after becoming sole emperor, he still saw himself more as a rumpled intellectual with little concern for proper imperial deportment than as a glamorous ruler with absolute powers. In his reply Julian described himself as "a lover of philosophy": "I am reluctant to undertake a life in administration." Summoning his former teachers to Constantinople was an indication that he would have preferred to resume his former life as a student: "I cherish Athens rather than this grandeur that now envelops me." Such comments may have justified Julian's attempt to downsize the court and the imperial administration, but the people and especially the senators at Constantinople probably preferred emperors who did not seem to challenge their own fragile prestige with casual behavior that might easily seem impertinent. They would have wanted Julian to behave more like Constantius at Rome, certainly respectful of the capital's residents and monuments, but still properly grand in his own appearance.[13]

Julian seems to have sensed that he was quickly wearing out his welcome at the capital, and before he left, he made one final attempt to promote the dignity of the senate and people. He stayed in Constantinople long enough to preside over the annual festival in early May that celebrated Constantine's foundation of the city. Then he set out for Antioch and the eastern frontier, perhaps thinking that he would have better opportunities to implement some of his plans in cities in Asia Minor.[14]


## Ancyra

A short residence could not undo the legacy of Constantine and Constantius at Constantinople. Since its first two imperial patrons had been Christians, their support for the construction of churches had imposed a definite Christian atmosphere over the new capital. Julian himself had removed his imperial robes and escorted Constantius' body to the Christian shrine that served as the imperial mausoleum. When he then offered a libation to the pagan gods, even one of his apologists had to admit that few followed his example. In addition, the senators in the capital, even pagan senators like Themistius, were too insecure about their standing to be at ease with an unconventionally informal emperor. Julian's first attempts to impose his reforms had had only limited success at Constantinople.[15]

In Asia Minor, however, he could visit cities that were both smaller and older than the capital, cities that might be expected to be more comfortable with their ancient traditions, and he could interact with decurions rather than senators. Decurions, the local aristocrats who served as municipal councilors in their native cities, had long been losing their authority and influence. The increasing size of the central administration, the confiscation of municipal resources for use on imperial projects, and the expectation that local aristocrats would make up shortfalls in municipal spending had all combined to make service on municipal councils an onerous burden. Because Julian's idea of Hellenism implied the importance of cities as the proper arenas for the promotion of pagan cults and classical culture, he was naturally sympathetic to reviving the vitality of cities. His sympathy included support for their local aristocrats. In the same way that he had associated himself with the senators at Constantinople, he would be equally solicitous of the decurions in provincial cities.

Already before leaving the capital he had issued a law in which he insisted that all landowners fulfill their public obligations, and he eliminated improper exemptions from service on municipal councils. He also relieved some of the financial pressure on cities and decurions by restoring public estates and alleviating some taxes. In Asia Minor, Julian would have many more opportunities to enhance the standing of cities and decurions through direct intervention. His tactics would include reducing the intrusiveness of the central administration, minimizing the authority and interference of provincial governors, promoting pagan cults and the accompanying priesthoods that local aristocrats often held, and giving local councils more control over the selection of teachers and the supervision of education. "Who does not know that a strong council is the soul of a city?" Libanius, one of his supporters, emphasized Julian's concern for cities: "his goal was not to rule but to benefit the cities." Some dedications would hail him as both "restorer of temples" and "reviver of municipal councils." At Constantinople Julian had not been very successful in introducing his reforms. But because he could have expected provincial aristocrats and decurions to be looking forward to his patronage, he left the capital in a good mood, "with hopes that exceeded human abilities."[16]

His trip through Asia Minor turned out to be a major disappointment. In some cases, before he could try to revive the prestige of decurions and priests, he first had to resurrect their cities and shrines. As Julian set out from the capital, he again visited Nicomedia, where he had spent some happy years as a young boy and where he had returned after being released from his detention in Cappadocia. In 358 while he had been off campaigning in Gaul a terrifying earthquake and fire had devastated the city and its suburbs. Julian now wept when he viewed the charred rubble, and he presented the city with generous gifts for repairs. In order to encourage pagan cults these gifts included statues of Apollo and Artemis. Julian then headed toward Galatia. A detour to Pessinus allowed him to worship at the temple of Cybele, the Great Mother of the gods, where he spent one night composing a long hymn in honor of the goddess. Before departing he promoted a local priestess to become the high priestess for the cult of the Great Mother.[17]

The first leg of his journey had provided Julian with the opportunities to help a city in disrepair and a famous pagan shrine. It had also been a sobering experience. The decurions and other citizens at Nicomedia were so demoralized that they greeted him in mourning clothes, clearly unable to rebuild with their own resources and equally clearly lobbying for a substantial subsidy by appealing to the emperor's sympathy. The shrine at Pessinus was already in decline, long overtaken by other cult centers, and Julian himself complained about the indifference of the locals and threatened them with his anger. In addition, some Christians confronted him directly. An ascetic reproached Julian and then had the audacity to express gratitude after the emperor ordered him to be punished. A young man upset the altar in the shrine at Pessinus and laughed at the emperor's purple robes. Challenging the emperor's paganism and ridiculing his authority were bad enough. Even worse, this young man then cut Julian's pretensions to the quick by offering some literary criticism. To his face the young man mocked the emperor's orations as "laughable, the work of a trickster." Already at the beginning of his journey Julian had found listless decurions, demoralized pagans, and confrontational Christians, and he had had to endure snide comments about his own learning. His journey became even more dreadful as he went on.[18]

His next stop was Ancyra, a provincial capital and the most important city in the region of Galatia. Ancyra should have been Julian's kind of town. In the early Roman empire distinguished orators and philosophers had visited to perform or teach. Men from local aristocratic families had acquired equestrian and senatorial rank, held offices in the imperial administration, and studied with illustrious teachers. During the fourth century young men from Galatia went off to study with prominent sophists like Himerius and Libanius, two of Julian's own teachers. In the early 360s some of Libanius' former students were serving as leading decurions at Ancyra, and Libanius once complimented them for setting the tone of the city with their "passion for all forms of culture" and their readiness to reward orators with both applause and financial compensation. Himerius too had taught students from "the peoples and cities of Galatia." Since he was now most likely a member of Julian's entourage, he was probably looking forward to showing off the emperor as a former student. All of his other former students at Ancyra would in turn be eager to display their legendary hospitality. "The inhabitants of Ancyra cherish strangers, and the only way they inconvenience people is by delaying them from leaving."[19]

At Ancyra Julian continued his policy of enhancing the standing of municipal notables and promoting pagan cults and Greek culture. In one law he announced that provincial governors could not begin new construction projects until they had completed the projects initiated by their predecessors. As local aristocrats had become increasingly unwilling or unable to fund new buildings, governors often took the initiative, and in the process earned great honors for themselves. Julian's law was hence an attempt not only to downplay the intervention of governors, but also perhaps to encourage local notables to become benefactors again. In another law, Julian claimed that the integrity of teachers was more important than their skill in eloquence. Since he was unable to evaluate all teachers in person, Julian insisted that teachers had to obtain the approval of their city's decurions. Both laws seem to have been attempts to enhance the prestige of decurions, and the second one linked their authority with the promotion of education. It also linked them with the promotion of pagan cults, since the emperor doubtless anticipated that one criterion for evaluating teachers' characters would be their adherence to paganism. "I think it is nonsensical," he confessed in another letter, "if those who teach the writings of these classical authors do not honor the gods whom the authors honored."[20]

Julian offered more overt support for pagan cults and pagan priests in a letter to the high priest of Galatia. In this letter he candidly conceded that Hellenism was not flourishing as he had hoped, and he suggested some remedies. The priests themselves were to live more virtuously, and they were to construct hostels in every city for the assistance of strangers and the poor. To help them fulfill this charity, Julian offered to supply grain and wine. With these edicts Julian seems to have wanted to demonstrate that his promotion of cities, decurions, Greek culture, and pagan cults could be successful. Everyone would benefit. Not surprisingly, Secundus Salutius, the prefect who was accompanying Julian, set up a dedicatory inscription at Ancyra that hailed the emperor as the "lord of the entire world." He probably also commissioned the erection of a statue of Julian.[21]

Yet Julian's stay at Ancyra was not fully reassuring about the eventual success of his reforms. Some of the decurions there certainly still maintained the customary tradition of serving their city. One decurion, because he considered the city to be as important as his own son, had spent much of his wealth on the city's behalf, and others served on embassies representing the city at the imperial court. As much as Julian may have hoped that these decurions would be models for others, he also discovered some complications. One conspicuous culprit was the provincial governor. At the time of Julian's visit the governor was most likely Maximus. By the end of his governorship Maximus was being praised for his extensive construction projects and for having recruited more teachers, and one of his friends even suggested that Ancyra should be renamed "the city of Maximus." Few local aristocrats could have competed with such a resourceful governor.[22]

Other obstacles to the success of Julian's proposals were decurions themselves. Not all were eager to help their cities. At Ancyra one wealthy local notable named Maximus (not to be confused with the governor Maximus) had retired to his rural estate. Since his son would become liable for service on the municipal council once he handed over much of his wealth, Maximus hoped his son would become a senator at Constantinople and thereby acquire exemption from having to serve as a decurion. Maximus clearly privileged his son's standing over the welfare of the city. Despite Julian's public support for promoting service as decurions, as he left Galatia men actually lined the road to complain that they had been unjustly forced to serve on their municipal councils. The pairing of active governors with disengaged decurions challenged the success of Julian's intentions.[23]

The prominence of Christianity presented yet another obstacle. At Ancyra, as in many other Greek cities, the only local notables who seemed willing and able to compete in prestige and in resources with the provincial governors and other imperial magistrates were now the bishop and other churchmen. Only a few years before Julian's visit bishop Basil of Ancyra had dedicated a new church during a ceremony attended by neighboring bishops. Local monks assisted inmates in the town prison and patients in a hospital, and poor people gathered in the courtyard of the church to receive daily rations. Because the emperor could see firsthand this glaring evidence for the prominence of Christianity during his stay at Ancyra, even he had to concede the difficulty of reviving pagan cults. In his letter to the high priest the paradigm Julian offered for the extension of pagan generosity was the impact of Christian charity. Even as he slighted Christianity by calling it "atheism" for its refusal to accept the pagan gods, he had to concede its success. "The expansion of atheism has been a result in particular of their care for strangers, their respect for the graves of the dead, and the feigned holiness of their lives." Although Julian tried to claim this generosity as a typically pagan attitude by citing a proof text from one of his own sacred scriptures, Homer's *Odyssey*, he seems to have sensed that in Galatia too his reforms were doomed. To suggest Christian altruism as a model for pagan generosity was effectively to acknowledge defeat.[24]

## Caesarea

Julian's experiences during his stay in Galatia had further deflated some of his expectations about the region and the potential success of his own plans. His next stop would be Cappadocia, about which he would have had mixed feelings even before his arrival.

Julian had spent his teenage years on an imperial estate near Caesarea In many respects his stay had closely resembled the leisured life of intellectual retirement on a rural estate that had for centuries been characteristic of landed aristocrats. Julian genuinely admired this sort of secluded life:

"nothing is more pleasant and more profitable than doing philosophy at leisure and without interruption." This imperial estate, although remote, had had comfortable amenities, and Julian had had his own teachers. He also had had access to the considerable library of Georgius, a local churchman. Georgius' library had included "many books on philosophy, many books on rhetoric," and "quite a few books by historians." Even though he eventually preferred to associate himself with the illustrious teachers he had known in Athens and other great university towns, Julian had in fact acquired his basic education in Greek literature during his years in Cappadocia.[25]

But now, years later, Julian remembered primarily how he had chafed at the isolation and the constant monitoring. Perhaps he was also a bit chagrined to remember that he had in addition read the many Christian books in Georgius' library. Julian had also acquired his basic education in Christianity during his years in Cappadocia. For Julian, Cappadocia represented the beginning of both his classical education and his Christian education. As he now returned to Cappadocia for the first time since his departure almost fifteen years earlier, Julian was perhaps hoping to exorcise his unpleasant memories of his Christian upbringing and revive his happier memories of his study of classical texts.

One way he could do so was by revisiting Georgius' library. Georgius had eventually served as bishop of Alexandria. Once Julian heard that Georgius had been murdered in December 361, he insisted that all of Georgius' books be sent to him at Antioch, so that he could save the classical texts but "completely obliterate" the Christian texts. Julian was now trying to erase, literally, the Christian half of his youthful study in Cappadocia. He also looked forward to meeting a friend. Julian had discouraged Philippus from coming to Constantinople because, as he had noted, he would soon be traveling through Philippus' region. Philippus was a native Cappadocian. Since he was also a rhetorician and poet in his homeland, and since he was a generation older than Julian, the emperor may have first met him during his earlier stay in Cappadocia. Perhaps Philippus had been one of his teachers. If so, Julian was anticipating being reunited with another former teacher and the classical books they had used, while at the same time destroying the Christian books he had read from Georgius' library.[26]

Philippus was also a pagan, and Julian probably expected his assistance for his program of promoting municipal notables, education, and pagan cults and downplaying the impact of imperial administrators. As in Galatia,

however, Julian was again unsuccessful in Cappadocia. During the previous winter Christians at Caesarea had destroyed a local pagan temple;
Julian now responded by removing the city's rank as a *polis,* a city. Since
this demotion would also have depreciated the standing of the city's decurions, the emperor's penalty neatly exposed a tension within his own vision
of the reforms necessary to invigorate Greek cities. If he demoted the city
to the "appearance of a village" for its Christian exuberance, then he was
also penalizing the city's decurions. The provincial governor furthermore
entangled Julian in his own private dispute with the newly consecrated
bishop of Caesarea. Since this new bishop had previously been a decurion, he was another example of a local notable using membership of the
clergy as a means of avoiding service on the municipal council. And other
churchmen were prepared to confront Julian, in particular Gregory the
Elder, who had himself most likely been a decurion before becoming bishop
of Nazianzus.[27]

In Cappadocia Julian hence found, and indeed exacerbated, exactly what
he had hoped to curtail: attacks on pagan shrines, an overbearing governor,
and influential bishops. He also discovered that he was unable to support
a pagan temple at Caesarea without at the same time feeling compelled to
restrict the influence of the city's decurions. A few years before his visit
the rhetorician Philippus had perhaps experienced these same changes in
a more direct confrontation. When Basil had returned from his studies at
Athens, he had outright disdained other notables in the region because
of his superior skills as an orator. Philippus may have been among the rhetoricians whom Basil had belittled, and perhaps he was now hoping that he
would finally have his redress by becoming another of those earlier acquain-
tances and teachers, like Himerius and Maximus, whom the emperor honored with his patronage.[28]

Julian, however, was upset, even disgusted, by his experiences in Cappadocia. Since his departure so many years earlier the region had obviously
gone downhill. This time, on his way out of Cappadocia, he invited Aristoxenus to meet him at Tyana. Aristoxenus was a philosopher and a pagan,
and Julian hoped that his presence would remind him that there was at
least one "true Hellene among the Cappadocians." Since Julian's notion of
Hellenism had both cultural and religious overtones, he was here indulging
in a snide comment about both the lack of Greek culture in Cappadocia
and the region's disrespect for paganism. For the second time in his life
Julian could hardly leave Cappadocia quickly enough.[29]

## Antioch

Once he crossed the Taurus Mountains, Julian could begin again to anticipate a more favorable response at his next stop. He soon met Celsus,
another former schoolmate and now the governor of Cilicia. Celsus' actions
had made him an exemplar of Julian's notion of an ideal governor. He had
subsidized pagan cults, and before he greeted Julian with an oration, they
sacrificed together at an altar. He had also enrolled new decurions in the
council of one of the cities in his province. Local aristocrats had been
avoiding service in various ways, some by fleeing to the mountains, others
by "hiding under their beds." Celsus now convinced them to serve not
by using force, but by stressing the "magnificent opportunities" and the
profits available for men who performed municipal liturgies. In his province
Celsus had hence successfully promoted pagan cults, classical culture, and
the standing of decurions. Julian was so pleased with this one triumphant
example of the successful application of his reforms that he invited Celsus
to accompany him to Tarsus in his own carriage.[30]

The final destination of Julian's journey was Antioch, where he seems
to have hoped he might have one last opportunity to remake a city. At Constantinople the senators had been too insecure to be comfortable with his
revamping of the court and his own informal behavior. Cities on the road
through Asia Minor had not been looking for more autonomy either. Local
aristocrats were avoiding service as decurions, and some cities preferred to
request financial support from the emperor or from imperial magistrates.
Nor had there been much enthusiasm for Julian's promotion of pagan cults.

At Antioch Julian found the same obstructions to his proposals and
some new obstacles too. There too pagan cults were in decline. When Julian
attended a festival at the temple of Apollo in a suburb, he found a single
priest who apologized that "the city had this time prepared nothing." In his
indignant response the emperor was still thinking about his experiences
at Caesarea, whose rank as a city he had recently removed. "It is disgraceful that such a magnificent city should have as little regard for the gods as a
tiny village near the borders of Pontus." After a fire broke out in the temple,
Julian blamed the Christians and retaliated by closing one of their churches.
A food shortage caused more problems. Because of a drought, local landowners were profiteering by hoarding their supplies. Julian appealed to
these landowners' sense of justice, fixed prices, and even had grain imported
from Egypt. Despite his good intentions, the emperor could not impose
a solution when he was part of the problem. Julian was now collecting so

many troops for his anticipated campaign against the Persians that their demand drove prices up. The response of many people in Antioch was to ridicule the emperor's policies, behavior, and even his appearance.[31]

Julian's residences in Constantinople and Antioch were the bookends of his short reign as sole emperor. In both cities he found hesitations about his reforms, in the capital because he was so radical in his deportment, in Antioch because he was so conservative in his religion. Because both cities were too large and cosmopolitan to correspond to the classical notion of a proper Greek city, Julian might have been able to shrug off this opposition as unrepresentative of the hundreds of small cities throughout the empire. In contrast, the truly eye-opening revelation about the probable failure of his reforms had been his journey through the Bible Belt of central and eastern Asia Minor. There he had discovered that ordinary cities and ordinary decurions in the heartland were also not going to be very receptive to his proposals. Julian was now running out of cities in which he might introduce his reforms. By the time he set off in March 363 on his invasion of the Persian empire, he had already announced that he would not be returning to Antioch for his next winter camp. This time he was right, since in June he was killed during a battle.[32]

Because Julian was a student of history, he was deeply aware of precedents and the actions of his imperial predecessors when proposing his own policies. In some of his reforms he seems to have deliberately tried to undermine the policies of his Christian predecessors. Julian offered amnesty to bishops whom Constantius had sent into exile, and in his laws he sometimes ordered the constitutions of his uncle Constantine to be abolished. Since Julian was a supporter of pagan cults, Constantius and Constantine seemed to be his natural rivals.[33]

Yet the true antithesis for Julian's reforms was not one of his Christian predecessors, but rather Diocletian, another pagan emperor. Diocletian and Julian were both self-conscious guardians of the past. Diocletian and his fellow emperors had prided themselves for their protection of "the splendor of the Roman name," and a town in North Africa hailed Julian as "the restorer of liberty and Roman religion." But from Diocletian's reign Julian had learned what not to do. Diocletian had accelerated the trend toward encasing the emperor in the formal protocol that Julian wanted to minimize. Diocletian had increased the size of the provincial administration whose impact Julian now wanted to lessen. Worst of all, Diocletian and his fellow emperors had issued edicts calling for the persecution of Christians. Julian repeatedly belittled Christians as "Galilaeans," but he did not initiate direct persecution. "I do not want the Galilaeans to be killed or unjustly beaten or to suffer any misfortune." "It is necessary for men to be persuaded and instructed by reason, not by beatings or insults or physical torture." Instead, Julian was more interested in cultural correctness than religious correctness. If others would concede his interpretation of the connection between classical culture and pagan cults, then paganism would naturally flourish and Christianity would wither. As long as he could impose his vision of Hellenism, Julian had no need to persecute Christians directly.[34]

During his campaign against the Persians Julian once suggested that he might eventually retire as emperor and become a private citizen again. Even though, in most respects, Julian had contradicted Diocletian's policies, he may have considered the idea of abdication from remembering his predecessor's successful retirement. Other great rulers from the past, including some emperors, provided other positive paradigms for Julian. Julius Caesar was an example of a successful general who had conquered Gaul. When Julian went to Gaul as a junior emperor, he had had no military experience; so he learned how to be a general perhaps by reading Julius Caesar's commentaries. Marcus Aurelius was an example of a philosopher emperor who, according to Julian, thought that the noblest ambition in life was "imitation of the gods." Not surprisingly, when Julian ranked earlier emperors, Marcus Aurelius headed the list. Another model was Alexander the Great, the conqueror of the Persian empire. Alexander's highest ambition, according to Julian, had been "to conquer everything." As Julian prepared for his own campaign against the Persians, he had Alexander on his mind.[35]

Julian had discovered one of the perks of being emperor, because he could now obscure the distinction between the fantasy world of mythology and ancient history and the real world of military campaigns. Julian led his campaigns with his books in hand. Rather than simply reading about Julius Caesar in Gaul, he could be Julian Caesar commanding his own battles in Gaul. This imitation or revival of past legendary exploits corresponded with his proposals about the promotion of classical culture and the revival of paganism. Conversion to Christianity stripped people of contact with their ancestral legends and traditional sacred shrines and required them to abandon the past and start anew. In contrast, Julian wanted people to embrace the past, especially the classical past. His imitation of Alexander the Great hence implied more than the possibility of winning military glory. Over the centuries Alexander had also acquired a reputation as a missionary of Greek culture in the eastern Mediterranean world and beyond. The myth of Alexander's responsibility for the spread of Greek culture into the Near East may have influenced Julian's plans. If his own reforms were meeting opposition within the Roman empire, perhaps it was now time for him to look elsewhere. Libanius, one of Julian's supporters at Antioch, outlined the expectations of the emperor's campaign precisely in cultural terms. "We thought that the entire Persian empire would become a part of the Roman empire and change its language, and that sophists in [the Persian city of] Susa would teach Persian children to be orators." Libanius also thought that Julian's military and cultural success in the Persian empire would translate into enthusiasm for paganism back in the Roman empire: "everyone would want to run to the pagan altars." If Julian were to return after successfully imitating both the military victories and the cultural evangelism of Alexander the conqueror, perhaps then he would finally be accepted within the Roman empire as another patron of Hellenism, an apostle of both Greek culture and paganism.[36]

Extensive learning had its practical limitations. Julian may have known ancient history and classical mythology, but he had failed to respond adequately to the pressing issues of contemporary Roman society. His experiences in Constantinople, the cities of Galatia and Cappadocia, and Antioch should have taught him the futility of his hopes for restoring the prestige of decurions, classical culture, and pagan cults. In these different settings, the booming new capital, the small provincial cities of central and eastern Asia Minor, and an old regional metropolis, most people had rejected his proposals. They were apparently not interested in trying to revive a gilded past.

Since Julian was such a traditionalist, the most poignant indignity would be his own ultimate dissociation from the classical past that he had venerated. Because of his early death and the succession of more Christian emperors, Christians would have the last word. Julian's support for paganism had so tainted their reactions that they were not prepared to acknowledge his authentic accomplishments, either his success as a commander or his patronage of classical culture. Rather than admitting that Julian's reign had represented continuity with imperial traditions and the classical heritage, they classified it as a momentary aberration. A clear sense of discontinuity marked his subsequent fame. Julian had wanted to forget his Christian upbringing in order to highlight only his support for Hellenism; Christians belittled his identification with classical culture in order to emphasize only his apostasy. As a result, in his posthumous reputation Julian would remain suspended between the classical culture he had admired and the Christianity he had abandoned. The epitaph on his tomb at Tarsus had described him, predictably, with a line from Homer's *Iliad*, "both a noble ruler and a brave warrior." Christians like Gregory of Nazianzus mocked both his military reputation and his religious preferences by characterizing him instead as an "apostate," a "deserter." Julian had wanted to be the first "Greek" emperor in a Roman empire. Christians stigmatized him as the last pagan persecutor in a Christian empire.[37]

# Chapter 10

# Basil's "Outline of Virtue"

Basil had received a sterling education in all aspects of classical culture, first in grammar from his own father in Pontus, then in rhetoric, philosophy, astronomy, geometry, and medicine from teachers at Caesarea in Cappadocia, Constantinople, and Athens. It had all come so easily to him: "because of his character, who had less need of culture?" Basil had departed from Athens apparently just before Julian arrived in 355, and he had then returned to Cappadocia. There he had rejected an invitation to teach at Neocaesarea, but did teach briefly as a rhetorician at Caesarea. Then he went off to his secluded retreat in Pontus. As he explained to his friend Gregory of Nazianzus, his new ascetic lifestyle would not include any additional study of classical literature. His objective was "separation from the entire world" in order "to sever the soul from any sympathy with the body." To accomplish this goal he had to discard "the knowledge derived from human teachings" and embrace "the system defined by divine teaching." Having just spent about twenty years studying classical literature, Basil now announced the need to retrain himself. For this extended vocational training his new textbook would be the Bible, since it supplied more than enough examples of proper behavior, such as Joseph as a paradigm of continence, Job of courage, and both Moses and David of boldness and gentleness. "The most important route toward the discovery of duty is the study of the divinely inspired Bible."[1]

## Rhetoric and Asceticism

Despite his intentions, Basil could not so readily slough off his classical education. He and Gregory studied the writings of the great Christian scholar Origen, and he soon composed his own learned theological treatise that refuted the doctrines of Eunomius. He became a priest and then bishop at

Caesarea. Yet for all his remarkable success at transforming himself into an ascetic, theologian, and cleric, Basil could not walk away that easily from the education of his early years. Eventually he too felt the need to explain more explicitly the relationship between classical culture and Christianity. The most compact formulation of his thoughts was in a treatise, which seems to have been originally an oration, that he addressed to young men. Basil composed this treatise most likely during the mid-360s when he was moving back and forth between his ascetic retirement, the writing of his theological treatise, and his clerical service as a priest.[2]

In this treatise Basil defined the relationship as a sequence. Although at the moment these young men were reading and studying classical litera-ture, "associating themselves with famous men of old through the texts they have left," the next step was to consider a different future for which they would prepare by studying biblical and ecclesiastical writings. Basil made a clear distinction between "external teachings," secular classical literature, and "holy and sacred teachings," Christian literature. But because he had conceded that these students would progress naturally from one set of writ-ings to the next, he felt no need to criticize the value of classical literature. In other contexts he and others would be more hesitant about classical writ-ings. His mother had once worried about the pernicious effects of allowing her daughter Macrina to read classical drama and epic poems. His brother Gregory of Nyssa would be dubious about the value of reading classical tragedies, since their plots too often revolved around patricide, matricide, or fratricide. Basil himself, when describing an education for young ascetics, suggested that children should be taught about biblical "miracles" rather than classical "myths." Even though he had his hesitations about the content of classical literature, Basil nevertheless did not condemn it wholesale for being pagan. Instead, he conceded that heroes from the Old Testament like Moses and Daniel had themselves first been trained in Egyptian teachings or in Chaldaean wisdom. He also suggested that classical texts and biblical writings were complementary. In his estimation, one was the colorful leaves of a tree, the other its ripe fruit.[3]

By emphasizing this sequence of study Basil had effectively demoted the significance of classical literature. Rather than marking the culmination of an educational career, the study of classical texts was simply another preliminary stage, a preparation for the next level that was reserved for "more mature listeners." This study was the equivalent of warm-up exer-cises, the playful drills before the actual combat. Because these young men in his audience were not yet old enough to pass on to the next level, Basil focused on defining the propaedeutic function of the classical literature they were currently studying. The basis for evaluating the content of these texts was "usefulness": "external learning is not useless for souls." Usefulness would be the criterion for acceptance or rejection of the content of classical texts. The deeds of good men that the poets described were worth admiring and imitating, but it was necessary to disregard disreputable deeds, "the adulteries of the gods and their love affairs." Basil's approach to classical literature was similar to Julian's reaction to Christian virtues. Just as Julian had insisted that pagan priests should imitate the generosity and charity of Christians, so Basil suggested that Christians might learn from the admirable behavior and values of pagans. To reinforce this distinction between praiseworthy and shameful behavior, Basil used some common illustrations, such as the bee that could collect honey while ignoring the beauty of the flowers, and the possibility of picking roses without being pricked by the thorns. The goal was always the same. "We must not select everything indiscriminately, but whatever is necessary."[4]

These recommendations about the usefulness of classical culture for young Christians were certainly respectable, but also a bit simplistic, "really a very slight performance." They become more intriguing, however, in the context of Basil's own life. In particular, this treatise raised unspoken questions about his past training as a rhetorician, his current interest in asceticism, and the relation between the two. When he had retreated to his life of asceticism and seclusion, Basil had abandoned his brief career as a rhetorician. Yet in this treatise he was again talking like a rhetorician. This treatise was similar to the sort of declamatory orations that rhetoricians performed in their classrooms. The topics of these orations were typically paradoxical or imaginary, designed to allow the rhetoricians to display their erudition and technique, dazzle the students in their audiences, but also instruct them by example. Rather than analyzing current political and social issues, the orators indulged in pure aesthetic eloquence, using all their vast erudition and skills to discuss hypothetical history, legal conundrums, and impossible questions of conscience. The illustrious rhetorician Himerius, one of Basil's teachers, had used such declamations in his teaching at Athens. He seems to have preferred to discourse on imaginary historical topics, and among his extant declamations are fragments of speeches in the guises of the Athenian general Themistocles and various Attic orators and an entire funeral oration in the guise of a magistrate from classical Athens. Proaeresius, another of Basil's teachers at Athens, had a reputation for "shaking the world with his improvised orations." He once suddenly halted an oration in order to argue exactly the opposite hypothesis. Students too would practice their rhetorical skills by arguing different points of view in declamations. When they were growing up in Cappadocia, Julian and his half-brother Gallus had argued the relative merits of Christianity and paganism. Julian typically presented the brief for paganism, "under the pretext of practicing at the weaker case." Although years later it would become apparent that the arguments of the young Julian had been a preview of his future ideas, at the time he had been a pious Christian, to all appearances arguing against his own convictions simply for the sake of argument.[5]

In this oration about the value of classical culture, Basil too seemed to have adopted an unexpected perspective. Since in previous centuries early Christianity had been generally suspicious of the influences of classical culture, Basil was now delivering a virtuoso declamation on another hypothetical, seemingly impossible question about a possible accommodation between the two. Yet Basil did not have to make up any odd, imaginary arguments, because he obviously already agreed that classical culture was of value for young Christians. In fact, his oration was itself a prime example of such usefulness, since he bolstered his arguments about the utility of classical literature by using many examples from those very writings. He included citations from or allusions to the poetry of Homer, Hesiod, Solon, and Theognis, the tragedy of Euripides, and the philosophy of Prodicus, Socrates, Plato, and Pythagoras. He included examples from Greek mythology, such as the story of Hercules' choice between virtue and vice, and from Greek history, such as a story about Pericles' forbearance. Basil's oration was meant to be both an example of and an apology for the usefulness of classical literature for Christian students.[6]

At the same time that Basil was looking back to his old training as a rhetorician, he was also aware of his new standing as a proponent of asceticism. Rhetorical training had always involved physical exercise and discipline in order to master deeper vocal tones, proper breathing, appropriate stances, and harmonious gestures. Toward the end of his oration Basil began to discuss "the care of the soul." The most important aspect of this spiritual exercise was freedom from "the passions of the body." This liberation required an austere diet, simple attire, and even disdain of good health. "I have heard from doctors that excellent health is dangerous." Basil furthermore insisted upon the rejection of both wealth and public acclaim, and he supported his assertions with more citations and examples from classical literature. The relevance of these claims about a lifestyle of denial to a discussion of the usefulness of classical texts is not readily apparent, except in the context of Basil's own preference for spiritual asceticism. When he had first gone to his ascetic retreat in Pontus, he had described his new austere lifestyle in similar terms. Now he was ready to incorporate a traditional education in classical literature into that ascetic lifestyle. His exhortations about the proper lifestyle to accompany the study of classical texts were similar to the recommendations that other authors, such as his brother Gregory of Nyssa, included in treatises extolling virginity. In Basil's estimation, not only was such study a preliminary for subsequent study of biblical and ecclesiastical texts, it was also preparation for the adoption of asceticism. The discipline of classical rhetoric was a preview of the discipline of an ascetic life.[7]

In the end, this treatise was less about classical culture and more about the progress of Basil's own life. If classical literature was useful primarily because it provided some examples of exemplary behavior, then in a Christian society it was redundant. In his description of his ascetic life in Pontus, Basil had already suggested that the Bible provided more than enough examples of virtuous behavior. Classical literature may have been helpful, and it was certainly seductive, since Basil repeatedly had to remind his audience, and himself, not to be distracted by "the pleasure of the words." But strictly speaking it was not necessary for Christian spirituality. At the conclusion of this treatise Basil conceded as much. "We will no doubt learn this better in our own writings; let us here trace only an outline of virtue based on external teachings." If classical literature hence had no intrinsically unique value, then Basil had to be relying upon a different justification for its usefulness.[8]

Rather than considering it in the abstract, at the point that he had to legitimate the study of classical culture Basil seems to have been thinking about his own life. In this treatise he was commenting not only on literature and education, but on his own life's story. Basil emphasized the importance of a traditional education in classical culture because that is what he had received. As a boy and a young man he had been trained in grammar and rhetoric, "hinting in an outline at the future beauty of his virtue." He had then progressed to study of biblical and ecclesiastical writings, as he suggested these young boys in his audience would, and he had composed his own theological treatises. Along the way he had adopted an ascetic lifestyle, as he recommended at the end of the oration. This treatise was hence a summation, and a justification, of the trajectory of Basil's own life as he had matured from a student of classical culture and a rhetorician into a Christian ascetic.[9]

## Theological Fanaticism

One of the oddities of this treatise is its apparent lack of interest in a particular moment. The treatise was argumentative but not polemical, learned but somewhat weary. Since the treatise provided no hints of a particular context, it is difficult to locate it with any confidence at a precise moment in Basil's career. In some respects the timelessness of the treatise seemed to have corresponded to Basil's general attitude toward classical literature. In terms of his interest in classical culture, the first half of Basil's life seems disconnected from the second half. Once he had been fanatical in his pursuit of a higher education, but after he ended his studies at Athens, he seems to have removed classical culture from his everyday life. This treatise marked a final indulging of his rhetorical prowess; it also nicely illustrated the contrast between his past life of classical culture and his current life of Christian asceticism.

As Basil talked about classical culture and Christianity, he was at the same time trying to match up the halves of his life. Julian had wanted to erase his boyhood education in Christianity by actually destroying the very Christian books he had read. Rather than finding any continuity in his transition from a Christian boyhood to his pagan adulthood, he hoped simply to eliminate the evidence for what he considered to have been a mistake in his early life. In contrast, rather than wanting to disavow his own boyhood education in classical texts, Basil decided to incorporate a traditional education into his overall scheme. For all his misgivings about classical culture, he sensed that he could not criticize or reject it without at the same time renouncing much of his own early life. His arguments about the usefulness of the study of classical literature were hence also arguments in favor of the usefulness of his own education. In this perspective, all along, even at Athens, he had been preparing himself to study the Bible and become an ascetic.

Basil's ideas subsequently became widely influential in Byzantine society, and later, in translation, even in Renaissance Europe. A century later some Christian young men who were law students at Beirut were reading this very treatise for an explanation of "how they might benefit from pagan texts." At Alexandria one student who read the (spurious) correspondence between Basil and the famous sophist Libanius thought that Basil had won their playful duel over whose letters were more delightful. He immediately followed Basil's lead by converting from the study of rhetoric to the study of theology. Basil's perspective would hence allow Christian intellectuals to go on studying classical literature and collecting ancient texts. In fact, in the later Byzantine period the episcopal library at his old see of Caesarea would become an important repository of classical texts and old books.[10]

At the time, however, not only had Basil separated his feelings about classical literature from his everyday life. He also seems to have worked out these arguments in isolation and for himself. Although Basil had been thinking about the meaning of his own education and the use of classical literature, he had not been directly engaged in the public wrangling over the role of classical culture associated with the reign of Julian. Julian seems not to have registered in his historical awareness, and in his genuine extant letters Basil never mentioned the emperor. Since Julian had quickly acquired a reputation as another persecuting emperor, and since Basil was deeply attracted to the ecclesiastical tradition of persecution and martyrdom, this was a distinctly odd oversight. Later traditions claimed that a local aristocrat named Eupsychius had taken the lead in destroying the temple of Fortune at Caesarea, and that he had been condemned to death because of Julian's anger. Once he became bishop at Caesarea, Basil presided over the festival in honor of "the blessed martyr Eupsychius" and his comrades, "whose memory is celebrated annually in our city and throughout the entire district." Basil often used the opportunity of this festival to convene a regional council to which he invited neighboring bishops. Yet in these letters Basil never mentioned the emperor Julian. Since in their panegyrics about martyrs preachers often referred to the presiding emperors anonymously as "tyrants," Basil may not have mentioned Julian in his commemorative orations on Eupsychius either. Instead, Basil preached on general theological issues. One man who attended a festival for St. Eupsychius would remember only Basil's comments about the Trinity. Basil had not defined himself in terms of Julian or the events of his reign. He was now a Christian theologian, and Julian was not a participant in the disputes over Christian theology.[11]

But since Julian would eventually become a symbol of the resurgence of paganism and Basil of the success of orthodox Christianity, it was clearly difficult for historians not to link them somehow. When Julian had passed through the region in 362, his entourage had included Eutychianus, a soldier from Cappadocia. In the next year Eutychianus apparently fought in Julian's campaigns against the Persians, and he subsequently composed a chronicle of the emperor's last days and death. In this account he included an apocryphal story about Basil's nightmare. After dreaming that he had seen Christ giving the command to St. Mercurius to kill Julian, Basil had woken up in distress. According to Eutychianus' legendary account, he had been upset because Julian had previously honored him as "his illustrious companion," and he had often written to him.[12]

In fact, Basil and Julian had not been students together, had not been friends, and had most likely not exchanged letters. On the other hand, they had not clashed either, or at least not over interpretations of classical culture. For Basil there was nothing to argue about. Julian was passionate about the association of classical culture with pagan cults, while Basil thought that familiarity with classical literature was, at best, a helpful preliminary exercise to understanding the Bible and Christian theology. Because Basil had such a charitable perspective on the usefulness of classical culture, he was not a central participant in the culture wars of the mid-fourth century. He was simply not enough of a zealot. Although in the past he had been devoted to the study of classical literature, now he reserved his fanaticism for arguing about Christian theology. His friend Gregory of Nazianzus would quarrel with Julian over the meaning of classical culture, but when Basil confronted an emperor, it would be over definitions of Christian orthodoxy.

# Chapter 11

# *Gregory of Nazianzus and the Philosopher Emperor*

During the winter of 361–362 Julian was consolidating his authority after surviving a civil war with his cousin, the emperor Constantius. One
of his first objectives had been to take up residence in Constantinople,
where he could ingratiate himself with the senators, magistrates, and residents of the capital of the eastern empire. Because Julian had been born
in Constantinople, he probably relished the opportunity of returning to his
hometown as the uncontested emperor.

During the same winter Gregory of Nazianzus had also received an
unexpected promotion at his hometown of Nazianzus. After ending his
studies in Athens, Gregory had returned to Cappadocia a few years earlier.
In his native region he had first satisfied people's requests by entertaining
them with a public oration: "I danced for my friends." After this display of
his rhetorical expertise he had several careers from which to choose. One
option was to participate in the civic life of his hometown by becoming a
decurion, a municipal magistrate, and a local benefactor. Another option
was to instruct local teenagers by becoming a rhetorician. Yet another
option was to assist his elderly father by becoming a cleric. As bishop of
Nazianzus his father was already strongly urging his son to accept "the
second throne." Even though any of these careers would have allowed him
to make full use of his extensive education in rhetoric, Gregory nevertheless
rejected these opportunities to serve as a municipal decurion or teacher
or cleric. After so many years of chafing under others' supervision, Julian
would quickly appreciate and even revel in the uninhibited freedom of
being a senior emperor and then sole emperor. In contrast, after so many
years of carefree and sometimes self-indulgent study at Athens and elsewhere, Gregory had difficulty coping with the more restrictive expectations
of his family and his fellow citizens.[1]

So he had left. Rather than immediately committing himself to any of
these careers in his hometown, Gregory decided to live, off and on, with Basil

at his retreat in Pontus. There they renewed their friendship, and they began to recast their learning into the service of Christian exegesis. Gregory seemed to want to remain a student indefinitely. Just as Julian had been deeply hesitant about giving up his studies at Athens and becoming an emperor, so Gregory was reluctant to initiate a municipal or clerical career. His ordination as a priest at Nazianzus in late 361 or early 362 genuinely upset his composure, and his response was to flee, once again, to Pontus. While Julian was at Constantinople trying to hone his skills as sole emperor, Gregory was in the mountains of Pontus coming to terms with his new priesthood.

## Confronting Julian

Gregory returned to Nazianzus by spring of 362. He soon delivered some sermons in which he defended both his initial reluctance to become a cleric and his subsequent decision to assume his duties, and stressed his concern for his elderly parents and his love for the congregation at Nazianzus. Another factor that may have influenced his decision to return was his apprehension about Julian. During the previous winter people in Cappadocia had had a preview of the impact of the new emperor's policies. Julian had sent his uncle on ahead as count of the East, charged with restoring pagan cults at Antioch. His passage through Cappadocia may well have precipitated the Christians at Caesarea, because of "their fervor for piety," to destroy a temple dedicated to the city's titular Fortune. Upon his return Gregory announced that he too was not afraid. "I do not fear the war that is coming from outside, nor that fulfillment of evil, the wild beast that is now rising up against the churches." These allusions suggest that Gregory had already heard about Julian's opposition to Christianity and probably too about the emperor's preparations to march to Antioch. His bravado now in the spring was only a mask for his, and others', worries.[2]

Gregory also had a direct interest in Julian's arrival, since his brother Caesarius was a doctor at the emperor's court. Julian's passage through Cappadocia in late spring hence raised personal concerns for the welfare of members of his family. At Caesarea Julian had imposed penalties for burning the pagan shrine, and he had interfered in a dispute between the governor and the bishop. Only after Gregory the Elder refused to back down did the emperor stop his intimidation of the city. Since Caesarius may still have been a member of Julian's entourage, at Nazianzus people grumbled about the propriety of their bishop's son serving at a pagan emperor's court.

As he reacted to the presence of the emperor in Cappadocia, Gregory's first objectives were to protect his father and his episcopal authority, and to convince his brother to abandon his career at the court.[3]

At the same time Gregory had to revisit his own past. Another likely member of Julian's entourage was Himerius, the famous rhetorician who had been one of Gregory's teachers at Athens. Himerius had joined Julian at Constantinople and, most likely, accompanied him on his journey to Antioch. At Athens it had been possible for devout young Christians like Gregory and Basil to study with the pagan Himerius, and Himerius may even have bid them adieu in a flattering farewell oration. During those years of study a shared interest in classical culture had minimized the significance of religious differences. Now that Himerius had openly joined the emperor, however, it was apparent that he had accepted Julian's exclusive association of classical culture with paganism. Gregory's teacher had become another proponent of the emperor's notion of Hellenism and his revival of pagan cults. Both a former teacher and a former fellow student were trying to turn classical culture into a religious issue.[4]

Because of the involvement of his father and brother and because of his own personal associations, Gregory could not avoid reacting to Julian's policies. His initial reaction was in another sermon that he delivered at Nazianzus, perhaps in mid-summer of 362 shortly after Julian's visit. In this sermon Gregory commemorated some of the resisters to the policies of king Antiochus Epiphanes during the period of the Maccabean revolts in the second century B.C. King Antiochus had supported those Jews who had wanted to Hellenize by accepting Greek culture, and he had eventually turned the Temple at Jerusalem into a sanctuary for Zeus. Not only did Gregory praise the strict Jews who had died for their opposition as martyrs, he also hinted that Julian's policies now offered a similar opportunity for Christians. In this sermon Gregory suggested that Julian was "another harsher Antiochus," "today's Antiochus." Already in the immediate aftermath of Julian's visit, rather than comparing him with any of the earlier Roman emperors who had persecuted Christians, Gregory preferred to associate him with a Greek king and his persecution of Jews. Since the antagonism between the king and the Jews had involved both respect for a traditional religion and concerns about the imposition of Greek culture, Gregory now implied that Christians could earn martyrdom by opposing Julian's policies about both religion and culture.[5]

As a pointed demonstration that Christians too could integrate classical culture with their biblical studies, in this sermon Gregory embellished his account of these Jewish martyrdoms with subtle allusions to Homer's *Iliad*. These allusions were discreet, however, because at the time he was perhaps hesitant to make too explicit this argument about martyrdom on behalf of cultural ideals. Such an unprecedented objective would have reminded his audience of the incongruity of listening to the admonitions of a priest who had been reluctant to become a cleric in part because of his own devotion to classical culture. Instead, in this sermon Gregory had tried to adopt the persona of a strict Old Testament prophet. Even though by doing so he was living up to the expectations of his mother, who had dedicated him at birth as a "new Samuel," this was a difficult role for him to play. His father could live up to this image. In fact, because of his earlier association with a semi-Jewish cult, his limited familiarity with classical culture, and his venerable age, Gregory the Elder seemed to have been custom-fitted to appear as the reincarnation of an Old Testament prophet. But after his long study of classical literature Gregory resembled no one so much as Julian himself, another overeducated young man.[6]

Beyond his concerns about the welfare of his family, Gregory now faced troubling personal questions about the role of classical culture in his new position as a cleric. Especially since it came so soon after he had assumed his priestly duties, the presence of Julian compelled Gregory to think again about the relationship between classical culture and service as a cleric.

## Interpreting Julian

Gregory faced some of these questions in two treatises about Julian that he composed about a year after the emperor's death. In the first of these treatises he intended to demonstrate "the evilness of the man" and in the second God's just retributions. The tone of these treatises was completely different from his earlier sermon about the Maccabean resistance. In that sermon Gregory had been defiant, but also cautious and uncertain. Because Julian had been only in his early thirties when he had become sole emperor and might have been expected to reign for decades, Christians seemingly had to prepare for another long bout of opposition. In addition, since Julian did not initiate any overt suppression of Christians, Gregory had had to redefine persecution. By suggesting that resistance to the emperor's policies about classical literature was also a form of martyrdom, Gregory had wanted to make sure that Christians would also fight for their right to use classical culture. In that sermon, delivered while Julian was still ruling, Gregory's response had been a simple parody of the emperor's totalitarian perspective. If Julian would identify Greek culture with paganism, then Gregory would associate it instead with Christianity and insist that cultural persecution was the equivalent of religious persecution.

After Julian's unexpectedly early death, however, Gregory, like other relieved Christians, could indulge in some gloating about the eventual success of "God's scale of justice." But even though the emperor's death had removed the threat of persecution either over Christianity or over the use of classical culture, this mood of triumphalism had not resolved Gregory's apprehensions about the relationship between Christianity and classical culture. He now used the opportunity of meditating on Julian's career and death in order to contemplate religion and culture.[7]

By the time Gregory composed these two treatises he had clearly done some research on Julian's life and reign. In order to understand "the magnitude of the danger," Gregory insisted that it was necessary to consider "the origins and the seeds of this evil." The starting point was Julian's survival of a massacre. After Constantine's death in 337, the army had murdered several collateral members of the imperial family in order to ensure the succession of Constantine's three sons. Julian and his half-brother Gallus had been spared, and eventually they had been sent into exile on an imperial estate in Cappadocia. There they had continued their instruction in Christianity, served as readers in the church, and constructed a shrine in honor of martyrs. When Gallus became a junior emperor, Julian was allowed to study with teachers in the old Greek world. Eventually Julian became a junior emperor himself. Gregory's rapid account of Julian's early years was predictably partisan, but not totally hostile. The oddity of this account is that it was simultaneously too critical and too sympathetic, and therefore doubly distorted. In retrospect, Gregory could not quite make up his mind about Julian.[8]

The distortions resulting from his criticism of Julian were most apparent in his praise of the emperor Constantius, Constantine's son and Julian's cousin. Even though Constantius had in fact been the instigator of the massacre of his relatives, Gregory credited him with having saved his cousins from the army. With this revisionist perspective he could then claim that in the aftermath Julian had been at fault, since he had subsequently been ungrateful to both God and Constantius. Throughout his reign Constantius had furthermore intruded constantly in ecclesiastical affairs, in particular in trying to impose a uniform doctrine of theological orthodoxy. Most recently, he had compelled bishops to accept a simplified credal formula, at the council of Constantinople in early 360, that soon caused dissension in Christian communities in Cappadocia. Gregory knew that Constantius had been an awkward and heavy-handed emperor for many who did not readily accept his preferred notion of orthodoxy. He nevertheless waved away that meddling. "If Constantius aggravated us a bit, he did so in order for us all to be one, to agree, and not to be separated or divided by schisms." Gregory explained away Constantius' intrusions by suggesting that it had been the emperor's subordinates who had misled "his simple soul that had no experience in religion and could not foresee any pitfalls." He furthermore characterized Constantius as the "most divine emperor, the emperor whom Christ loved most." In order to provide a contrast to Julian's evil reign, Gregory had to offer a favorable reinterpretation of Constantius' reign. In his revised reading of the past, Constantius had been generous in sparing Julian, and he had been a devout Christian emperor. Gregory could then criticize Julian for having taken revenge on his benefactor and rejected Christianity.[9]

Despite this criticism Gregory also seemed at times sympathetic to Julian, perhaps because he could see reflections of his own life in the emperor's life. Julian had grown up on an estate in Cappadocia, and he had shared his study of both Christian writings and classical literature with his brother Gallus. Gregory himself during the previous few years had been living on Basil's family's estate in Pontus, where they had immersed themselves in ecclesiastical writings. Gregory also understood devotion to a brother, even a brother whose career went off in disconcerting directions. He furthermore admired Julian's willingness to share the hardships and food of his troops, and he hinted that Julian would have made a good ascetic. When he looked at Julian, Gregory saw a version of himself. To avoid that identification, Gregory again had to turn any possible virtues into criticisms. He claimed that because Gallus had remained a Christian, Julian had eventually considered even his brother as an enemy, and he insisted that Julian had showed no respect for Christian ascetics.[10]

In these treatises Gregory was searching for a way to interpret Julian. His attempt at writing history was not very successful. Even though he had obviously done some research on Julian's early life, he skewed his interpretation in order to construct Constantius as a properly laudable emperor. In order to differentiate himself from Julian, Gregory furthermore had to repress any tinges of sympathy. His hostility to Julian had made him too laudatory of Constantius, and his affinities with Julian had made him too skeptical of the emperor's motives.

Another mode that Gregory adopted in these treatises was, again, his role as an Old Testament prophet. At the beginning of the first treatise Gregory identified himself with the prophet Isaiah. "He testified to Israel when it was in revolt, I to a tyrant who was in revolt and has suffered a misfortune worthy of his impiety." At the end of the second treatise, Gregory exhorted his audience to learn from these threats and improve their own lives: "let us use the moment wisely." Even though this posturing as a shrill prophet allowed Gregory to be suitably indignant about Julian's behavior and appropriately gloating about his eventual demise, he could not, predictably, sustain such a raw demeanor. Yet another mode that Gregory adopted was to present himself as a prosecutor. As he began his survey of Julian's career in his first treatise Gregory claimed that he was setting out an "indictment." These accusations included the usual charges of impiety and disloyalty. In addition, he attributed to Julian's responsibility some specific examples of persecution. These included the defilement of Christian virgins, the lynching of a priest who had destroyed a pagan temple at Arethusa, and the arrest of Christians after a riot. At the end of his second treatise Gregory concluded his indictment by noting that he had presented it on a "column." Since Julian was no longer alive to answer these charges, this column was now simply a marker, a reminder to others of Julian's "revolt against God" and a tombstone to his failure.[11]

Because Gregory had presented himself in so many different guises, as a historian, a prophet, and a prosecutor, these two treatises were predictably digressive and baggy, simultaneously hysterical and pedantic, fiercely caustic and pompously ponderous. These are perhaps Gregory's least likable writings, full of an anger and a triumphant mockery that verged on smugness and even outright meanness. To read them is to cringe both from embarrassment at Gregory's petulance and from boredom with his longwindedness. The only topic in the treatises that genuinely engaged Gregory was his defense of classical culture from the threats he thought that Julian had posed.

## Confronting Classical Culture

Much of this discussion of classical culture focused around the meanings and significance of *logos* (and, sometimes, its plural form, *logoi*). Since *logos* was a word with many significations, Gregory was careful to distinguish them; but at the same time he was not above eliding some of these meanings in order to advance his own arguments. At the beginning of the first treatise Gregory stepped right into this multiplicity of meanings. His *logos*, this "oration," was meant to be a sacrifice of gratitude to God that would be a contrast to Julian's bloody sacrifices on the altars of pagan gods. Through the *logoi*, the "words," in this oration Gregory would in addition be able to honor the Logos, Jesus Christ the "Word," "who is happy in particular with this title." Through this oration he also wanted to punish Julian for his "crime against *logoi*, 'culture,'" which was itself a consequence of the emperor's lack of *logos*, "reason." With these puns Gregory was able to associate his oration and its words with homage to Jesus Christ the Word and present it as an act of defense for classical culture and human reason. In addition, the slight-of-hand associated with these multiple meanings allowed him to imply that the identification of Jesus Christ with the Logos entailed a natural connection between Christianity and classical culture. Because Jesus Christ had been the embodiment, the fulfillment, of "reason" and "culture," there could not be any antagonism between classical culture and Christianity.[12]

In contrast, in Gregory's estimation Julian had been deceitful in his understanding of *logos*. Gregory claimed that Julian "had dishonestly transferred the [meaning of this] word to the [realm of] imagination, as if the *logos*, the 'language,' of the Hellenes was [an aspect] of religious worship and not of speaking." On the basis of this association between the Greek language and pagan cults Julian had wanted to prohibit Christians from using *logoi*, "culture," entirely. Although Julian obviously could use these multiple meanings to his advantage too, his logic was not as disingenuous as Gregory made it sound. In previous centuries early Christian apologists had already made this connection between "Greek" and "non-Christian" by using "Hellenes" as the equivalent of "pagans," and Gregory himself, later in this treatise, would use "Hellenes" as a synonym for "pagans." Because early apologists had also already argued that certain aspects of classical Greek mythology were too immoral for use by Christians, in some respects Julian's attempt to separate classical culture from Christianity was simply an extension of earlier Christian misgivings.[13]

In fact, not all learned Christians were as upset as Gregory at Julian's attempt to prevent Christians from teaching and using classical literature. Some saw it as an opportunity to affirm their commitment to Christianity. The Christian rhetorician Proaeresius gave up his official teaching post at Athens, even though Julian offered him an exemption. Apollinarius, who had been a rhetorician before becoming bishop of Laodicea, and his father,

Apollinarius the Elder, who had been a grammarian before serving as a priest, reacted to Julian's prohibitions by rewriting the Bible in the style of various classical authors. The father transformed the early history of Israel into a Homeric epic and composed comedies, tragedies, and odes based on biblical books, and the son turned the gospels into Platonic dialogues. "Apollinarius took themes from the holy Scriptures and composed works that were similar in tone and language to the works that the Hellenes hold in esteem." In contrast, other learned Christians decided to abandon Christianity. The rhetorician Hecebolius had been a Christian when he taught Julian at Constantinople during the reign of Constantius. During Julian's reign he became a pagan. Pegasius was a bishop who had once given the young Julian a tour of the shrines to Homeric heroes at Troy. When Julian became sole emperor, Pegasius became a pagan priest. Christians who either abandoned classical literature or disavowed their Christianity had essentially accepted Julian's exclusive linkage of classical culture with paganism.[14]

Gregory was not prepared to follow these examples by either giving up classical literature or rejecting Christianity. Even though he too identified pagans as Hellenes, he was not prepared to let Julian then claim the Greek language, classical literature, and Greek culture in general exclusively for paganism. Like Julian, he too enjoyed reading the *Iliad*. At the beginning of his first treatise Gregory's only rebuttal was to sneer at the emperor's cowardice. In his perspective, Julian was simply afraid to engage in head-to-head arguments, as if allowing Christians access to all the resources of classical rhetoric and philosophy would certainly undermine his own religious arguments. Even without the use of classical culture, however, Gregory thought that Julian's support for paganism was a weak case. "By issuing this edict he prevented us from using [classical] Attic Greek, but he did not stop us from speaking the truth."[15]

At the end of the treatise Gregory returned to his discussion of Julian's interpretation of culture. Although he had already criticized the emperor at length by posing as a historian, a prophet, and a prosecutor, he now conceded that in his true self he was "someone who took pleasure in culture." He again ridiculed Julian's arguments for claiming exclusive possession of *logos*, Greek culture and language. "Culture belongs to us, he says, and so does 'being a Hellene,' one characteristic of which is worshipping the [pagan] gods." Gregory rejected this association of culture and paganism in various arguments. He made a distinction between Hellenes as Greek-speakers and Hellenes as pagans, and suggested that Greek culture belonged to the former rather than to the latter. He noted that because the Greek language included many dialects and styles and because paganism included so many cults, it was difficult to tell which Greek language and which cults Julian was trying to link. He claimed that both the Greek language and pagan cults had borrowed so many components from non-Greeks that it was impossible to make and enforce claims about proprietary usage. Even poetry was not an invention of the Greeks. The implied conclusion to these arguments was that educated Christians also had a right to use and enjoy the Greek language, classical literature, and classical culture.[16]

Gregory then tried to turn the emperor's arguments upside-down by insisting that Julian had modeled his own proposals about the spread of culture and paganism on the practices of Christians. His attack on Julian's plan to use classical literature as the equivalent of a scriptural basis for pagan cults ridiculed two characteristics of the proposal. According to Gregory, Julian had wanted to establish a school in every city, each of which would include a pulpit, front and back benches, "readings and interpretations of Hellenic doctrines," and even the prescribed recitation of prayers. He also claimed that Julian had intended to found hospices, convents for virgins, and monasteries. Gregory's first complaint was that Julian's ideas were not even original, since he was merely imitating "whatever is clearly characteristic of our [Christian] ecclesiastical order." Even his proposed schools looked like churches. His second criticism mocked any attempts to teach "theology and morality" on the basis of classical texts that included so many stories about the gods' immoral and disreputable behavior. With all these examples of scandalous behavior it would be difficult to promote the virtues of harmony within cities, respect for parents, rejection of wealth, and individual chastity and continence. In contrast, Christian teachings provided all the right doctrines for encouraging these virtues. At the end of this treatise Gregory concluded that classical literature could not provide the theological basis for pagan cults. Since classical texts were hence not religious at all, Christians too could use and enjoy them.[17]

After they had returned from Athens to Cappadocia, both Basil and Gregory had had to reevaluate their lives. Basil had soon abandoned a career as a rhetorician and instead retreated to a life of ascetic seclusion in Pontus. Gregory had had a harder struggle with his relationship with classical culture, and he had had to balance his love of classical culture against his obligation of caring for his parents and his hesitation about being coopted into the clergy. During the same period Julian too had been reconsidering the role of classical culture in his life. After spending a few years studying with famous teachers he had become a junior emperor, a military commander in Gaul, and then sole emperor. As one dedication would put it, he had come to the emperorship from philosophy. Careers as ascetics, clerics, and emperors were not the conventional outcomes of an extensive education in classical culture. Gregory conceded as much in his occasional ironical descriptions of Julian as "the sophist of evil," "the philosopher emperor," "the new-fangled sophist." No one expected a sophist or philosopher to become an emperor; then again, a sophist who became a Christian ascetic and cleric was also extraordinary. Thinking about Julian and classical culture hence helped Gregory think about himself and classical culture, in part because he could sense the incongruities in both of their careers.[18]

In the end, Gregory never adequately resolved the larger issue of the relationship between classical culture and Christianity in general. Julian had insisted that classical texts were religious texts. Not only had he wanted to use them as the underpinning for pagan cults, he had also tried to separate them from Christianity. Yet Julian had remained a bit unsure about the exclusiveness of the relationship between classical culture and paganism, and the exasperated shrillness of his edicts and letters was a sign of his uncertainty. He was even annoyed at the name of his rivals. Julian consistently preferred to use another name for Christians, in part perhaps because he had sensed one of the unstated implications of the identification of Jesus Christ as the Logos. If Jesus Christ had really been the incarnation of *logos*, reason and culture, then it would have been easy for "Christians" to claim that they were "followers of culture." Julian instead referred to them as "Galilaeans," a name that both belittled Christianity as a small regional sect and separated it from any association with culture and philosophy. Gregory, predictably, mocked Julian's insistence on this new name as "especially adolescent and stupid." In addition, by ridiculing the shameful content of classical texts Gregory effectively removed their capacity to serve as religious texts. Basil had wanted to turn the study of classical texts into a preparation for the study of biblical and ecclesiastical texts; Gregory simply left it as an autonomous field with no necessary religious implications.[19]

## Christian Culture and Friendship

Gregory should have been careful about what he wished for. Previous emperors had confronted Christianity on religious issues, pagan emperors by initiating persecutions, Christian emperors by meddling in disputes over orthodoxy and heresy. Julian, in contrast, had challenged Christianity on cultural issues and compelled educated Christians like Gregory to think hard about the relationship between Christianity and classical culture. After Julian's death Christians continued to argue about the merits and demerits of studying classical literature. Some essentially accepted Julian's identification of Greek culture and paganism and encouraged their fellow believers to avoid classical texts entirely. Julian had linked paganism and Greek literature to exclude Christians from access to classical texts; fundamentalist Christians conceded the linkage and excluded classical culture from a Christian education. Other Christians were more accommodating, in particular by adopting Basil's vision of a pedagogical advancement from classical texts to ecclesiastical texts.

But the urgency of this issue had died with Julian, the only emperor of the fourth century who could claim a thorough education in Greek classical culture. At Constantinople Julian had endowed a new library with his own books. He soon tried to replenish his stock of classical texts by acquiring the books of Georgius, his former mentor in Cappadocia, who had recently been lynched in Alexandria. At Antioch Julian may have deposited these very books in a temple that he had remodeled into a library. In addition to pagan temples and shrines, libraries were to be the legacy of Julian's reforms. But when Jovian succeeded Julian, he had the library at Antioch burned down "with all its books." The involvement of emperors in the arguments about the relationship between Christianity and classical culture also went up in smoke. The next two emperors in the East, Valens and Theodosius, were not only professional soldiers with limited familiarity with classical culture. They were also native Latin speakers, and hence most unlikely to raise any questions about the role of Greek classical culture in a Christian empire. Their involvement with Christianity again focused on the issue of orthodoxy and heresy.[20]

Gregory was free to go on enjoying classical culture. In some of his letters he even cited biblical verses and quotations from classical poems back to back, once combining snippets from the *Iliad* with a verse from a Psalm. Gregory knew that his letters were enticing. When he put together a collection, he first compared his volume to the sensuous charms of the magical girdle of Aphrodite, the goddess of love. Then, with an impish chuckle, he backpedaled: his letters of course concerned "rhetoric, not seduction." Subsequent readers were nevertheless entranced by his letters, orations, and poems, and Gregory acquired a reputation as a literary stylist. One Byzantine commentator noted that some theologians were so proud of their deep familiarity with Gregory's orations that they were known as "imitators of

Gregory." This commentator then explained his own motivation to study Gregory's poems: "Imitate my Gregory, Christ says. He was not the speaker. I was." Among the many books in the library of Eustathius Boilas, a native Cappadocian and a Byzantine official during the eleventh century, was a volume of Gregory's poems. Gregory's combination of deep emotions and wide learning has influenced modern poets too. The greatest of the modern Greek poets drew inspiration from reading Gregory. "'Two poems of mine were shipwrecked because I could not find a copy of Gregory Nazianzen,' Cavafy used to say to his friends."[21]

Since Gregory's two treatises about Julian had focused on his ideas about classical culture, it is not surprising that they also touched on a related notion, his ideas about friendship. After he had returned to Cappadocia from his years of study overseas, he had soon, even if with some misgivings, joined Basil at his retreat in Pontus. That time together had been an attempt to recreate some of their experiences as students together at Athens. It had also allowed Gregory to postpone having to think about the value of his education in classical culture. His procrastination ended, abruptly and unexpectedly, during the winter of 361–362, when he became a priest and Julian emerged as emperor in the East. Because Gregory had known Julian as a fellow student at Athens, and because Julian now tried to prevent Christians from teaching and using classical culture, his reign compelled Gregory to reconsider the significance of "Athens" and all it represented.

Julian too had identified himself with Athens, which he described as his "true fatherland." After he became emperor, he used the image of "Athens" as a contrast to the extravagance of the court, and he invited some of his former teachers at Athens to join him at the capital and then to accompany him on his journey through Asia Minor. When this imperial entourage reached Cappadocia, Gregory would have seen his world turned upside-down, with a former fellow student and a former teacher not just supporting paganism but claiming that classical literature was now reserved for the exclusive use of pagans. Gregory found it difficult to imagine that another student from Athens could be so perverse in his understanding of classical culture. Since his own experiences at Athens had been so formative, Gregory could not allow Julian to appropriate this image and distort his memories.[22]

So he reinterpreted Julian's visit to Athens. After the emperor's death he mentioned that he had indeed seen Julian at Athens, but now he used the encounter to question Julian's devotion to classical culture. In this later evaluation Gregory claimed that Julian had had a double motivation for going to Athens, with one goal "perfectly appropriate," his interest in the schools in Greece, but the other "quite secret, and known only to a few people." "He wanted to consult the diviners and the rogues in Greece about his future." While in Greece Julian had in fact participated in the cult of Demeter and Persephone at Eleusis. Now, by suggesting that Julian had already then been more of a religious charlatan than a student of classical culture, Gregory was able to save his memories of Athens, and his own devotion to classical culture, from being tainted by the emperor's subsequent actions. Since Julian had not behaved like a cultured gentleman when emperor, he had doubtless not learned the true culture that was taught at Athens. Gregory claimed that he had already back then sensed Julian's duplicity. "Before he had done anything, I had recognized in him the sort of man that I later observed in his actions." In Gregory's opinion, Julian's stay in Athens had had nothing to do with classical culture.[23]

Gregory wanted to distinguish classical culture from both politics and religion and leave it as a neutral discipline, available for use by both Christians and pagans. In his perspective, the passion for classical literature that they had shared at Athens should have made Julian his cultural soulmate, despite their differences over religious beliefs. Both his indignation and his sympathy suggest that Gregory never quite gave up on Julian. He would not have reacted with such vehemence and such ambivalence if he had not sensed what they still shared. Even if now, in the mid-360s, Gregory had decided that Julian's subsequent pronouncements had ruined their cultural affinity, at least he still had another soulmate from his days at Athens. While composing these treatises against Julian he seems to have received assistance from Basil, and at the end of the second treatise he signed off in both of their names. "Basil and Gregory [send] these words to you." In Gregory's estimation, these treatises were another indication of the bond that the two had formed during their years together as students and ascetics.[24]

Gregory still venerated Athens as the beacon of classical culture, and also as the incubator for his friendship with Basil. By now their friendship had survived their adoption of asceticism and their ordinations as priests. Even Julian's threats had only reinforced their bond. Gregory thought that the one secure guarantee of his commitment to classical culture would be his friendship with Basil. Surely Basil would always be true.

# Epilogue:
## Admonishment and Compassion

In fact, Basil would not be a reliable friend. Within a few years Gregory would have to endure the breakdown of their friendship, and then the recriminations that would follow. In his later years, when he composed a panegyric about Basil and a series of autobiographical poems that helped him come to terms with the vicissitudes of his life, he would anguish incessantly about Basil and their ruined friendship. His dispute with Julian, meanwhile, faded from his memory, in part because Julian's death had removed the possibility of a challenge from an emperor to the use of classical culture by Christians. In his autobiographical poems Gregory would never again mention Julian, or even hint at this confrontation. The only other emperor with whom Gregory interacted directly was Theodosius at Constantinople. In a sermon Gregory may have alluded to the example of Julian to caution the emperor against his preference for peremptory coercion, but at least Theodosius was an orthodox Christian who supported Gregory's theological doctrines. As a native Latin speaker from Spain, Theodosius was furthermore not about to challenge Gregory or other Greek churchmen over their fascination with classical Greek culture.[1]

Confrontations were how men measured themselves. Men found their identities in the drama, the performance, of their relationships. Since those relationships always involved comparisons, they often became confrontational. Even the best of relationships, initiated with the best of intentions and the deepest of feelings, might eventually go wrong. Gregory of Nyssa had misgivings about his marriage, and ended up writing a treatise about the virtues of virginity that also reflected on the ambiguities of his relationships with his older sister and older brother, Macrina and Basil. Gregory of Nazianzus had no choice but to use the failure of his friendship with Basil to investigate the course of his own life. Tensions in relationships generated the most intimate scrutiny of the self.

Confrontations were also how others measured these men. Rivalries helped shaped men's public reputations and images. As a bishop Basil defined his episcopal authority in terms of his success at confronting an emperor like Valens, high-ranking magistrates like the prefect Modestus and the vicar Demosthenes, and local notables who were hoarding grain. In addition, he often defined his theology in feuds with other theologians, most notably his rival and fellow Cappadocian, Eunomius. Gregory of Nazianzus initially presented himself in terms of his relationship with his father, whose clerical career he was reluctant to imitate even as he remained devoted to caring for him. Gregory also had misgivings about his addiction to classical culture, which he worked out in his treatises against Julian. Emperors were obviously a common object of contemplation, as useful to think with as to think about. Basil distinguished himself from Valens over Christianity orthodoxy, and Gregory of Nazianzus from Theodosius over the techniques for enforcing orthodoxy. Gregory also distinguished himself from Julian over classical culture. For Basil and Gregory, emperors represented religion and culture. They notably did not confront emperors specifically over the nature of Roman rule. Their sense of self, and hence their public disputations, focused on Christianity and Greekness, not Romanness.

In my trilogy of books about late Roman Cappadocia, *Families and Friends* ends with Gregory's reflections about friendship and *Becoming Christian* concludes with his musings about himself and the trajectory of his life. The final chapter in this book discusses his meditations about classical culture. Although Gregory did not hesitate to argue with his opponents in treatises about the role of Greek culture and the nature of doctrinal orthodoxy, he was consistently rather reluctant to confront them personally. Basil was not reluctant at all. One later evaluation distinguished Basil for his hectoring admonishment and Gregory for his sympathetic compassion. Basil was seemingly compulsive about challenging others directly, Gregory about scrutinizing himself. As a result, because Basil had the contentious personality to initiate the sort of direct showdowns that exposed underlying realities of power and authority, he has been an invaluable escort for learning about the workings of Roman rule in Cappadocia and about the hard conniving of local notables. In contrast, because of his personal sensitivity and introspection Gregory has been a wonderful guide to relationships between friends, ideas about classical culture, and attempts to find a consistent self. Friendship, culture, identity: even though in different guises, Gregory was always writing about himself.[2]

# Abbreviations

| | |
|---|---|
| ACW | Ancient Christian Writers (Westminster) |
| *Becoming Christian* | R. Van Dam, *Becoming Christian: The Conversion of Roman Cappadocia* (University of Pennsylvania Press, forthcoming) |
| Budé | Collection des Universités de France publiée sous le patronage de l'Association Guillaume Budé (Paris) |
| CChr. | Corpus christianorum (Turnhout) |
| CPG | *Clavis patrum graecorum.* CChr. (Turnhout). Vols. 1–5, ed. M. Geerard (1974–1987); Supplementum, ed. M. Geerard and J. Noret (1998) |
| CSEL | Corpus scriptorum ecclesiasticorum latinorum (Vienna) |
| *Families and Friends* | R. Van Dam, *Families and Friends in Late Roman Cappadocia* (University of Pennsylvania Press, forthcoming) |
| FC | Fathers of the Church (Washington, D.C.) |
| GCS | Die grieschischen christlichen Schriftsteller der ersten Jahrhunderte (Berlin) |
| GNO | Gregorii Nysseni opera (Leiden) |
| IGR | *Inscriptiones graecae ad res romanas pertinentes.* Vols. 1, 3–4, ed. R. Cagnat et al. (Paris, 1906–1927) |
| ILS | *Inscriptiones latinae selectae.* 3 volumes in 5, ed. H. Dessau (reprint, Berlin, 1962). |
| LCL | Loeb Classical Library (Cambridge, Mass. and London) |
| NPNF | A Select Library of Nicene and Post-Nicene Fathers of the Christian Church (reprint, Grand Rapids, Mich.) |
| PG | *Patrologia graeca* (Paris) |
| PL | *Patrologia latina* (Paris) |
| PLRE | *The Prosopography of the Later Roman Empire* (Cambridge). Vol. 1, *A.D. 260–395*, ed. A. H. M. Jones, J. R. Martindale, and J. Morris (1971). Vol. 2, *A.D. 395–527*, ed. J. R. Martindale (1980). Vol. 3, *A.D. 527–641*, ed. J. R. Martindale (1992) |
| SChr. | Sources chrétiennes (Paris) |
| *Studia Pontica* 3.1 | *Studia Pontica III: Recueil des inscriptions grecques et latines du Pont et de l'Arménie*, Fascicule 1, ed. J. G. C. Anderson, F. Cumont, and H. Grégoire (Brussels, 1910) |
| Teubner | Bibliotheca scriptorum graecorum et romanorum Teubneriana (Leipzig and Stuttgart) |
| TTH | Translated Texts for Historians (Liverpool) |

In the notes, B = Basil of Caesarea, GNaz = Gregory of Nazianzus, and GNys = Gregory of Nyssa.

# Notes

## Introduction

1. Kaplan (1992) 14: "l'Asie Mineure est le royaume de la neige." Worthless: *Anthologia Graeca* 11.238. Kappa: Constantine VII Porphyrogenitus, *De thematibus* II, ed. Pertusi (1952) 66 = *Suda* K.324. Deceitful: Isidore of Pelusium, *Ep.* 1.281, *PG* 78.348A-B, commenting on Gigantius, a Cappadocian who had served as a provincial governor in Egypt in the early fifth century: see *PLRE* 2:512. Trimalchio: Petronius, *Satyricon* 69.2. Quotation about sad name from Syme (1982) 181. Note the telling exclusion of central and eastern Asia Minor from a description of Rome's Mediterranean empire in Horden and Purcell (2000) 23: "Rome dominated the Mediterranean region and gradually extended her power well beyond its boundaries—notably to Britain, Gaul and the Danube basin."

2. For a visit by Ammianus, see Ammianus Marcellinus, *Res gestae* 23.6.19, suggesting autopsy of a spring at Tyana.

3. For discussion of their friendship, see *Families and Friends*, Chapter 10.

## Badlands Introduction

1. For the Persian invasions of Cappadocia in the mid-third century, see *Res gestae divi Saporis* 18–19, 26, 32, ed. Maricq (1958) 311–15; also SHA, *Tyranni triginta* 2, and *Oracula Sibyllina* 13.89–94, mentioning Caesarea and Tyana; with Lieu (1986), on the permeability of the eastern frontier. For the Arab invasions, see Chapter 1.

2. Herman (1987), discusses the personal relationships that were the foundation of imperial control; for the interaction between imperial magistrates and local dynasts in the neighboring regions of Cilicia and Isauria, see Shaw (1990), Lenski (1999a, b), and Hopwood (1999a, b).

3. For the imperial estates, see Chapter 5, and Jones (1964) 416, "In the sixth century the greater part of the province of Cappadocia Prima belonged to the crown."

## Chapter 1. Local Notables and Imperial Rule

1. Viper: *Anthologia Graeca* 11.237. Isthmus: Strabo, *Geographia* 12.1.3.

2. Strabo, *Geographia* 12.2.9, noted that the city of Mazaca (later known as Caesarea) used the laws of Charondas, a legendary lawgiver at Catana during the

archaic period; hence the tart observation in Jones (1971) 178, about the tardiness of Hellenization in Cappadocia: "the Mazacenes were no doubt at much the same stage of civilization in the second century [B.C.] as the Catanians in the seventh."

3. Beetles: Pliny the Elder, *Historia naturalis* 28.78. Note the statue of Mercury erected at the Cilician Gates, with a dedication begging for deliverance from "clouds of locusts" swarming from the plateau to the coastal plains: Varinlioglu (1988), reprinted in *L'année épigraphique 1988* (1991) 282–83, no. 1048. Giving thanks: B, *Hom.* 4.2. Snowfalls: B, *Hom. in hexaemeron* 6.8. Reeking with snow: B, *Ep.* 349 = Libanius, *Epistularum commercium* 15; tombs: B, *Ep.* 350 = Libanius, *Epistularum commercium* 16; both letters were included in the (probably) spurious correspondence between Basil and Libanius. Long night: GNaz, *Ep.* 4.4. Mountain passes: B, *Ep.* 156.2. Easter: B, *Ep.* 198.1. Two months: B, *Ep.* 48. Hot springs: B, *Ep.* 137; cf. GNaz, *Ep.* 125.4.

4. Mount Argaeus: Strabo, *Geographia* 12.2.7. Coins minted at Caesarea during the imperial period often depicted Mount Argaeus: see Sydenham (1933) 19–21. Severe winters: *Expositio totius mundi et gentium* 40, with Kaplan (1992) 14–24, on the climate. Blizzard: B, *Ep.* 80. On the Forty Martyrs, see *Becoming Christian*, Chapter 7. For bathhouses and Romanization, see Mitchell (1993) 1:216–17.

5. Descriptions of springtime: GNys, *Ep.* 10.1, 12.1. Sunbeams: GNys, *Ep.* 10.2. Attractive region: B, *Hom. in Hexaemeron* 2.3. Glade known as Ἔρως: *Anthologia Graeca* 9.668–69. Epitaph: Kaibel (1878) 259, no. 640 = Peek (1955) 286, no. 1018, dated to the second century A.D., with discussion in Robert (1974) 388–93.

6. Taxes from Cappadocia: see Chapter 3. Rafters: GNys, *Ep.* 26.2, 27.4. Livestock: B, *Hom.* 7.2, mentioning camels, horses, cattle, sheep, and pigs. Export of grain: [B,] *Ep.* 365, for the transport of grain on the Halys River. Import of olive oil: B, *Regulae fusius tractatae* 19.2. Local wine: GNaz, *Ep.* 57, mentioning an ordinary "wine from the hills." Wine purchased in Syria and Armenia: John of Ephesus, *Lives of the Eastern Saints* 8, tr. Brooks (1923–1925) 130. For comprehensive surveys of the natural resources of the region, see Broughton (1938) 607–27, Magie (1950) 492–93, 1351–52, Franck (1966) 67–81, and Teja (1974) 23–34, (1980) 1091–1102. For the agricultural prosperity of the region, especially around Caesarea, see Erinç and Tunçdilek (1952) 185.

7. Poor: GNys, *Ep.* 15.1. Caves as granaries in Cappadocia: Varro, *De re rustica* 1.57.2, Pliny the Elder, *Historia naturalis* 18.306; for the possibility that caves were used as homes, see Rodley (1985) 5–7, and Mathews and Mathews (1997). Animals and weather: B, *Hom. in Hexaemeron* 9.3, with *Becoming Christian*, Chapter 6. Jewish martyrs: GNaz, *Orat.* 15.8. Cheese: GNaz, *Carm.* II.2.4.67–68.

8. For these early satrapies, see the list in Herodotus, *Hist.* 3.90.2–3, with the comments of Briant (1996) 402–17. For "Cilicians" in Strabo's *Geographia*, see Desideri (1991); satrapies and subjects, Kuhrt (1995) 689–701; the "caractère irrédentiste" of Cappadocia and Armenia under Persian rule, Briant (1996) 761–64.

9. Alternative names: Strabo, *Geographia* 11.14.15, 12.1.4, with Franck (1966) 9–19. Mithridates the Founder: Strabo, *Geographia* 12.3.41; Appian, *Mithridatica* 9, described the first Mithridates as a member "of the royal Persian clan"; for the Mithridatic kings of Pontus, see Bosworth and Wheatley (1998). Ariarathes: Strabo, *Geographia* 12.1.2, "Ariarathes was the first to be called king of the Cappadocians."

For a fine survey of the interaction between geography and history in Cappadocia from the Hittites to the Ottoman Turks, see de Planhol (1981).

10. Selection of king Ariobarzanes I: Strabo, *Geographia* 12.2.11, Justin, *Epitoma* 38.2.8, with Sullivan (1980), a comprehensive survey of Cappadocian kings under Roman patronage. Appointment of Archelaus: Strabo, *Geographia* 12.2.11, Dio, *Hist.* 49.32.3. Although both Tacitus, *Annales* 2.42, and Dio, *Hist.* 57.17.3–7, placed king Archelaus' death in A.D. 17, the appropriate context for the formation of the province is Germanicus' trip to the East in 18: see Tacitus, *Annales* 2.56, with Gwatkin (1930) 17, and Magie (1950) 1349n.1.

11. Sulla in Cappadocia: Plutarch, *Sulla* 5.3, Appian, *Mithridatica* 57, with Sullivan (1990) 352n.50, on the date of his visit. Abdication of Ariobarzanes I: Valerius Maximus, *Facta et dicta memorabilia* 5.7.ext.2. Pay-offs by Ariobarzanes III to Pompey and Brutus: Cicero, *Ep. ad Atticum* 5.18.4, 6.1.3, 6.2.7, 6.3.5; note also Cicero, *Ep. ad familiares* 15.4.15, for the kingdom of Cappadocia as a "client" of Cato the Younger. Family of Archelaus: Magie (1950) 211–31, 371, 411, 435. Claim of ancestry: Josephus, *Bellum Iudaicum* 1.476.

12. Strabo, *Geographia* 12.2.3, temple at Comana, which Strabo had once visited, 12.2.6, temple of Zeus at Venasa; note also the priesthood of Ma at Comana in Pontus, "modeled" after the priesthood at Comana in Cappadocia: Strabo, *Geographia* 12.3.32–36. Plot: Cicero, *Ep. ad familiares* 15.4.6, with Syme (1995) 145–46, for a possible identification of this rebellious priest.

13. Opposition from Cappadocians: Plutarch, *Lucullus* 14.6, Appian, *Mithridatica* 10. Principality for Ariarathes: [Julius Caesar,] *Bellum Alexandrinum* 66, although two years later Ariarathes was nevertheless in Rome trying to "purchase some kingdom from Caesar": see Cicero, *Ep. ad Atticum* 13.2a.2. Appointment of Lycomedes: [Julius Caesar,] *Bellum Alexandrinum* 66, Strabo, *Geographia* 12.3.35, 38, with Magie (1950) 1264n.21, and Syme (1995) 166–74, on the confusion between Comana in Cappadocia and Comana in Pontus. Death of king Ariobarzanes III, who was succeeded for a few years by his brother Ariarathes: Appian, *Bella civilia* 4.63, Dio, *Hist.* 47.33.4. Usurpation of Sisines: Strabo, *Geographia* 12.2.6, with Syme (1995) 148–50, on his identity as "a baron of the western marches." Rumors about Marcus Antonius' affairs, circulated as propaganda by his opponents: Martial, *Epigram.* 11.20. Seduction of the son of Cato the Younger: Plutarch, *Cato Minor* 73. Octopus: B, *Hom. in Hexaemeron* 7.3.

14. Hiring of Aulus Gabinus: Cicero, *Oratio de provinciis consularibus* 4.9. Prefectures: Strabo, *Geographia* 12.1.4. "First friends": Rott (1908) 370–71, no. 78 = Berges and Nollé (2000) 1:206–9, no. 30, with Syme (1995) 146–47; note also Diodorus of Sicily, *Bibliotheca historica* 31.21, for Ariarathes V showing the usual solicitude for "friends, magistrates, and other lesser officials," and Cicero, *Ep. ad familiares* 15.2.6, 15.4.6, for other friends and supporters. Strabo's family: Strabo, *Geographia* 11.2.18, 12.3.33, with Clarke (1997) 99, and Dueck (2000) 5–8. Fortresses: Strabo, *Geographia* 12.2.9, "many garrisons, some belonging to the kings, others to their friends," with Harper and Bayburtluoglu (1968) 150, for the possible site of one garrison on a mountain overlooking Comana. Note Syme (1995) 109: "No king of Cappadocia, whatever his calibre, was at ease among his neighbours or his barons."

15. Stock breeders: Strabo, *Geographia* 12.2.9. Archelaus' treatise: Varro, *De re rustica* 2.3.5, 3.11.4, 3.12.4, 3.16.4, Pliny the Elder, *Historia naturalis* 8.202, 218, 18.22. Local notables: note Cicero, *Ep. ad Atticum* 6.1.3, mentioning that two or three of the friends of the Cappadocian king were very wealthy.

16. On the fate of royal properties and temple lands, see Broughton (1938) 650–51, (1951), and Kreissig (1967); Mitchell (1993) 1:149–62, provides an excellent survey of the development of large estates in Galatia and surrounding regions. Anderson (1903) 68, mentions an (apparently still unpublished) boundary stone of the emperor Maurice that perhaps indicated the existence of an imperial estate formed from temple lands near Comana in Pontus; for another possible boundary stone of an imperial estate, see French (1991) 55, no. 5b. For Cappadocians in the imperial administration, see Chapter 3. The evidence for individual landowners in Cappadocia under the empire is limited: see Broughton (1938) 675–76. At Tyana was the wealthy family of Apollonius: Philostratus, *Vita Apollonii* 1.4. Another family associated with Titus Flavius Aelianus Apollonius apparently had estates north of Comana: see Harper (1968) 104. Wealth and happiness: B, *Hom. in Hexaemeron* 5.1. Gold: B, *Hom.* 6.5.

17. Details of houses: B, *Hom.* 7.2, GNys, *Hom. in Ecclesiasten* 3.4, with the commentary and bibliography in Drobner (1996) 137–77; also B, *Hom.* 7.4: "whenever I enter the house of a man who has recently become wealthy . . . and I see that it is glittering with various decorations. . . ." Flowers and fans: GNaz, *Orat.* 14.17.

18. Family's properties in three provinces: GNys, *Vita Macrinae* 5. Retreat in Pontus: B, *Ep.* 14. Iris River: B, *Ep.* 223.5. Gardening: GNaz, *Ep.* 5.5, with *Families and Friends*, Chapter 1, on the location of Basil's retreat. Gregory's estates at Arianzus and Kanotala: GNaz, *Testamentum, PG* 37.389C, 392D, with Coulie (1985) 10–28, and Van Dam (1995) 129; on the location of Nazianzus, see Hild and Restle (1981) 244, and Equini Schneider (1994). Amphilochius' estate at Ozizala: GNaz, *Ep.* 25–27, with Hild and Restle (1981) 252. Other estates: Zosimus, *Historia nova* 4.4.3, "wealthy estates" near Caesarea belonging to the usurper Procopius; Philostorgius, *HE* 10.6, Eunomius' exile to his estate near Caesarea. The survey of archaeological sites in Cappadocia in Equini Schneider (1995) highlights fortresses and roads.

19. Olympias: *Vita Olympiadis* 5; for a possible connection between Olympias and the family of Gregory of Nazianzus, see *Families and Friends*, Chapter 2. Seleucia: John Chrysostom, *Ep. ad Olympiadem* 9.2f–3b. Rome: Ammianus Marcellinus, *Res gestae* 28.4.12. Estate: GNys, *Ep.* 20.12, nature, 15, fish. The heading to this letter identified the recipient (and the owner of the villa) as the *scholasticus* (legal advocate) Adelphius, who can be identified probably with the Adelphius who received GNaz, *Ep.* 204, and possibly with the Adelphius who was later governor of Galatia: see Chapter 3. Gregory claimed that the name of this estate, "sacred Vanota," was a "Galatian name": see GNys, *Ep.* 20.1. The estate was, however, not in Galatia, as suggested by *PLRE* 1:13, "Adelphius 2," but in Cappadocia. Thierry (1981a), Hild and Restle (1981) 302, and Maraval (1990) 259n.3, have now identified the site with the "Venasa" mentioned by GNaz, *Ep.* 246.2, located between Nyssa and Caesarea at the modern town of Avanos on the Halys River. Thierry (1977) 130–34, mentions some Roman ruins, a sarcophagus, and small bronze images of an eagle and Zeus found at the site; Rossiter (1989), analyzes the architectural features of the villa; for general

discussions, see Bergmann (1991) on landscape and control over the forces of nature, and Ellis (1991) on domestic architecture as a manifestation of power and status.

20. Reputation: GNaz, *Epitaph.* 21 = *Anthologia Graeca* 8.100.4, εὐίπποις ... Καππαδόκαις, with Chapter 4. Mount Argaeus: Claudian, *In Rufinum* 2.31. Annual tribute: Strabo, *Geographia* 11.13.8. Cappadocian cavalry: Plutarch, *Eumenes* 4. Constantius' gifts: Philostorgius, *HE* 3.4, with Shahîd (1984) 86–106, on the Southern Semites. Palmatian horses: *CTh* 15.10.1, issued in January 371 to Publius Ampelius, the prefect of Rome who may have been a landowner in Cappadocia: see Van Dam (1996) 21–22; also *CTh* 10.6.1 = *CJ* 11.76. For the "Villa of Palmatius," see *Itinerarium Burdigalense* 577.6, with Jones (1964) 706, Hild and Restle (1981) 140–41, and Chapter 4, for legends about Palmatius.

21. Gregory's ride: GNys, *Ep.* 1.6–7, with Drobner (1996) 36–39, on Gregory's knowledge of horses. Association with magistrates, generals, and rhetoricians: B, *Hom.* 3.5. Patron: GNys, *Ep.* 17.14–15. Fines: GNaz, *Ep.* 198.4. Pedigrees: B, *Hom.* 7.2. Races on frozen lakes: GNys, *Encomium in XL martyres* 1B, *PG* 46.768A, with Hyland (1990) 124, for "hipposandals" fitted with ice crampons. Brands: B, *Hom. in psalmos* 48.7, *PG* 29.448C–449A.

22. GNys, *Ep.* 17.28, annual incomes; *Ep.* 20.3, Blessed Isles, 8, shrine.

23. On king Ariarathes V, see Dittenberger (1915–1924) 2:237, no. 666, citizenship; Dittenberger (1903–1905) 1:562–67, no. 352, patronage; and Diodorus of Sicily, *Bibliotheca historica* 31.19.8, "for a long time unknown to the Greeks, Cappadocia then offered a home to learned men," with Habicht (1997) 282.

24. Strabo, *Geographia* 12.2.7, Tyana, "Eusebeia near the Taurus [Mountains]," 7–9, Mazaca, "Eusebeia near [Mount] Argaeus," with Jones (1971) 178, and Berges and Nollé (2000) 2:313–14, on the renaming as Eusebeia. In ca. 77 B.C. king Tigranes of Armenia forcibly transferred people from Cappadocia to his new capital of Tigranocerta: see Strabo, *Geographia* 12.2.9, Plutarch, *Lucullus* 21.4, 26.1, Appian, *Mithridatica* 67, with Magie (1950) 321, 339. Strabo, *Geographia* 11.14.15, claimed that these settlers came from "twelve Greek cities," among them presumably cities in Cappadocia.

25. Caesarea: Suetonius, *Augustus* 60, with Magie (1950) 1353n.9, for the date of the renaming as Caesarea. For surveys of Cappadocian cities, see Jones (1971) 177–82, and Teja (1980) 1102–9; Magie (1950) 1353n.9, suggests a later date for Comana and Archelais, and Maraval (1975), discusses Nyssa. For the identification of Nazianzus as Diocaesarea, see Chapter 5.

26. On Hanisa, see Robert (1963) 457–503; also Jones (1971) 175, and Mitchell (1993) 1:83. Festival: GNaz, *Ep.* 246.2, 6 (= [B,] *Ep.* 169); for the estate and the location of Venasa, see above.

27. Equestrian procurator: Tacitus, *Annales* 12.49, Dio, *Hist.* 57.17.7. Senatorial legate: Suetonius, *Vespasian* 8.4, with Magie (1950) 574, 1435n.22. Quotation from Mitchell (1993) 1:98.

28. Greekness: Philostratus, *Vita Apollonii* 1.4, a description of Tyana as πόλις Ἑλλὰς ἐν τῷ Καππαδοκῶν ἔθνει. Dedications at Comana: *IGR* 3:46, no. 121 = Harper (1968) 96, no. 1.03, to emperor Hadrian passed under the chairmanship of Maebuzanes; Harper (1968) 98, no. 1.06, to emperor Decius; *IGR* 3:46, no. 122 = Harper (1968) 99, no. 1.08, to Valerian, son of emperor Gallienus; *IGR* 3:47, no. 125 =

Harper (1968) 94–96, no. 1.01, to a provincial governor passed under the chairman-ship of Mitras, son of Appas; with *Becoming Christian*, Chapter 4, on the survival of oriental names in Cappadocia. Lists: GNys, *Ep.* 17.28, with the caution of Berges and Nollé (2000) 2:509, on the differences in political structure of Cappadocian cities.

29. Names on monuments: B, *Hom. in psalmos* 48.7, *PG* 29.448c–449a. Dedi-cation: *Studia Pontica* 3.1:41, no. 27, with *PLRE* 1:462, "Jovinus 3."

30. Description of Caesarea: Sozomen, *HE* 5.4. *IGR* 4:537, no. 1645, an inscrip-tion from Philadelphia, mentioned a κοινὸν Καππαδόκων, a "league of Cappado-cians," that met at Caesarea; dated by Deininger (1965) 82, to the second or third century. Agora, porticoes, gymnasiums: B, *Ep.* 74.3. A drunken soldier in the agora: B, *Hom.* 14.7. Schools: GNaz, *Orat.* 43.13. Temples: Sozomen, *HE* 5.4. Agoras, porti-coes, two- and three-story houses: GNaz, *Orat.* 43.80. "The suburb of Caesarea": B, *Ep.* 223.5. Extensive wall: Procopius, *De aedificiis* 5.4.7–14. For depictions of the region's "Fortune" on coins and gemstones, see Sydenham (1933) 18–19, and Weiss (1985) 30–31. Leopards: B, *Homilia dicta in Lacisis* 9, *PG* 31.1456c–d, "Often I watched the most hostile of beasts in the stadiums"; but the attribution of this sermon to Basil is dubious. Coins minted at Caesarea during the early imperial period commemorated the city as *metropolis, neokoros* ("temple warden"), and *entichios* ("enclosed by walls"): see Sydenham (1933) 23, 88, 93–136. Bernardakis (1908), dis-tinguishes between the ancient and Byzantine city on the rise and the Seljuk, Ottoman, and modern city in the plain; the survey in Hild and Restle (1981) 193–96, focuses primarily on the city's walls; Thierry (1981b), surveys primarily later Byzan-tine monuments and iconography.

31. For the regional priests known as Cappadocarchs, see *Digest* 27.1.6.14. Retinues and horses: B, *Hom.* 7.2. B, *Hom.* 18.1, description of the stadium as "the ornament in the suburbs," 3–5, races, 6, crowds "outside the walls," with Van Dam (1996) 28–30, on this governor. This stadium and the city's baths were still used in the twelfth century: see Vryonis (1971) 19n.109.

32. Obligations: B, *Ep.* 84, with the survey in Jones (1964) 724–31.

33. Julian's restoration of municipal lands: *CTh* 10.3.1, *CJ* 11.70.1; of municipal lands and taxes: Ammianus Marcellinus, *Res gestae* 25.4.15. Confiscation of temple lands: *CTh* 5.13.3, 10.1.8. Valens' refund in the province of Asia: Riccobono (1941) 511–13, no. 108, with Schulten (1906) 40–61; restoration of one-third of revenues: *CTh* 4.13.7, 15.1.18, with Jones (1964) 146–47, 732–33, and Heather (1994) 22–24.

34. Division: GNaz, *Carm.* II.1.11.458–59.

35. For the strategic location of Podandus, see Harper (1970), and Hild and Restle (1981) 261–62; the excellent map of western Cappadocia in Mitchell (1993) 2:66, is a clear commentary on the importance of Podandus. Jones (1971) 182, 432n.17, suggests that eastern Cappadocia had already been attached to Lesser Arme-nia before becoming Armenia Secunda; Kopecek (1974) 320–21, and Mitchell (1993) 2:163n.59, date the formation of Armenia Secunda before Valens' partition of Cappadocia, even though it is first attested in *CTh* 13.11.2 = *CJ* 11.48.10, issued in 386. Decurions for the new city of Tymandus in Pisidia: *ILS* 2:526, no. 6090 = Buckler, Calder, and Guthrie (1933) 86–87, no. 236, with *PLRE* 1:504, "Lepidus 2," for the date. Basilinopolis: Schwartz (1933–1935) 418. Migration to Podandus: B, *Ep.* 75, with Gain (1985) 296n.31, 297n.33, for the interpretation of οἱ πολιτευόμενοι as decurions.

Captives, exile: B, *Ep.* 74.3; the "three portions" that Basil distinguished referred to three categories of decurions at Caesarea, those who fled, those who migrated, and those who stayed. Community: B, *Ep.* 76.

36. Sinkhole: B, *Ep.* 74.3.

37. B, *Ep.* 74.2, dividing an animal, 3, reconsideration. Revenues: GNaz, *Carm.* II.1.11.461. Orcistus and Nacolea in Phrygia: *ILS* 2:526–27, no. 6091 = Calder (1956) 69–72, no. 305.

38. Affliction of jealousy: Herodian, *Hist.* 3.2.8, with Robert (1977), on the rivalry between Nicaea and Nicomedia, and the general surveys in Sheppard (1984–1986) 230–37, Harl (1987) 21–30, 75–82, Sartre (1991) 190–98, and Mitchell (1993) 1:204–6. For Perge, see Roueché (1989b). Neocaesarea: GNys, *Vita Gregorii Thaumaturgi, PG* 46.897D. Rivalry between Laodicea and Apamea: Libanius, *Orat.* 18.187.

39. For Julian's threats, see Chapters 6, 9. "Mother church": GNaz, *Ep.* 50.4–5. History of Nazianzus: GNaz, *Ep.* 141.2–3.

40. Lost amenities: B, *Ep.* 74.3. Spectacle: B, *Ep.* 76. Primacy: GNaz, *Carm.* II.1.11.460.

41. Solitude and anticipation: B, *Ep.* 75.

42. Basil mentioned "our city" in *Ep.* 74.3, 76, "the city that brought you into life" in *Ep.* 75, and πατρίς in all three letters; for the recipients of these letters, Martinianus, Aburgius, and Sophronius, see Chapter 3.

43. The Cappadocian king Ariobarzanes I was the first eastern monarch to call himself Φιλορώμαιος: see Sullivan (1980) 1129, and Braund (1984) 105–16. For the harsh treatment of Cappadocia, see Plutarch, *Crassus* 18.4, Cicero, *Ep. ad familiares* 15.1.6, "Cappadocia est inanis"; note also Cicero, *Ep. ad Atticum* 6.1.4: "no kingdom is more plundered, no king is more destitute."

44. Guardian for Archelaus: Dio, *Hist.* 57.17.3–7. Summons and accusation: Tacitus, *Annales* 2.42, Philostratus, *Vita Apollonii* 1.12, with Gwatkin (1930) 7–16, Teja (1980) 1086–87, and Sullivan (1980) 1149–61, for surveys of Archelaus' reign. Dedication to Archelaus Philopatris Ktistes Soter: Dittenberger (1903–1905) 1:570–71, no. 358 = Harper (1968) 99–101, no. 2.01, with Syme (1995) 152. Knees: B, *Ep.* 76, with Smith (1998) 87, on the choice: "'Friend to the Romans' was fine, but 'friend of the fatherland' was surely better."

45. For the subsequent classification of Podandus as a ῥεγεών in the province of Cappadocia Prima, see Hierocles, *Synecdemus* 699.3, with Jones (1971) 184, 187–88, for the interpretation of *regio* as an imperial estate. For the strategic location of Tyana, see Berges and Nollé (2000) 1:9–22. Council at Tyana: B, *Ep.* 226.3, 244.5, 263.3, with Barnes (1993) 162, 291n.64, for the date; bishop Eusebius of Caesarea apparently presided, since Sozomen, *HE* 6.12.2, listed him first among the bishops who attended. "Foremost city": B, *Ep.* 138.2, a description of Iconium before its promotion as a provincial capital. For the importance of such a promotion, see Mitchell (1993) 1:258: "the cities that gained most of all were the provincial capitals."

46. Apollonius' shrine and imperial honors: Philostratus, *Vita Apollonii* 1.5, 8.31, SHA, *Aurelian* 24. Pilgrim: *Itinerarium Burdigalense* 577.7–578.1. Rank of metropolis and resident governor: John Malalas, *Chronographia* 13.345, 347, 14.365, describing the consequences of the creation of other new provinces by Theodosius I and Theodosius II.

47. Modestus: see Berges and Nollé (2000) 1:202–3, no. 26, a dedication found at a nearby town but perhaps originally from Tyana: "this building was also initiated from its foundations during the tenure of Domitius Modestus, the most distinguished praetorian prefect." Municipal council: B, *Ep.* 97. Bandits: GNaz, *Orat.* 43.58. Foreigner: B, *Ep.* 98.2.

48. Catalogue of bishops: B, *Ep.* 92.1, with the identifications of Hauschild (1990) 216n.394. Metropolitan city as center: GNaz, *Ep.* 41.6. Anthimus' circle: GNaz, *Ep.* 50.3–5.

49. Civil war, meddling: GNaz, *Ep.* 183.1, 5. Feud between Helladius and Theodorus: Severus of Antioch, *Ep.* 2.2, tr. Brooks (1903–1904) 1:205.

50. Feud between Firmus and Eutherius: Calvet-Sebasti and Gatier (1989) 42–48. Intervention: Theodoret of Cyrrhus, *Commonitorium ad Alexandrum Hierapolitanum*, ed. Schwartz (1922–1923) 87, and Azéma (1998) 156–58; *PLRE* 2:687, suggests that the *comes* Longinus was count in Isauria, Azéma (1998) 157n.5, that he was a local notable. Tyana as Christoupolis: Laurent (1963–1972) 1:317, no. 436, and *Notitiae graecae episcopatuum* 1.21, 250, with Hild and Restle (1981) 298–99.

51. Request for Basil's assistance: B, *Ep.* 74.1, with Coppola (1923), on the publication of Basil's letters, and MacMullen (1988) 83–84, on the public display of letters.

52. For Basil and Valens, see Chapters 6–7. Arabs and Caesarea: Michael the Syrian, *Chron.* 11.10, tr. Chabot (1899–1910) 2:441, with Haldon and Kennedy (1980) 92–106, on the reduction of cities into fortresses. Rank of Caesarea: *Notitiae graecae episcopatuum* 4.2.

## Chapter 2. The Rewards of Giving

1. Silk: B, *Hom. in Hexaemeron* 8.8. Imperial mill and weavers: GNaz, *Orat.* 43.57, with Jones (1964) 836.

2. B, *Hom.* 6.7, cloak and sandal; *Hom.* 7.2, long mantles, 4, chests. Silk, gold threads, and dye: GNys, *Hom. in Ecclesiasten* 3.5. Macrina's robe: GNys, *Vita Macrinae* 30. Gregory's clothing: GNaz, *Testamentum, PG* 37.392D, 393B–C.

3. Rags: GNys, *Contra Eunomium* 2.128. Funeral: B, *Hom.* 7.9. Theft: B, *Ep.* 286. Old cloak: B, *Ep.* 113. Exports and rabbit pelts: *Expositio totius mundi et gentium* 40, with Rougé (1966) 271–73. Woven bark: Strabo, *Geographia* 3.5.10, with quotation from Broughton (1938) 823.

4. For the restoration of the aqueduct at Amaseia by one of the Severan emperors, see *Studia Pontica* 3.1:122, no. 100, with Nicholson and Nicholson (1993). Aqueduct and bath at Tyana: Hild and Restle (1981) 299, and Berges and Nollé (2000) 1:36–71. Bernardakis (1908) 25–26, suggests a bath and aqueduct at Caesarea. Aqueducts and honor: B, *Hom. in psalmos* 61.4, *PG* 29.477A; also 48.7, *PG* 29.448C: "Do you not see those who are ... building aqueducts, and how their names are placed on their earthly structures?"

5. Wetness: B, *Hom. in Hexaemeron* 2.3. Flooding by Halys River: [B,] *Ep.* 365. Swollen river: GNys, *De virginitate* 4.6. Lycus River: GNys, *Vita Gregorii Thaumaturgi, PG* 46.929B; note that wolves had a reputation for being untamable: see B,

*Hom. in Hexaemeron* 9.3. Euphrates River: Pseudo-Dionysius, *Chronicle Part III*, tr. Witakowski (1996) 64–65. Hailstorms and unseasonable rain: B, *Hom.* 6.5, *Ep.* 240.1. Thousand bushels: Lucian, *Icaromenippus* 26.

6. Drought and ditches: B, *Hom.* 6.5; for the drought described in *Hom.* 8, see below. Thistles: GNys, *Hom. in Ecclesiasten* 4.3. Well-diggers: B, *Hom. in Hexaemeron* 1.7. Fields of Egypt: GNaz, *Carm.* II.2.4.44–45. Irrigation: GNys, *Hom. in Ecclesiasten* 3.4; GNys, *Ep.* 17.27–28, refers to cisterns, not aqueducts as suggested by Goggin (1947) 11–12. For the remains of underground tunnels, see Bixio and Castellani (1995). Armies: GNys, *Vita Gregorii Thaumaturgi, PG* 46.925D; Gregory Thaumaturgus resolved this dispute by turning the lake into dry meadows and fields (928A). For the suggestion that a fertile plain east of Nicopolis is perhaps a dried-up lake, see Cumont and Cumont (1906) 318.

7. Prosperity: B, *Hom. in psalmos* 29.5, *PG* 29.316B, with Durliat (1990) 287–319, on municipal institutions for supplying grain. Cabbage: B, *Ep.* 186. Basil's diet: GNaz, *Orat.* 43.61. Regions: GNaz, *Orat.* 43.34.

8. For recommendations about stockpiling, see Duncan-Jones (1982) 37–38, and Halstead (1987) 86; also Purcell (1995) 169, and Horden and Purcell (2000) 267, for the connection between "control of storage" and local elite power. B, *Hom.* 6.4, children, 5, cisterns; *Hom.* 7.4, rotting grain; *Hom.* 8.4, contracting labor; *Ep.* 86, theft, with Van Dam (1996) 35–37, for the context. Granaries: GNaz, *Carm.* I.2.28.70–75.

9. Wickedness, fields, violence: B, *Hom.* 7.5, with Holman (1999c) 213–21, for Basil's recommendations about loans and debt. Lender and collector: GNaz, *Carm.* I.2.28.33–34. Fishing line: GNys, *Hom. in Ecclesiasten* 4.3. For similar comments about the usury and debt that followed a food shortage, see GNaz, *Orat.* 16.18–19, with Coulie (1985) 95–118.

10. Stomach: GNys, *De oratione dominica* 4, *PG* 44.1169B. Sky, grief: B, *Hom.* 8.2, with Mitchell (1993) 1:143–47, for a fine survey of climate and soil in central Asia Minor. For the distinction between famine and food shortage, see Garnsey (1988) 6: "famines were rare, but . . . subsistence crises falling short of famine were common."

11. B, *Hom.* 8.2, granaries, 4, giving. For the dating of B, *Hom.* 9, 6, 8 (in that order) to spring and summer of 369, see Bernardi (1968) 60–62, who also includes *Hom.* 7, a general sermon on the wealthy; for a general survey of Basil's ideas about wealth, Giet (1941) 96–151.

12. Adam's sin: B, *Hom.* 8.7, with Holman (1999b), for an excellent survey of ideas about sin and starvation in this homily. Oppression, free will: B, *Hom.* 9.1, 3.

13. Gallus: Ammianus Marcellinus, *Res gestae* 14.7.2, 5. Julian's measures: Julian, *Misopogon* 368C–370C. Flogging in 382: Libanius, *Orat.* 1.205–10. General surveys of the situation at Antioch: Petit (1955) 105–22, Liebeschuetz (1972) 126–32, and Durliat (1990) 360–75.

14. Cicero in Cilicia: Cicero, *Ep. ad Atticum* 5.21.8.

15. Titles of honor: B, *Hom.* 6.3.

16. Clothes: Asterius of Amaseia, *Hom.* 1.4. Ignoring needy: B, *Hom.* 6.6.

17. Privy: B, *Hom.* 6.6. Defecation: Artemidorus, *Onirocriticon* 2.26. For generosity toward the poor and social outcasts (sometimes called "lepers") as therapy for the wealthy, see Holman (1999a) 308: "the leper's body becomes a healing agent

in homeopathic spiritual therapy that is able to absorb the spiritual diseases of the rich ... and to transmit redemptive healing in return."

18. Tombstone: *Studia Pontica* 3.1:34, no. 20; also Thierry (1977) 116, for the tombstone of a deaconess in Cappadocia who "distributed her own bread to the needy."

19. B, *Hom.* 6.8, accusations on Judgment Day; *Hom.* 7.6, resources before judge, heart of stone; *Hom.* 8.9, eternity in fire, penalty, truthful voice.

20. GNaz, *Orat.* 43.35, oratory, 36, grain-giver.

21. Easter: GNaz, *Orat.* 2.4. Reactions: B, *Hom.* 8.3.

22. GNaz, *Orat.* 43.35, comparisons, 36, 72, Joseph. Israelites: Evagrius, *HE* 2.6. Description of manna: GNys, *De vita Moysis* 2, PG 44.368C. For the commonness of ideas about providing for the poor throughout the Near East, see Garsoïan (1981); for the attitudes of the Cappadocian Fathers, Meredith (1998).

23. Church at Nazianzus: see *Families and Friends*, Chapter 2. Relics: B, *Ep.* 49. Martyrs' shrine: GNys, *Ep.* 25. Basil's complex: B, *Ep.* 94, with Scicolone (1982), on the politics, and Van Dam (1996) 53–54, for the date. Poorhouse: B, *Ep.* 150.3, 176, Sozomen, *HE* 6.34. For the possible connection between Basil's sermons and his selection as bishop, see Gribomont (1977) 184, "On pourrait interpréter ces homélies comme des programmes électoraux."

24. Poverty: GNys, *Ep.* 25.16: "By scrutinizing the contracts we seem to be stingy." St. Julitta's milk: B, *Hom.* 5.2, PG 31.241B. Provision of poor: GNaz, *Testamentum*, PG 37.389A. B, *Ep.* 142, small property; *Ep.* 143, poorhouse at Amaseia; *Ep.* 150.3, distribution of wealth; *Ep.* 285, estate belonging to the poor. Poorhouse and estates: GNaz, *Ep.* 211, with Van Dam (1996) 47–49, for the date, location, and recipient. Common storehouse: GNaz, *Orat.* 43.63. Daley (1999), provides a fine survey of the Cappadocian Fathers' emphasis on the need for charity.

25. Ruler's image: GNys, *De beneficentia = De pauperibus amandis* 1, PG 46.460C. Valens' donation: Theodoret, *HE* 4.19.13.

26. Local poorhouse: Epiphanius, *Panarion* 75.2.3, accumulation, 3.1–2, living in countryside, referring to the priest Aerius and bishop Eustathius of Sebasteia.

27. Father of a thousand children: B, *Hom.* 6.3. New city: GNaz, *Orat.* 43.63. For later traditions about the location of Basilias, see Bernardakis (1908) 25, with *Families and Friends*, Chapter 4, and *Becoming Christian*, Chapter 5. For discussion of bishops and the poor, see Brown (1992) 89–103.

## Chapter 3. Service in the Imperial Administration

1. Halys River: Arrian, *Periplus* 15.1, with Stadter (1980) 11–13, 32–41. For the Halys River separating Cappadocia from Galatia and Pontus, see [B,] *Ep.* 365. For a mosaic found near the Euphrates east of Hierapolis, with the inscription βασιλεὺς ποταμὸς Εὐφράτης, see von Oppenheim and Lucas (1905) 58–59, and Cumont and Cumont (1906) 339n.3.

2. Taxes: Tacitus, *Annales* 1.78, 2.42. Corbulo: Tacitus, *Annales* 13.8, winter camps, 35, recruits, 14.26, Tigranes, "a descendant [great-grandson] of Archelaus," with Gwatkin (1930) 41–54, on Corbulo's campaigns, and Isaac (1992) 36–38, on the

stationing of troops. For an epitaph found at Trapezus of a soldier from Caesarea who had served in a legion at Satala during the late second or early third century, see Bryer and Winfield (1985) 1:181, with Mitford (1974) 164: "Central Cappadocia and Pontus may be seen as one of the recruiting areas for the legion."

3. Satire: Martial, *Epigram.* 12.29(26).1–6.

4. For the pattern of promotion in Galatia, see Mitchell (1993) 1:154–58. The wealthy family of Apollonius at Tyana in the first century A.D. was described as "an old family descended from the settlers," but its background was not Italian: see Philostratus, *Vita Apollonii* 1.4. For a veteran who settled near Faustinopolis during the second century, see the inscription commemorating his wife in Drew-Bear (1991) 139–41 = Berges and Nollé (2000) 1:278, no. 119. Descendants of royal dynasties: see Harper (1968) 109–10, 129, nos. 2.18, 6.15, dedications at Comana mentioning Tiberius Iulius Archelaus, perhaps a descendant of king Archelaus, with Halfmann (1979) 47. Equestrians: Martial, *Epigram.* 10.76.3, a sneer at "an equestrian from Cappadocian slave markets"; Juvenal, *Saturae* 7.15, a reference to "Cappadocian equestrians," although the authenticity of this line is suspect: see Courtney (1980) 352. Ti. Claudius Gordianus: Halfmann (1979) 197–98, no. 130, and Berges and Nollé (2000) 2:431–33. "Gordiani" in Cappadocia and emperor Gordianus: Robert (1963) 526n.9, and Syme (1971) 166–70, (1980); note also the martyr Gordius, a native of Caesarea: see B, *Hom.* 18.2, with Halkin (1961), and *Becoming Christian*, Chapter 4. Aurelius Cl. Hermodorus: Harper (1964) 167–68, (1968) 133–34, no. 6.29; for his family's tomb, see Harper and Bayburtluoglu (1968) 150–55. For the possibility of identifying this Hermodorus with the Aurelius Hermodorus who was governor of Noricum Mediterraneum in 311 (*PLRE* 1:422), see Harper (1964) 168, and Eck (1972/1973) 331.

5. Senatorial families: Halfmann (1982) 619. Blockade of Isauria: SHA, *Tyranni triginta* 26.6, "quasi limes."

6. For this increase in the size of the administration and army, see Jones (1964) 51–52, 60.

7. Anniversary games at Rome: Aurelius Victor, *De Caesaribus* 28, Eutropius, *Breviarium* 9.3, SHA, *Gordiani* 33. "Second Rome": Socrates, *HE* 1.16. Stripped bare: Jerome, *Chronicon* s.a. 330. Ax and crumbs: *Vita Constantini*, ed. Guidi (1907) 337. Imperial resources: *Origo Constantini imperatoris* 6.30. Size of senate: Themistius, *Orat.* 34.13, with Skinner (2000), on the attractiveness of Constantinople to provincial notables.

8. Many men: *Expositio totius mundi et gentium* 44.

9. Anthimus: GNaz, *Ep.* 128.3, ἐξ ἐπιφανοῦς στρατείας. The translation of this phrase in Gallay (1964–1967) 2:18, suggests that Anthimus had served in the army; *PLRE* 1:70, "Anthimus," suggests that he was "perhaps a former *officialis*"; Hauser-Meury (1960) 33, "Anthimus II," is undecided whether he served in the army or an imperial department. For the argument that στρατεία or στρατιά was the equivalent of *officium* and στρατιώτης of *officialis*, see Roueché (1989a) 74–75, and Van Dam (1996) 31–32. Briso (or Brison): B, *Ep.* 302, a letter of consolation to his widow. Hauschild (1993) 239n.570, is perhaps misled by the flattery into suggesting he had held a high military office. Cledonius: GNaz, *Carm.* II.2.1.127, with *PLRE* 1:213, "Cledonius 2," and Hauser-Meury (1960) 55, "Cledonius III," who suggests that

this monk Cledonius might be identified with the Cledonius who received GNaz, *Ep.* 101–2. Maxentius: GNaz, *Epitaph.* 126–27 = *Anthologia Graeca* 8.159–60, with *PLRE* 1:571, "Maxentius 2." Firminus: in *Ep.* 116 Basil encouraged Firminus to say farewell to στρατεία, ὅπλα, and the labors of the στρατόπεδον, which are probably to be taken as references to service in the bureaucracy at the imperial court rather than military service. Hauschild (1973) 160n.64, suggests that *Ep.* 117 was Firminus' response to Basil. Pouchet (1992a) 297–98, suggests that this Firminus can be identified with the Firminus from Cappadocia who finally retired as an *officialis* in 392 to become a sophist: see Libanius, *Ep.* 1048.2, with *PLRE* 1:339, "Firminus 3." Helladius: Basil once asked the prefect Modestus to exempt a man named Helladius from service as a *peraequator* (*Ep.* 281). Since Basil described this *peraequator* Helladius as ὁ πρωτεύων, *PLRE* 1:412, "Helladius 2," and Pouchet (1992a) 611n.5, identify him as a *principalis*, a leading decurion, at Caesarea. This is an unlikely identification. If Jones (1964) 537, is correct in arguing that the emperors Valentinian and Valens preferred to use equestrians and members of the order of *comites* as *peraequatores*, then the *peraequator* Helladius was probably already a *honoratus* at the time of his appointment. So he should be identified with the Helladius who was a *comes* (B, *Ep.* 109) and a "member of the prefect's household" (B, *Ep.* 107): see *PLRE* 1:412, "Helladius 3." In that case Modestus probably selected this *comes* Helladius, a member of his staff, to be *peraequator* in Cappadocia because he was a native of the region. It is then unlikely that this Helladius who served as a *comes* and *peraequator* can be identified with the Helladius who succeeded Basil as bishop of Caesarea, as suggested by Kopecek (1973) 458, (1974) 337–40, since all the known bishops from the region had previously had no higher than curial rank. Nicobulus the Elder: GNaz, *Carm.* II.2.4.118–21, military career and family, with *Families and Friends*, Chapter 2; GNaz, *Ep.* 196.4, "who assisted you magistrates for a long time," with *PLRE* 1:629, "Nicobulus 1." For Nicobulus' sons, see *Families and Friends*, Chapter 3.

10. Publius Ampelius was probably a landowner in Cappadocia, but he was most likely not a governor there: see Van Dam (1996) 27–28. Theodosius' edict: *CJ* 9.29.3, with the dating of Seeck (1919) 95, 255.

11. Magnilianus: *PLRE* 1:532. Philagrius' tenure in Egypt: *PLRE* 1:694, "Fl. Philagrius 5," and Barnes (1993) 29, 45–48, 252n.43; his residence in Cappadocia during his vicarate from 348 to 350: Libanius, *Orat.* 1.66. Gregory of Nazianzus delivered *Orat.* 21 sometime while serving as leader of the Nicene community at Constantinople: see Bernardi (1968) 155–57, Mossay and Lafontaine (1980) 99–103, and Chapter 8. According to GNaz, *Orat.* 21.28, Philagrius, "a two-time prefect," attended the festivities celebrating Athanasius' return to Alexandria, after yet another exile, in February 362. Not only did Gregory praise Philagrius for "his affection and his honor that surpassed that affection," but he was unaware that Philagrius had died before 358: see Libanius, *Ep.* 372.2. For Gregory's ignorance and the chronological confusion, see Hauser-Meury (1960) 145n.293, and Mossay and Lafontaine (1980) 170n.1.

12. Martinianus' career: *PLRE* 1:564, "Martinianus 5." For Basil's appeal, see Chapters 6–7. Epitaphs: GNaz, *Epitaph.* 40–53 = *Anthologia Graeca* 8.104–17. In *Ep.* 64, 72, Basil appealed for the support of Hesychius, who was apparently a local aristocrat in Cappadocia. Hauschild (1990) 202n.290, suggests that this Hesychius might

be identified with the Hesychius who became a provincial governor in the later 380s: see *PLRE* 1:429, "Hesychius 4."

13. Evagrius' career: *PLRE* 1:285, "Evagrius 5." Hauser-Meury (1960) 64, "Evagrius I," and Delmaire (1989a) 36, identify this *comes* Evagrius with the Evagrius who thanked Gregory of Nazianzus for having taught his son: see GNaz, *Ep.* 3. Since Gregory apparently taught this boy soon after his return from Athens to Cappadocia, Evagrius was most likely a native of the region. Arcadius: B, *Ep.* 15. The heading to this letter identified Arcadius as a κόμης πριβάτων, and Basil's reference to "our mother city," presumably Caesarea, implied that Arcadius was a Cappadocian. For the date and circumstances of this letter, see Chapter 6. Caesarius: see *Families and Friends*, Chapter 3.

14. Sophronius as *notarius*: Ammianus Marcellinus, *Res gestae* 26.7.2, with Chapter 6; as *magister officiorum*: B, *Ep.* 32, 76, 96, 177, 180, 192, 272, GNaz, *Ep.* 22, 29, with Clauss (1980) 190–91, and *Families and Friends*, Chapter 9; as prefect: *PLRE* 1:847, "Sophronius 3," and Dagron (1974) 251, who suggests he was prefect possibly in 379. Aburgius: B, *Ep.* 33, 75, 147, 178, 304. Although *PLRE* 1:5 and Forlin Patrucco (1983) 394, suggest that Aburgius held an important office at the court, Delmaire (1989a) 61–62, argues that he was the *comes Orientis* in ca. 375. For Aburgius' possible prefecture, see B, *Ep.* 196 = [GNaz,] *Ep.* 241, "now preparing provisions for the army, now appearing before the emperor in dazzling robes," with the discussion of *PLRE* 1:5; Barnes (1997) 9n.18, suggests he did not become prefect. Aburgius' later influence: Libanius, *Ep.* 907, 960.

15. Caesarius: see *Families and Friends*, Chapter 3. Adelphius' offers: GNaz, *Ep.* 204.6. Gallay (1964–1967) 2:95n.1, *PLRE* 1:13, "Adelphius 2," and Maraval (1990) 258n.2, suggest that this Adelphius might be identified with the advocate Adelphius who received GNys, *Ep.* 20 (see Chapter 1). Gallay (1964–1967) 2:95n.1, *PLRE* 1:13, "Adelphius 3," and Teske (1997) 108n.174, also suggest the possibility of identification with the Adelphius who had been a student of Libanius and who became governor of Galatia in 392: see Libanius, *Ep.* 1049. Distinguished man: B, *Hom. in Hexaemeron* 5.2.

16. Libanius' students: Libanius, *Orat.* 62.27–28. For the details and calculations of Libanius' students, see Petit (1956) 112–35.

17. Mushrooms: GNaz, *Carm.* II.1.41.5–7. Gregory directed the criticism in this poem against Maximus, his rival at Constantinople: see Gallay (1943) 169n.6, for the date, and Chapter 8. Clergy: Jones (1964) 910–12, size of clerical staffs, 934, "the staffing of the church absorbed far more manpower than did the secular administration." For "rural bishops," see *Becoming Christian*, Chapter 2.

18. Amphilochius: see *Families and Friends*, Chapters 2, 9. Optimus' transfer: *CTh* 16.1.3, Socrates, *HE* 7.36. Greek language: Libanius, *Ep.* 1544.1. Another court: GNaz, *Orat.* 7.15, with *Families and Friends*, Chapter 3.

19. Bishop Archelaus: Photius, *Bibliotheca* 52, with Calvet-Sebasti and Gatier (1989) 39n.59. Helladius: Firmus of Caesarea, *Ep.* 12, to Helladius, *Ep.* 26, to Helladius: "you made me your friend from boyhood." *PLRE* 2:534–35, "Helladius 3," suggests that Helladius was a provincial governor, Calvet-Sebasti and Gatier (1989) 57, an important magistrate at Constantinople.

20. Sirens: B, *Ep.* 1, with Forlin Patrucco (1983) 251, identifying this "city on the Hellespont" as Constantinople, Hauschild (1990) 161n.3, less plausibly, as Lampsacus.

Luxury and sweat: Libanius, *Orat.* 1.279, with Petit (1957) 349–50, on his concern about men from Antioch moving to the capital. Morning star: GNaz, *Carm.* II.1.1.177–78.

21. For Maurice's career, see Whitby (1988) 3–9, and *PLRE* 3:855–60; for his recruitment in Cappadocia, Whitby (1995) 84–85. A late source also described Phocas, Maurice's successor, as a Cappadocian: see *Patria Konstantinoupoleos* 3.13, 184, with *PLRE* 3:1030, "probably . . . a term of abuse."

22. Epigram: John the Lydian, *De magistratibus* 3.57 = *Anthologia Graeca* 11.238, a critique of John the Cappadocian, the powerful prefect of the East during the 530s.

## Chapter 4. The Highlander

1. Land of beautiful horses: Ruge (1919) 1911, although note the alternative etymology in de Planhol (1981) 27–29. Legend: Polybius, *Hist.*, frag. 54, quoted by Constantine VII Porphyrogenitus, *De thematibus* II, ed. Pertusi (1952) 64: "Neocaesarea, Colonia, and Melitene are all said to be Cappadocia. This is a Persian name. A Persian man [was with] king Artaxerxes or someone else during a hunt. A lion bounded out and seized the king's horse. By chance the Persian was in the wild beast's path. He drew his sword, rescued the king who was in close danger, and killed the lion. This Persian then ascended to the highest peak and looked over the entire region, as far as the human eye could see to the east and the west and to the north and the south. He received it all as a gift from the king. Polybius says this in his history." For discussion of this legend, see Briant (1996) 145–47.

2. Families and cults: Robert (1975), and Mitchell (1993) 2:29–30, 73. Valens: GNaz, *Orat.* 43.45. Magusaeans: B, *Ep.* 258.4; also Herodian, *Hist.* 6.4.6, for the settlement of Persians in Phrygia. Persian fruit: GNys, *Ep.* 20.11. Halys River: GNys, *Ep.* 20.5, Himerius, *Orat.* 18.2–3, with Chuvin (1994) 172–74, for the legend of an Indian empire in eastern Asia Minor. Greeting: B, *Ep.* 349 = Libanius, *Epistularum commercium* 15. Reverence: Strabo, *Geographia* 11.13.9.

3. Valerianus Paetus: Dio, *Hist.* 80.4.7, with Mitchell (1993) 1:155, for the family's property. Palmatius: Hesychius of Miletus, *Historia romana*, frag. 1, with the discussion in Berges and Nollé (2000) 2:297–304, 497, and Chapter 1, for Palmatian racehorses. Eustathius Maleinus: John Scylitzes, *Synopsis historiarum*, ed. Thurn (1973) 340, with Honigmann (1936) 268–71, for the extent of the family's estates, Hendy (1985) 100–107, on the distribution of magnates, Kaplan (1981) 143–52, on the family's prominence, and Cheynet (1986), on its associations with the powerful Phocas family.

4. *Digenes Akrites*, Grottaferrata version 7.2, offshoot, 8.202–300, funeral and tomb, Escorial version 1092, "the marvelous Cappadocian." For discussion of possible historical contexts, see Magdalino (1993), Beaton (1996), and Jeffreys (1998) XXX–XLI.

5. Meeting with emperor Basil: *Digenes Akrites*, Grottaferrata version 4.971–1089. Quotation about marcher lord from Bryer (1993) 102.

6. Lion as "emperor": Julian, *Misopogon* 339B.

7. Note that the emperor too was earlier described as a "great highlander":

*Digenes Akrites*, Grottaferrata version 4.56. For suggestions about the identification of this emperor, see Jeffreys (1998) 389.

8. *Digenes Akrites*, Grottaferrata version 6.700–701, saints, 7.42–108, villa. For the local legends about St. Georgius (George), see the Epilogue to *Becoming Christian*.

9. Digenes' father was also considered a "second Samson": *Digenes Akrites*, Grottaferrata version 4.24. For the association of the ninth-century emperor Basil I with images of Samson, see Brubaker (1999) 179–84.

## Empire and Province Introduction

1. Man of steel: Libanius, *Orat.* 59.96; also Socrates, *HE* 2.12–13, Sozomen, *HE* 3.7, for the circumstances at Constantinople. Libanius, *Orat.* 1.14–15, Libanius' trip in late 336, 279, death of Cimon.

2. Acacius' reluctance: Libanius, *Ep.* 1222.2, with Van Dam (1996) 19–22, for his appointment as *comes domorum*. Philippus: Libanius, *Ep.* 1223, with Chapter 9.

3. Anonymous Cappadocian orator: Libanius, *Orat.* 1.35. Bemarchius: *Suda* B.259. For the rivalry between Libanius and Bemarchius, see Libanius, *Orat.* 1.31, 39–44. Eustochius: *Suda* E.3755, "the events of the emperor Constans and the antiquarian lore of Cappadocia and other peoples"; for a possible reference to Eustochius' encyclopedia, see Stephanus of Byzantium, *Ethnica*, s.v. Παντικάπαιον, ed. Meineke (1849) 501–502.

4. Again: GNaz, *Ep.* 148.1, with Van Dam (1996) 41–42, on Asterius' office. On the increasing ambitions of late Roman emperors, see Corcoran (1996) 198–203.

## Chapter 5. Provincial Governors and Tax Assessors

1. For a survey of changes in the province of Cappadocia, see Rémy (1986) 30–33, 51–61, 65–73.

2. Bits: Lactantius, *De mortibus persecutorum* 7.4. Jones (1971) 182, 432n.17, suggests that eastern Cappadocia had already been attached to Armenia Minor before becoming Armenia Secunda; Kopecek (1974) 320–21, and Mitchell (1993) 2:163 n.59, date the formation of Armenia Secunda before Valens' partition of Cappadocia, even though it is first attested in *CTh* 13.11.2 = *CJ* 11.48.10, issued in 386. The existence of the province of Lycaonia is first attested in B, *Ep.* 138.2, describing the rank of Iconium as a new capital city: "formerly it was the foremost city after the most important city, but now it presides over a region that has been assembled from various pieces and has received administration over its own province." Hauschild (1973) 14, and Pouchet (1992a) 271, date this letter to 373; Holl (1904) 16–17, associates the creation of Lycaonia with the division of Cappadocia. For the details of the division, reunification, and second division of Cappadocia, see Honigmann (1961) 28–31, and Van Dam (1996) 7–12, 65–66.

3. As a comparison of the relative importance of vicars and governors for the residents of Cappadocia, note that during the three decades after their return from Athens to their native region Basil and Gregory of Nazianzus mentioned only

three or four vicars of Pontica, perhaps one-fifth of the vicars who served during the period; other sources mentioned at least three more vicars. In contrast, Basil, Gregory of Nazianzus, and Gregory of Nyssa mentioned almost twenty governors in Cappadocia, about half of the governors who served during the period; other sources mentioned only one other governor: for details, see Van Dam (1996). For the importance of provincial governors, note also Bagnall (1993) 63: "The imperial government, from a provincial point of view, consisted fundamentally in provincial governorships and their attached offices."

4. For collection of rents on imperial estates by officials of the *res privata*, see *CTh* 10.1.11, issued in 367; Jones (1964) 417, associates this edict with Cappadocia. For the transfer of the collection of rents from provincial governors back to magistrates of the *res privata* because of the accumulation of arrears, see *CTh* 5.14.31, issued in 382. Note also *CTh* 6.30.2 = *CJ* 12.23.3, issued in 379, for a rearrangement of the staff of the *comes domorum*, with Forlin Patrucco (1972), on the imperial estates.

5. GNaz, *Orat.* 43.58, mentioned "the revenues and tolls of the Taurus Mountains." The tolls came perhaps from supervision of mountain passes, and miners were probably expected to supply iron ore for the armor factory at Caesarea: see Jones (1964) 834–39. B, *Ep.* 110, mentioned a "levy of iron" expected from the inhabitants of the Taurus Mountains. For discussion of other taxes, see below.

6. Definition of a good judge: B, *Ep.* 96, about an anonymous governor, with Van Dam (1996) 33–34; since Basil was writing to a fellow Christian, he went on to claim that a governor's most important function was to "restore the affairs of Christians to their old honor." Benefit friends: B, *Ep.* 86, addressed to an anonymous governor, with Van Dam (1996) 35–37. Governor and Judge: GNaz, *Ep.* 142.

7. Short tenures of governors: see Jones (1964) 379–83. Commander and governor: GNys, *Ep.* 19.16, mentioning a κόμης who commanded a detachment of troops and a ἡγεμών. Maraval (1990) 254n.1, suggests that this *comes* was a military commander, a *comes rei militaris*, perhaps similar to Terentius, the *comes* and *dux* in Armenia with whom Basil corresponded during the early and mid-370s: see Chapter 7. *PLRE* 1 does not include this anonymous governor or this anonymous *comes*.

8. Birds: GNaz, *Ep.* 224.1–2, to Africanus, probably a provincial governor: see Van Dam (1996) 22–23. Gregory cited this proverb apparently from Aristotle's discussion of friendship: see Aristotle, *Ethica Nicomachea* 8.1155a34–35. Euripides: B, *Ep.* 63, citing Euripides, fragment 902, ed. Nauck (1964) 650–51. According to the heading of this letter the recipient was a "governor of Neocaesarea" whom *PLRE* 1:1024, "Anonymus 122," identifies as the governor of Pontus Polemoniacus. Proverb: B, *Ep.* 186–87, to Antipater, a governor of Cappadocia or Cappadocia Prima during Basil's episcopacy: see Van Dam (1996) 40–41. Appeals: B, *Ep.* 96, on behalf of an anonymous governor, *Ep.* 147–49, on behalf of Maximus, with Van Dam (1996) 33–34, 60–61. Themistius: GNaz, *Ep.* 24, dated to the late 360s.

9. Hesiod: GNaz, *Ep.* 195.1. Shadow: B, *Ep.* 84. Epigram: *Anthologia Graeca* 16.74. Gregory the Elder: GNaz, *Orat.* 18.34. Gentleness: GNaz, *Orat.* 17.10, directed perhaps at the *peraequator* Julianus (discussed below). Note Brown (1992) 24: "no representative of the imperial majesty could be certain that his authority would be upheld by those who had sent him"; 46: "Appeals to a shared love of the Muses tactfully disguised the weakness of the provincial governor's own position."

10. Direct administration: B, *Ep.* 94, to Helias. Acclamations: *CTh* 1.16.6 = *CJ* 1.40.3, with Harries (1999) 96–98, on accountability. Note B, *Ep.* 281, for a request that the prefect Modestus send a copy of his decision to the provincial governor. On the roles of governors, see Corcoran (1996) 234–53, Carrié (1998), Roueché (1998), and Harries (1999) 153–71; for "dwarf governors" and "giant subjects," see Lendon (1997) 222–35.

11. Benefactor: GNaz, *Ep.* 14, dated to before 372 by Gallay (1964–1967) 1:21n.1; this letter is a bit blunt, perhaps because it was one of Gregory's first to an imperial magistrate and because he was writing on behalf of two relatives. Flattery: GNaz, *Ep.* 224.3, with Vogler (1992), on the absence of important details in these letters. Titles: Hauser-Meury (1960) 186–88, for Gregory of Nazianzus, Gain (1985) 399–402, for Basil, Maraval (1971) 274–75, for Gregory of Nyssa, with Zilliacus (1949) 61–81, on the confusion between flattery and titles. Examples from ancient history: B, *Ep.* 94, 272.3, Alexander refused to take slanders seriously; B, *Ep.* 112.2, leniency of Croesus and Cyrus; GNaz, *Ep.* 198.1, the philosopher Pythagoras, who sacrificed a clay ox to avoid shedding more blood; GNys, *Ep.* 8.1, Alexander and his friends. For Alexander's journey through Cappadocia, see *Becoming Christian*, Chapter 4. Note that in his prayers Gregory likewise encouraged even God to perform up to His previous miracles: see Demoen (1997). "Excellence" and salutation: B, *Ep.* 84; in this letter Basil claimed that the salutations addressed to a magistrate were supposed to be different from those addressed to private citizens: "we must try to profit from his power." Monuments: GNaz, *Ep.* 154.4.

12. Quotation from Brown (1992) 45.

13. Invitation: GNaz, *Ep.* 130.4, a hope that "the most pious emperor" will excuse him from attending a council at Constantinople in summer 382.

14. Improper consecration: GNaz, *Ep.* 125.5. Threat to city's rank: GNaz, *Ep.* 141; *Ep.* 142 was another appeal to Olympius on behalf of the city's magistrates. In *Ep.* 141.3 Gregory noted that the city being threatened was "Diocaesarea." Hild and Restle (1981) 171, identify this Diocaesarea as a site about twenty-five miles east of Nazianzus; Gallay (1943) 13–16, (1964–1967) 2:154, and Galsterer-Kröll (1972) 130, argue more plausibly that Diocaesarea was another name for Nazianzus. See also Szymusiak (1972) 548, for a Roman milestone (still unpublished?) that apparently mentioned both Diocaesarea and Nazianzus.

15. Generosity: GNaz, *Ep.* 105.1. Wisdom and courage: GNaz, *Ep.* 140.2. Gentleness: GNaz, *Ep.* 105.2; also 104.1, 141.1. Virtues of magistrate: GNaz, *Ep.* 154.1. God's qualities: GNaz, *Ep.* 140.1. Repayment: GNaz, *Ep.* 104.1.

16. Appeal: GNaz, *Ep.* 141.2, kings, 3, Persians, 5, friend, 9, old city.

17. Dismay: GNaz, *Ep.* 154.2. Deference: GNaz, *Ep.* 144.1, 145.3. For the chronology of Olympius' governorship and his possible role in the reunification of Cappadocia, see Van Dam (1996) 10–12, 64–66. Olympius should not be identified with the Olympianus who may have been a governor in Cappadocia and whom Gregory praised for his rhetorical talent: GNaz, *Ep.* 234.2, with Van Dam (1996) 63–64.

18. Fellowship of culture: GNaz, *Ep.* 199.2.

19. Nemesius: GNaz, *Carm.* II.2.7.1–6, legal and rhetorical skills, 13–17, substitute, 248–49, poems and Bible; *Ep.* 200.1, philosopher, 4, promise, with Demoen (1996) 128–41, on Gregory's awareness of his audience: "Gregory reserves the

biblical exempla for Christians, but does not reserve the pagan ones for Hellenes" (140). Devotion: GNys, *Ep.* 11.1, with Calvet-Sebasti (1996) 379, on letters between Christians and pagans: "Le genre épistolaire n'est pas . . . le lieu d'un combat." For Nemesius' career and the argument that he should not be identified with the Nemesius who was bishop of Emesa in the later fourth century, see Van Dam (1996) 61–62.

20. Afflictions: GNaz, *Carm.* II.1.19.89–98. Many-headed Hydra: B, *Ep.* 284, 315 (perhaps a pun on the "capitation" tax), with Forlin Patrucco (1973), for Basil's references to taxes.

21. The references linking governors and taxation are all ambiguous or indirect: B, *Ep.* 84, to an anonymous governor of Cappadocia or Cappadocia Prima concerning an old man forced to serve on a municipal council and therefore to collect revenues; B, *Ep.* 98.2, mentioning Maximus, a former governor of Cappadocia or Cappadocia Prima, and his "persecutions," which might refer to the collection of taxes; GNaz, *Ep.* 196.5, to Hecebolius, a governor of Cappadocia Prima or Cappadocia Secunda in the mid-380s, mentioning "threats" against orphans that might refer to the pressure of taxes; GNaz, *Ep.* 211, a request to Cyriacus, possibly a governor of Cappadocia Prima during the mid-380s, about exempting two estates belonging to a poorhouse from "all hardship," which might refer to imperial taxes. Provision of soldiers: B, *Ep.* 3, with Van Dam (1996) 43–45, on the identification of Candidianus, the recipient.

22. For Basil's letters to Modestus, see Chapters 6–7. *Numerarii:* B, *Ep.* 142, 143; since two *numerarii* administered each sub-department, these two correspondents were perhaps colleagues: see Jones (1964) 450. *Tractator:* B, *Ep.* 144. Levy of mares: the heading to B, *Ep.* 303, identified the recipient as a κόμης πριβατῶν; he should be identified not as a *comes domorum,* as suggested by Pouchet (1992a) 626, but as a *comes rei privatae.* If Basil was writing to the *comes rei privatae,* then the men he represented were perhaps lessees of imperial properties who were usually excused from many taxes: see Jones (1964) 419–20, 452. There is no compelling reason to identify this anonymous *comes* either with the *comes rei privatae* Fortunatianus, as suggested by *PLRE* 1:1010, "Anonymus 27," and Delmaire (1989a) 59, or with the *comes rei privatae* Arcadius who received B, *Ep.* 15, as suggested by Forlin Patrucco (1983) 319. Gregory may also have requested assistance from a *comes rei privatae* in confirming the sale of an estate: see GNaz, *Ep.* 14, with Delmaire (1989a) 44, who argues that the Caesarius who received this letter was the *comes rei privatae* in 363–364, and *PLRE* 1:168–69, "Caesarius 1."

23. B, *Ep.* 36–37, on the equalization of the property of Basil's foster-brother; *Ep.* 83, on the assessment of a property; *Ep.* 85, on tax collectors requiring oaths from peasants; *Ep.* 88, on the collection of a tax in gold, with Van Dam (1986) 65n.58, on the nature of this tax; *Ep.* 284, on immunity for monks; *Ep.* 299, encouraging a man to conduct the tax assessments at Ibora (near which Basil's family happened to own property); *Ep.* 309, on the assessment of a property; *Ep.* 311, on the assessment of a property; *Ep.* 312, on a man's assessment; *Ep.* 313, on assessments in Galatia, where Basil happened to own a property. Note also B, *Ep.* 21, for an analogy with "collectors of public tribute" who demanded fourfold (as a penalty? as extortion?).

24. Amphilochius: GNaz, *Ep.* 9.3, dated to the mid-360s. Nectarius: GNaz, *Ep.*

151, dated after mid-381, with Hauser-Meury (1960) 84, for the identification of the "losses" as taxes. The τῶν οἰκείων κόμης whom Nectarius was to influence has been identified probably correctly as the *comes rei privatae* by Hauser-Meury (1960) 84, 126n.243, less plausibly as the *comes domesticorum* (a military officer) by PLRE 1:1011, "Anonymus 32," or as the *comes domorum* by Delmaire (1989b) 220–21.

25. For the pattern of appointing local aristocrats as tax assessors, see the career of Helladius in Chapter 3. Hellenius as assessor at Nazianzus: B, *Ep.* 98. GNaz, *Carm.* II.2.1.15–17, thanks, 278–79, 359, native of Armenia, 285–86, "my old friendship," 295–97, Basil's role, 363–68, honors. Armenian students: GNaz, *Orat.* 43.17–18. There is no evidence that Hellenius became the governor of Cappadocia Secunda, as suggested by PLRE 1.413, "Hellenius 1," or that he might be identified with the Hellenius who was vicar of Rome in 386, as suggested by PLRE 1:413, "Hellenius 2": see Van Dam (1996) 54–56.

26. Fellow students: GNaz, *Orat.* 19.16; Gregory also knew Julianus' mother (*Carm.* II.2.2.17). GNaz, *Ep.* 67.1, friendship and Nicobulus, 2, request and precedent; *Ep.* 68.2, parents. This *peraequator* Julianus had previously held some office (cf. GNaz, *Carm.* II.2.2.5–6), but it was not necessarily a provincial governorship, as suggested by Seeck (1906) 191–92, "Julianus VIII," and Hauser-Meury (1960) 16, 110n.211. This *peraequator* Julianus should hence be distinguished from the Julianus who had held governorships in Phrygia and Euphratensis: see PLRE 1:471–72, "Iulianus 14, 17," and Van Dam (1996) 38–39.

27. Invitation: GNaz, *Ep.* 68.1. GNaz, *Orat.* 19.5, "the holy martyrs ... whom the present festival [honors]." Only the heading of this oration mentioned the ἐξισωτής (= *peraequator*) Julianus by name; the oration itself refers only to the ἀπογραφεύς (= *censitor*) who was to act "justly and generously" (*Orat.* 19.12).

28. GNaz, *Orat.* 19.12–13, Christ's birth, 15, God's census. Gregory repeated these themes in a poem to Julianus: *Carm.* II.2.2.10–12, 15–16. Gallay (1943) 128, dates *Orat.* 19 after Christmas 374; Bernardi (1968) 132–33, discounts the reference to Christ's birth as an indication of the oration's date.

29. Characteristics of an oration to a magistrate: Menander Rhetor, *Treatise* II.414–18, ed. Russell and Wilson (1981) 164–70. School days: GNaz, *Orat.* 19.16. Surpass me: GNaz, *Orat.* 17.13. In *Orat.* 17.8–9 Gregory addressed some "rulers and magistrates" in the audience and told one specific magistrate that he had received his sword from Christ. Gallay (1943) 123–24, and Bernardi (1968) 121–24, date this oration to 373 or early 374, during the period when Gregory was helping his father at Nazianzus. Coulie (1985) 75–86, dates the oration after Gregory the Elder's death in spring 374, and suggests that the magistrate addressed in *Orat.* 17 was the *peraequator* Julianus; see also Van Dam (1996) 37–39, for other identifications.

30. GNaz, *Orat.*19.1, seclusion, 3, "my flock," 10, pastures, 16, writing. Sacrifice: GNaz, *Ep.* 67.2. Gentleness: GNaz, *Orat.* 17.12.

31. Thanks and Grand Remitter: GNaz, *Ep.* 69, with Holman (2001) 107, on the transformation of "tax language into gift language."

32. Draining away: GNaz, *Ep.*146.1; cf. *Ep.* 104.2, "I come to bestow a favor rather than to receive one."

33. Hands: GNaz, *Ep.* 147.3.

34. Nazianzus: GNaz, *Ep.* 141.3. For the conventions of epistolography, see

*Families and Friends*, Chapter 8. Increasing prestige of letters: note B, *Ep.* 198.1, for a letter carried by *officiales* and a reply sent by a *peraequator*.

35. Extension of hands: GNaz, *Ep.* 140.4, on the presentation of a suppliant to a provincial governor: "he has placed himself beneath my hands and, through my hands, beneath yours," with Brilliant (1963) 189–95, on gestures of submission. For depictions of this gesture of generosity in manuscript illustrations of Byzantine emperors, see Mullett (1992) 204: "What is represented almost always is not the moment of composition or the moment of reading but the process of letter-exchange epitomized in the transaction of delivery, the primary reception of the text." Hand of friendship: GNaz, *Ep.* 239.1.

## Chapter 6. Emperors in Cappadocia

1. For imperial visits to Rome during the fourth century, see Barnes (1975), and Halfmann (1986) 61–62.

2. Imperial arrival: Athanasius, *De incarnatione verbi* 9. Constantius at Rome: Ammianus Marcellinus, *Res gestae* 16.10.1–20, esp. 13 for his behavior to the people: "he also respectfully observed the obligatory deference." Constantius' hunt: Julian, *Orat.* 2.53B: "I watched you killing many bears and panthers and lions," with Bidez (1930) 24, for the location of this hunt in Cappadocia. For the meeting of Constantius and bishop Athanasius at Caesarea, see Athanasius, *Apologia ad Constantium* 5, dated to spring 338 by Barnes (1993) 41–45. For the visit by king Arsak of Armenia in 360, see below.

3. Constantius certainly or probably visited Cappadocia in autumn 337, spring 338, early 342, autumn 343, late winter 347, autumn 349, and autumn 350: for his journeys, see Barnes (1993) 219–20. Ammianus Marcellinus, *Res gestae* 20.4.1, Constantius leaves for eastern frontier, 9.1–5, news at Caesarea.

4. GNaz, *Orat.* 4.34, divine emperor, 37, Christians, 39, simplicity; also *Orat.* 5.16, blaming Constantius' subordinates; with Chapter 11, for Gregory's evaluation of Constantius. For the council at Constantinople, see *Becoming Christian*, Chapter 1. Exiles: Socrates, *HE* 2.42, Sozomen, *HE* 4.24–26. Fury: Ammianus Marcellinus, *Res gestae* 20.9.2.

5. Ammianus Marcellinus, *Res gestae* 20.11.1–4, visit of king Arsak to Cappadocia, 5, Amida; 21.15.1–3, death in Cilicia, 16.20–21, funeral procession. According to GNaz, *Orat.* 5.16, some people claimed to hear angels chanting Psalms as Constantius' cortege crossed the Taurus Mountains.

6. Taxes at Antioch: Julian, *Misopogon* 365B, 367C–D. Chalcedon: Socrates, *HE* 3.12, Sozomen, *HE* 5.4. For Julian's journey through Asia Minor, see also Chapter 9.

7. Hannibalianus: *Epitome de Caesaribus* 41.20, *Origo Constantini imperatoris* 6.35, *Chronicon Paschale* s.a. 335. Hewsen (1978–1979) 110, interprets his title of *rex regum* as king of Armenia, although Barnes (1981) 259, (1985) 132, suggests he was intended to replace the king of Persia.

8. Julian's exile at Macellum and enrollment as reader: Sozomen, *HE* 5.2, with Hadjinicolaou (1951), and Hild and Restle (1981) 226–27, for the location of Macellum, and Bouffartigue (1992) 29–39, for the chronology of his stay. Eunuchs:

Eunapius, *Vitae sophistarum* 473. "The way": Julian, *Ep.* 47.434D. GNaz, *Orat.* 4.24–26, martyrium, 52, baptism, 97, reader; *Orat.* 43.13, Basil and Gregory at Caesarea.

9. Macellum: Julian, *Ep. ad Athenienses* 271B–D. Georgius' death and library: Julian, *Ep.* 21.379C, *Ep.* 23, with Chapter 9.

10. Julianus: Julian, *Ep.* 29, sent to his uncle in spring 362 from Constantinople. Images of Tyche had appeared on coinage minted at Caesarea in the mid-third century: see Bland (1991) 215. Penalties: Sozomen, *HE* 5.3–4, with Chapters 9–10, for more discussion of the destruction of this temple.

11. Petitioners: Ammianus Marcellinus, *Res gestae* 22.9.8–11. Dispute at Caesarea: GNaz, *Orat.* 18.33–34. This governor can be identified as Ulpianus: see Van Dam (1996) 75–76. Note that some of the imperial bureaucrats at Caesarea had supported the choice of bishop Eusebius: see Van Dam (1996) 30–32. Julian's threat to enroll clerics as bureaucrats may hence have been some kind of sarcastic penalty: if imperial underlings were going to support the bishop, then the emperor would place clerics under the governor's authority. A few years later Gregory of Nazianzus could not resist his own pun: Julian had been upset because at the moment of his own good fortune, this temple to "Fortune" at Caesarea had suffered a misfortune (*Orat.* 4.92). Twenty years later Gregory again seemed to hint at Julian's regard for Gregory the Elder: see GNaz, *Carm.* II.1.19.55–56, "my father, whom even someone who was very far from the fold venerated, respecting his white hair and the corresponding splendor of his spirit."

12. Julian at Athens: GNaz, *Orat.* 5.23. "Incarnation of evil": GNaz, *Orat.* 2.87, with Bernardi (1978) 11–17, arguing that Gregory composed this treatise before Julian's arrival in Cappadocia. Christian emperors: GNaz, *Orat.* 4.98.

13. GNaz, *Orat.* 15.5, only king, 12, "today's Antiochus," with Chapter 11, and *Families and Friends*, Chapter 2, for the context and date of this sermon.

14. Criticism and seduction of Basil and Gregory: GNaz, *Orat.* 5.39. Aristoxenus: Julian, *Ep.* 35. For Caesarius' career, see *Families and Friends*, Chapter 3.

15. Celsus and Basil: Libanius, *Epistularum commercium* 2.2 = B, *Ep.* 336.1, with Chapter 9. Celsus and Julian: Ammianus Marcellinus, *Res gestae* 22.9.13. Panegyric and sacrifice: Libanius, *Orat.* 18.159, *Ep.* 736.3.

16. Ammianus Marcellinus, *Res gestae* 22.14.3, mocking, 23.2.5, plans and burial, 25.9.12, burial. On Julian and Hercules, see Athanassiadi (1981) 132–33; on Hercules as the founder of Tarsus, Jones (1978) 72. Julian and Trajan: Julian, *Caesares* 311C, 327A–328B. Trajan's death: Dio, *Hist.* 68.33.3. For Procopius, Julian's relative, see below. GNaz, *Orat.* 5.18, cortege and shrine, *Orat.* 21.33, earthquake. According to Philostorgius, *HE* 8.1, Julian's tomb was across the road from the tomb of Maximinus, an emperor who had persecuted Christians: see *Families and Friends*, Chapter 1.

17. Ammianus Marcellinus, *Res gestae* 25.5.8, Jovian's reputation, 10.4–9, Tarsus, Tyana, 10.14–15, Christianity, Constantius.

18. Ammianus Marcellinus, *Res gestae* 26.6.11, dated Valens' departure to the end of winter, although in fact *CTh* 12.6.8 was still issued from Constantinople on July 30, 365; 26.7.2, at Caesarea. For Basil and Eusebius, see *Families and Friends*, Chapter 1; the influence of Valens' visit on Basil's dispute with the heresiarch Eunomius, *Becoming Christian*, Chapter 1.

19. Ammianus Marcellinus, *Res gestae* 21.16.20–21, Jovian, 23.3.2, 26.6.2, rumor, 7.16, family. Estate: Zosimus, *Historia nova* 4.4.3.

20. For Valens' lack of experience upon becoming emperor, see Zosimus, *Historia nova* 4.4.1.

21. Constantius' family: Ammianus Marcellinus, *Res gestae* 26.7.10, 9.3. Support of Gauls: Ammianus Marcellinus, *Res gestae* 26.7.4, with Sivan (1993) 98–99. For Procopius' supporters, see Grattarola (1986) 90–94; his connections with Constantine's family, Austin (1972) 189–91. Support from barbarians: Ammianus Marcellinus, *Res gestae* 26.10.3, Eunapius, *Fragmenta historica* 37, Zosimus, *Historia nova* 4.7.

22. *Pannonius degener.* Ammianus Marcellinus, *Res gestae* 26.7.16. For Constantine's origins in Moesia, see Barnes (1981) 3; for Constantinople as "la ville de la légitimité constantinienne," Dagron (1974) 26; for Julian's veneration for Constantinople as his birthplace, Ammianus Marcellinus, *Res gestae* 22.9.2, 25.3.23. Julian was only too aware of the stigma of his own ancestry, because he once argued that "although my family was Thracian, I am a Greek in my behavior": see Julian, *Misopogon* 367c. In the West he was certainly considered a Greek, since in Gaul his army had once mocked him as an "Asiatic" and a "little Greek": Ammianus Marcellinus, *Res gestae* 17.9.3, with Chapter 9, for Julian's notion of Hellenism. Goat's breath: Julian, *Epigram.* 1 = *Anthologia Graeca* 9.368. Insults: Libanius, *Orat.* 20.25; also 19.15. Beer drinker: Ammianus Marcellinus, *Res gestae* 26.8.2. Panegyric: Libanius, *Orat.* 1.163–65.

23. Hyperechius: Ammianus Marcellinus, *Res gestae* 26.8.5, with *PLRE* 1:449–50, Foss (1977a) 43–44, and Delmaire (1997) 118–20, on Procopius' supporters. Araxius may have been a native of Cappadocia or Pontus, since his daughter Vetiana was later a member of Macrina's monastic community: see GNys, *Vita Macrinae* 28, with Seeck (1906) 82–83, *PLRE* 1:94, and *Families and Friends*, Chapter 7. Although Philostorgius, *HE* 9.5, 8, claimed that at the beginning of Valens' reign Eunomius had sheltered Procopius on his estate outside Chalcedon, Ammianus Marcellinus, *Res gestae* 26.6.5, noted that Procopius stayed at Chalcedon with Strategius, a senator at Constantinople; for further discussion of Eunomius and Procopius, see *Becoming Christian*, Chapter 1.

24. Sophronius: Ammianus Marcellinus, *Res gestae* 26.7.2, with Chapter 3. Arcadius: B, *Ep.* 15, with Chapter 3. Contrary to *PLRE* 1:99 and Delmaire (1989a) 52, the letter does not suggest that Basil was now living in seclusion; it is better to assume, with Fedwick (1981) 11, and Forlin Patrucco (1983) 319, that Basil was already serving at Caesarea. In fact, an appropriate moment for Basil to request Arcadius' support would be shortly after his return to Caesarea in 365 to help bishop Eusebius. The next known *comes rei privatae* in the East is Alexandrianus, in office at least by May 367: see *PLRE* 1:44, and Delmaire (1989a) 55. Zeno: Theodoret, *Historia religiosa* 12.1, Pontus, 2, "the belt of a magistrate," with *PLRE* 1:992, "Zenon 6," and Canivet and Leroy-Molinghen (1977–1979) 1:461n.2, who identify Zeno as an *agens in rebus*. Primus the Younger and Arinthaeus: *Studia Pontica* 3.1:121, no. 99, an epitaph at Amaseia of Primus the Younger's daughter, dated to 376 or 377, that also mentioned other members of the family with senatorial rank that they perhaps acquired under Valens. Note the mistakes in *PLRE* 1, "Anonyma 10," "Arinthea," "Earinus," "Marius 3," and "Sabina 1": this daughter was the niece (not cousin) of Earinus and Sabina,

and the cousin (not niece) of Marius and Arenthea (not Arinthea). Her cousin Arenthea may have been the sister or daughter of Flavius Arinthaeus; if so, then Arinthaeus too was perhaps a native of Pontus. For Arinthaeus' career, see *PLRE* 1:102–3. Antonius Tatianus: see Roueché (1989a) 39–42.

25. Caesarius: see *Families and Friends*, Chapter 3. Valens also spruced up Julian's tomb, perhaps now: see Libanius, *Orat.* 24.10.

26. For the journeys of the imperial court during 370–372, see Seeck (1919) 239–43, May (1973) 50–54, and Van Dam (1986) 74–75; the account in Rousseau (1994) 351–53, is unreliable. In 371 Valens apparently campaigned against the Persians before going on to Antioch "at the end of summer": see Ammianus Marcellinus, *Res gestae* 29.1.4, correcting Barnes (1998) 253. Libanius, *Orat.* 1.144–45, seems to imply that Valens arrived at Antioch already before mid-August: see Van Dam (1986) 75–76.

27. For Modestus' career, see *PLRE* 1:605–8. Trials: Libanius, *Ep.* 37, *Orat.* 14.19–20, Ammianus Marcellinus, *Res gestae* 19.12.6. Gift from "two emperors": Libanius, *Ep.* 1216.1–2. House: Libanius, *Ep.* 1483.2. As a former prefect of the city Modestus would have been a prominent senator at Constantinople, but when Procopius presented himself at the senate house, only a few men of low rank appeared: see Ammianus Marcellinus, *Res gestae* 26.6.18. For the connection between Modestus and the water supply of Constantinople, see Mango (1995). Dagron (1974) 242–47, suggests that Modestus was prefect of Constantinople for a second time in the late 360s before becoming prefect of the East.

28. For Pannonian supporters promoted by Valentinian in the West, see Matthews (1975) 32–49.

29. Valens' ignorance of Greek: Themistius, *Orat.* 6.71C–D, Themistius apologizes for his inability to speak Latin to Valens; *Orat.* 8.105C, Valens did not speak "our words"; *Orat.* 10.129C, Valens had more respect for "our words" than for the words of "those who share your language." Petronius: Ammianus Marcellinus, *Res gestae* 26.6.7–9; also *CTh* 7.22.7, issued to Petronius in April 365 and "posted at Beirut." Festus, governor of Syria: Libanius, *Orat.* 1.156.

30. Olympius Palladius: see Seeck (1906) 228, and *PLRE* 1:662. Aelius Palladius: see *PLRE* 1:661. Clearchus: see Seeck (1906) 108–9, and *PLRE* 1:211–12. Vindaonius Magnus: see Seeck (1906) 199–200, and *PLRE* 1:536. Fortunatianus as philosopher, rhetorician, poet: Libanius, *Ep.* 694, 1425. Friendship with Modestus: Libanius, *Ep.* 364, mentioning Fortunatianus, who praised a man who had praised another man who had praised Modestus. *Comes*: *CTh* 7.13.2, 10.16.3, 10.19.5, 15.2.2, and Ammianus Marcellinus, *Res gestae* 29.1.5; other references for Fortunatianus in Seeck (1906) 159–60, *PLRE* 1:369, and Delmaire (1989a) 57–59.

31. Dedication: *L'année épigraphique 1907* (1908) 46, no. 164, from Chersonesus Taurica on the north coast of the Black Sea. This inscription is dated between 369 and 375 and identified the dedicator as "vir] clarissimus co[mes et magister." *PLRE* 1:1009–10, "Anonymus 21," suggests that this general might have been the *magister utriusque militiae* in the East, and that he might be identified with Julius, a *magister equitum et peditum* in the East during the 370s. Like Modestus, Julius had earlier opposed the usurper Procopius: see Ammianus Marcellinus, *Res gestae* 26.7.5, and *PLRE* 1:481, "Julius 2."

32. Modestus' paganism: Libanius, *Ep.* 791.2, misgivings; *Ep.* 804.4, "now you have acknowledged the gods whom you were admiring for a long time." Baptism: GNaz, *Orat.* 43.48. Vindaonius Magnus: Theodoret, *HE* 4.22. On Eunomius, see *Becoming Christian*, Chapter 1. Ship: Socrates, *HE* 4.16, Sozomen, *HE* 6.14. Robes rather than god: Themistius, *Orat.* 5.67D, in a panegyric for the emperor Jovian in 364. Themistius was arguing for toleration in religion, in contrast to the changes repeatedly demanded by previous emperors: see Dagron (1968) 163–72.

33. Elation: GNys, *Contra Eunomium* 1.127. Dedication of the Church of the Holy Apostles: Jerome, *Chronicon* s.a. 370, and *Chronicon Paschale* s.a. 370. Even after his successes over the Goths, Valens was still uneasy about his standing as emperor at Constantinople, a city closely associated with the dynasty of Constantine. The Church of the Holy Apostles was next to the mausoleum containing the tombs of Constantine and Constantius, and presiding over its dedication on April 9 allowed Valens to appropriate some of their prestige. But note that by the end of April Valens was already in Antioch: see *CTh* 10.19.5, issued at Antioch on April 30, with *PLRE* 1:369, "Fortunatianus 1." By leaving so quickly Valens had clearly decided to avoid having to preside over the festival on May 11 in Constantinople that celebrated the city's foundation and its founder, Constantine.

34. GNys, *Contra Eunomium* 1.131–38, first confrontation, 139–41, second confrontation. Dialogue: GNaz, *Orat.* 43.48–51. Basil's liver: GNys, *In Basilium fratrem* 10, with Van Dam (1986) 74–76, for discussion of the chronology, and Pouchet (1992b) 7–15, arguing that Basil became bishop in September 370. GNys, *Contra Eunomium* 1.139, belittled Demosthenes as "the man in charge of the food and the chief of the cooks," GNaz, *Orat.* 43.47, as the "chief cook"; Theodoret, *HE* 4.19.12, described him as "the administrator of the imperial food." Both Gregory of Nyssa and Gregory of Nazianzus called Demosthenes "Nabuzaradan," referring to the captain of the guard for the Babylonian king Nebuchadnezzar (cf. 2 Kings 25:8–20). Perhaps they considered this an appropriate comparison because the Septuagint had translated Nabuzaradan's office mentioned in 2 Kings 25 (= Septuagint 4 Kings 25) and Jeremiah 40:1 (= Septuagint 47:1) as ἀρχιμάγειρος, "chief cook." Demosthenes was certainly an influential member of the emperor's personal staff, perhaps even its high-ranking head, the *praepositus sacri cubiculi*, "superintendent of the sacred bedchamber," or perhaps the *castrensis*, a eunuch in charge of domestic accounts: see Hauser-Meury (1960) 60–61, and *PLRE* 1:249, "Demosthenes 1." The complaints in B, *Ep.* 79, about the threats of the prefect and the "administrator of the bedchamber" presumably referred to Modestus and Demosthenes: see May (1973) 55.

According to GNaz, *Orat.* 43.51, Modestus reported to Valens that "it is necessary to test another man, someone less distinguished." This concession was probably not a recommendation to support another candidate as bishop of Caesarea, as suggested by Rousseau (1994) 352n.9. In the context of Modestus' other comments about threats and violence it was more likely a recommendation to proceed with intimidating another bishop: see Bernardi (1992) 233n.3.

35. Armenian families: Eunapius, *Vitae sophistarum* 486, on Proaeresius, with *Families and Friends*, Chapter 1. For Constantine's nephew Hannibalianus and the meeting with Arsak, see above. Primate of primates: *Buzandaran Patmut'iwnk'* 4.4, in Garsoïan (1989) 111. For Armenian history, see Chaumont (1969) 147–64, on the

consecration of Gregory the Illuminator, and Garsoïan (1989) 375–76, Gregory the Illuminator, 395, Nerses, with *Becoming Christian*, Chapter 9. Hauschild (1990) 217n.394, suggests that the bishop "Narses" who joined Basil in signing B, *Ep.* 92, may have been the primate Nerses. Ancient custom: B, *Ep.* 122.

36. Ammianus Marcellinus, *Res gestae* 27.12.9–15, Pap and Arinthaeus, 29.1.1–4, campaigns in 371. On the interactions between the Roman empire and the Persian empire, see Blockley (1987), (1992) 5–45, 116–17.

37. *Clibanarii*: Ammianus Marcellinus, *Res gestae* 16.2.5, 10.8, with Eadie (1967), on armored cavalry, and Hyland (1990) 148–56, on armored horses. Statues: Julian, *Orat.* 1.37D, 2.57C. Persian iron cavalry: Ammianus Marcellinus, *Res gestae* 19.1.2, 7.4, 25.1.11–13, 3.4.

38. Factory at Caesarea: *Notitia Dignitatum orientalis* 11.26, "Clibanaria, Caesarea Cappadociae," with Jones (1964) 834–36, and James (1988). The *magister officiorum* assumed control over the arms factories certainly by the later fourth century: see Jones (1964) 369. For Sophronius, see Chapter 3. Valens as tribune: Ammianus Marcellinus, *Res gestae* 26.4.2, with Jones (1964) 625–26, and Scharf (1990), on the office, and Davies (1969), on the supply of horses. Cappadocian studs: Claudian, *Carmina minora* 30 = *Laus Serenae* 190–93, on Stilicho, who was *comes sacri stabuli* in ca. 384: see *PLRE* 1:854. Requisitions: *CTh* 11.17.1. Horse at Antioch: Theodoret, *Historia religiosa* 8.11–12. Trajan's horse: Ammianus Marcellinus, *Res gestae* 16.10.15.

39. Tax rates: Themistius, *Orat.* 8.112D–113C, with Vanderspoel (1995) 168, who dates the oration to March 368, and Jones (1964) 145–47, 414, 417, 732–33, for the new arrangements. Gold coins: *CTh* 12.6.12–13, with Hendy (1985) 386–94, on the concentration of the production of coinage in precious metals at court mints.

40. For the new provinces, see Chapter 5.

41. Auxonius' reputation: Zosimus, *Historia nova* 4.10.4.

42. Sophronius: B, *Ep.* 76, with Chapter 1, for more discussion of Basil's appeals.

43. Aristides' appeal: Philostratus, *Vitae sophistarum* 582. Julian at Nicomedia: Ammianus Marcellinus, *Res gestae* 22.9.4, with Chapter 9. Valens and Ephesus: Riccobono (1941) 511–13, no. 108, with Schulten (1906) 51–52, and Foss (1979) 188–91, a general survey of earthquakes at late antique Ephesus.

44. Maximinus' march: Lactantius, *De mortibus persecutorum* 45.2–3. Jovian: Philostorgius, *HE* 8.8. Monks: Sozomen, *HE* 6.34.

45. Accusations and trials: Ammianus Marcellinus, *Res gestae* 29.1.5–2.20 (quotation at 29.1.40). Celebration of Kalends: Gleason (1986) 108–13. Ancestral regulation: GNys, *Ep.* 14.1.

46. Soldiers celebrating the Kalends: Asterius of Amaseia, *Hom.* 4.7. Persian troops: Ammianus Marcellinus, *Res gestae* 27.12.18.

47. Payment of taxes: *CTh* 11.4.1, issued on April 4, 372, at "Seleucia," presumably Seleucia Pieria, the port of Antioch.

48. Celebration of Epiphany: GNaz, *Orat.* 43.52–53. Constantius at Rome: Ammianus Marcellinus, *Res gestae* 16.10.9–10.

49. Autonomy: B, *Ep.* 94. For the estates, see Chapter 2. Imperial edict: B, *Ep.* 99.1, 4; for additional nuances of this meeting between Basil and Valens, see Van Dam (1986) 53–58. Less plausible is the argument of Garsoïan (1983) 149–58, who

suggests that Basil was to provide bishops for the Armenian provinces in the Roman empire, rather than for the kingdom of Armenia; for counterarguments, see Giet (1941) 363–66.

50. Edict, and Modestus' request: GNaz, *Orat.* 43.54–55. Taxes: B, *Ep.* 104, 110, 281; Basil wrote these letters probably during the census that preceeded the start of a new indiction in September 372. Friendship: B, *Ep.* 109, 111.

51. Imperial estates: B, *Ep.* 104, τῷ βασιλικῷ οἴκῳ.

52. Patron and benefactor: B, *Ep.* 279, 280.

## *Chapter 7. Basil and Valens' Court at Antioch*

1. Arrival: GNys, *Vita Gregorii Thaumaturgii, PG* 46.920A. Complaint: Firmus of Caesarea, *Ep.* 12, with Chapter 3, on the identification of Helladius, the recipient. For the impact of the journeys of Roman emperors, see Millar (1977) 31–40, Halfmann (1986) 65–89, and Ziegler (1996) 126–27. For later Byzantine expeditions, especially as described by Constantine VII Porphyrogenitus, see Hendy (1985) 272–75, 304–15: "the through passage of the baggage-train was not something to be looked forward to" (314).

2. Modestus: GNaz, *Orat.* 43.48.

3. Meeting at Tomi: Sozomen, *HE* 6.21. GNys, *Contra Eunomium* 1.130, candor, 333, differences in rank. John the Baptist: GNys, *In Basilium fratrem* 14, with De Salvo (1983), on Basil's candor.

4. For Valens' lack of education, see Ammianus Marcellinus, *Res gestae* 31.14.5. Interpreter, culture: Themistius, *Orat.* 8.105D–106A, with Errington (2000) 878–93, for the relationship between Valens and Themistius, and Chapter 6, for Valens' limited familiarity with Greek. On the *Breviaria* of Eutropius and Festus, see Schmidt (1989). Note that one historian would think that Valens' death in battle was a direct consequence of his ignorance about history: see Eunapius, *Fragmenta historica* 44.1.

5. B, *Ep.* 74, Martinianus; *Ep.* 147, Aburgius; with Chapter 3, for their careers. For another bilingual correspondent, note GNaz, *Ep.* 173.1, on the prefect Postumianus: "You are most competent in culture, whichever one you prefer."

6. Emperor without the purple: Eunapius, *Vitae sophistarum* 490, with Jones (1964) 371–72, on the powers of prefects. Nursling: Libanius, *Ep.* 37.7. For a less charitable assessment of Modestus' learning, see Ammianus Marcellinus, *Res gestae* 30.4.2.

7. Evaluation: B, *Ep.* 111. Comparison with emperors: GNys, *De oratione dominica* 1, *PG* 44.1128D. Match the request: GNaz, *Ep.* 23.1–2. Private matters: B, *Ep.* 107. Delight: B, *Ep.* 281. Gentleness: B, *Ep.* 110. Hand and knees: B, *Ep.* 104. For the honorific titles in Basil's letters, see Gain (1985) 399–401.

8. For misleading interpretations of flattery, note MacMullen (1990) 71, "almost unintelligibly obsequious" (an otherwise excellent collection of examples of "the ample style"); and Gain (1985) 402: "l'impression d'un exercice de style un peu précieux, d'un raffinement de langage destiné à flatter." For flattery instead as a means for shaping behavior, see Dagron (1968) 84n.2: "Thémistios félicite de préférence les empereurs pour les qualités qui leur manquent manifestement le plus, ce

qui est une manière de leur en recommander l'usage." For a promising discussion of acclamations as part of "a continual process of negotiation," see Aldrete (1999) 162.

9. Gaius: Suetonius, *Gaius Caligula* 29.1. Teacher: B, *Hom. in Hexaemeron* 9.5. Valens in Cappadocia: GNys, *Contra Eunomium* 1.123. Tip of tongue: Ammianus Marcellinus, *Res gestae* 29.1.19.

10. Ammianus Marcellinus, *Res gestae* 29.1.20, anger, 30.6, Valentinian's death.

11. On the trials at Scythopolis, see Matthews (1989) 217–18. Many men: Ammianus Marcellinus, *Res gestae* 29.1.12, with Brown (1992) 48–61, on anger and decorum.

12. Ferocity: Ammianus Marcellinus, *Res gestae* 29.1.10. At Antioch Valens was perhaps especially concerned about the lingering prominence of supporters of Julian, who may also have supported Procopius: see Matthews (1989) 224–25.

13. Ammianus Marcellinus, *Res gestae* 29.1.27, wild animal, 2.18, Valens' failure to learn from history. Ancient myths: Himerius, *Orat.* 48.19, describing Hermogenes, with Barnes (1987) 218–20, for the argument that this was an appeal before the emperor Gallus. Gallus' education: Socrates, *HE* 3.1; for more discussion of Gallus at Antioch, see *Becoming Christian*, Chapter 1.

14. Ammianus Marcellinus, *Res gestae* 29.1.11, blossoms of Cicero; 31.14, Valens' virtues and vices. Aphrahat: Theodoret, *HE* 4.26.1–6, *Historia religiosa* 8.8, with Brock (1994), on the use of Greek and Syriac in the Near East.

15. Punch: Sozomen, *HE* 6.18. On the enforcement of imperial laws, see Harries (1999) 88, "From the perspective of the small-town politician, religious or secular, the emperor's will was a tool to be manipulated."

16. For Valens' buildings at Antioch, see Downey (1961) 403–10, 632–40. Persecution at Antioch: Socrates, *HE* 4.2, 17, Sozomen, *HE* 6.7, 18, Theodoret, *HE* 4.24–25, *Historia religiosa* 2.15, 19. Themistius' oration pleading for toleration: Socrates, *HE* 4.32, Sozomen, *HE* 6.36–37. Pouchet (1992a) 209n.3, 259, and Hauschild (1990) 29–30, suggest that Meletius had departed for exile by spring 372.

The trials for treason at Antioch may eventually have affected a cleric from Cappadocia. Basil appealed for assistance on behalf of a man named Eusebius in *Ep.* 177 to Sophronius, the *magister officiorum*, and in *Ep.* 178 to Aburgius. The letter to Aburgius argued that even though many men had been "exposed in most dangerous activities," Eusebius deserved a trial; Pouchet (1992a) 309, suggests that this Eusebius was not Eusebius of Samosata, but a reader at Caesarea caught up in the accusations of treason and magic.

17. B, *Ep.* 48, letters about Antioch; *Ep.* 66.2, Athanasius and Antioch; *Ep.* 258, to Epiphanius; *Ep.* 212.2, land and sea. After Athanasius' death Basil wrote about Antioch to Peter, his successor as bishop of Alexandria: see B, *Ep.* 266.2. For Basil's overtures to western bishops, see Grumel (1922), Taylor (1973), May (1973) 64–68, Gribomont (1975), Fedwick (1979) 107–13, and de Vries (1981).

18. B, *Ep.* 99.3, visit to Meletius' ἀγρός at Getasa, most likely in summer 372; for the location of Getasa, see Hauschild (1973) 156n.18. Meletius' hometown was Melitene, the metropolitan capital of Armenia Secunda in eastern Cappadocia, and he had previously served briefly as bishop at Sebasteia: see Philostorgius, *HE* 5.1, 5. Accusations at Antioch: B, *Ep.* 120. Appeals: B, *Ep.* 129.2. In *Ep.* 213.2 Basil mentioned that he was expecting a summons to the court, and that "this bishop" urged him to

gather his eastern supporters and hurry to the emperor. Pouchet (1988) 496–98, (1992a) 194, identifies "this bishop" as Meletius and dates the letter to autumn 375; Hauschild (1973) 183nn.332–33, suggests that "this bishop" was a bishop in Syria and dates the letter to early 375.

19. For Eusebius' visit in 370, see *Families and Friends*, Chapter 1. Basil's visit to Samosata: B, *Ep.* 105; also *Ep.* 138.1, 145, both letters sent to Eusebius in late 373 and hinting at a visit a year earlier. For Valens' tour, see *CTh* 14.13, issued in August 373 from Hierapolis, less than one hundred miles south of Samosata and previously used by the emperor Julian as a staging point for a campaign against Persia: see Ammianus Marcellinus, *Res gestae* 23.2.6, Zosimus, *Historia nova* 3.12.1. Birds and invitation: B, *Ep.* 145. Gregory of Nazianzus was too ill to visit with Eusebius when he passed through Cappadocia in 374: see GNaz, *Ep.* 64.1; perhaps he was still grieving over his father's death.

20. B, *Ep.* 118, to Jovinus, bishop of Perrhe, with Fedwick (1993) 477, for the uncertainty in the heading to this letter about the bishop's name and see; *Ep.* 127, visit from Jovinus; *Ep.* 132, to Abram, bishop of Batnae; *Ep.* 181, to Otreius, bishop of Melitene; *Ep.* 184, to Eustathius, bishop of Himmeria; *Ep.* 185, to Theodotus, bishop of Beroea; *Ep.* 220–21, to the people of Beroea; *Ep.* 222, to the people of Chalcis; *Ep.* 254, to Pelagius, bishop of Laodicea, who subsequently was exiled to Arabia: see Theodoret, *HE* 4.13.2–3; *Ep.* 255, to Vitus, bishop of Carrhae; *Ep.* 264, 267, to Barses, bishop of Edessa, who was already in exile: see Theodoret, *HE* 4.16.1–2.

21. B, *Ep.* 134, to the priest Paeonius, possibly at Antioch: see Pouchet (1992a) 356; *Ep.* 135, to Diodorus, a priest at Antioch; *Ep.* 140, to the church at Antioch; *Ep.* 253, to priests at Antioch; *Ep.* 256, to priests, deacons, and monks, with Canivet (1977) 113–15, for the location of their monastery at Gindaros, about thirty miles northeast of Antioch.

22. B, *Ep.* 99, to Terentius; *Ep.* 148–49, to Traianus, who can probably be identified with the military count: see *PLRE* 1:921–22; *Ep.* 179, to Arinthaeus, probably to be identified as the general Flavius Arinthaeus whom Basil may have met at Caesarea in early 372: see Chapter 6; *Ep.* 152–53, to Victor, whom Basil perhaps had first met when he had marched Julian's army from Constantinople to Antioch in 362: see Zosimus, *Historia nova* 3.11.3, with *PLRE* 1:957–59; *Ep.* 112, to Andronicus, identified in the heading to the letter as a governor, probably of Armenia Prima, since Basil had hoped to see him at Sebasteia; cf. *Ep.* 306, whose recipient, identified in the heading as the "governor of Sebasteia," was probably the governor of Armenia Prima. Support for Nicene theology: Theodoret, *HE* 4.28.2, Traianus and monk, 32, Terentius, 33, Traianus, Arinthaeus, Victor. After Arinthaeus' death Basil sent condolences to his widow: B, *Ep.* 269, with Woods (2001), suggesting an earlier date for Arinthaeus' death. Sophronius: B, *Ep.* 96, Sophronius should recommend a man "to the emperor"; *Ep.* 180, Sophronius should receive a "petition for the emperors"; *Ep.* 192, hopes to see Sophronius; *Ep.* 272.1, flatterers and bees. Aburgius: B, *Ep.* 147, 178, 196, with Delmaire (1989a) 61–62, on his office, and Chapter 3. Note B, *Ep.* 274, to Himerius, who may have succeeded Sophronius as *magister officiorum*: see *PLRE* 1: 437, "Himerius 5," and Clauss (1980) 109, 161.

23. Reminder: B, *Ep.* 99, mentioning Terentius' "friendly letter."

24. Consecration by Anthimus: B, *Ep.* 120–22. Fire and smoke: B, *Ep.* 222.

25. B, *Ep.* 225: the στρατιῶται who seized Gregory were probably bureaucrats on the vicar's staff, not soldiers. In this letter Basil described the recipient as a magistrate in "our homeland"; only the heading to the letter named him as Demosthenes: see Fedwick (1993) 398. This vicar Demosthenes should not be identified with the Demosthenes who had confronted Basil a few years earlier, as suggested by Pouchet (1992a) 380, and Demoen (1994) 305. None of the Cappadocian Fathers explicitly identified the two. In addition, if the earlier Demosthenes had been a *cubicularius*, one of the chamberlains in the emperor's bedchamber (see Chapter 6), then he was most likely a eunuch and a barbarian, characteristics that would have made his selection as a vicar (or other civilian magistrate) unlikely: see Jones (1964) 567. Nor is this vicar Demosthenes necessarily to be identified with the unnamed vicar who had Basil's bedroom searched after the bishop sheltered a widow: see Van Dam (1996) 39–40.

The chronology and sequence of events leading to the deposition of Gregory of Nyssa are endlessly debatable. Hauschild (1973) 9–10, (1993) 7–9, argues that Demosthenes convened the council at Galatia in December 374 and visited Antioch in the following January and February, and that the council at Nyssa that led to Gregory's replacement met in April 375. Pouchet (1992a) 373–92, argues more plausibly that Gregory was arrested and went into seclusion in spring of 375, that Demosthenes convened the council in Galatia during the following winter, and that the council at Nyssa replaced Gregory in spring of 376. May (1971) 54, and Maraval (1990) 21, place Gregory's arrest between the council in Galatia in late 375 and the council at Nyssa and his replacement in early 376. Daniélou (1965) 34–38, dates the council at Nyssa that deposed Gregory in early 377.

26. B, *Ep.* 237: the council in Galatia met "in the middle of winter"; the council at Nyssa included "men from Galatia and Pontus," who were presumably bishops. In this letter Basil referred to the activities of a vicar, but provided no name; a later scribal gloss identified the vicar as Demosthenes: see Pouchet (1992a) 374–75. B, *Ep.* 226.2, mentioned a meeting of Basil's opponents at Ancyra, which was probably this council in Galatia, and a letter delivered from Basil's opponents to the vicar's staff, apparently when he was at Caesarea. For the perception of the vicar as a court official rather than a regional magistrate like a provincial governor, note that Gregory of Nazianzus classified the vicar with the emperor and the prefect when describing Basil's "war with the world": GNaz, *Orat.* 43.58.

27. Enemies: B, *Ep.* 231. Terentius: B, *Ep.* 214.2; cf. *Ep.* 215–16, mentioning letters to Terentius. Abram: B, *Ep.* 132. Appeals to court: B, *Ep.* 247.

28. Evagrius: B, *Ep.* 138.2, visit; *Ep.* 156.3, separation. Jerome, *Ep.* 3.3, trip through Asia Minor, dated to 368 by Booth (1981), to the summer of 373 by Kelly (1975) 36–38, and Scourfield (1986), to the summer of 374 by Cavallera (1922) 1:25. Jerome and Evagrius: Jerome, *Vita Malchi* 3 (*PL* 23.53C–54A), *Ep.* 7.1, 15.5. Arrogance: Jerome, *Chronicon* s.a. 376. Jerome composed his *Chronicon* at Constantinople in ca. 380: see Cavallera (1922) 1:63–68, 2:20, and Kelly (1975) 72–75; but by placing his entry about Basil under the year 376, he seems deliberately to have wanted to associate his evaluation of Basil with his stay in Syria. Jerome's later estimation of Basil was more cautiously laudatory: see Jerome, *De viris illustribus* 116.

29. Many friends: B, *Ep.* 117; this letter was apparently a response to *Ep.* 116 by

Firminus, who was planning to leave service at the court but is otherwise unknown. Perhaps he was related to another Firminus, a native of Cappadocia who also left service in the imperial administration during the early 390s: see Chapter 3. Court's decisions: B, *Ep.* 129.2.

30. Criticism of new bishops: B, *Ep.* 239.1. B, *Ep.* 231, "Doara has received back the old muleteer." Deferrari (1926–1934) 3:361n.6, identifies this "muleteer" as Demosthenes; Hauschild (1993) 203n.179, suggests that he was the new bishop belittled as a "household slave" in B, *Ep.* 239.1, Pouchet (1992a) 565, that he was the Georgius mentioned in B, *Ep.* 239.1, whom he identifies as the former bishop of Doara; Devos (1993) 74–80, identifies him as the bishop who had preceeded the deposed bishop of Doara and who had now returned to his see.

31. Appeal: B, *Ep.* 227. Expulsion: B, *Ep.* 238, 240.2, 242.2, with Van Dam (1985a), 68–69, 79, for penalties on heretics. Angel of Satan: B, *Ep.* 248. Disturbances, sea monster: B, *Ep.* 231, with Devos (1992) 251–54, on the date.

32. Compliments: B, *Ep.* 225.

33. On the military importance of Samosata for linking Cappadocia and Syria, see Syme (1995) 105.

34. Silk robes: GNys, *De beatitudinibus* 1, PG 44.1204B. Cloaks: Asterius of Amaseia, *Hom.* 1.3.3, with *Families and Friends*, Chapter 3, on Naucratius' reputation as a hunter. Church: Nilus of Sinai, *Ep.* 4.61, PG 79.577B–580A, with PLRE 2:799, "Olympiodorus 3"; Nilus recommended that the shrine be decorated instead with a cross and scenes from the Bible. Commodus at Rome: Dio, *Hist.* 73.18–21, Herodian, *Hist.* 1.15. Gratian: Ammianus Marcellinus, *Res gestae* 31.10.19; his portrait: Ausonius, *Epigram.* 30, with the commentary of Green (1991) 379, 381.

35. Marcus Antonius: Plutarch, *Antonius* 29.4. Hadrianotherae: Dio, *Hist.* 69.10.2, SHA, *Hadrian* 20.13, with Stadter (1980) 50–59, and Birley (1997) 137–38, 184–85, 240–41, 284, on Hadrian's hunts. For an explicit connection between hunting and the imposition of Roman might, see Plutarch, *Pompey* 12.5. Yourcenar (1954) 6, nicely summarized the importance of hunting for Hadrian: "My hunts ... have helped me as emperor to judge the courage or the resources of high officials." Imperial icons: GNaz, *Orat.* 4.80.

36. Personalities: note B, *Ep.* 79, for a complaint that the prefect and the "administrator of the bedchamber" (presumably referring to Modestus and Demosthenes) had supported Basil's opponents ἰδιοπαθῶς, "from personal motives." Quotations from Geertz (1983) 125, 135, 138.

37. Licinius' lions: Sozomen, *HE* 4.16. Galerius' bears: Lactantius, *De mortibus persecutorum* 21.5. Julian: GNaz, *Orat.* 2.87. Valentinian's bears: Ammianus Marcellinus, *Res gestae* 29.3.9, with Matthews (1989) 258–61, on Ammianus' animal imagery. Basil and Modestus: GNaz, *Orat.* 43.48, "presenting the appearance of a lion," 50, boldness; with Gleason (1995) 61–62, 73, on manliness and leonine deportment.

## Chapter 8. Gregory of Nazianzus at Constantinople

1. Wild animals: Ammianus Marcellinus, *Res gestae* 31.8.9, with Wolfram (1988) 117–31, and Heather (1991) 122–47, on the Gothic settlements and raids. The

court at Antioch had remained informed about the Goths through letters and visits by imperial magistrates. In particular, in spring or summer of 376 the vicar of Thrace and the *praepositus* of a storage depot for imperial revenues at Philippopolis traveled through Cappadocia to Thrace, perhaps conveying Valens' decision about this Gothic settlement: see B, *Ep.* 237.1, with *PLRE* 1:1015, "Anonymus 60," for the anonymous vicar; *PLRE* 1 did not include the anonymous *praepositus*. In late 376 Basil noted that the presence of "enemies," presumably the Goths, prevented travel by land between Constantinople and Rome: see B, *Ep.* 215.

2. Headaches: Ammianus Marcellinus, *Res gestae* 30.2.2; on Persia and Armenia, see Blockley (1987) 227–30. Modestus was last attested as prefect in *CJ* 8.10.8 and 11.62.5, issued respectively on October 20 and November 2, 377; note that the months are incorrectly reversed in *PLRE* 1:607, followed by Rousseau (1994) 362n.10, and Barnes (1997) 9n.18. Errington (1997) 24–33, dates Valens' recall as early as summer 377, Snee (1985) 402, and Maraval (1988) 29, to September or October, Barnes (1997) 4–6, to early spring 378.

3. Gregory's triumph: GNys, *Ep.* 6.6, with Maraval (1990) 22–23, for the suggestion that Gregory was describing his return from exile in late 377. Retreat: B, *Ep.* 268, "we hear about the passage of the court," with Millar (1977) 42–43, Gain (1985) 292, and Barnes (1997) 9–13, for the translation of στρατόπεδον as "imperial court" (= *comitatus*), not "army."

4. Valens' support for Demophilus: Socrates, *HE* 4.14–15, Sozomen, *HE* 6.13. Chanting: Philostorgius, *HE* 9.10. Reputation as speaker: *Suda* Δ.470. Sermon: Philostorgius, *HE* 9.14. Pretense: B, *Ep.* 48.

5. GNaz, *Carm.* II.1.12.77–78, unnamed man, 93–94, his exile. In his commemorative oration about Basil, Gregory would hint that he had become an "exile" at Constantinople "not without the approval of that distinguished champion of the truth": see *Orat.* 43.2. In a prayer about his trip to Constantinople, Gregory mentioned the life of leisure he was giving up and his hope of returning to his friends and relatives: see *Carm.* II.1.3.2, 20. Gregory eventually left Constantinople in summer 381; since he described the length of his stay as three years (*Carm.* II.1.12.101), he may well have gone, or agreed to go, to the capital before Basil's death. Pouchet (1992b) 23–26, suggests that Gregory had gone to Constantinople already early in 378, Barnes (1997) 13, in autumn 378, Bernardi (1995) 153, 175–77, in early 379. For a general survey of Gregory's tenure in Constantinople, see Mossay (1977).

6. Devastation: GNaz, *Orat.* 22.2, dated after Easter 379 and considered the earliest of Gregory's extant orations from Constantinople by Gallay (1943) 139–43, and Bernardi (1968) 144, (1995) 185–88; dated sometime during Gregory's tenure at Constantinople by Mossay and Lafontaine (1980) 205, 222n.1. Imperial patronage: GNaz, *Orat.* 25.3; in *Orat.* 32.33 Gregory addressed the "rulers of the people" in his audience, who were presumably magistrates. Baptism: GNaz, *Orat.* 40.26. Criticism: GNaz, *Orat.* 33.8, 36.1, *Carm.* II.1.11.696–702.

7. Stoning: GNaz, *Ep.* 77.3, with Gallay (1943) 138. Barbarians: GNaz, *Orat.* 33.2. For contemporary attitudes in the aftermath of the battle of Adrianople, see Lenski (1997).

8. Military recruitment: Jones (1964) 156, and Errington (1996) 5–7. Orthodoxy: *CTh* 16.1.2 = *CJ* 1.1.1, issued February 27, 380. GNaz, *Carm.* II.1.11.750–59,

Maximus' appearance, 810–12, meals, 970–71, new converts, 974–75, conversion. Athanasius as "the guide of your confession": GNaz, *Orat.* 25.11, with Mossay (1982), on Maximus' orthodoxy. *Orat.* 25 was delivered in honor of the philosopher "Heron," whom Jerome, *De viris illustribus* 117, identified as Maximus: see Hauser-Meury (1960) 119n.231. Gregory's admission that he had once honored Maximus with a "great encomium" might be a reference to this oration: see GNaz, *Carm.* II.1.11.954–55. Gallay (1943) 161–65, argues that Gregory delivered *Orat.* 25 in mid-379 while he and Maximus were friends, and that Maximus then acquired Peter's support, perhaps after a trip to Egypt; Szymusiak (1966) 185, dates the oration to autumn 379. Bernardi (1968) 168–72, argues that Gregory was still friendly with Maximus in March 380, when he sent him as his representative to bishop Peter of Alexandria, whom Theodosius had just named in his imperial edict as a guarantor of orthodoxy, and that *Orat.* 25 was an encomium on Maximus' departure.

9. GNaz, *Carm.* II.1.11.824–27, priest, 858–60, letters from Peter, 875–83, Thasos, 887–97, sailors, 1007, edict, 1009, dog, 1021, prefect. Lobbyists at Thessalonica: Zosimus, *Historia nova* 4.25.1, 27.1. Chagrin: *CTh* 10.10.15, issued November 16, 380. Delegation from senate: Themistius, *Orat.* 14. Other appeals from Constantinople: *CTh* 10.18.2, on the discovery of buried treasure, issued in Janurary 380 to the people of Constantinople. Gallay (1943) 165n.6, and Bernardi (1968) 172n.174, argue that Maximus visited Theodosius at Thessalonica before mid-July. In fact, although Theodosius did leave Thessalonica then for a visit to other cities, he returned by mid-September, when Maximus could have visited: see Seeck (1919) 255. *PLRE* 1:473, "Iulianus 19," suggests that this prefect in Egypt may perhaps be identified with Julianus, attested as prefect of Egypt (only) in March 380; but note the skepticism of Hauser-Meury (1960) 185. Maximus later tried to find support in the West: see Jerome, *De viris illustribus* 127, for a treatise he presented to the emperor Gratian, with McLynn (1994) 110–11, 141–43, and Errington (1997) 67–72. He also launched another attack on Gregory: see GNaz, *Carm.* II.1.41, for Gregory's sarcastic response.

10. Emperors: GNaz, *Orat.* 25.9–10. Schism: GNaz, *Carm.* II.1.11.1051.

11. Students at Athens: GNaz, *Orat.* 43.15–16. Holy temple: Eunapius, *Vitae sophistarum* 483, with Frantz (1988) 42–47, Camp (1989), and Karivieri (1994), on houses used as schools in Athens. For the limits of Gregory's influence on Jerome, see Kelly (1975) 70–71, Mathieu (1988), Moreschini (1988), Adkin (1991), and Rebenich (1997). Flowed to sermons: GNaz, *Carm.* II.1.6.4–5, with Lim (1995) 158–71, on Gregory's rhetoric and the creation of a community at Constantinople, and *Becoming Christian*, Chapter 6, for the quality of Gregory's preaching.

12. GNaz, *Carm.* II.1.11.1261–72, farmer's rewards, 1273–74, end of account, 1279, arrival of emperor. Theodosius' "sudden" arrival might suggest that he was not expected: see Errington (1997) 36–41.

13. Turning post: GNaz, *Orat.* 38.10, dated to Christmas 379 by Gallay (1943) 153–59, to Christmas 380 by Bernardi (1968) 199–205, and Moreschini and Gallay (1990) 16–22. For the announcements of these victories, see *Consularia Constantinopolitana* s.a. 379, 380; for the liklihood of victory races, see McCormick (1986) 41–42.

14. Arrival on November 24: Socrates, *HE* 5.6, and *Chronicon Paschale* s.a. 378. Skepticism over Theodosius' victories: Zosimus, *Historia nova* 4.33.1, with the

interpretation of McCormick (1986) 42n.30. For commemoration of Theodosius' victories on his monuments at Constantinople, see Geyssen (1998).

15. Constantine's baptism: Eusebius, *Vita Constantini* 4.62.5. Theodosius' baptism: Socrates, *HE* 5.6, Sozomen, *HE* 7.4. Theodosius and Constantine's robe: George the Monk, *Chronicon* 9.8, ed. de Boor (1978) 2:563.

16. For the correspondence between Ascholius and Damasus about events at Constantinople, see Damasus, *Ep.* 5–6, *PL* 13.365–70, with Pietri (1972), who highlights Theodosius' increasing autonomy from Damasus after moving to Constantinople. For Theodosius' western supporters, see Matthews (1975) 109–15; for his inexperience, McLynn (1994) 109: "Strikingly unqualified to govern the east,... he was acutely dependent upon local expertise."

17. Delegation: Themistius, *Orat.* 14.182B–D. Themistius delivered this panegyric at Thessalonica in spring 379: see Dagron (1968) 23, and Vanderspoel (1995) 195.

18. Expulsion of Demophilus: Socrates, *HE* 5.7, Sozomen, *HE* 7.5. GNaz, *Carm.* II.1.11.1311–12, remark, 1325–95, mob and march.

19. Envy: GNaz, *Orat.* 36.5, delivered perhaps in mid-December, 380: see Bernardi (1968) 193, and Moreschini and Gallay (1985) 40–41; for discussion, see Gómez Villegas (1997). Statue of Julian: *Parastaseis syntomoi chronikai* 46.

20. Theodosius: GNaz, *Carm.* II.1.11.1282–1301, evaluation, 1306, first meeting, 1320–21, happiness and apprehension, 1407–35, gentleness. Expulsion of Evagrius in 370: Socrates, *HE* 4.14–15, Sozomen, *HE* 6.13. Although Bernardi (1968) 165, identifies the βασιλικὸν δόγμα mentioned in GNaz, *Orat.* 33.13, with *CTh* 16.1.2 (issued in early 380), Moreschini and Gallay (1985) 21–22, 185n.4, Snee (1985) 412n.95, and Barnes (1997) 15, date this sermon to summer 379. For Theodosius' tendency to resort to the use of soldiers, see Brown (1992) 103–15.

21. Proverb: GNaz, *Orat.* 36.11. Oration to Valens: Themistius, *Orat.* 7.89D, delivered during the winter of 366–367, with Dagron (1968) 150–53, for Themistius' knowledge of the Bible. Themistius cited Proverbs 21:1 again in *Orat.* 11.147C, a panegyric delivered at Antioch in 373 in honor of the tenth anniversary of Valens' accession, as well as in *Orat.* 19.229A, a panegyric in honor of Theodosius delivered at Constantinople in 384. For the dates of these orations, see Vanderspoel (1995) 162, 177, 213.

22. Recommendation: GNaz, *Orat.* 37.23. Bernardi (1968) 216–17, and Moreschini and Gallay (1985) 48, argue that *CTh* 16.5.6 = *CJ* 1.1.2, issued on January 10, 381, was a response to Gregory's oration.

23. Arrival of Athanaric: Ammianus Marcellinus, *Res gestae* 27.5.10, Zosimus, *Historia nova* 4.34.4–5; for the date of January 11, see *Consularia Constantinopolitana* s.a. 381. Generosity: Themistius, *Orat.* 15.190C–D, with Vanderspoel (1995) 199–204, who dates this oration to January 19, 381.

24. Monuments in the Forum of Theodosius, also known as the Forum of the Bull: *Notitia urbis Constantinopolitanae* 8.13, *Chronicon Paschale* s.a. 393, 394, John Malalas, *Chronographia* 16.13, with Janin (1964) 64–68, 81–82, and Mango (1985) 43–45. Praise of building projects: Themistius, *Orat.* 18.222C, dated to summer 384 by Vanderspoel (1995) 210–11, to probably the winter of 384–385 by Dagron (1968) 23–24. Anniversary celebration: *Chronicon Paschale* s.a. 330, with Dagron (1974) 37–42, and Krautheimer (1983) 61–62.

25. Dedication: *ILS* 1:182, no. 821, with Janin (1964) 189–91; for photographs and perceptive comments on the reliefs, see Safran (1993).

26. Opening date: Socrates, *HE* 5.8, with Ritter (1965) 41, 85. Meletius' early arrival: Socrates, *HE* 5.8, Sozomen, *HE* 7.7, with Ritter (1965) 33–40. Theodosius' vision: Theodoret, *HE* 5.6.1–2. Greeting: Theodoret, *HE* 5.7.2–3. A few months later a grieving Theodosius participated in the funeral procession for Meletius at Constantinople: see GNys, *Oratio funebris in Meletium episcopum*, PG 46.861D–864A.

27. GNaz, *Carm.* II.1.11.1680–89, reactions at council, 1745, illness. In *CTh* 16.1.3, issued July 30, 381, Theodosius defined orthodoxy in terms of the preferences of various prominent bishops, but did not mention a bishop for Antioch.

28. GNaz, *Carm.* II.1.11.1871–1904, meeting with emperor; *Ep.* 130.4, request and illness; cf. *Orat.* 42.21, for a comparison between the "holy war" and the "barbarian war."

29. "Second Rome": Socrates, *HE* 1.16. "New Rome": Council of Constantinople, *Canon.* 3. Founder: Themistius, *Orat.* 18.223A–B, referred to a "third city," the first two having been founded by the legendary Byzas and the emperor Constantine. Equestrian statue of Theodosius: *Anthologia Graeca* 16.65, with Krautheimer (1983) 55–56, 62–67, on Constantine as the sun god, and Mango (1985) 25, on the statue and column. Gregory noted that the people of Constantinople were inordinately proud of "that splendid and admired column": see GNaz, *Orat.* 33.6. Since he was most likely referring to Constantine's porphyry column, his comment can lay claim to being the earliest literary allusion: see Fowden (1991).

30. Churches: Council of Constantinople, *Canon.* 2, with Mathisen (1997) 667–68. Treaty: *Consularia Constantinopolitana* s.a. 382, treaty dated to October 3, with Heather (1991) 157–81. Friend: Jordanes, *Getica* 146, with Errington (1996), for a survey of Theodosius' negotiations with the Goths.

31. Letter of thanks: Council of Constantinople, *Epistula synodalis ad Theodosium imperatorem* (*CPG* 4:26, no. 8598), ed. Pitra (1864–1868) 1:507–8.

32. Priesthood: GNaz, *Orat.* 42.19, with Bernardi (1968) 226–35, (1988), (1992) 7–25, suggesting that Gregory later edited this oration, and McLynn (1998) 474–77, on Gregory's stance as an independent outsider at the capital.

33. Church of the Holy Apostles: GNaz, *Orat.* 36.12, "you might be the city of God, and you might be painted on the hands of the Lord," with Bernardi (1968) 198. Church of Holy Wisdom: GNaz, *Orat.* 42.26.

34. Yearning and Bethlehem: GNaz, *Carm.* II.1.16.61–62. Ornament: GNaz, *Ep.* 88.1, with Gallay (1964–1967) 1:xxxvi–xxxvii, discussing the authenticity of this letter. Teach the emperor: GNaz, *Ep.* 202.22. Desert: GNaz, *Orat.* 42.24. Other indications of his yearning for the Anastasia: GNaz, *Carm.* II.1.5, 6, 15.49–52, 27.12, with *Becoming Christian*, Chapter 10.

35. Legal standing of bishops: *CTh* 11.39.8 = *CJ* 1.3.7, "pars actorum habitorum in consistorio," issued June 29. Orthodox bishops: *CTh* 16.1.3, issued July 30. Council at Constantinople in June 383: Socrates, *HE* 5.10; Sozomen, *HE* 7.12, added that Theodosius reinforced his decision by an imperial edict, presumably *CTh* 16.5.11, issued on July 25. Seat in church: Sozomen, *HE* 7.25.9. Decree from heaven: Themistius, *Orat.* 16.207B, with Vanderspoel (1995) 205, for the date.

36. Invitation: GNaz, *Ep.* 130, to Procopius, possibly a vicar: see Van Dam

(1996) 66–67; *Ep.* 131, to Olympius, governor of Cappadocia. For the occasion, see Theodoret, *HE* 5.8.10, mentioning a council that met "again in that city during the next summer" after the general council at Constantinople in 381. GNaz, *Carm.* II.1.17.59, companion, 91–92, councils. For the order of *comites*, see Jones (1964) 526–28, and Roueché (1989a) 30–31.

37. Land of Cappadocia: GNaz, *Carm.* II.1.10.35–36, a poem composed during his departure from Constantinople. Nectarius: GNaz, *Ep.* 88, 91, 151, 185, 186, 202. Cleric: GNaz, *Ep.* 164, to Timotheus, perhaps a priest at Constantinople, with Hauser-Meury (1960) 174. Generals: GNaz, *Ep.* 132, 181, to Saturninus, who also became consul in 383; *Ep.* 133–34, to Victor; *Ep.* 136–37, to Modares; *Ep.* 225, to Ellebichus. Magistrates: GNaz, *Ep.* 103, 170, perhaps also *Ep.* 110, 119, to Palladius, the *magister officiorum*, with Hauser-Meury (1960) 140–41, and Clauss (1980) 177–78; *Ep.* 93, 135, to Sophronius, the prefect of Constantinople; *Ep.* 173, to Postumianus, the prefect of the East in 383. Friends: GNaz, *Ep.* 95, to Leontius; *Ep.* 96, to Hypatius, who visited Constantinople in 381 after serving as prefect of Rome; *Ep.* 168, to Photius; *Ep.* 169, to Strategius; quotation from *Ep.* 97, to Heraclianus. Weaknesses: GNaz, *Ep.* 94.3, to Alypius, identified as a friend at Constantinople by Hauser-Meury (1960) 29. McLynn (1997) 302, attributes to Gregory a stronger "properiety interest in the capital"; see also Elm (2000), on Gregory's contacts with friends at Constantinople.

38. Trapezus: Arrian, *Periplus* 1.3–4, with Mitford (1974) 160–3, for discussion of the dedicatory inscription, and Birley (1997) 155. Caesarea: B, *Ep.* 46.4. Nazianzus: GNaz, *Ep.* 141.9, for the destruction of statues, probably imperial statues.

39. Statues at Constantinople: Dagron (1984) 128–32. Relics of Samuel: Jerome, *Contra Vigilantium* 5, *PL* 23.343C–D, and *Chronicon Paschale* s.a. 406, 411. Epitaphs at Constantinople: Feissel (1995).

40. Gate of palace: *Petitiones Arianorum* 4, *PG* 26.821C, an appeal to Jovian from opponents of Athanasius. Invitations: Libanius, *Orat.* 20.46–47, to Theodosius and his son. Imperial palace and ascetic: John Rufus, *Plerophoriae* 88, tr. Nau (1912) 142–44. Theodosius may even have issued an edict that restricted emperors from commanding wars in person: see John the Lydian, *De magistratibus* 2.11, 3.41. For visits by the emperor Arcadius to Ancyra in the summers of 396–398 and 405, see Seeck (1919) 291–95, 309. During one trip Arcadius was annoyed to find that provincial magistrates were already allowing others to use imperial lodges in his absence: see *CTh* 7.10.1, issued from Ancyra in July 405. For exiles to Cappadocia during the fifth century, see Hild and Restle (1981) 68. John Chrysostom was first exiled to "the very isolated town" of Cucusus, just north of the Taurus Mountains: see Palladius, *Dialogus de vita Iohannis Chrysostomi* 11, with the description of Meyer (1985) 187n.384, "apparently the Siberia of the Eastern Empire." For the "fortress of oblivion," a detention center for Persian notables, see Procopius, *Bella* 1.5.7–8. Visit by Heraclius in 612: Georgius of Sykeon, *Vita Theodori Syceotae* 153–54, 166; Nicephorus, *Breviarium* 2; Sebeos, *Pamut'iwn*, tr. Thomson and Howard-Johnston (1999) 1:81, 83; with Foss (1977a) 68–72, for Heraclius' campaigns on the eastern frontier.

41. New garrisons at Caesarea and Mocissus: Procopius, *De aedificiis* 5.4.14, 16. Taxes and banditry: Arrian, *Periplus* 11.2, with Bosworth (1976) 70–72, on barbarian bandits. Edict of 536: Justinian, *Novellae* 30.2–4, magistrates, 5, imperial estates, 6, gold and clothing, 11, campaigns, with Kaplan (1981) 126–37, (1992) 140–42, 149–52.

42. For the rise of great Cappadocian landowners and their challenges to the Byzantine emperors during the tenth and eleventh centuries, see Morris (1976), Kaplan (1992) 326–38, 359–68, the excellent survey in Howard-Johnston (1995), and Chapter 4.

43. For the decline of cities in Asia Minor from the later sixth century, see Foss (1975), (1977b), and the comprehensive survey in Brandes (1989).

## Culture Wars Introduction

1. "Loquacious and rarely silent": Ammianus Marcellinus, *Res gestae* 25.4.17. Such virtue: Libanius, *Orat.* 18.307.

2. Disciple: Julian, *Ep.* 4.385B. "Filosofi[ae] magistro": *ILS* 1:167, no. 751, near Pergamum. Horse race: Julian, *Misopogon* 351D, referring to his teacher Mardonius. Amulets: Julian, *Ep.* 29. Destiny: Ammianus Marcellinus, *Res gestae* 15.8.17, citing *Iliad* 5.83. Alone: Julian, *Orat.* 8.241D, citing *Iliad* 11.401. Constantius: Julian, *Orat.* 2.50A, with Athanassiadi (1981) 63, "this elephantine hint." See Lamberton (1986) 134–39, for Julian's interpretation of Homer, and Bouffartigue (1992) 143–56, for the extent of his reading.

3. Quotation about cultural system from Geertz (1975) 89.

4. Licinius' characterization of culture: *Epitome de Caesaribus* 41.8.

5. Teachers at Athens: GNaz, *Orat.* 43.21.

## Chapter 9. Julian in Asia Minor

1. Acclamations: Zosimus, *Historia nova* 3.11. Installation of consuls: Mamertinus, *Gratiarum actio* = *Panegyrici latini* 3.28–30.

2. Liberty for state: Mamertinus, *Gratiarum actio* = *Panegyrici latini* 3.30.3. Threats: Julian, *Ep. ad Themistium* 259B. Nicomedia: Libanius, *Orat.* 18.13–15. Bodyguard, visit to Maximus at Ephesus: Eunapius, *Vitae sophistarum* 474–75.

3. Reader: Socrates, *HE* 3.1. Aetius: Philostorgius, *HE* 3.27. Visits Gallus: Ammianus Marcellinus, *Res gestae* 15.2.7. Acropolis: Julian, *Ep. ad Athenienses* 275A, with Athanassiadi (1981) 13–51, for an excellent survey of Julian's early intellectual development. Rivals in Gaul: Matthews (1989) 87–93.

4. Secundus: see *PLRE* 1:814–17, "Saturninius Secundus Salutius 3." Invitation to Aetius: Julian, *Ep.* 15; to Eutherius: Julian, *Ep.* 10, with *PLRE* 1:314–15, "Eutherius 1." Invitation to Proaeresius: Julian, *Ep.* 14; presumably Julian offered to show him captured letters that supposedly proved Constantius' treachery in inviting barbarians to attack Gaul and keep Julian preoccupied there: see Ammianus Marcellinus, *Res gestae* 21.3.4–5, with Nixon and Rodgers (1994) 401n.38. Invitation to Priscus: Eunapius, *Vitae sophistarum* 477, with *PLRE* 1:730, "Priscus 5."

5. Mithraic mysteries: Himerius, *Orat.* 41.1, with Barnes (1987) 221–22. Maximus' reputation: Eunapius, *Vitae sophistarum* 475, with *PLRE* 1:583–84, "Maximus 21." Julian, *Ep.* 8.415C, veneration of gods, 415D, order from gods.

6. Robes: Ammianus Marcellinus, *Res gestae* 20.4.22.

7. Ammianus Marcellinus, *Res gestae* 22.4.9–10, barbers, 22.7.1, humbled himself, 3, senate, Maximus' arrival. Himself as senator: *CTh* 9.2.1. Libanius, *Orat.* 18.130, staff, eunuchs, 131–45, functionaries, 154, debates, 155–56, greets Maximus, 191–92, purple robes and crown; with Dvornik (1955), (1966) 2:659–66, on Julian's reactionary political ideas.

8. Founders: *CTh* 2.12.1.

9. Quotation from the succinct survey of Hellenism in Bowersock (1990) 7. For Greek culture in Cappadocia, see Chapter 1.

10. Gods: Julian, *Ep.* 36.422D–423A. Brothers: Libanius, *Orat.* 18.157. Rhetorical tricks: Julian, *Ep.* 55, in an attack on Diodorus, later bishop of Tarsus.

11. Pagan shrine: Libanius, *Orat.* 18.127. Library: Zosimus, *Historia nova* 3.11.3, with Mango (1985) 39–40, for the harbor. Books and shrine: Julian, *Orat.* 3.123D–124A. Julian also supported a school of music in Alexandria: see Julian, *Ep.* 49.

12. Criticism: Ammianus Marcellinus, *Res gestae* 22.7.1, 3. For the senate at Constantinople, see Jones (1964) 545–52, on the origins of eastern senators, and Vanderspoel (1995) 61–70, on the changes in the later 350s. Constantius' address to senate at Rome: Ammianus Marcellinus, *Res gestae* 16.10.13, with Dagron (1968) 205–12, and Vanderspoel (1995) 101–3, on Themistius at Rome. Hercules and Dionysus: Julian, *Ep. ad Themistium* 253C, with Vanderspoel (1995) 118–26, on the dating of this letter.

13. Julian, *Ep. ad Themistium* 260B, Athens, 266C–D, philosophy, reluctance.

14. Dedication of Constantinople on May 11: see Chapter 8. Departure: Julian issued his last datable constitution from Constantinople, *CTh* 13.3.4, on May 12.

15. Constantius' funeral: GNaz, *Orat.* 5.17. Libation: Libanius, *Orat.* 18.120–21.

16. *CTh* 10.3.1, public estates; 11.16.10, obligations; 12.1.50, 13.1, alleviation of taxes, with the discussion of Pack (1986) 118–59. Libanius, *Orat.* 18.23, benefit cities, 146–50, exemptions, 147, strong council. Dedications from Phoenicia: Negev (1969), and Dietz (2000), dated to spring 363 by Bowersock (1978) 123–24. Hopes: Ammianus Marcellinus, *Res gestae* 22.9.1.

17. Destruction of Nicomedia: Ammianus Marcellinus, *Res gestae* 17.7.1–8, with Foss (1995), and *Becoming Christian*, Chapter 4. Julian's visit: Ammianus Marcellinus, *Res gestae* 22.9.3–5; note also *CTh* 7.4.8, issued from Nicomedia. Statues: *Parastaseis syntomoi chronikai* 47. Visit to Pessinus: Ammianus Marcellinus, *Res gestae* 22.9.5. One night: Julian, *Orat.* 5.178D. Promotion of Callixeine: Julian, *Ep.* 42.

18. Decline of Pessinus: Mitchell (1993) 2:20–22. Threat: Julian, *Ep.* 22.431D–432A. Ascetic: Palladius, *Historia Lausiaca* 45. Young man: GNaz, *Orat.* 5.40. Julian himself insisted that there had been no persecution in Galatia: see Julian, *Ep.* 41.436A–B.

19. Excellent surveys of Ancyra in Foss (1977a), and Mitchell (1993) 2:84–91, at p. 85: "Ancyra occupied a respectable place in the second division as a cultural as well as an administrative centre." Compliment: Libanius, *Ep.* 1517.3, with Petit (1956) 129–32, on Libanius' students at Ancyra. Students from Galatia: Himerius, *Orat.* 69.8, with Barnes (1987) 222, for the suggestion that Himerius was in Julian's entourage. Strangers at Ancyra: Libanius, *Ep.* 607.1.

20. Governors' projects: *CTh* 15.1.3, issued June 29, with Petit (1955) 291–93, on governors as municipal patrons, and Liebeschuetz (1972) 132: "the governors everywhere took the councils' place in the control of public works." Evaluation of

teachers: *CTh* 13.3.5 = *CJ* 10.53.7, issued June 17. Since these laws did not mention the place of publication, the chronology of Julian's journey is relevant. Seeck (1919) 210, suggests that Julian issued these laws after his arrival at Antioch. It is more likely that Julian issued them from or near Ancyra. Basil, a priest at Ancyra, was thought to have been martyred during Julian's visit: see Sozomen, *HE* 5.11. According to a later account of his martyrdom, Julian left Ancyra just before Basil was executed on June 28: see *Passio Basilii presbyteri* 3.20, with de Gaiffier (1956) 11, Foss (1977a) 39n.40, and Woods (1992). Bidez (1930) 400n.1, Pack (1986) 261–62, and Barnes (1998) 163n.98, agree that Julian arrived in Antioch only in mid-July; the first extant law listing Antioch as its place of publication is *CTh* 1.16.8 = *CJ* 3.3.5, issued on July 28. Nonsensical: Julian, *Ep.* 36.423A.

21. Letter to highpriest Arsacius: Julian, *Ep.* 22 = Sozomen, *HE* 5.16, with Nicholson (1994), for Julian's emphasis on the personal piety of priests. Julian composed this letter probably while at Ancyra, as suggested by Foss (1977a) 39–40, rather than sending it later from Antioch, as suggested by Mitchell (1993) 2:90. Dedication: *ILS* 1:168, no. 754.

22. Achillius' wealth: Libanius, *Ep.* 767, an appeal to the governor Maximus for relief, with Foss (1977a) 44–46, on decurions at Ancyra. Praise of governor Maximus: Libanius, *Ep.* 1230.2, with Foss (1977a) 46–47, and *PLRE* 1:583, "Maximus 19"; also Smith (1999) 172–73, on the prominence of governors at Aphrodisias.

23. Landowner Maximus' wealth: Libanius, *Ep.* 298.3; his son: Libanius, *Ep.* 731; with Seeck (1906) 182–83, "Hyperechius I," 210–11, "Maximus XII,", and *PLRE* 1:449–50, "Hyperechius." Complaints: Ammianus Marcellinus, *Res gestae* 22.9.8, with Hunt (1998) 66, on the implausibility of these proposals: "Julian's professed goal of strong and effective city councils was at odds with the centralized nature of imperial autocracy in the late Roman empire."

24. New church: Sozomen, *HE* 4.13. Assistance: Palladius, *Historia Lausiaca* 68, with Mitchell (1993) 2:91–95, on Christianity at Ancyra.

25. Julian, *Ep.* 3, doing philosophy; *Ep.* 23, philosophy and rhetoric; *Ep.* 38, historians, Christian books; with Smith (1995) 23–36, on Julian's education, and Chapter 6, on Julian's exile in Cappadocia.

26. Georgius' books: Julian, *Ep.* 23, obliteration; *Ep.* 38, at Antioch. Julian sent *Ep.* 23 to Ecdicius Olympus, who became prefect of Egypt in 362 sometime after early February: see *PLRE* 1:393, "Gerontius 2," 647–48, "Ecdicius Olympus." Letter to Philippus: Julian, *Ep.* 30. This Philippus is probably to be identified with the Cappadocian Philippus who had been a fellow student with Libanius: see Seeck (1906) 240, "Philippus II," and *PLRE* 1:695, "Philippus 3."

27. Appearance of village: Libanius, *Orat.* 16.14. For the confrontations in Cappadocia, see Chapter 6, and *Families and Friends*, Chapters 1–2; for Julian's readiness to remove the rank of a city because of its opposition to Christianity, see Sozomen, *HE* 5.3, on the demotion of Maiumas in Palestine, with Van Dam (1985b) 6–13.

28. For Basil's earlier confrontation and his tendency to criticize men of his father's generation, see *Families and Friends*, Chapter 1. Philippus may now have accompanied Julian to Antioch, and there given recitals of his poems: see Wiemer (1995) 50n.181, suggesting the identification of Philippus with the poet mentioned in Libanius, *Ep.* 779.2.

29. Letter to Aristoxenus: Julian, *Ep.* 35.

30. Meeting with Celsus: Ammianus Marcellinus, *Res gestae* 22.9.13. Altar: Libanius, *Orat.* 18.159, *Ep.* 736.3. New decurions: Libanius, *Ep.* 696.1–3. This governor Celsus may perhaps be identified with the Celsus who once accompanied Basil to Athens: see B, *Ep.* 336.1 = Libanius, *Epistularum commercium* 2.2, with Seeck (1906) 105, and Chapter 6. By 363 Celsus had become governor of Syria, perhaps appointed by Julian: see *PLRE* 1:193–94, "Celsus 3."

31. Temple of Apollo, Pontus: Julian, *Misopogon* 361D–362B. Fire: Ammianus Marcellinus, *Res gestae* 22.13.1–2. Food shortage: Julian, *Misopogon* 368C–370A; impact of army: Socrates, *HE* 3.17; with Petit (1955) 109–18, and Downey (1961) 380–96, for Julian's stay at Antioch, and Wiemer (1995) 269–355, for a thorough review of this food shortage. Ridicule of Julian: Gleason (1986).

32. For Julian's discomfort at Antioch, note Bowersock (1978) 93: "Antioch was no place for a puritanical pagan." For his plans to winter at Tarsus, see Chapter 6.

33. Amnesty: Julian, *Ep.* 24, 41. Constantine: *CTh* 2.5.2, 3.1.3.

34. Roman name: *Mosaicarum et Romanarum legum collatio* 6.4.8. Restorer of liberty: *ILS* 1:168, no. 752. Julian, *Ep.* 37, Galilaeans; *Ep.* 41.438B, reason; with Smith (1995) 207–16, for Julian's thinking about persecution. For the traditions about martyrs during Julian's reign, see Brennecke (1988) 114–57. For Diocletian's persecutions, see Digeser (2000) 54–56, and *Families and Friends*, Chapter 1.

35. Julian, *Caesares* 317C, Marcus Aurelius' appearance, 320A–322A, Caesar's conquests, 330B, conquer everything, 335C, rank of Marcus Aurelius; with Bouffartigue (1992) 409–11, who doubts that Julian had read Julius Caesar. For Julian's imitation of Alexander, see Athanassiadi (1981) 192–200.

36. Books in hand: according to Libanius, *Orat.* 18.233, during his eastern campaign Julian determined strategy by reading "from a book" about "the stupidity of an earlier Roman general"; this general was Crassus, the site of whose defeat Julian visited: see Ammianus Marcellinus, *Res gestae* 23.3.1. For rewriting the past by Christians, see *Becoming Christian*, Chapters 3–4. Cultural expectations: Libanius, *Orat.* 18.282. For Alexander and the myth of Greek cultural domination in the Near East, see Fowden (1993) 21–22.

37. Epitaph: Zosimus, *Historia nova* 3.34.4 = *Anthologia Graeca* 7.747, citing *Iliad* 3.179. Apostate: GNaz, *Orat.* 4.1.

## Chapter 10. Basil's "Outline of Virtue"

1. Less need: GNaz, *Orat.* 43.23. B, *Ep.* 2.2, separation, 3, route, examples. For Basil's early life and education, see *Families and Friends*, Chapter 1.

2. Basil addressed his treatise to παῖδες (*Ad adulescentes* 1.1, 2.1), and later suggested that when Hercules had chosen between virtue and vice, "he was almost the same young age as you are now" (*Ad adulescentes* 5.12). His audience, at least for the original oration, hence consisted of teenagers, most likely only boys, whom Basil addressed as "students." For παῖδες as the equivalent of "students," see Petit (1956) 33–35. Basil also claimed that "because I am by natural relationship to you just after your parents, I offer you no less goodwill than do your parents" (*Ad adulescentes*

1.2). This description does not necessarily imply that these boys were Basil's nephews, as suggested by Wilson (1975) 7. Teachers and clerics were also seen as "fathers": see B, *Ep.* 300, for himself "in the second row of fathers," with *Families and Friends*, Chapter 1. Moffatt (1972), suggests that Basil composed this treatise in 362–363, Fedwick (1979) 140–41, in the mid-360s, Pouchet (1992a) 172–74, between 365 and 368, Wilson (1975) 9, less plausibly, at the end of his life; Rousseau (1994) 49, locates the treatise in "a period of pastoral responsibility." Fedwick (1981) 18, leaves it undated. For Eunomius, see *Becoming Christian*, Chapter 1.

3. B, *Ad adulescentes* 1.4, famous men, 2.8, distinction, 3.2, leaves and fruit, 3.3–4, Moses and Daniel; with Harl (1967), on Moses as a model for the transition from profane culture to asceticism, Fortin (1981), on Basil's specious interpretations of classical texts, and Kaster (1988) 78, "Basil does ... external culture the favor of allowing it to remain both clearly secular and clearly useful in Christian terms." For Macrina, see *Families and Friends*, Chapter 6. Tragedies: GNys, *De virginitate* 3.10. Miracles and myths: B, *Regulae fusius tractatae* 15.3.

4. B, *Ad adulescentes* 1.5, usefulness, 2.3, listeners, 2.6, drills and combat, 4.1, souls, 4.5, gods, 4.7–8, bees and roses, 8.1, select everything. Note Brown (1992) 123, describing Basil's evaluation of an education in Greek culture as "a moral and intellectual boot camp."

5. Estimation of Basil's treatise by Laistner (1951) 52. Himerius, *Orat.* 1–2, 5–6, with Kennedy (1974), on the practice of declamations, Kennedy (1983) 141–49, an appreciation of Himerius, Barnes (1987) 224, for the circumstances of Himerius' orations, and *Families and Friends*, Chapter 1. For similar declamations by Libanius, see Russell (1996) 1–15. Proaeresius' improvisations: GNaz, *Epitaph.* 5.4; his orations: Eunapius, *Vitae sophistarum* 489. Julian and Gallus: GNaz, *Orat.* 4.30, with Chapter 6.

6. B, *Ad adulescentes* 5.12–14, Hercules, 7.2, Pericles. Note also the flourish of pedantic skepticism about a story in a poem attributed to Homer, "if indeed this work is by Homer": B, *Ad adulescentes* 8.11.

7. B, *Ad adulescentes* 9.1, care of soul, 2, passions, 15, health, 17–23, wealth, 24–27, acclaim. On mastery of the voice, see Rousselle (1983), and Gleason (1995) 82–102.

8. B, *Ad adulescentes* 4.3, pleasure, 10.1, outline of virtue.

9. Hinting: GNaz, *Orat.* 43.12, describing Basil's study with his father; the similarity in terminology suggests that Gregory may have been familiar with Basil's treatise: see Ruether (1969) 165n.2. For Basil's restrained use of rhetorical techniques in his writings, see Campbell (1922).

10. Zachariah Scholasticus, *Vita Severi Antiocheni,* tr. Kugener (1903) 13, conversion of Severus, later bishop of Antioch, 53–54, students at Beirut; with Schucan (1973) 42–48, for the influence of Basil's treatise in Byzantine society, and Klein (1997), for its later influence. For the library compiled by Arethas, bishop of Caesarea in the early tenth century, see Bidez (1934), and Lemerle (1971) 213–39.

11. Eupsychius' martyrdom: Sozomen, *HE* 5.11, with Brennecke (1988) 150–52, for speculation about Eupsychius' motives, and de Gaiffier (1956) 12–13, for later traditions. B, *Ep.* 100, blessed martyr, council; *Ep.* 142, council; *Ep.* 176, council; *Ep.* 200, invitation; *Ep.* 252, memory, invitation to bishops in Pontus; with Devos (1992) 256–58, on the date of the festival, and *Families and Friends*, Chapter 1. Sermon: GNaz, *Ep.* 58.7.

12. Eutychianus and Basil's dream: John Malalas, *Chronographia* 13.23–25, pp. 332–34; similar story in *Chronicon Paschale* p. 552, and John of Nikiu, *Chronicon* 80.19–26, tr. Charles (1916) 78–79, with Delehaye (1909) 91–101, on the cult of St. Mercurius, Baynes (1937), Brennecke (1988) 96n.3, and Muraviev (2001), for discussion of this and other legends, and *Becoming Christian*, Chapter 9, for the afterlife of this story about St. Mercurius. *PLRE* 1:319, "Eutychianus 2" and "Eutychianus 3," rightly distinguishes this soldier Eutychianus from the grammarian Eutychianus who had attended the inauguration ceremonies of Constantinople in 330 and who accompanied Julian to the East. The extant correspondence of Julian and Basil includes three letters that they supposedly exchanged: Julian, *Ep.* 26 = [B,] *Ep.* 39, Julian, *Ep.* 81 = [B,] *Ep.* 40, B, *Ep.* 41. Pouchet (1992a) 174, argues that the Basil who received Julian, *Ep.* 26, was not Basil of Caesarea, and that the other two letters were imaginary school exercises; Vanderspoel (1999) 468–69, accepts Julian, *Ep.* 26, as an authentic letter from Julian to Basil of Caesarea; for the debate, see Forlin Patrucco (1983) 409–13.

## Chapter 11. Gregory of Nazianzus and the Philosopher Emperor

1. GNaz, *Carm.* II.1.11.265–66, 274, oration and dancing, 344, "second throne," with *Families and Friends*, Chapter 2, for additional context. In GNaz, *Ep.* 3, Gregory accepted a father's compliments for having taught *logoi*, "culture" or "oratory," to his son. This is apparently Gregory's earliest extant letter, dated to 359 by Gallay (1964–1967) 1:2.

2. Fervor: GNaz, *Orat.* 4.92. No fear: GNaz, *Orat.* 2.87.

3. See *Families and Friends*, Chapter 2, for Gregory's family.

4. On Himerius, see Chapter 9, and *Families and Friends*, Chapter 1.

5. Antiochus: GNaz, *Orat.* 15.5, 12, with Habicht (1989) 346–50, on king Antiochus' policies. For additional discussion of Julian's visit, see Chapter 6, and *Families and Friends*, Chapter 2.

6. For the Homeric allusions in GNaz, *Orat.* 15, see Vinson (1994) 167–70.

7. Evilness, justice: GNaz, *Orat.* 5.1. Bernardi (1983) 35, and Kurmann (1988) 6–12, argue that Gregory completed *Orat.* 4–5 shortly after the accession of the emperor Valens in early spring 364.

8. Danger and origins: GNaz, *Orat.* 4.20. Gregory did not specify his sources for this information about Julian's career. For some of the events from Julian's years in Cappadocia he had talked to "eyewitness": "there are many who have transmitted this wonderful [story] to me" (*Orat.* 4.29). For a survey of Gregory's possible sources, see Bernardi (1983) 41–50; but it is unlikely he had read Julian's treatises: see Bernardi (1978).

9. GNaz, *Orat.* 4.21, ungrateful, 34, most divine, 37, aggravation, 42, revenge on benefactor; *Orat.* 5.16, simple soul, with Brennecke (1988) 84–85, on Gregory's revisionist interpretation of Constantius. Gregory seemingly absolved Constantius of participation in the massacre of his relatives by suggesting that he had spared Gallus and Julian "in part to offer an excuse for the revolutionaries at the beginning of his reign, as if they had acted against his wish" (*Orat.* 4.22). Julian himself held

Constantius directly responsible as "the executioner of our entire family": see Julian, *Ep. ad Athenienses* 270C–D, 281B. Note also GNaz, *Carm.* 1.2.25.290–303: Gregory praised the leniency of "the most pious" Constantius and blamed "a magistrate" for having given bad advice. For the dissension at Caesarea and Nazianzus, see *Families and Friends*, Chapters 1–2.

10. GNaz, *Orat.* 4.45, brother, 71, ascetics, with Norris (1991) 5, "[Gregory] Nazianzen and Julian shared so many common features that their differences needed emphasis."

11. GNaz, *Orat.* 4.2, Isaiah, 20, indictment, 87, virgins, 88–91, Marcus of Arethusa, 93, arrest; *Orat.* 5.34, use the moment, 42, column, with Kurmann (1988) 18–20, on invective and indictment.

12. GNaz, *Orat.* 4.3–4, meanings of *logos*.

13. GNaz, *Orat.* 4.5, Julian's transfer, 88, 91, 93, Hellenes contrasted to Christians, with Athanassiadi and Frede (1999) 6–7, on Christian apologists.

14. Proaeresius: Eunapius, *Vitae sophistarum* 493, Jerome, *Chronicon* s.a. 363. Apollinarius: Socrates, *HE* 3.16; quotation from Sozomen, *HE* 5.18. Hecebolius: Socrates, *HE* 3.1, 13. After Julian's death Hecebolius returned to Christianity and dismissed his former student as an "incompetent sophist": Socrates, *HE* 3.23. Pegasius: Julian, *Ep.* 19.

15. Copy of *Iliad*: GNaz, *Ep.* 31.7. Edict: GNaz, *Orat.* 4.5–6.

16. GNaz, *Orat.* 4.100, pleasure in culture, 102, culture belongs to us, 103, different pagan cults, 103–4, distinction between Hellenic people and Hellenic religion, 105, different styles, 107, borrowing of alphabet, 108, poetry, 109, borrowing of pagan practices.

17. GNaz, *Orat.* 4.111, imitations, 115, theology and morality, 119–21, counterexamples, 123–24, "our teachings."

18. Dedication to Julian at Iasos in Caria: Dittenberger (1903–1905) 2:174–75, no. 520 = Blümel (1985) 1:33–34, no. 14, τὸν ἐκ φιλοσοφίας βασιλεύοντα. GNaz, *Orat.* 4.27, sophist of evil, 91, philosopher emperor, 112, new-fangled sophist; cf. *Orat.* 5.30, "your reasoning, which is both imperial and sophistic"; with Elm (2001), on Gregory's and Julian's attempts to redefine philosophy.

19. Galilaeans: GNaz, *Orat.* 4.76, with Bouffartigue (1992) 653–58, on Julian and *logos*.

20. For Julian and his books, see Chapter 9. Jovian and Julian's library: Eunapius, *Fragmenta historica* 29.1 = *Suda* I.401.

21. Citations: GNaz, *Ep.* 178.4, citing Ecclesiasticus 4:32 and *Anthologia Graeca* 9.537; *Ep.* 180.1, citing *Iliad* 9.437, 21.109, and Psalms 45.4; with Wyss (1946) 154–55, (1983), for excellent accounts of Gregory's familiarity with classical literature, Ruether (1969) 55–128, for the influence of rhetoric on Gregory's writings, and Demoen (1996), for Gregory's extensive use of examples from classical literature. Girdle: GNaz, *Ep.* 52.2. Cosmas of Jerusalem, *Commentarii in Gregorii Nazianzeni carmina*, PG 38.343, Γρηγοριολόγοι, 345, imitate, with Demoen (1993), on Gregory's attitudes toward classical poetry, Van Dam (1998), a short survey of Gregory's poems, and *Becoming Christian*, Chapter 10. For the library of Eustathius Boilas, see Vryonis (1957), and Lemerle (1977). For Cavafy's comment, see Seferis (1966) 140.

22. True fatherland: Julian, *Orat.* 3.118D.

23. Julian at Athens: GNaz, *Orat.* 5.23, with Chapter 6. Cult at Eleusis: Eunapius, *Vitae sophistarum* 475–76.

24. GNaz, *Orat.* 5.40, Basil and Gregory, with *Families and Friends*, Chapter 10, on Athens and their friendship. Bernardi (1983) 36–37, suggests that Basil collaborated with Gregory on these treatises when he visited Nazianzus to help resolve a dispute with monks: see *Families and Friends*, Chapters 1–2.

## Epilogue

1. For Gregory and Theodosius, see Chapter 8; for Basil's and Gregory's friendship, *Families and Friends*, Chapter 10; for Gregory's later poems, *Becoming Christian*, Chapter 10.

2. Evaluation: Sidonius, *Ep.* 4.3.7, "ut Basilius corripit, ut Gregorius consolatur."

# Editions and Translations

In this book all translations from Greek and Latin texts are by the author. In this list of editions and translations full references for books and articles already cited in the notes are in the Bibliography.

## The Cappadocian Fathers

### Basil of Caesarea

*Ad adulescentes* (= *Hom.* 22): ed. and tr. R. J. Deferrari and M. R. P. McGuire, in Deferrari (1926–1934), vol. 4, pp. 378–435—ed. F. Boulenger, in Wilson (1975), pp. 19–36.

*Epistulae*: ed. and tr. Deferrari (1926–1934)—ed. and tr. [French] Y. Courtonne, *Saint Basile, Lettres*, 3 vols. Budé (1957–1966)—tr. [German] Hauschild (1973), (1990), (1993)—*Ep.* 1–46, ed. and tr. [Italian] Forlin Patrucco (1983).

*Homilia* 3: ed. *PG* 31.197–217—tr. M. M. Wagner, *Saint Basil, Ascetical Works*. FC 9 (1950), pp. 431–46.

*Homilia* 4: ed. *PG* 31.217–37.

*Homilia* 5: ed. *PG* 31.237–61.

*Homilia* 6: ed. *PG* 31.261–77—ed. and tr. [French] Y. Courtonne, *Saint Basile, Homélies sur la richesse. Edition critique et exégétique* (Paris, 1935), pp. 14–37.

*Homilia* 7: ed. *PG* 31.277–304—ed. and tr. [French] Y. Courtonne, *Saint Basile, Homélies sur la richesse. Edition critique et exégétique* (Paris, 1935), pp. 38–71.

*Homilia* 8: ed. *PG* 31.304–28.

*Homilia* 9: ed. *PG* 31.329–53.

*Homilia* 14: ed. *PG* 31.444–64.

*Homilia* 18: ed. *PG* 31.489–508.

*Homilia* 22: see *Ad adulescentes*.

*Homiliae in Hexaemeron*: ed. E. Amand de Mendieta and S. Y. Rudberg, *Basilius von Caesarea: Homilien zum Hexaemeron*. GCS, Neue Folge, 2 (1997)—ed. and tr. [French] S. Giet, *Basile de Césarée: Homélies sur l'Hexaéméron*. SChr. 26 (1950)—tr. B. Jackson, in *St. Basil: Letters and Select Works*. NPNF, 2nd series, 8 (1895; reprint, 1978), pp. 52–107—tr. A. C. Way, *Saint Basil, Exegetic Homilies*. FC 46 (1963), pp. 3–150.

*Homiliae in psalmos*: ed. *PG* 29.209–494—tr. A. C. Way, *Saint Basil: Exegetic Homilies*. FC 46 (1963), pp. 151–359.

*Regulae fusius tractatae*: ed. *PG* 31.901–1052—tr. W. K. L. Clarke, *The Ascetic Works of Saint Basil* (London, 1925), pp. 152–228—tr. M. M. Wagner, *Saint Basil: Ascetical Works*. FC 9 (1950), pp. 232–337.

*Gregory of Nazianzus*

*Carmina:*

I.2.1–40 = *Carmina moralia*: ed. *PG* 37.521–968.

II.1.1–99 = *Carmina de se ipso*: ed. *PG* 37.969–1452—*Carm.* II.1.1, 11, 12: tr. D. M.
Meehan, *Saint Gregory of Nazianzus: Three Poems. Concerning His Own Affairs,
Concerning Himself and the Bishops, Concerning His Own Life.* FC 75 (1987)—
*Carm.* II.1.11: ed. and tr. [German] C. Jungck, *Gregor von Nazianz: De vita sua*
(Heidelberg, 1974)—*Carm.* II.1.11, 19, 34, 39, 92: tr. C. White, *Gregory of Nazianzus: Autobiographical Poems.* Cambridge Medieval Classics 6 (Cambridge,
1996)—*Carm.* II.1.12: ed. and tr. [German] B. Meier, *Gregor von Nazianz: Über
die Bischöfe (Carmen 2,1,12). Einleitung, Text, Übersetzung, Kommentar.* Studien
zur Geschichte und Kultur des Altertums, Neue Folge, 2. Reihe: Forschungen
zu Gregor von Nazianz 7 (Paderborn, 1989).

II.2.1–8 = *Carmina quae spectant ad alios*: ed. *PG* 37.1451–1600.

*Epistulae*: ed. P. Gallay, *Gregor von Nazianz: Briefe.* GCS 53 (1969)—*Ep.* 1–100, 103–
201, 203–42, 244–49: ed. and tr. [French] Gallay (1964–1967); *Ep.* 101–2, 202: ed.
and tr. [French] P. Gallay and M. Jourjon, *Grégoire de Nazianze: Lettres théo-
logiques.* SChr. 208 (Paris, 1974)—tr. [German] M. Wittig, *Gregor von Nazianz:
Briefe.* Bibliothek der griechischen Literatur, Abteilung Patristik, Bd. 13 (Stuttgart, 1981)—selections tr. C. G. Browne and J. E. Swallow, in *S. Cyril of Jerusalem. S. Gregory Nazianzen.* NPNF, 2nd series, 7 (1894; reprint, 1978), pp. 437–82.

*Epitaphia*: ed. *PG* 38.11–82—*Epitaph.* 1–3, 6–78, 80–128 are included in *Anthologia
Graeca* 8: ed. and tr. W. R. Paton, *The Greek Anthology*, vol. 2. LCL (1917),
pp. 400–73 (see *CPG* 2:191–92, for a concordance).

*Orationes*: *Orat.* 1–3: ed. and tr. [French] Bernardi (1978)—*Orat.* 4–5: ed. and tr.
[French] Bernardi (1983)—*Orat.* 6–12: ed. and tr. [French] M.-A. Calvet-
Sebasti, *Grégoire de Nazianze: Discours 6–12.* SChr. 405 (1995)—*Orat.* 7: ed. and
tr. [French] F. Boulenger, *Grégoire de Nazianze: Discours funèbres en l'honneur
de son frère Césaire et de Basile de Césarée* (Paris, 1908), pp. 2–57—*Orat.* 13–19:
ed. *PG* 35.852–1064—*Orat.* 20–23: ed. and tr. [French] Mossay and Lafontaine
(1980)—*Orat.* 24–26: ed. and tr. [French] J. Mossay and G. Lafontaine, *Grégoire
de Nazianze: Discours 24–26.* SChr. 284 (1981)—*Orat.* 32–37: ed. and tr. [French]
Moreschini and Gallay (1985)—*Orat.* 38–41: ed. and tr. [French] Moreschini
and Gallay (1990)—*Orat.* 42–43: ed. and tr. [French] Bernardi (1992)—*Orat.*
43: ed. and tr. [French] F. Boulenger, *Grégoire de Nazianze: Discours funèbres en
l'honneur de son frère Césaire et de Basile de Césarée* (Paris, 1908), pp. 58–231—
*Orat.* 1–3, 7–8, 12, 16, 18, 21, 27–31, 33–34, 37–43, 45: tr. C. G. Browne and J. E.
Swallow, in *S. Cyril of Jerusalem. S. Gregory Nazianzen.* NPNF, 2nd series, 7
(1894; reprint, 1978), pp. 203–434.

*Testamentum*: ed. *PG* 37.389–96—ed. Pitra (1864–1868), vol. 2, pp. 155–59—tr.
[French] F. Martroye, "Le testament de saint Grégoire de Nazianze," *Mémoires
de la Société nationale des antiquaires de France* 76 (1924), pp. 219–25; translation reprinted in H. Leclercq, "Nazianze," in *Dictionnaire d'archéologie
chrétienne et de liturgie*, ed. F. Cabrol and H. Leclercq, vol. 12.1 (Paris, 1935), col.
1057–59—tr. Van Dam (1995), pp. 143–48.

*Gregory of Nyssa*

*Contra Eunomium*: ed. W. Jaeger, *Gregorii Nysseni Contra Eunomium libri, Pars prior: Liber I et II (vulgo I et XIIʙ)*, and *Gregorii Nysseni Contra Eunomium libri, Pars altera: Liber III (vulgo III–XII). Refutatio confessionis Eunomii (vulgo Lib. II).* GNO 1–2 (2nd ed., 1960)—tr. W. Moore, H. A. Wilson, H. C. Ogle, and M. Day, in *Select Writings and Letters of Gregory, Bishop of Nyssa*. NPNF, 2nd series, 5 (1893; reprint, 1976), pp. 35–100, 250–314, 135–248 [in that order]—*Contra Eunomium* 1: tr. S. G. Hall, in *El "Contra Eunomium I" in la producción literaria de Gregorio de Nisa. VI Coloquio internacional sobre Gregorio de Nisa*, ed. L. F. Mateo-Seco and J. L. Bastero (Pamplona, 1988), pp. 35–135.

*De beatitudinibus*: ed. J. F. Callahan, *Gregorii Nysseni De oratione dominica, De beatitudinibus*. GNO 7.2 (1992), pp. 77–170; reference numbers from *PG* 44.1193–1301—tr. H. C. Graef, *St. Gregory of Nyssa, The Lord's Prayer. The Beatitudes.* ACW 18 (1954), pp. 85–175.

*De beneficentia* (= *De pauperibus amandis* 1): ed. A. Van Heck, in *Gregorii Nysseni Sermones*. GNO 9 (1967), pp. 93–108; reference numbers from *PG* 46.453–69.

*De oratione dominica*: ed. J. F. Callahan, *Gregorii Nysseni De oratione dominica, De beatitudinibus*. GNO 7.2 (1992), pp. 5–74; reference numbers from *PG* 44.1120–93—tr. H. C. Graef, *St. Gregory of Nyssa: The Lord's Prayer. The Beatitudes.* ACW 18 (1954), pp. 21–84.

*De virginitate*: ed. J. P. Cavarnos, in *Gregorii Nysseni opera ascetica*. GNO 8.1 (1952), pp. 248–343—ed. and tr. [French] M. Aubineau, *Grégoire de Nysse: Traité de la virginité*. SChr. 119 (1966)—tr. V. W. Callahan, *Saint Gregory of Nyssa: Ascetical Works*. FC 58 (1967), pp. 6–75.

*De vita Moysis*: ed. H. Musurillo, *Gregorii Nysseni De vita Moysis*. GNO 7.1 (1964); reference numbers from *PG* 44.297–430—tr. A. J. Malherbe and E. Ferguson, *Gregory of Nyssa: The Life of Moses*. Classics of Western Spirituality (New York, 1978).

*Encomia in XL martyres* 1ᴀ, 1ʙ, 2: ed. O. Lendle, in *Gregorii Nysseni Sermones, pars II*. GNO 10.1 (1990), pp. 135–69; reference numbers from *PG* 46.749–88.

*Epistulae*: ed. G. Pasquali, *Gregorii Nysseni Epistulae*. GNO 8.2 (2nd ed., 1959)—ed. and tr. [French] Maraval (1990)—*Ep.* 29–30, 2, 4–18, 20, 25, 3, 1 [in that order]: tr. W. Moore, H. C. Ogle, and H. A. Wilson, in *Select Writings and Letters of Gregory, Bishop of Nyssa*. NPNF, 2nd series, 5 (1893; reprint, 1976), pp. 33–34, 382–83, 527–48.

*Homiliae in Ecclesiasten*: ed. P. Alexander, in *Gregorii Nysseni In inscriptiones Psalmorum, In sextum Psalmum, In Ecclesiasten homiliae*. GNO 5 (1962), pp. 277–442—ed. and tr. [French] P. Alexander and F. Vinel, *Grégoire de Nysse: Homélies sur l'Ecclésiaste*. SChr. 416 (1996), pp. 106–435—tr. S. G. Hall and R. Moriarty, in *Gregory of Nyssa: Homilies on Ecclesiastes. An English Version with Supporting Studies. Proceedings of the Seventh International Colloquium on Gregory of Nyssa (St Andrews, 5–10 September 1990)*, ed. S. G. Hall (Berlin and New York, 1993), pp. 32–144.

*In Basilium fratrem*: ed. and tr. J. A. Stein, *Encomium of Saint Gregory Bishop of Nyssa on His Brother Saint Basil Archbishop of Cappadocian Caesarea*. Catholic

University of America Patristic Studies 17 (Washington, D.C., 1928)—ed. O. Lendle, in *Gregorii Nysseni Sermones, pars II.* GNO 10.1 (1990), pp. 107–34.

*Oratio funebris in Meletium episcopum:* ed. A. Spira, in *Gregorii Nysseni Sermones.* GNO 9 (1967), pp. 441–57; reference numbers from *PG* 46.852–64—tr. W. Moore, in *Select Writings and Letters of Gregory, Bishop of Nyssa.* NPNF, 2nd series, 5 (1893; reprint, 1976), pp. 513–17.

*Vita Gregorii Thaumaturgii:* ed. G. Heil, in *Gregorii Nysseni Sermones, pars II.* GNO 10.1 (1990), pp. 1–57; reference numbers from *PG* 46.893–957—tr. M. Slusser, *St. Gregory Thaumaturgus: Life and Works.* FC 98 (1998), pp. 41–87.

*Vita Macrinae:* ed. V. W. Callahan, in *Gregorii Nysseni opera ascetica.* GNO 8.1 (1952), pp. 370–414—tr. V. W. Callahan, *Saint Gregory of Nyssa: Ascetical Works.* FC 58 (1967), pp. 163–91—ed. and tr. [French] Maraval (1971).

## Ancient Authors and Texts

Ammianus Marcellinus, *Res gestae:* ed. and tr. J. C. Rolfe, *Ammianus Marcellinus,* 3 vols. LCL (1935–1940).

*Anthologia Graeca:* ed. and tr. W. R. Paton, *The Greek Anthology,* 5 vols. LCL (1916–1918).

Appian, *Bella civilia* and *Mithridatica:* ed. and tr. H. White, *Appian's Roman History,* vols. 2–4. LCL (1912–1913).

Aristotle, *Ethica Nicomachea:* ed. and tr. H. Rackham, *Aristotle: The Nicomachean Ethics.* LCL (1926).

Arrian, *Periplus Ponti Euxini:* ed. A. G. Roos, rev. G. Wirth, *Flavii Arriani quae exstant omnia,* vol. 2, *Scripta minora et fragmenta.* Teubner (1967), pp. 103–28.

Artemidorus, *Onirocritica:* ed. R. A. Pack, *Artemidori Daldiani Oneirocriticon libri V.* Teubner (1963)—tr. R. J. White, *The Interpretation of Dreams: Oneirocritica by Artemidorus* (Park Ridge, N.J., 1975).

Asterius of Amaseia, *Homiliae* 1–14: ed. C. Datema, *Asterius of Amasea: Homilies I–XIV. Text, Introduction and Notes* (Leiden, 1970).

Athanasius, *Apologia ad Constantium:* ed. and tr. [French] J. M. Szymusiak, *Athanase d'Alexandrie: Deux Apologies. A l'empereur Constance. Pour sa fuite.* SChr. 56bis (1987), pp. 86–175—tr. A. Robertson, *Select Writings and Letters of Athanasius, Bishop of Alexandria.* NPNF, 2nd series, 4 (1892; reprint, 1991), pp. 238–53.

———, *De incarnatione verbi:* ed. and tr. R. W. Thomson, *Athanasius,* Contra gentes *and* De incarnatione. Oxford Early Christian Texts (Oxford, 1971), pp. 134–277—ed. and tr. [French] C. Kannengiesser, *Athanase d'Alexandrie: Sur l'incarnation du Verbe.* SChr. 199 (1973), pp. 258–469.

Aurelius Victor, *De Caesaribus:* ed. F. Pichlmayr and R. Gruendel, *Sexti Aurelii Victoris Liber de Caesaribus.* Teubner (1970), pp. 77–129—tr. H. W. Bird, *Liber de Caesaribus of Sextus Aurelius Victor.* TTH 17 (1994).

Ausonius, *Epigrammata:* ed. and tr. H. G. Evelyn White, *Ausonius,* vol. 2. LCL (1921), pp. 154–217.

*Buzandaran Patmut'iwnk':* tr. Garsoïan (1989).

*Chronicon Paschale:* ed. L. Dindorf, *Chronicon Paschale ad exemplar Vaticanum,* vol.

1. Corpus Scriptorum Historiae Byzantinae (Bonn, 1832)—tr. M. Whitby and M. Whitby, *Chronicon Paschale 284–628 AD*. TTH 7 (1989).

Cicero, *Epistulae ad Atticum*: ed. and tr. D. R. Shackleton Bailey, *Cicero's Letters to Atticus*, 7 vols. (Cambridge, 1965–1970).

————, *Epistulae ad familiares*: ed. D. R. Shackleton Bailey, *Cicero: Epistulae ad familiares*, 2 vols. (Cambridge, 1977)—tr. D. R. Shackleton Bailey, *Cicero's Letters to His Friends* (Atlanta, 1988).

————, *Oratio de provinciis consularibus*: ed. and tr. R. Gardner, *Cicero*, vol. 13. LCL (1958), pp. 538–603.

*CJ* = *Codex Justinianus*: ed. P. Krueger, *Codex Iustinianus*. Corpus Iuris Civilis 2 (11th ed., 1954; reprint, Hildesheim, 1989).

Claudian, *Carmina minora* 30 = *Laus Serenae*: ed. and tr. M. Platnauer, *Claudian*, vol. 2. LCL (1922), pp. 238–57.

————, *In Rufinum*: ed. and tr. M. Platnauer, *Claudian*, vol. 1. LCL (1922), pp. 24–97.

Constantine VII Porphyrogenitus, *De thematibus*: ed. Pertusi (1952).

*Consularia Constantinopolitana*: ed. R. W. Burgess, *The* Chronicle *of Hydatius and the* Consularia Constantinopolitana. *Two Contemporary Accounts of the Final Years of the Roman Empire* (Oxford, 1993), pp. 215–45.

Cosmas of Jerusalem, *Commentarii in Gregorii Nazianzeni carmina*: ed. *PG* 38.341–680.

Council of Constantinople, *Canones* and *Epistula synodalis ad Theodosium imperatorem*: ed. Pitra (1864–1868), vol. 1, pp. 507–9.

*CTh* = *Codex Theodosianus*: ed. Th. Mommsen, *Codex Theodosianus 1.2: Theodosiani libri XVI cum Constitutionibus Sirmondi[a]nis* (Berlin, 1905)—tr. C. Pharr et al., *The Theodosian Code and Novels and the Sirmondian Constitutions* (1952; reprint, Westport, Conn., 1969), pp. 3–486.

*Digenes Akrites*: ed. and tr. Jeffreys (1998).

*Digest*: ed. Th. Mommsen and P. Krueger, *Institutiones et Digesta*. Corpus Iuris Civilis 1 (Berlin, 13th ed., 1920)—tr. A. Watson et al., *The Digest of Justinian*, 2 vols., rev. ed. (Philadelphia, 1998).

Dio, *Historiae Romanae*: ed. and tr. E. Cary, *Dio's Roman History*, 9 vols. LCL (1914–1927).

Diodorus of Sicily, *Bibliotheca historica*: ed. and tr. C. H. Oldfather, C. L. Sherman, C. B. Welles, R. M. Geer, and F. R. Walton, *Diodorus of Sicily*, 12 vols. LCL (1933–1967).

Epiphanius, *Panarion* (+ *Rescriptum ad Acacium et Paulum* and *Recapitulatio brevis*): ed. K. Holl, *Epiphanius (Ancoratus und Panarion)*, 3 vols. GCS 25, 31, 37 (1915–1933)—tr. F. Williams, *The Panarion of Epiphanius of Salamis*, 2 vols. Nag Hammadi and Manichaean Studies 35–36 (Leiden, 1987–1994)—selections tr. P. R. Amidon, *The* Panarion *of St. Epiphanius, Bishop of Salamis: Selected Passages* (New York and Oxford, 1990).

*Epitome de Caesaribus*: ed. F. Pichlmayr and R. Gruendel, *Sexti Aurelii Victoris Liber de Caesaribus*. Teubner (1970), pp. 133–76.

Eunapius, *Fragmenta historica*: ed. and tr. R. C. Blockley, *The Fragmentary Classicising Historians of the Later Roman Empire: Eunapius, Olympiodorus, Priscus and Malchus, II: Text, Translation and Historiographical Notes*. ARCA Classical and

Medieval Texts, Papers and Monographs 10 (Liverpool, 1983), pp. 6–127.

————, *Vitae sophistarum*: ed. and tr. W. C. Wright, *Philostratus and Eunapius: The Lives of the Sophists*. LCL (1921), pp. 342–565.

Eusebius of Caesarea, *Vita Constantini*: ed. F. Winkelmann, *Eusebius Werke 1.1: Über das Leben des Kaisers Konstantin*. GCS (2nd ed., 1991)—tr. A. Cameron and S. G. Hall, *Eusebius: Life of Constantine. Introduction, Translation, and Commentary* (Oxford, 1999).

Eutropius, *Breviarium*: ed. H. Droysen, *Eutropi Breviarium ab urbe condita cum versionibus graecis et Pauli Landolfique additamentis*. Monumenta Germaniae Historica, Auctores antiquissimi 2 (Berlin, 1879)—tr. H. W. Bird, *Eutropius: Breviarium*. TTH 14 (1993).

Evagrius, *HE = Historia ecclesiastica*: ed. J. Bidez and L. Parmentier, *The Ecclesiastical History of Evagrius with the Scholia* (London, 1898)—tr. M. Whitby, *The Ecclesiastical History of Evagrius Scholasticus*. TTH 33 (2000).

*Expositio totius mundi et gentium*: ed. and tr. [French] J. Rougé, *Expositio totius mundi et gentium*. SChr. 124 (1966).

Firmus of Caesarea, *Epistulae*: ed. and tr. [French] Calvet-Sebasti and Gatier (1989).

Georgius of Sykeon, *Vita Theodori Syceotae*: ed. and tr. [French] A.-J. Festugière, *Vie de Théodore de Sykéon*, 2 vols. Subsidia Hagiographica 48 (Brussels, 1970)— partial tr. E. Dawes and N. H. Baynes, *Three Byzantine Saints: Contemporary Biographies Translated from the Greek* (London and Oxford, 1948), pp. 88–185.

Herodian, *Historia*: ed. and tr. C. R. Whittaker, *Herodian*, 2 vols. LCL (1969–1970).

Herodotus, *Historia*: ed. and tr. A. D. Godley, *Herodotus*, 4 vols. LCL (1920–1925).

Hesychius of Miletus, *Historia romana atque omnigena*: ed. C. Müller, *Fragmenta historicorum graecorum* 4 (Paris, 1851), pp. 145–55.

Hierocles, *Synecdemus*: ed. G. Parthey, *Hieroclis Synecdemus et Notitiae graecae episcopatuum: Accedunt Nili Doxapatrii Notitia patriarchatuum et locorum nomina immutata* (Berlin, 1866), pp. 3–51—ed. A. Burckhardt, *Hieroclis Synecdemus: Accedunt fragmenta apud Constantinum Porphyrogennetum servata et nomina urbium mutata*. Teubner (1893), pp. 1–48; reprinted in E. Honigmann, *Le Synekdèmos d'Hiéroklès et l'opuscule géographique de Georges de Chypre: Texte, introduction, commentaire et cartes*. Corpus Bruxellense Historiae Byzantiniae, Forma Imperii Byzantini, Fascicle 1 (Brussels, 1939), pp. 12–48.

Himerius, *Orationes*: ed. A. Colonna, *Himerii declamationes et orationes cum deperditarum fragmentis* (Rome, 1951).

*Itinerarium Burdigalense*: ed. P. Geyer and O. Cuntz, in *Itineraria et alia geographica*, vol. 1. CChr., Series latina 175 (Turnholt, 1965), pp. 1–26.

Jerome, *Chronicon*: ed. R. Helm, *Eusebius Werke 7: Die Chronik des Hieronymus. Hieronymi Chronicon*. GCS 47 (2nd ed., 1956)—*Chron.* s.a. 327 to end: tr. M. D. Donalson, *A Translation of Jerome's* Chronicon *with Historical Commentary* (Lewiston, Pa., 1996), pp. 39–57.

————, *De viris illustribus*: ed. E. C. Richardson, *Hieronymus: Liber de viris inlustribus. Gennadius: Liber de viris inlustribus*. Texte und Untersuchungen 14.1 (Leipzig, 1896), pp. 1–56—tr. T. P. Halton, *Saint Jerome: On Illustrious Men*. FC 100 (Washington, D.C., 1999).

————, *Epistulae*: ed. I. Hilberg, *Sancti Eusebii Hieronymi Epistulae*, 3 vols. CSEL

54–56 (1910–1918)—ed. and tr. [French] J. Labourt, *Jérôme: Correspondance*, 8 vols. Budé (1949–1963)—selections tr. W. H. Fremantle, *St. Jerome: Letters and Select Works*. NPNF, 2nd series, 6 (1892; reprint, 1954), pp. 1–295.

——, *Vita Malchi*: ed. *PL* 23. 55–60—tr. C. White, *Early Christian Lives* (Harmondsworth, 1998), pp. 75–84.

John Chrysostom, *Epistulae ad Olympiadem*: ed. and tr. [French] A.-M. Malingrey, *Jean Chrysostome: Lettres à Olympias. Seconde édition augmentée de la Vie anonyme d'Olympias*. SChr. 13bis (1968), pp. 106–389.

John of Ephesus, *Lives of the Eastern Saints*, ed. and tr. Brooks (1923–1925).

John the Lydian, *De magistratibus reipublicae Romanae*: ed. and tr. A. C. Bandy, *Ioannes Lydus: On Powers, or The Magistracies of the Roman State. Introduction, Critical Text, Translation, Commentary, and Indices* (Philadelphia, 1983), pp. 2–257.

John Malalas, *Chronographia*: ed. L. Dindorf, *Ioannis Malalae Chronographia*. Corpus Scriptorum Historiae Byzantinae 13 (Bonn, 1831); reprinted in *PG* 97.65–717—tr. E. Jeffreys, M. Jeffreys, and R. Scott, *The Chronicle of John Malalas: A Translation*. Byzantina Australiensia 4 (Melbourne, 1986).

John of Nikiu, *Chronicon*: tr. Charles (1916).

Jordanes, *Getica*: ed. Th. Mommsen, *Iordanis Romana et Getica*. Monumenta Germaniae Historica, Auctores antiquissimi 5.1 (Berlin, 1882), pp. 53–138—tr. C. C. Mierow, *The Gothic History of Jordanes in English Version with an Introduction and a Commentary* (2nd ed., Princeton, 1915; reprint, Cambridge, 1960), pp. 51–142.

Josephus, *Bellum Iudaicum*: ed. and tr. H. St. J. Thackeray, *Josephus*, vols. 2–3. LCL (1927–1928).

Julian, *Caesares, Epigrammata, Epistulae, Epistula ad Athenienses, Epistula ad Themistium, Misopogon, Orationes*: ed. and tr. W. C. Wright, *The Works of the Emperor Julian*, 3 vols. LCL (1913–1923).

[Julius Caesar,] *Bellum Alexandrinum*: ed. and trans. A. G. Way, *Caesar: Alexandrian, African and Spanish Wars*. LCL (1955), pp. 10–135.

Justin, *Epitoma*: ed. O. Seel, *M. Iuniani Iustini Epitoma Historiarum Philippicarum Pompei Trogi: Accedunt prologi in Pompeium Trogum*. Teubner (2nd ed., 1972).

Justinian, *Novellae*: ed. R. Schoell and W. Kroll, *Novellae*. Corpus Iuris Civilis 3 (8th ed., 1963; reprint, Hildesheim, 1993).

Juvenal, *Saturae*: ed. W. V. Clausen, *A. Persi Flacci et D. Iuni Iuvenalis Saturae*. Oxford Classical Texts (Oxford, 1959)—tr. P. Green, *Juvenal: The Sixteen Satires* (Harmondsworth, 1967).

Lactantius, *De mortibus persecutorum*: ed. and tr. J. L. Creed, *Lactantius: De Mortibus Persecutorum*. Oxford Early Christian Texts (1984).

Libanius, *Epistulae* and *Epistularum commercium*: ed. R. Foerster, *Libanii opera*, vols. 10–11. Teubner (1921–1922)—selection ed. and tr. A. F. Norman, *Libanius: Autobiography and Selected Letters*, 2 vols. LCL (1992).

——, *Orationes*: ed. R. Foerster, *Libanii opera*, vols. 1–4. Teubner (1903–1908)—*Orat*. 1: ed. and tr. A. F. Norman, *Libanius: Autobiography and Selected Letters*, vol. 1. LCL (1992), pp. 52–337—*Orat*. 2, 12–24, 30, 33, 45, 47–50: ed. and tr. A. F. Norman, *Libanius: Selected Works*, 2 vols. LCL (1969–1977)—*Orat*. 3, 11, 31, 34,

36, 42–43, 58, 62: tr. A. F. Norman, *Antioch as a Centre of Hellenic Culture as Observed by Libanius.* TTH 34 (2000).

Lucian, *Icaromenippus:* ed. and tr. A. M. Harmon, *Lucian,* vol. 2. LCL (1915), pp. 268–323.

Mamertinus, *Gratiarum actio:* see *Panegyrici Latini.*

Martial, *Epigrammata:* ed. and tr. D. R. Shackleton Bailey, *Martial: Epigrams,* 3 vols. LCL (1993).

Menander Rhetor, *Treatises* I–II: ed. and tr. Russell and Wilson (1981), pp. 2–225.

Michael the Syrian, *Chronica:* ed. and tr. [French] Chabot (1899–1910).

*Mosaicarum et Romanarum legum collatio:* ed. J. Baviera, *Fontes iuris romani antejustiniani, Pars altera: Auctores* (Florence, 1968), pp. 544–89.

Nicephorus, *Breviarium:* ed. and tr. C. Mango, *Nikephoros Patriarch of Constantinople: Short History. Text, Translation, and Commentary.* Corpus Fontium Historiae Byzantinae 13 (Washington, D.C., 1990).

*Notitia Dignitatum:* ed. O. Seeck, *Notitia Dignitatum accedunt Notitia urbis Constantinopolitanae et Laterculi provinciarum* (Berlin, 1876), pp. 1–225.

*Notitia urbis Constantinopolitanae:* ed. O. Seeck, *Notitia Dignitatum accedunt Notitia urbis Constantinopolitanae et Laterculi provinciarum* (Berlin, 1876), pp. 229–43.

*Notitiae graecae episcopatuum:* ed. G. Parthey, *Hieroclis Synecdemus et Notitiae graecae episcopatuum: Accedunt Nili Doxapatrii Notitia patriarchatuum et locorum nomina immutata* (Berlin, 1866), pp. 55–261.

*Oracula Sibyllina:* ed. J. Geffcken, *Die Oracula Sibyllina.* GCS 8 (1902)—tr. J. J. Collins, "Sibylline Oracles (Second Century B.C.—Seventh Century A.D.)," in *The Old Testament Pseudepigrapha,* vol. 1, *Apocalyptic Literature and Testaments,* ed. J. H. Charlesworth (Garden City, N.Y., 1983), pp. 327–472.

*Origo Constantini imperatoris* (= *Anonymus Valesianus,* Pars prior): ed. and tr. J. C. Rolfe, *Ammianus Marcellinus,* vol. 3. LCL (1939), pp. 508–31—tr. J. Stevenson, in *From Constantine to Julian: Pagan and Byzantine Views. A Source History,* ed. S. N. C. Lieu and D. Montserrat (London and New York, 1996), pp. 43–48.

Palladius, *Dialogus de vita Iohannis Chrysostomi:* ed. and tr. [French] A.-M. Malingrey and P. Leclercq, *Palladios: Dialogue sur la vie de Jean Chrysostome,* 2 vols. SChr. 341–42 (1988)—tr. Meyer (1985).

———, *Historia Lausiaca:* ed. C. Butler, *The Lausiac History of Palladius,* vol. 2, *The Greek Text Edited with Introduction and Notes.* Texts and Studies 6.2 (1904)— tr. R. T. Meyer, *Palladius: The Lausiac History.* ACW 34 (1964).

*Panegyrici Latini:* ed. and tr. [French] E. Galletier, *Panégyriques latins,* 3 vols. Budé (1949–1955)—ed. R. A. B. Mynors, *XII Panegyrici Latini.* Oxford Classical Texts (Oxford, 1964)—tr. Nixon and Rodgers (1994), pp. 41–516.

*Parastaseis syntomoi chronikai:* ed. T. Preger, *Scriptores originum Constantinopolitanarum,* vol. 1. Teubner (1901), pp. 19–73—tr. A. Cameron and J. Herrin, *Constantinople in the Early Eighth Century: The* Parastaseis Syntomoi Chronikai (Leiden, 1984), pp. 56–165.

*Passio Basilii presbyteri:* ed. *Acta sanctorum,* Martii tomus 3 (Paris and Rome, 1865), pp. 378–81.

*Patria Konstantinoupoleos:* ed. T. Preger, *Scriptores originum Constantinopolitanarum,* vol. 2. Teubner (1907), pp. 135–283.

Petronius, *Satyricon*: ed. and tr. M. Heseltine, in *Petronius. Seneca: Apocolocyntosis*, rev. E. H. Warmington. LCL (1969), pp. 2–379.

Philostorgius, *HE = Historia ecclesiastica*: ed. J. Bidez, *Philostorgius Kirchengeschichte: Mit dem Leben des Lucian von Antiochien und den Fragmenten eines arianischen Historiographen*. GCS 21 (1913); rev. F. Winkelmann, 2nd ed. (1972), 3rd ed. (1981)—tr. E. Walford, *The Ecclesiastical History of Sozomen, Comprising a History of the Church, from A.D. 324 to A.D. 440. Translated from the Greek: with a Memoir of the Author. Also the Ecclesiastical History of Philostorgius, as Epitomised by Photius, Patriarch of Constantinople.* Bohn's Ecclesiastical Library (London, 1855), pp. 429–521.

Philostratus, *Vita Apollonii*: ed. and tr. F. C. Conybeare, *Philostratus: The Life of Apollonius of Tyana. The Epistles of Apollonius and the Treatise of Eusebius*, 2 vols. LCL (1912).

——, *Vitae sophistarum*: ed. and tr. W. C. Wright, *Philostratus and Eunapius: The Lives of the Sophists*. LCL (1921), pp. 2–315.

Photius, *Bibliotheca*: ed. and tr. [French] R. Henry, *Photius: Bibliothèque*, 8 vols., and Index, ed. J. Schamp. Budé (1959–1991).

Pliny the Elder, *Historia naturalis*: ed. and tr. H. Rackham, W. H. S. Jones, and D. E. Eichholz, *Pliny: Natural History*, 10 vols. LCL (1938–1963).

Plutarch, *Antonius, Cato Minor, Crassus, Eumenes, Lucullus, Pompey, Sulla*: ed. and tr. B. Perrin, *Plutarch's Lives*, 11 vols. LCL (1914–1926).

Procopius, *Bella, De aedificiis*: ed. and tr. H. B. Dewing, *Procopius*, 7 vols. LCL (1914–1940).

Pseudo–Dionysius, *Chronicle Part III*: tr. Witakowski (1996).

Sebeos, *Pamut'iwn*: tr. R. W. Thomson, in R. W. Thomson and J. Howard-Johnston, *The Armenian History Attributed to Sebeos*, 2 vols. TTH 31 (1999).

Severus of Antioch, *Epistulae*: tr. Brooks (1903–1904).

SHA = Scriptores Historiae Augustae, *Aurelian, Gordiani, Tyranni triginta*: ed. and tr. D. Magie, *The Scriptores Historiae Augustae*, 3 vols. LCL (1921–1932).

Sidonius, *Epistulae*: ed. and tr. W. B. Anderson, *Sidonius: Poems and Letters*, 2 vols. LCL (1936–1965).

Socrates, *HE = Historia ecclesiastica*: ed. G. C. Hansen, with M. Sirinian, *Sokrates: Kirchengeschichte*. GCS, Neue Folge, 1 (1995)—tr. A. C. Zenos, in *Socrates, Sozomenus: Church Histories*. NPNF, 2nd series, 2 (1890; reprint, 1973), pp. 1–178.

Sozomen, *HE = Historia ecclesiastica*: ed. J. Bidez, *Sozomenus: Kirchengeschichte*. GCS 50 (1960); rev. G. C. Hansen. GCS, Neue Folge, 4 (2nd ed., 1995)—tr. C. D. Hartranft, in *Socrates, Sozomenus: Church Histories*. NPNF, 2nd series, 2 (1890; reprint, 1973), pp. 236–427.

Strabo, *Geographia*: ed. and tr. H. L. Jones, *The Geography of Strabo*, 8 vols. LCL (1917–1932).

*Suda*: ed. A. Adler, *Suidae Lexicon*, 5 vols. (1928–1938).

Suetonius, *Augustus, Gaius Caligula, Vespasian*: ed. and tr. J. C. Rolfe, *Suetonius*, 2 vols. LCL (1914).

Tacitus, *Annales*: ed. C. D. Fisher, *Cornelii Taciti Annalium ab excessu divi Augusti libri*. Oxford Classical Texts (Oxford, 1906)—tr. M. Grant, *Tacitus: The Annals of Imperial Rome* (Harmondsworth, rev. ed., 1977).

Themistius, *Orationes*: ed. G. Downey and A. F. Norman, *Themistii Orationes quae supersunt*, 2 vols. Teubner (1965–1971)—*Orat.* 8.112d–120b, 10: tr. D. Moncur, in P. Heather and J. Matthews, *The Goths in the Fourth Century.* TTH 11 (1991), pp. 26–50—*Orat.* 17, 20–34: tr. R. J. Penella, *The Private Orations of Themistius* (Berkeley, 2000).

Theodoret of Cyrrhus, *HE = Historia ecclesiastica*: ed. L. Parmentier, *Theodoret: Kirchengeschichte.* GCS 19 (1911); 2nd ed. rev. F. Scheidweiler. GCS 44 (1954); 3rd ed. rev. G. C. Hansen. GCS, Neue Folge, 5 (1998)—tr. B. Jackson, in *Theodoret, Jerome, Gennadius, Rufinus: Historical Writings, Etc.* NPNF, 2nd series, 3 (1892; reprint, 1989), pp. 33–159.

————, *Historia religiosa*: ed. and tr. [French] Canivet and Leroy-Molinghen (1977–1979)—tr. R. M. Price, *A History of the Monks of Syria by Theodoret of Cyrrhus.* Cistercian Studies Series 88 (Kalamazoo, Mich., 1985).

Valerius Maximus, *Facta et dicta memorabilia*: ed. and tr. D. R. Shackleton Bailey, *Valerius Maximus: Memorable Doings and Sayings*, 2 vols. LCL (2000).

Varro, *De re rustica*: ed. and tr. W. D. Hooper, rev. H. B. Ash, *Marcus Porcius Cato: On Agriculture. Marcus Terentius Varro: On Agriculture.* LCL (1934), pp. 160–529.

*Vita Olympiadis*: ed. and tr. [French] A.-M. Malingrey, *Jean Chrysostome: Lettres à Olympias. Seconde édition augmentée de la Vie anonyme d'Olympias.* SChr. 13bis (1968), pp. 406–49—tr. E. A. Clark, *Jerome, Chrysostom, and Friends: Essays and Translations.* Studies in Women and Religion 2 (New York, 1979), pp. 127–42.

Zachariah Scholasticus, *Vita Severi Antiocheni*: ed. and tr. [French] Kugener (1903)— selections tr. R. A. D. Young, "Zacharias: The Life of Severus," in *Ascetic Behaviour in Greco-Roman Antiquity: A Sourcebook*, ed. V. L. Wimbush (Minneapolis, 1990), pp. 315–27.

Zosimus, *Historia nova*: ed. L. Mendelssohn, *Zosimi comitis et exadvocati fisci Historia nova.* Teubner (1887)—ed. and tr. [French] F. Paschoud, *Zosime: Histoire nouvelle*, 3 vols. in 5. Budé (1971–1989)—tr. R. T. Ridley, *Zosimus: New History. A Translation with Commentary.* Byzantina Australiensia 2 (Canberra, 1982).

# Bibliography

Adkin, N. (1991). "Gregory of Nazianzus and Jerome: Some Remarks." In *Georgica: Greek Studies in Honour of George Cawkwell*, ed. M. A. Flower and M. Toher, pp. 13–24. Institute of Classical Studies, Bulletin Supplement 58. London.

Aldrete, G. S. (1999). *Gestures and Acclamations in Ancient Rome.* Baltimore and London.

Anderson, J. G. C. (1903). *A Journey of Exploration in Pontus.* = *Studia Pontica* 1. Brussels.

Athanassiadi, P. (1981). *Julian and Hellenism: An Intellectual Biography.* Oxford.

Athanassiadi, P., and M. Frede (1999). "Introduction." In *Pagan Monotheism in Late Antiquity*, ed. P. Athanassiadi and M. Frede, pp. 1–20. Oxford.

Austin, N. J. E. (1972). "A Usurper's Claim to Legitimacy: Procopius in A.D. 365/6." *Rivista storica dell'antichità* 2:187–94.

Azéma, Y., ed. and tr. (1998). *Théodoret de Cyr: Correspondance IV (Collections conciliaires).* SChr. 429. Paris.

Bagnall, R. S. (1993). *Egypt in Late Antiquity.* Princeton, N.J.

Barnes, T. D. (1975). "Constans and Gratian in Rome." *Harvard Studies in Classical Philology* 79:325–33.

———. (1981). *Constantine and Eusebius.* Cambridge, Mass.

———. (1985). "Constantine and the Christians of Persia." *Journal of Roman Studies* 75:126–36. Reprinted in T. D. Barnes, *From Eusebius to Augustine. Selected Papers 1982–1993*, Chapter 6. Aldershot, 1994.

———. (1987). "Himerius and the Fourth Century." *Classical Philology* 82:206–25. Reprinted in T. D. Barnes, *From Eusebius to Augustine: Selected Papers 1982–1993*, Chapter 16. Aldershot, 1994.

———. (1993). *Athanasius and Constantius: Theology and Politics in the Constantinian Empire.* Cambridge, Mass.

———. (1997). "The Collapse of the Homoeans in the East." In *Studia Patristica Vol. XXIX, Papers Presented at the Twelfth International Conference on Patristic Studies Held in Oxford 1995. Historica, Theologica et Philosophica, Critica et Philologica*, ed. E. A. Livingstone, pp. 3–16. Leuven.

———. (1998). *Ammianus Marcellinus and the Representation of Historical Reality.* Ithaca, N.Y.

Baynes, N. H. (1937). "The Death of Julian the Apostate in a Christian Legend." *Journal of Roman Studies* 27:22–29. Reprinted in N. H. Baynes, *Byzantine Studies and Other Essays*, pp. 271–81. London, 1955.

Beaton, R. (1996). "Cappadocians at Court: Digenes and Timarion." In *Alexios I Komnenos I: Papers*, ed. M. Mullett and D. Smythe, pp. 329–38. Belfast Byzantine Texts and Translations 4.1. Belfast.

Berges, D., and J. Nollé (2000). *Tyana: Archäologisch-historische Untersuchungen zum südwestlichen Kappadokien*, 2 vols. Inschriften griechischer Städte aus Kleinasien 55.1–2. Bonn.

Bergmann, B. (1991). "Painted Perspectives of a Villa Visit: Landscape as Status and Metaphor." In *Roman Art in the Private Sphere: New Perspectives on the Architecture and Decor of the Domus, Villa, and Insula*, ed. E. K. Gazda and A. E. Haeckl, pp. 49–70. Ann Arbor, Mich.

Bernardakis, G. (1908). "Notes sur la topographie de Césarée de Cappadoce." *Echos d'Orient* 11:22–27.

Bernardi, J. (1968). *La prédication des Pères Cappadociens: La prédicateur et son auditoire*. Paris.

———, ed. and tr. (1978). *Grégoire de Nazianze: Discours 1–3*. SChr. 247. Paris.

———, ed. and tr. (1983). *Grégoire de Nazianze: Discours 4–5, Contre Julien*. SChr. 309. Paris.

———. (1988). "La composition et la publication du Discours 42 de Grégoire de Nazianze." In *Mémorial Dom Jean Gribomont (1920–1986)*, pp. 131–43. Studia Ephemeridis "Augustinianum" 27. Rome.

———, ed. and tr. (1992). *Grégoire de Nazianze: Discours 42–43*. SChr. 384. Paris.

———. (1995). *Saint Grégoire de Nazianze: Le théologien et son temps (330–390)*. Paris.

Bidez, J. (1930). *La vie de l'empereur Julien*. Paris.

———. (1934). "Aréthas de Césarée, éditeur et scholiaste." *Byzantion* 9:391–408.

Birley, A. R. (1997). *Hadrian: The Restless Emperor*. London and New York.

Bixio, R., and V. Castellani (1995). "New Typologies of Cappadocian Undergrounds: The Redoubts and the Hydric Installations." *Araştirma Sonuçlari Toplantisi* 13:271–87.

Bland, R. (1991). "The Last Coinage of Caesarea in Cappadocia." In *Ermanno A. Arslan Studia Dicata, Parte I, Monetazione greca e greco-imperiale*, ed. R. Martini and N. Vismara, pp. 213–58. Glaux 7. Milan.

Blockley, R. C. (1987). "The Division of Armenia Between the Romans and the Persians at the End of the Fourth Century A.D." *Historia* 36:222–34.

———. (1992). *East Roman Foreign Policy: Formation and Conduct from Diocletian to Anastasius*. ARCA Classical and Medieval Texts, Papers and Monographs 30. Leeds.

Blümel, W. (1985). *Die Inschriften von Iasos*, 2 vols. Inschriften griechischer Städte aus Kleinasien 28.1–2. Bonn.

de Boor, C., ed. (1978). *Georgii Monachi Chronicon*, 2 vols. Corrected ed. P. Wirth. Teubner. Stuttgart.

Booth, A. D. (1981). "The Chronology of Jerome's Early Years." *Phoenix* 35:237–59.

Bosworth, A. B. (1976). "Vespasian's Reorganization of the North-East Frontier." *Antichthon* 10:63–78.

Bosworth, A. B., and P. V. Wheatley (1998). "The Origins of the Pontic House." *Journal of Hellenic Studies* 118:155–64.

Bouffartigue, J. (1992). *L'empéreur Julien et la culture de son temps*. Collection des Etudes Augustiniennes, Série antiquité 133. Paris.

Bowersock, G. W. (1978). *Julian the Apostate*. London.

————. (1990). *Hellenism in Late Antiquity.* Jerome Lectures 18. Ann Arbor, Mich.

Brandes, W. (1989). *Die Städte Kleinasiens im 7. und 8. Jahrhundert.* Amsterdam.

Braund, D. (1984). *Rome and the Friendly King: The Character of the Client Kingship.* London and New York.

Brennecke, H. C. (1988). *Studien zur Geschichte der Homöer: Der Osten bis zum Ende der homöischen Reichskirche.* Beiträge zur Historischen Theologie 73. Tubingen.

Briant, P. (1996). *Histoire de l'empire perse de Cyrus à Alexandre.* Paris.

Brilliant, R. (1963). *Gesture and Rank in Roman Art: The Use of Gestures to Denote Status in Roman Sculpture and Coinage.* Memoirs of the Connecticut Academy of Arts and Sciences 14. New Haven, Conn.

Brock, S. P. (1994). "Greek and Syriac in Late Antique Syria." In *Literacy and Power in the Ancient World,* ed. A. K. Bowman and G. Woolf, pp. 149–60. Cambridge.

Brooks, E. W., tr. (1903–1904). *The Sixth Book of the Select Letters of Severus Patriarch of Antioch in the Syriac Version of Athanasius of Nisibis, Vol. II (Translation),* 2 vols. London and Oxford.

————, ed. and tr. (1923–1925). *John of Ephesus: Lives of the Eastern Saints.* Patrologia Orientalis 17.1, pp. 1–307, 18.4, pp. 511–698 [309–496], 19.2, pp. 151–285 [497–631]. Paris.

Broughton, T. R. S. (1938). "Roman Asia Minor." In *An Economic Survey of Ancient Rome,* ed. T. Frank, 4:499–918. Baltimore.

————. (1951). "New Evidence on Temple-Estates in Asia Minor." In *Studies in Roman Economic and Social History in Honor of A. C. Johnson,* ed. P. R. Coleman-Norton, pp. 236–50. Princeton, N.J.

Brown, P. (1992). *Power and Persuasion in Late Antiquity: Towards a Christian Empire.* Madison, Wis.

Brubaker, L. (1999). *Vision and Meaning in Ninth-Century Byzantium: Image as Exegesis in the Homilies of Gregory of Nazianzus.* Cambridge.

Bryer, A. (1993). "The Historian's *Digenes Akrites.*" In *Digenes Akrites. New Approaches to Byzantine Heroic Poetry,* ed. R. Beaton and D. Ricks, pp. 93–102. Aldershot.

Bryer, A., and D. Winfield (1985). *The Byzantine Monuments and Topography of the Pontos,* 2 vols. Dumbarton Oaks Studies 20. Washington, D.C.

Buckler, W. H., W. M. Calder, and W. K. C. Guthrie (1933). *Monumenta Asiae Minoris antiqua, Vol. IV. Monuments and Documents from Eastern Asia and Western Galatia.* Manchester.

Calder, W. M. (1956). *Monumenta Asiae Minoris antiqua, Vol. VII, Monuments from Eastern Phrygia.* Manchester.

Calvet-Sebasti, M.-A. (1996). "Comment écrire à un païen? L'exemple de Grégoire de Nazianze et de Théodoret de Cyr." In *Les apologistes chrétiens et la culture grecque,* ed. B. Pouderon and J. Dore, pp. 369–81. Théologie historique 105. Paris.

Calvet-Sebasti, M.-A., and P.-L. Gatier, ed. and tr. (1989). *Firmus de Césarée: Lettres.* SChr. 350. Paris.

Camp, J. M. (1989). "The Philosophical Schools of Roman Athens." In *The Greek Renaissance in the Roman Empire,* ed. S. Walker and A. Cameron, pp. 50–55. Institute of Classical Studies, Bulletin Supplement 55. London.

Campbell, J. M. (1922). *The Influence of the Second Sophistic on the Style of the Sermons of St. Basil the Great.* Catholic University of America Patristic Studies 2. Washington, D.C.

Canivet, P. (1977), *Le monachisme syrien selon Théodoret de Cyr.* Théologie historique 42. Paris.

Canivet, P., and A. Leroy-Molinghen, ed. and tr. (1977–1979). *Théodoret de Cyr: Histoire des moines de Syrie,* 2 vols. SChr. 234, 257. Paris.

Carrié, J.-M. (1998). "Le gouverneur romain à l'époque tardive: Les directions possibles de l'enquête." *Antiquité tardive* 6:17–30.

Cavallera, F. (1922). *Saint Jérôme, sa vie et son oeuvre,* 2 vols. Spicilegium Sacrum Lovaniense, Etudes et Documents 1–2. Louvain and Paris.

Chabot, J.-B., ed. and tr. (1899–1910). *Chronique de Michel le Syrien patriarche jacobite d'Antioche (1166–1199),* 4 vols. Paris.

Charles, R. H. (1916). *The Chronicle of John, Bishop of Nikiu, Translated from Zotenberg's Ethiopic Text.* London and Oxford.

Chaumont, M.-L. (1969). *Recherches sur l'histoire d'Arménie de l'avènement des Sassanides à la conversion du royaume.* Paris.

Cheynet, J.-C. (1986). "Les Phocas." In *Le Traité sur la guerilla (De velitatione) de l'empereur Nicéphore Phocas (963–969),* ed. G. Dagron and H. Mihaescu, pp. 289–315. Paris.

Chuvin, P. (1994). "Local Traditions and Classical Mythology in the Dionysiaca." In *Studies in the* Dionysiaca *of Nonus,* ed. N. Hopkinson, pp. 167–76. Proceedings of the Cambridge Philological Society, Supplementary Vol. 17. Cambridge.

Clarke, K. (1997). "In Search of the Author of Strabo's *Geography*." *Journal of Roman Studies* 87:92–110.

Clauss, M. (1980). *Der Magister Officiorum in der Spätantike (4.–6. Jahrhundert): Der Amt und sein Einfluß auf die kaiserliche Politik.* Munich.

Coppola, G. (1923). "L'archetipo dell'epistolario di Basilio." *Studi italiani di filologia classica* n.s. 3:137–50.

Corcoran, S. (1996). *The Empire of the Tetrarchs: Imperial Pronouncements and Government AD 284–324.* Oxford.

Coulie, B. (1985). *Les richesses dans l'oeuvre de Saint Grégoire de Nazianze: Etude littéraire et historique.* Publications de l'Institut orientaliste de Louvain 32. Louvain.

Courtney, E. (1980). *A Commentary on the Satires of Juvenal.* London.

Cumont, F., and E. Cumont (1906). *Voyage d'exploration archéologique dans le Pont et la Petite Arménie.* = *Studia Pontica* 2. Brussels.

Dagron, G. (1968). "L'empire romain d'Orient du IV$^e$ siècle et les traditions politiques de l'hellénisme: Le témoignage de Thémistios." *Travaux et mémoires* 3:1–242.

———. (1974). *Naissance d'une capitale: Constantinople et ses institutions de 330 à 451.* Bibliothèque byzantine, Etudes 7. Paris.

———. (1984). *Constantinople imaginaire: Etudes sur le recueil des* Patria. Bibliothèque byzantine, Etudes 8. Paris.

Daley, B. E. (1999). "Building a New City: The Cappadocian Fathers and the Rhetoric of Philanthropy." *Journal of Early Christian Studies* 7:431–61.

Daniélou, J. (1965). "Grégoire de Nysse à travers les lettres de saint Basile et de saint Grégoire de Nazianze." *Vigiliae Christianae* 19:31–41.

Davies, R. W. (1969). "The Supply of Animals to the Roman Army and the Remount System." *Latomus* 28:429–59.

Deferrari, R. J., ed. and tr. (1926–1934). *Saint Basil: The Letters*, 4 vols. LCL. Cambridge, Mass.

Deininger, J. (1965). *Die Provinziallandtage der römischen Kaiserzeit*. Munich and Berlin.

Delehaye, H. (1909). *Les legendes grecques des saints militaires*. Paris.

Delmaire, R. (1989a). *Les responsables des finances impériales au Bas-Empire romain (IVᵉ–VIᵉ s.)*. *Etudes prosopographiques*. Collection Latomus 203. Brussels.

———. (1989b). *Largesses sacrées et res privata: L'aerarium impérial et son administration du IVᵉ au VIᵉ siècle*. Collection de l'Ecole française de Rome 121. Paris and Rome.

———. (1997). "Les usurpateurs du Bas-Empire et le recruitement des fonctionnaires (Essai de reflexion sur les assises du pouvoir et leurs limites)." In *Usurpationen in der Spätantike: Akten des Kolloquiums "Staatsreich und Staatlichkeit" 6.–10. März 1996 Solothurn/Bern*, ed. F. Paschoud and J. Szidat, pp. 111–26. Historia, Einzelschriften 111. Stuttgart.

Demoen, K. (1993). "The Attitude Towards Greek Poetry in the Verse of Gregory Nazianzen." In *Early Christian Poetry: A Collection of Essays*, ed. J. den Boeft and A. Hilhorst, pp. 235–52. Supplements to Vigiliae Christianae 22. Leiden.

———. (1994). "Exemples d'antonomasie dans l'oraison funèbre de s. Basile de Césarée (*BHG* 245): Un nom peut en cacher un autre." *Analecta Bollandiana* 112:304–8.

———. (1996). *Pagan and Biblical Exempla in Gregory Nazianzen: A Study in Rhetoric and Hermeneutics*. CChr., Lingua Patrum 2. Turnhout.

———. (1997). "The Paradigmatic Prayer in Gregory Nazianzen." In *Studia Patristica. Vol. XXXII, Papers Presented at the Twelfth International Conference on Patristic Studies Held in Oxford 1995. Athanasius and His Opponents, Cappadocian Fathers, Other Greek Writers After Nicaea*, ed. E. A. Livingstone, pp. 96–101. Leuven.

De Salvo, L. (1983). "Basilio di Cesarea e Modesto: un vescovo di fronte al potere statale." In *Basilio di Cesarea: La sua età, la sua opera e il Basilianesimo in Sicilia. Atti del Congresso internazionale (Messina 3–6 XII 1979)*, 1:137–53. Messina.

Desideri, P. (1991). "Strabo's Cilicians." In *De Anatolia Antiqua: Eski Anadolu 1*, ed. J. des Courtils, J.-C. Moretti, and F. Planet, pp. 299–304. Bibliothèque de l'Institut français d'études anatoliennes d'Istanbul 32. Paris.

Devos, P. (1992). "Aspects de la correspondance de s. Basile de Césarée avec s. Eusèbe de Samosate et avec s. Amphiloque d'Iconium." *Analecta Bollandiana* 110:241–59.

———. (1993). "Doèk dans l'hagiographie byzantine, chez s. Augustin et dans une lettre de s. Basile." *Analecta Bollandiana* 111:69–80.

Dietz, K. (2000). "Kaiser Julian in Phönizien." *Chiron* 30:807–55.

Digeser, E. D. (2000). *The Making of a Christian Empire: Lactantius and Rome*. Ithaca, N.Y.

Dittenberger, W. (1903–1905). *Orientis graeci inscriptiones selectae: Supplementum sylloges inscriptionum graecarum*, 2 vols. Leipzig.

———. (1915–1924). *Sylloge inscriptionum graecarum*, 4 vols. 3rd ed. Leipzig.

Downey, G. (1961). *A History of Antioch in Syria from Seleucus to the Arab Conquest.* Princeton, N.J.

Drew-Bear, T. (1991). "Inscriptions de Cappadoce." In *De Anatolia Antiqua: Eski Anadolu 1*, ed. J. des Courtils, J.-C. Moretti, and F. Planet, pp. 131–49. Bibliothèque de l'Institut français d'études anatoliennes d'Istanbul 32. Paris.

Drobner, H. R. (1996). *Archaeologia Patristica. Die Schriften der Kirchenväter als Quellen der Archäologie und Kulturgeschichte: Gregor von Nyssa*, Homiliae in Ecclesiasten. Sussidi allo studio delle antichità cristiane pubblicati a cura del Pontificio Istituto di Archeologia Cristiana. Vatican City.

Dueck, D. (2000). *Strabo of Amasia: A Greek Man of Letters in Augustan Rome.* London and New York.

Duncan-Jones, R. (1982). *The Economy of the Roman Empire: Quantitative Studies.* 2nd ed. Cambridge.

Durliat, J. (1990). *De la ville antique à la ville byzantine: Le problème des subsistances.* Collection de l'Ecole française de Rome 136. Rome.

Dvornik, F. (1955). "The Emperor Julian's 'Reactionary' Ideas on Kingship." In *Late Classical and Mediaeval Studies in Honor of Albert Mathias Friend, Jr.*, ed. K. Weitzman, pp. 71–81. Princeton, N.J.

———. (1966). *Early Christian and Byzantine Political Philosophy: Origins and Background*, 2 vols. Dumbarton Oaks Studies 9. Washington, D.C.

Eadie, J. W. (1967). "The Development of Roman Mailed Cavalry." *Journal of Roman Studies* 57:161–73.

Eck, W. (1972/1973). Review of *PLRE* 1. *Zephyrus* 23–24:325–36.

Ellis, S. P. (1991). "Power, Architecture, and Decor: How the Late Roman Aristocrat Appeared to His Guests." In *Roman Art in the Private Sphere: New Perspectives on the Architecture and Decor of the Domus, Villa, and Insula*, ed. E. K. Gazda and A. E. Haeckl, pp. 117–34. Ann Arbor, Mich.

Elm, S. (2000). "A Programmatic Life: Gregory of Nazianzus' *Orations* 42 and 43 and the Constantinopolitan Elites." In *Elites in Late Antiquity*, ed. M. R. Salzman and C. Rapp. = *Arethusa* 33:411–27.

———. (2001). "Orthodoxy and the True Philosophical Life: Julian and Gregory of Nazianzus." In *Studia Patristica Vol. XXXVII. Papers Presented at the Thirteenth International Conference on Patristic Studies Held in Oxford 1999. Cappadocian Writers, Other Greek Writers*, ed. M. F. Wiles and E. J. Yarnold, with P. M. Parvis, pp. 69–85. Leuven.

Equini Schneider, E. (1994). "Classical Sites in Anatolia: 1993 Archaeological Survey in Cappadocia." *Araştirma Sonuçlari Toplantisi* 12:429–40.

———. (1995) "Classical Sites in Anatolia: 1994 Archaeological Survey in Cappadocia." *Araştirma Sonuçlari Toplantisi* 13:15–33.

Erinç, S., and N. Tunçdilek (1952). "The Agricultural Regions of Turkey." *Geographical Review* 42:179–203.

Errington, R. M. (1996). "Theodosius and the Goths." *Chiron* 26:1–27.

———. (1997). "Church and State in the First Years of Theodosius I." *Chiron* 27:21–72.

———. (2000). "Themistius and His Emperors." *Chiron* 30:861–904.

Fedwick, P. J. (1979). *The Church and the Charisma of Leadership in Basil of Caesarea.* Toronto.

———. (1981). "A Chronology of the Life and Works of Basil of Caesarea." In *Basil of Caesarea: Christian, Humanist, Ascetic. A Sixteen-Hundredth Anniversary Symposium,* ed. P. J. Fedwick, 1:3–19. Toronto.

———. (1993). *Bibliotheca Basiliana universalis: A Study of the Manuscript Tradition of the Works of Basil of Caesarea, I: The Letters.* Turnhout.

Feissel, D. (1995). "Aspects de l'immigration à Constantinople d'après les épitaphes protobyzantines." In *Constantinople and Its Hinterland: Papers from the Twenty-Seventh Spring Symposium of Byzantine Studies, Oxford, April 1993,* ed. C. Mango, G. Dagron, and G. Greatrex, pp. 367–77. Society for the Promotion of Byzantine Studies, Publications 3. Aldershot.

Forlin Patrucco, M. (1972). "Domus divina per Cappadociam." *Rivista di filologia et di istruzione classica* 100:328–33.

———. (1973). "Aspetti del fiscalismo tardo-imperiale in Cappadocia: la testimonianza di Basilo di Cesarea." *Athenaeum* n.s. 51:294–309.

———. (1983), ed. and trans. *Basilio di Cesarea: Le lettere,* vol. 1. Turin.

Fortin, E. L. (1981). "Christianity and Hellenism in Basil the Great's Address *Ad Adulescentes.*" In *Neoplatonism and Early Christian Thought: Essays in Honour of A. H. Armstrong,* ed. H. J. Blumenthal and R. A. Markus, pp. 189–203. London.

Foss, C. (1975). "The Persians in Asia Minor and the End of Antiquity." *English Historical Review* 90:721–47. Reprinted in C. Foss, *History and Archaeology of Byzantine Asia Minor,* Chapter 1. Aldershot, 1990.

———. (1977a). "Late Antique and Byzantine Ankara." *Dumbarton Oaks Papers* 31:29–87. Reprinted in C. Foss, *History and Archaeology of Byzantine Asia Minor,* Chapter 6. Aldershot, 1990.

———. (1977b). "Archaeology and the 'Twenty Cities' of Byzantine Asia." *American Journal of Archaeology* 81:469–86. Reprinted in C. Foss, *History and Archaeology of Byzantine Asia Minor,* Chapter 2. Aldershot, 1990.

———. (1979). *Ephesus After Antiquity: A Late Antique Byzantine and Turkish City.* Cambridge.

———. (1995). "Nicomedia and Constantinople." In *Constantinople and Its Hinterland. Papers from the Twenty-Seventh Spring Symposium of Byzantine Studies, Oxford, April 1993,* ed. C. Mango, G. Dagron, and G. Greatrex, pp. 181–90. Society for the Promotion of Byzantine Studies, Publications 3. Aldershot.

Fowden, G. (1991). "Constantine's Porphyry Column: The Earliest Literary Allusion." *Journal of Roman Studies* 81:119–31.

———. (1993). *Empire to Commonwealth: Consequences of Monotheism in Late Antiquity.* Princeton, N.J.

Franck, L. (1966). "Sources classiques concernant la Cappadoce." *Revue hittite et asianique* 24:5–122.

Frantz, A. (1988). *The Athenian Agora: Results of Excavations Conducted by the American School of Classical Studies at Athens, Volume XXIV. Late Antiquity: A.D. 267–700.* Princeton.

French, D. (1991). "The Definition of Territories: Cappadocia." In *La Cappadoce méridionale jusqu'à la fin de l'époque romaine. Etat des recherches. Actes du Colloque d'Istanbul (Institut Français d'Etudes Anatoliennes) 13–14 avril 1987*, ed. B. Le Guen-Pollet and O. Pelon, pp. 49–59. Paris.

de Gaiffier, B. (1956). "«Sub Iuliano Apostata» dans le martyrologe romain." *Analecta Bollandiana* 74:5–49.

Gain, B. (1985). *L'église de Cappadoce au IVᵉ siècle d'après la correspondance de Basile de Césarée (330–379)*. Orientalia Christiana Analecta 225. Rome.

Gallay, P. (1943). *La vie de saint Grégoire de Nazianze*. Lyon and Paris.

———. (1964–1967), ed. and trans. *Saint Grégoire de Nazianze: Lettres*, 2 vols. Budé. Paris.

Galsterer-Kröll, B. (1972). "Untersuchungen zu den Beinamen der Städte des Imperium Romanum." *Epigraphischen Studien* 9:44–145.

Garnsey, P. (1988). *Famine and Food Supply in the Graeco-Roman World: Responses to Risk and Crisis*. Cambridge.

Garsoïan, N. G. (1981). "Sur le titre de *Protecteur des pauvres*." *Revue des études arméniennes* n.s. 15:21–32. Reprinted in N. G. Garsoïan, *Armenia Between Byzantium and the Sasanians*, Chapter 6. London, 1985.

———. (1983). "Nerses le Grand, Basile de Césarée et Eustathe de Sébaste." *Revue des études arméniennes* n.s. 17:145–69. Reprinted in N. G. Garsoïan, *Armenia Between Byzantium and the Sasanians*, Chapter 7. London, 1985.

———. (1989). *The Epic Histories Attributed to P'awstos Buzand (Buzandaran Patmut'iwnk')*. Cambridge, Mass.

Geertz, C. (1975). "Religion as a Cultural System." In C. Geertz, *The Interpretation of Cultures: Selected Essays*, pp. 87–125. London.

———. (1983). "Centers, Kings and Charisma: Reflections on the Symbolics of Power." In C. Geertz, *Local Knowledge: Further Essays in Interpretive Anthropology*, pp. 121–46. New York.

Geyssen, J. (1998). "Presentations of Victory on the Theodosian Obelisk Base." *Byzantion* 68:335–45.

Giet, S. (1941). *Les idées et l'action sociales de saint Basile*. Paris.

Gleason, M. W. (1986). "Festive Satire: Julian's *Misopogon* and the New Year at Antioch." *Journal of Roman Studies* 76:106–19.

———. (1995). *Making Men: Sophists and Self-Presentation in Ancient Rome*. Princeton.

Goggin, T. A. (1947). *The Times of Saint Gregory of Nyssa as Reflected in the Letters and the Contra Eunomium*. Catholic University of America, Patristic Studies 79. Washington, D.C.

Gómez Villegas, N. (1997). "La corte de Constantinopla y su obispo: A propósito de la Or. 36 de Gregorio de Nacianzo." In *Vescovi e pastori in epoca teodosiana. In occasione del XVI centenario della consacrazione episcopale di S. Agostino, 396–1996. XXV Incontro di studiosi dell'antichità cristiana, Roma, 8–11 maggio 1996*, 2:359–70. Studia Ephemeridis "Augustinianum" 58. Rome.

Grattarola, P. (1986). "L'usurpazione di Procopio e la fine dei Costantinidi." *Aevum* 60:82–105.

Green, R. P. H. (1991). *The Works of Ausonius*. Oxford.

Gribomont, J. (1975). "Rome et l'Orient: Invitations et reproches de s. Basile." *Seminarium* 27 (n.s. 15):336–52.

———. (1977). "Un aristocrate révolutionnaire, évêque et moine: s. Basile." *Augustinianum* 17:179–91.

Grumel, V. (1922). "Saint Basile et le siège apostolique." *Echos d'Orient* 21:280–92.

Guidi, M. (1907). "Un ΒΙΟΣ di Costantino." *Rendiconti della Reale Accademia dei Lincei,* Classe di scienze morali, storiche e filologiche, Serie quinta, 16:304–40, 637–62.

Gwatkin, W. E., Jr. (1930). *Cappadocia as a Roman Procuratorial Province.* Princeton, N.J.

Habicht, C. (1989). "The Seleucids and Their Rivals." In *The Cambridge Ancient History, Second Edition, Volume VIII, Rome and the Mediterranean to 133 b.c.,* ed. A. E. Astin, F. W. Walbank, M. W. Frederiksen, and R. M. Ogilvie, pp. 324–87. Cambridge.

———. (1997). *Athens from Alexander to Antony,* trans. D. L. Schneider. Cambridge, Mass.

Hadjinicolaou, A. (1951). "Macellum, lieu d'exil de l'empereur Julien." *Byzantion* 21:15–22.

Haldon, J. F., and H. Kennedy (1980). "The Arab-Byzantine Frontier in the Eighth and Ninth Centuries: Military Organisation and Society in the Borderlands." *Zbornik Radova Vizantoloskog Instituta* 19:79–116.

Halfmann, H. (1979). *Die Senatoren aus dem östlichen Teil des Imperium Romanum bis zum Ende des 2. Jahrhunderts n. Chr.* Hypomnemata, Heft 58. Gottingen.

———. (1982). "Die Senatoren aus den kleinasiatischen Provinzen des römischen Reiches vom 1. bis 3. Jahrhundert (Asia, Pontus-Bithynia, Lycia-Pamphylia, Galatia, Cappadocia, Cilicia)." In *Atti del Colloquio Internazionale AIEGL su Epigrafia e ordine senatorio. Roma, 14–20 maggio 1981,* vol. 2 = *Tituli* 5:603–49. Rome.

———. (1986). *Itinera Principum: Geschichte und Typologie der Kaiserreisen im römischen Reich.* Heidelberger Althistorische Beiträge und Epigraphische Studien 2. Stuttgart.

Halkin, F. (1961). "Un second saint Gordius?" *Analecta Bollandiana* 79:5–15. Reprinted in F. Halkin, *Martyrs grecs IIe–VIIIe s.,* Chapter 7. London, 1974.

Halstead, P. (1987). "Traditional and Ancient Rural Economy in Mediterranean Europe: Plus ça change?" *Journal of Hellenic Studies* 107:77–87.

Harl, K. W. (1987). *Civic Coins and Civic Politics in the Roman East A.D. 180–275.* Berkeley.

Harl, M. (1967). "Les trois quarantaines de la vie de Moïse, schéma idéal de la vie du moine-évêque chez les Pères Cappadociens." *Revue des études grecques* 80:407–12.

Harper, R. P. (1964). "Roman Senators in Cappadocia." *Anatolian Studies* 14:163–68.

———. (1968). "Tituli Comanorum Cappadociae." *Anatolian Studies* 18:93–147.

———. (1970). "Podandus and the Via Tauri." *Anatolian Studies* 20:149–53.

Harper, R. P., and I. Bayburtluoglu (1968). "Preliminary Report on Excavations at Şar, Comana Cappadociae, in 1967." *Anatolian Studies* 18:149–58.

Harries, J. (1999). *Law and Empire in Late Antiquity.* Cambridge.

Hauschild, W.-D., tr. (1973). *Basilius von Caesarea, Briefe,* Zweiter Teil. Bibliothek der griechischen Literatur, Abteilung Patristik, Bd. 3. Stuttgart.

————, tr. (1990). *Basilius von Caesarea, Briefe,* Erster Teil. Bibliothek der griechischen Literatur, Abteilung Patristik, Bd. 32. Stuttgart.

————, tr. (1993). *Basilius von Caesarea, Briefe,* Dritter Teil. Bibliothek der griechischen Literatur, Abteilung Patristik, Bd. 37. Stuttgart.

Hauser-Meury, M.-M. (1960). *Prosopographie zu den Schriften Gregors von Nazianz.* Bonn.

Heather, P. (1991). *Goths and Romans 332–489.* Oxford.

————. (1994). "New Men for New Constantines? Creating an Imperial Elite in the Eastern Mediterranean." In *New Constantines: The Rhythm of Imperial Renewal in Byzantium, 4th–13th Centuries. Papers from the Twenty-Sixth Spring Symposium of Byzantine Studies, St Andrews, March 1992,* ed. P. Magdalino, pp. 11–33. Society for the Promotion of Byzantine Studies, Publications 2. Aldershot.

Hendy, M. F. (1985). *Studies in the Byzantine Monetary Economy c. 300–1450.* Cambridge.

Herman, G. (1987). *Ritualised Friendship and the Greek City.* Cambridge.

Hewson, R. H. (1978–1979). "The Successors of Tiridates the Great: A Contribution to the History of Armenia in the Fourth Century." *Revue des études arméniennes* n.s. 13:99–126.

Hild, F., and M. Restle (1981). *Kappadokien (Kappadokia, Charsianon, Sebasteia und Lykandos).* = *Tabula Imperii Byzantini,* ed. H. Hunger, Bd. 2. Österreichische Akademie der Wissenschaften, philosophisch-historische Klasse, Denkschriften, Bd. 149. Vienna.

Holl, K. (1904). *Amphilochius von Ikonium in seinem Verhältnis zu den grossen Kappadoziern.* Tubingen and Leipzig.

Holman, S. R. (1999a). "Healing the Social Leper in Gregory of Nyssa's and Gregory of Nazianzus's ʿπερὶ φιλοπτωχίας.'" *Harvard Theological Review* 92:283–309.

————. (1999b). "The Hungry Body: Famine, Poverty, and Identity in Basil's *Hom. 8.*" *Journal of Early Christian Studies* 7:337–63.

————. (1999c). "'You Speculate on the Misery of the Poor': Usury as Civic Injustice in Basil of Caesarea's Second Homily on Psalm 14," In *Organised Crime in Antiquity,* ed. K. Hopwood, pp. 207–28. London.

————. (2001). "Taxing Nazianzus: Gregory and the Other Julian." In *Studia Patristica, Vol. XXXVII, Papers Presented at the Thirteenth International Conference on Patristic Studies Held in Oxford 1999. Cappadocian Writers, Other Greek Writers,* ed. M. F. Wiles and E. J. Yarnold, with P. M. Parvis, pp. 103–9. Leuven.

Honigmann, E. (1936). "Un itinéraire arabe à travers le Pont." In *Mélanges Franz Cumont.* = *Annuaire de l'Institut de philologie et d'histoire orientales et slaves* 4:261–71.

————. (1961). *Trois mémoires posthumes d'histoire et de géographie de l'Orient chrétien,* ed. P. Devos. Subsidia Hagiographica 35. Brussels.

Hopwood, K. (1999a). "Ammianus Marcellinus on Isauria." In *The Late Roman World and Its Historian: Interpreting Ammianus Marcellinus,* ed. J. W. Drijvers and D. Hunt, pp. 224–35. London and New York.

————. (1999b). "Bandits Between Grandees and the State: The Structure of Order in Roman Rough Cilicia." In *Organised Crime in Antiquity*, ed. K. Hopwood, pp. 177–206. London.

Horden, P., and N. Purcell (2000). *The Corrupting Sea: A Study of Mediterranean History*. Oxford.

Howard-Johnston, J. D. (1995). "Crown Lands and the Defence of Imperial Authority in the Tenth and Eleventh Centuries." In *Bosphorus: Essays in Honour of Cyril Mango*, ed. S. Efthymiadis, C. Rapp, and D. Tsougarakis. = *Byzantinische Forschungen* 21:75–100.

Hunt, D. (1998). "Julian." In *The Cambridge Ancient History, Volume XIII: The Late Empire, A.D. 337–425*, ed. A. Cameron and P. Garnsey, pp. 44–77. Cambridge.

Hyland, A. (1990). *Equus: The Horse in the Roman World*. New Haven, Conn.

Isaac, B. (1992). *The Limits of Empire: The Roman Army in the East*. Rev. ed. Oxford.

James, S. (1988). "The *Fabricae*: State Arms Factories of the Later Roman Empire." In *Military Equipment and the Identity of Roman Soldiers: Proceedings of the Fourth Roman Military Equipment Conference*, ed. J. C. Coulston, pp. 257–331. British Archaeological Reports, International Series 394. Oxford.

Janin, R. (1964). *Constantinople byzantin: Développement urbain et répertoire topographique*. Archives de l'Orient chrétien 4. 2nd ed. Paris.

Jeffreys, E., ed. and tr. (1998). *Digenis Akritis: The Grottaferrata and Escorial Versions*. Cambridge Medieval Classics 7. Cambridge.

Jones, A. H. M. (1964). *The Later Roman Empire 284–602: A Social, Economic and Administrative Survey*, 2 or 3 vols. (continuous pagination). Oxford and Norman, Okla.

———. (1971). *The Cities of the Eastern Roman Provinces*. 2nd ed. Oxford.

Jones, C. P. (1978). *The Roman World of Dio Chrysostom*. Cambridge, Mass.

Kaibel, G., ed. (1878). *Epigrammata graeca ex lapidibus conlecta*. Berlin.

Kaplan, M. (1981). "Les grands proprietaires de Cappadoce (VIᵉ–XIᵉ siècles)." In *Le aree omogenee della civiltà rupestre nell'ambito dell'Impero Bizantino: La Cappadocia. Atti del quinto Convegno internazionale di studio sulla civiltà rupestre medioevale nell Mezzogiorno d'Italia (Lecce-Nardò, 12–16 ottobre 1979)*, ed. C. D. Fonseca, pp. 125–58. Galatina.

———. (1992). *Les hommes et la terre à Byzance du VIᵉ au XIᵉ siècle: Propriété et exploitation du sol*. Byzantina Sorbonensia 10. Paris.

Karivieri, A. (1994). "The 'House of Proclus' on the Southern Slope of the Acropolis: A Contribution." In *Post-Herulian Athens: Aspects of Life and Culture in Athens A.D. 267–529*, ed. P. Castrén, pp. 115–39. Papers and Monographs of the Finnish Institute at Athens 1. Helsinki.

Kaster, R. A. (1988). *Guardians of Language: The Grammarian and Society in Late Antiquity*. Berkeley, Calif.

Kelly, J. N. D. (1975). *Jerome: His Life, Writings, and Controversies*. London.

Kennedy, G. A. (1974). "The Sophists as Declaimers." In *Approaches to the Second Sophistic: Papers Presented at the 105th Annual Meeting of the American Philological Association*, ed. G. W. Bowersock, pp. 17–22. University Park, Pa.

———. (1983). *Greek Rhetoric Under Christian Emperors*. Princeton, N.J.

Klein, R. (1997). "Die Bedeutung von Basilius' Schrift 'Ad adolescentes' für die Erhaltung der heidnisch-griechischen Literatur." *Römische Quartalschrift* 92:162–76.

Reprinted in R. Klein, *Roma Versa per Aevum. Ausgewählte Schriften zur heidnischen und christlichen Spätantike*, ed. R. von Haehling and K. Scherberich, pp. 617–37. Spudasmata, Bd. 74. Hildesheim, 1999.

Kopecek, T. A. (1973). "The Social Class of the Cappadocian Fathers." *Church History* 42:453–66.

———. (1974). "Curial Displacements and Flight in Later Fourth Century Cappadocia." *Historia* 23:319–42.

Krautheimer, R. (1983). *Three Christian Capitals: Topography and Politics*. Berkeley, Calif.

Kreissig, H. (1967). "Hellenistische Grundbesitzverhältnisse im oströmischen Kleinasien." *Jahrbuch für Wirtschaftsgeschichte* 1:200–206.

Kugener, M.-A., ed. and tr. (1903). *Sévère patriarche d'Antioche 512–518: Textes syriaques publiés, traduits et annotés, Première partie: Vie de Sévère par Zacharie le scholastique. Patrologia Orientalis* 2:7–115. Paris.

Kuhrt, A. (1995). *The Ancient Near East c. 3000–330 BC*, 2 vols. London and New York.

Kurmann, A. (1988). *Gregor von Nazianz: Oratio 4, Gegen Julian. Ein Kommentar*. Schweizerische Beiträge zur Altertumswissenschaft 19. Basel.

Laistner, M. L. W. (1951). *Christianity and Pagan Culture in the Later Roman Empire. Together with an English Translation of John Chrysostom's* Address on Vainglory and the Right Way for Parents to Bring Up their Children. Ithaca, N.Y.

Lamberton, R. (1986). *Homer the Theologian: Neoplatonist Allegorical Reading and the Growth of the Epic Tradition*. Berkeley, Calif.

Laurent, V. (1963–1972). *Le corpus des sceaux de l'empire byzantin, Tôme V, L'église*, 3 vols. Paris.

Lemerle, P. (1971). *Le premier humanisme byzantin: Notes et remarques sur enseignement et culture à Byzance des origines au X^e siècle*. Bibliothèque byzantine, Etudes 6. Paris.

———. (1977). "Le testament d'Eustathios Boïlas (avril 1059)." In P. Lemerle, *Cinq études sur le XI^e siècle*, pp. 15–63. Paris.

Lendon, J. E. (1997). *Empire of Honour: The Art of Government in the Roman World*. Oxford.

Lenski, N. (1997). "*Initium mali Romano imperio*: Contemporary Reactions to the Battle of Adrianople." *Transactions of the American Philological Association* 127:129–68.

———. (1999a). "Assimilation and Revolt in the Territory of Isauria, from the 1st Century BC to the 6th Century AD." *Journal of the Economic and Social History of the Orient* 42:413–65.

———. (1999b). "Basil and the Isaurian Uprising of A.D. 375." *Phoenix* 53:308–29.

Liebeschuetz, J. H. W. G. (1972). *Antioch: City and Imperial Administration in the Later Roman Empire*. Oxford.

Lieu, S. N. C. (1986). "Captives, Refugees and Exiles: A Study of Cross-Frontier Civilian Movements and Contacts Between Rome and Persia from Valerian to Jovian." In *The Defence of the Roman and Byzantine East: Proceedings of a Colloquium Held at the University of Sheffield in April 1986*, ed. P. Freeman and D. Kennedy, pp. 475–505. British Archaeological Reports, International Series 297. Oxford.

Lim, R. (1995). *Public Disputation, Power, and Social Order in Late Antiquity.* Berkeley, Calif.

MacMullen, R. (1988). *Corruption and the Decline of Rome.* New Haven, Conn.

———. (1990). *Changes in the Roman Empire: Essays in the Ordinary.* Princeton, N.J.

Magdalino, P. (1993). "*Digenes Akrites* and Byzantine Literature: The Twelfth-Century Background to the Grottaferrata Version." In *Digenes Akrites: New Approaches to Byzantine Heroic Poetry*, ed. R. Beaton and D. Ricks, pp. 1–14. Aldershot.

Magie, D. (1950). *Roman Rule in Asia Minor to the End of the Third Century After Christ*, 2 vols. Princeton, N.J.

Mango, C. (1985). *Le développement urbain de Constantinople (IVᵉ–VIIᵉ siècles).* Travaux et Mémoires du Centre de recherche d'histoire et civilisation de Byzance. Collège de France, Monographies 2. Paris.

———. (1995). "The Water Supply of Constantinople." In *Constantinople and Its Hinterland: Papers from the Twenty-Seventh Spring Symposium of Byzantine Studies, Oxford, April 1993*, ed. C. Mango, G. Dagron, and G. Greatrex, pp. 9–18. Society for the Promotion of Byzantine Studies, Publications 3. Aldershot.

Maraval, P., ed. and tr. (1971). *Grégoire de Nysse: Vie de sainte Macrine.* SChr. 178. Paris.

———. (1975). "Nysse en Cappadoce." *Revue d'histoire et de philosophie religieuses* 55:237–47.

———. (1988). "La date de la mort de Basile de Césarée." *Revue des études augustiniennes* 34:25–38.

———, ed. and tr. (1990). *Grégoire de Nysse: Lettres.* SChr. 363. Paris.

Maricq, A. (1958). "Classica et orientalia, 5: Res gestae divi Saporis." *Syria* 35:295–360.

Mathews, T. F., and A.-C. D. Mathews (1997). "Islamic-Style Mansions in Byzantine Cappadocia and the Development of the Inverted T-Plan." *Journal of the American Society of Architectural Historians* 56:294–315.

Mathieu, J.-M. (1988). "Grégoire de Nazianze et Jérôme: Commentaire de l'*In Ephesios* 3,5,32." In *Jérôme entre l'Occident et l'Orient: XVIᵉ centenaire du départ de saint Jérôme de Rome et de son installation à Bethléem. Actes du Colloque de Chantilly (septembre 1986)*, ed. Y.-M. Duval, pp. 115–27. Paris.

Mathisen, R. W. (1997). "Barbarian Bishops and the Churches 'In barbaricis gentibus' During Late Antiquity." *Speculum* 72:664–97.

Matthews, J. (1975). *Western Aristocracies and Imperial Court A.D. 364–425.* Oxford.

———. (1989). *The Roman Empire of Ammianus.* Baltimore.

May, G. (1971). "Die Chronologie des Lebens und der Werke des Gregor von Nyssa." In *Ecriture et culture philosophique dans la pensée de Grégoire de Nysse*, ed. M. Harl, pp. 51–66. Leiden.

———. (1973). "Basilios der Grosse und der römische Staat." In *Bleibendes im Wandel der Kirchengeschichte: Kirchenhistorische Studien*, ed. B. Moeller and G. Ruhbach, pp. 47–70. Tubingen.

McCormick, M. (1986). *Eternal Victory: Triumphal Rulership in Late Antiquity, Byzantium, and the Early Medieval West.* Cambridge.

McLynn, N. (1994). *Ambrose of Milan: Church and Court in a Christian Capital.* Berkeley, Calif.

———. (1997). "The Voice of Conscience: Gregory Nazianzen in Retirement." In

*Vescovi e pastori in epoca teodosiana. In occasione del XVI centenario della consacrazione episcopale di S. Agostino, 396–1996. XXV Incontro di studiosi dell'antichità cristiana, Roma, 8–11 maggio 1996,* 2:299–308. Studia Ephemeridis "Augustinianum" 58. Rome.

――――. (1998). "A Self-Made Holy Man: The Case of Gregory Nazianzen." *Journal of Early Christian Studies* 6:463–83.

Meineke, A., ed. (1849). *Stephani Byzantii Ethnicorum quae supersunt.* Berlin.

Meredith, A. (1998). "The Three Cappadocians on Beneficence: A Key to Their Audiences." In *Preacher and Audience: Studies in Early Christian and Byzantine Homiletics,* ed. M. B. Cunningham and P. Allen, pp. 89–104. A New History of the Sermon 1. Leiden.

Meyer, R. T., tr. (1985). *Palladius: Dialogue on the Life of St. John Chrysostom.* ACW 45. New York.

Millar, F. (1977). *The Emperor in the Roman World (31 B.C.–A.D. 337).* London.

Mitchell, S. (1993). *Anatolia: Land, Men, and Gods in Asia Minor,* 2 vols. Oxford.

Mitford, T. B. (1974). "Some Inscriptions from the Cappadocian *Limes.*" *Journal of Roman Studies* 64:160–75.

Moffatt, A. (1972). "The Occasion of St Basil's *Address to Young Men.*" *Antichthon* 6:74–86.

Moreschini, C. (1988). "*Praeceptor meus.* Tracce dell'insegnamento di Gregorio Nazianzeno in Gerolamo." In *Jérôme entre l'Occident et l'Orient: XVI^e centenaire du départ de saint Jérôme de Rome et de son installation à Bethléem: Actes du Colloque de Chantilly (septembre 1986),* ed. Y.-M. Duval, pp. 129–38. Paris.

Moreschini, C., and P. Gallay, ed. and tr. (1985). *Grégoire de Nazianze: Discours 32–37.* SChr. 318. Paris.

――――, ed. and tr. (1990). *Grégoire de Nazianze: Discours 38–41.* SChr. 358. Paris.

Morris, R. (1976). "The Powerful and the Poor in Tenth-Century Byzantium: Law and Reality." *Past and Present* 73:3–27.

Mossay, J. (1977). "Gregor von Nazianz im Konstantinopel (379–381 A.D.)." *Byzantion* 47:223–38.

――――. (1982). "Note sur Héron-Maxime, écrivain ecclésiastique." *Analecta Bollandiana* 100:229–36.

Mossay, J., and G. Lafontaine, ed. and tr. (1980). *Grégoire de Nazianze: Discours 20–23.* SChr. 270. Paris.

Mullett, M. (1992). "The Language of Diplomacy." In *Byzantine Diplomacy: Papers from the Twenty-Fourth Spring Symposium of Byzantine Studies, Cambridge, March 1990,* ed. J. Shepard and S. Franklin, pp. 203–16. Society for the Promotion of Byzantine Studies, Publications 1. Aldershot.

Muraviev, A. (2001). "The Syriac Julian Romance as a Source of the Life of St. Basil the Great." In *Studia Patristica, Vol. XXXVII, Papers Presented at the Thirteenth International Conference on Patristic Studies Held in Oxford 1999. Cappadocian Writers, Other Greek Writers,* ed. M. F. Wiles and E. J. Yarnold, with P. M. Parvis, pp. 240–49. Leuven.

Nau, F., ed. and tr. (1912). *Jean Rufus, évêque de Maiouma: Plérophories. Témoignages et révélations contre le Concile de Chalcedoine. Patrologia Orientalis* 8:1–208. Paris.

Nauck, A., ed. (1964). *Tragicorum graecorum fragmenta*. Reprinted with Supplementum, ed. B. Snell. Hildesheim.

Negev, A. (1969). "The Inscription of the Emperor Julian at Ma'ayan Barukh." *Israel Exploration Journal* 19:170–73.

Nicholson, O. (1994). "The 'Pagan Churches' of Maximinus Daia and Julian the Apostate." *Journal of Ecclesiastical History* 45:1–10.

Nicholson, O., and C. Nicholson (1993). "The Aqueduct at Amasya in Pontus." *Anatolian Studies* 43:143–46.

Nixon, C. E. V., and B. S. Rodgers (1994). *In Praise of Later Roman Emperors: The Panegyrici Latini. Introduction, Translation, and Historical Commentary with the Latin Text of R. A. B. Mynors*. Berkeley, Calif.

Norris, F. W. (1991). *Faith Gives Fullness to Reasoning: The Five Theological Orations of Gregory Nazianzen*. Tr. L. Wickham and F. Williams. Supplements to Vigiliae Christianae 13. Leiden.

von Oppenheim, M. F., and H. Lucas (1905). "Griechische und lateinische Inschriften aus Syrien, Mesopotamien und Kleinasien." *Byzantinische Zeitschrift* 14:1–72.

Pack, E. (1986). *Städte und Steuern in der Politik Julians: Untersuchungen zu den Quellen eines Kaiserbildes*. Collection Latomus 194. Brussels.

Peek, W., ed. (1955). *Griechische Vers-Inschriften, Band I, Grab-Epigramme*. Berlin.

Pertusi, A., ed. (1952). *Constantino Porfirogenito: De thematibus. Introduzione—Testo critico—Commento*. Studi et Testi 160. Vatican City.

Petit, P. (1955). *Libanius et la vie municipale à Antioche au IV^e siècle après J.-C.* Institut français d'archéologie de Beyrouth, Bibliothèque archéologique et historique 62. Paris.

———. (1956). *Les étudiants de Libanius*. Etudes prosopographiques 1. Paris.

———. (1957). "Les sénateurs de Constantinople dans l'oeuvre de Libanius." *L'antiquité classique* 26:347–82.

Pietri, C. (1972). "Damase et Théodose: Communion orthodoxe et géographie politique." In *Epektasis: Mélanges patristiques offerts au Cardinal Jean Daniélou*, ed. J. Fontaine and C. Kannengiesser, pp. 627–34. Paris. Reprinted in C. Pietri, *Christiana respublica: Eléments d'une enquête sur le christianisme antique*, 1:347–54. Collection de l'Ecole française de Rome 234. Paris and Rome, 1997.

Pitra, J. B., ed. (1864–1868). *Iuris ecclesiastici graecorum historia et monumenta iussu Pii IX. pont. max.*, 2 vols. Rome.

de Planhol, X. (1981). "La Cappadoce: Formation et transformations d'un concept géographique." In *Le aree omogenee della civiltà rupestre nell'ambito dell'Impero Bizantino: La Cappadocia. Atti del quinto Convegno internazionale di studio sulla civiltà rupestre medioevale nell Mezzogiorno d'Italia (Lecce-Nardò, 12–16 ottobre 1979)*, ed. C. D. Fonseca, pp. 25–38. Galatina.

Pouchet, R. (1988). "Essai de décryptage de la Lettre 213 de s. Basile." In *Mémorial Dom Jean Gribomont (1920–1986)*, pp. 487–502. Studia Ephemeridis "Augustinianum" 27. Rome.

———. (1992a). *Basile le Grand et son univers d'amis d'après sa correspondance: Une stratégie de communion*. Studia Ephemeridis "Augustinianum" 36. Rome.

———. (1992b). "La date de l'élection épiscopale de saint Basile et celle de sa mort." *Revue d'histoire ecclésiastique* 87:5–33.

Purcell, N. (1995). "The Roman *Villa* and the Landscape of Production." In *Urban Society in Roman Italy*, ed. T. J. Cornell and K. Lomas, pp. 151–79. London.

Rebenich, S. (1997). "Asceticism, Orthodoxy and Patronage: Jerome in Constantinople." In *Studia Patristica, Vol. XXXIII, Papers Presented at the Twelfth International Conference on Patristic Studies Held in Oxford 1995. Augustine and His Opponents, Jerome, Other Latin Fathers After Nicaea, Orientalia*, ed. E. A. Livingstone, pp. 358–377. Leuven.

Rémy, B. (1986). *L'évolution administrative de l'Anatolie aux trois premiers siècles de notre ère.* Collection du Centre d'études romaines et gallo-romaines, nouvelle serie 5. Lyon.

Riccobono, S., ed. (1941). *Fontes iuris romani antejustiniani, Pars prima: Leges.* Florence.

Ritter, A. M. (1965). *Das Konzil von Konstantinopel und sein Symbol: Studien zur Geschichte und Theologie des II. Ökumenischen Konzils.* Forschungen zur Kirchen- und Dogmengeschichte 15. Göttingen.

Robert, L. (1963). *Noms indigènes dans l'Asie-Mineure gréco-romaine: Première partie.* Bibliothèque archéologique et historique de l'Institut français d'archéologie d'Istanbul. Paris.

———. (1974). "Géographie et philologie ou la terre et le papier." In L. Robert, *Opera minora selecta: Epigraphie et antiquités grecques*, 4:383–403. Amsterdam.

———. (1975). "Une nouvelle inscription grecque de Sardes: Règlement de l'autorité perse relatif à un culte de Zeus." *Comptes rendus de l'Académie des inscriptions*, pp. 306–30. Reprinted in L. Robert, *Opera minora selecta: Epigraphie et antiquités grecques*, 5:211–49. Amsterdam, 1989.

———. (1977). "La titulature de Nicée et de Nicomédie: La gloire et la haine." *Harvard Studies in Classical Philology* 81:1–39. Reprinted in L. Robert, *Opera minora selecta: Epigraphie et antiquités grecques*, 5:485–509. Amsterdam, 1989.

Rodley, L. (1985). *Cave Monasteries of Byzantine Cappadocia.* Cambridge.

Rossiter, J. J. (1989). "Roman Villas of the Greek East and the Villa in Gregory of Nyssa *Ep.* 20." *Journal of Roman Archaeology* 2:101–10.

Rott, H. (1908). *Kleinasiatische Denkmäler aus Pisidien, Pamphylien, Kappadokien und Lydien.* Studien über christliche Denkmäler, Neue Folge 5–6. Leipzig.

Roueché, C. (1989a). *Aphrodisias in Late Antiquity: The Late Roman and Byzantine Inscriptions Including Texts from the Excavations at Aphrodisias Conducted by Kenan T. Erim.* Journal of Roman Studies Monographs 5. London.

———. (1989b). "Floreat Perge." In *Images of Authority: Papers Presented to Joyce Reynolds on the Occasion of Her Seventieth Birthday*, ed. M. M. MacKenzie and C. Roueché, pp. 206–28. Proceedings of the Cambridge Philological Society, Supplementary Vol. 16. Cambridge.

———. (1998). "The Functions of the Governor in Late Antiquity: Some Observations." *Antiquité tardive* 6:31–36.

Rougé, J., ed. and tr. (1966). *Expositio totius mundi et gentium.* SChr. 124. Paris.

Rousseau, P. (1994). *Basil of Caesarea.* Berkeley, Calif.

Rousselle, A. (1983). "Parole et inspiration: Le travail de la voix dans le monde romain." *History and Philosophy of the Life Sciences* 5:129–57.

Ruether, R. R. (1969). *Gregory of Nazianzus: Rhetor and Philosopher.* Oxford.

Ruge, W. (1919). "Kappadokia." In *Paulys Real-Encyclopädie der classischen Altertumswissenschaft.* Neue Bearbeitung begonnen von G. Wissowa, ed. W. Kroll, vol. 10: col. 1910–17. Stuttgart.

Russell, D. A. (1996). *Libanius, Imaginary Speeches: A Selection of Declamations.* London.

Russell, D. A., and N. G. Wilson, ed. and tr. (1981). *Menander Rhetor.* Oxford.

Safran, L. (1993). "Points of View: The Theodosian Obelisk Base in Context." *Greek, Roman, and Byzantine Studies* 34:409–35.

Sartre, M. (1991). *L'Orient romain: Provinces et sociétés provinciales en Méditerranée orientale d'Auguste aux Sévères (31 avant J.-C–235 après J.-C.).* Paris.

Scharf, R. (1990). "Der *comes sacri stabuli* in der Spätantike." *Tyche* 5:135–47.

Schmidt, P. L. (1989). "Eutropius" and "Rufius Festus, *Breviarum de breviario rerum gestarum populi Romani.*" In *Restauration und Ernauerung: Die lateinische Literatur von 284 bis 374 n. Chr.,* ed. R. Herzog, pp. 201–7, 207–10. Handbuch der lateinischen Literatur der Antike, ed. R. Herzog and P. L. Schmidt, vol. 5. Handbuch der Altertumswissenschaft, Achte Abteilung, Fünfter Band. Munich.

Schucan, L. (1973). *Das Nachleben von Basilius Magnus «Ad adolescentes»: Ein Beitrag zur Geschichte des christlichen Humanismus.* Travaux d'Humanisme et Renaissance 133. Geneva.

Schulten, A. (1906). "Zwei Erlasse des Kaisers Valens über die Provinz Asia." *Jahreshefte des österreichischen archäologischen Institutes* 9:40–70.

Schwartz, E., ed. (1922–1923). *Acta conciliorum oecumenicorum 1.4: Concilium universale Ephesenum. Collectionis Casinensis sive Synodici a Rustico diacono compositi pars altera.* Berlin and Leipzig.

———, ed. (1933–1935). *Acta conciliorum oecumenicorum, Tomus alter, Volumen primum.* Berlin and Leipzig.

Scicolone, S. (1982). "Basilio e la sua organizzazione dell'attività assistenziale a Cesarea." *Civiltà classica et cristiana* 3:353–72.

Scourfield, J. H. D. (1986). "Jerome, Antioch, and the Desert: A Note on Chronology." *Journal of Theological Studies* n.s. 37:117–21.

Seeck, O. (1906). *Die Briefe des Libanius zeitlich geordnet.* Leipzig.

———. (1919). *Regesten der Kaiser und Päpste für die Jahre 311 bis 476 n. Chr. Vorarbeit zu einer Prosopographie der christlichen Kaiserzeit.* Stuttgart.

Seferis, G. (1966). *On the Greek Style: Selected Essays in Poetry and Hellenism,* tr. R. Warner and T. D. Frangopoulos. Boston and Toronto.

Shahîd, I. (1984). *Byzantium and the Arabs in the Fourth Century.* Washington, D.C.

Shaw, B. D. (1990). "Bandit Highlands and Lowland Peace: The Mountains of Isauria-Cilicia." *Journal of the Economic and Social History of the Orient* 33:199–233, 237–70.

Sheppard, A. R. R. (1984–1986). "*Homonoia* in the Greek Cities of the Roman Empire." *Ancient Society* 15–17:229–52.

Sivan, H. (1993). *Ausonius of Bordeaux: Genesis of a Gallic Aristocracy.* London and New York.

Skinner, A. (2000). "The Birth of a 'Byzantine' Senatorial Perspective." In *Elites in Late Antiquity,* ed. M. R. Salzman and C. Rapp. = *Arethusa* 33:363–77.

Smith, R. (1995). *Julian's Gods: Religion and Philosophy in the Thought and Action of Julian the Apostate*. London and New York.

———. (1999). "Telling Tales: Ammianus' Narrative of the Persian Expedition of Julian." In *The Late Roman World and Its Historian: Interpreting Ammianus Marcellinus*, ed. J. W. Drijvers and D. Hunt, pp. 89–104. London and New York.

Smith, R. R. R. (1998). "Cultural Choice and Political Identity in Honorific Portrait Statues in the Greek East in the Second Century A.D." *Journal of Roman Studies* 88:56–93.

Snee, R. (1985). "Valens' Recall of the Nicene Exiles and Anti-Arian Propaganda." *Greek, Roman, and Byzantine Studies* 26:395–419.

Stadter, P. A. (1980). *Arrian of Nicomedia*. Chapel Hill, N.C.

Sullivan, R. D. (1980). "The Dynasty of Cappadocia." In *Aufstieg und Niedergang der römischen Welt*, vol. 2.7.2, ed. H. Temporini, pp. 1125–68. Berlin and New York.

———. (1990). *Near Eastern Royalty and Rome, 100–30 BC*. Phoenix, Supplementary Vol. 24. Toronto.

Sydenham, E. A. (1933). *The Coinage of Caesarea in Cappadocia*. London.

Syme, R. (1971). *Emperors and Biography: Studies in the Historia Augusta*. Oxford.

———. (1980). "An Eccentric Patrician." *Chiron* 10:427–48. Reprinted in R. Syme, *Roman Papers*, vol. 3, ed. A. R. Birley, pp. 1316–36. Oxford, 1984.

———. (1982). "The Career of Arrian." *Harvard Studies in Classical Philology* 86:181–211. Reprinted in R. Syme, *Roman Papers*, vol. 4, ed. A. R. Birley, pp. 21–49. Oxford, 1988.

———. (1995). *Anatolica: Studies in Strabo*, ed. A. Birley. Oxford.

Szymusiak, J. M. (1966). "Pour une chronologie des discours de s. Grégoire de Nazianze." *Vigiliae Christianae* 20:183–89.

———. (1972). "Les sites de Nazianze et Karbala." In *Epektasis: Mélanges patristiques offerts au Cardinal Jean Daniélou*, ed. J. Fontaine and C. Kannengiesser, pp. 545–48. Paris.

Taylor, J. (1973). "St Basil the Great and Pope Damasus I—I" and "St Basil the Great and Pope St Damasus I—Part II." *Downside Review* 91:186–203, 262–74.

Teja, R. (1974). *Organización económica y social de Capadocia en el siglo IV, según los Padres Capadocios*. Salamanca.

———. (1980). "Die römische Provinz Kappadokien in der Prinzipatszeit." In *Aufstieg und Niedergang der römischen Welt*, vol. 2.7.2, ed. H. Temporini, pp. 1083–1124. Berlin and New York.

Teske, D., tr. (1997). *Gregor von Nyssa: Briefe*. Bibliothek der griechischen Literatur, Abteilung Patristik, Bd. 43. Stuttgart.

Thierry, N. (1977). "Un problème de continuité ou de rupture: La Cappadoce entre Rome, Byzance et les Arabes." *Comptes rendus de l'Académie des inscriptions et belles-lettres*, pp. 98–144.

———. (1981a). "Avanos-Vénasa—Cappadoce." In *Geographica Byzantina*, ed. H. Ahrweiler, pp. 119–29. Byzantina Sorbonensia 3. Paris.

———. (1981b). "Monuments de Cappadoce de l'antiquité romaine au Moyen Age byzantin." In *Le aree omogenee della civiltà rupestre nell'ambito dell'Impero Bizantino: La Cappadocia. Atti del quinto Convegno internazionale di studio sulla civiltà rupestre medioevale nell Mezzogiorno d'Italia (Lecce-Nardò, 12–16 ottobre 1979)*, ed. C. D. Fonseca, pp. 39–73. Galatina.

Thomson, R. W., and J. Howard-Johnston, tr. (1999). *The Armenian History Attributed to Sebeos*, 2 vols. TTH 31. Liverpool.

Thurn, H., ed. (1973). *Ioannis Scylitzae Synopsis historiarum*. Corpus Fontium Historiae Byzantinae, Series Berolinensis 5. Berlin and New York.

Van Dam, R. (1985a). *Leadership and Community in Late Antique Gaul*. Berkeley, Calif.

———. (1985b). "From Paganism to Christianity at Late Antique Gaza." *Viator* 16:1–20.

———. (1986). "Emperor, Bishops, and Friends in Late Antique Cappadocia." *Journal of Theological Studies* n.s. 37:53–76.

———. (1995). "Self-Representation in the Will of Gregory of Nazianzus." *Journal of Theological Studies* n.s. 46:118–48.

———. (1996). "Governors of Cappadocia During the Fourth Century." In *Late Antiquity and Byzantium*, ed. R. W. Mathisen. = *Medieval Prosopography* 17:7–93.

———. (1998). Review of C. White, tr., *Gregory of Nazianzus: Autobiographical Poems* (Cambridge, 1996). *Medieval Review* 98.05.09. Available at www.hti.umich.edu/t/tmr.

Vanderspoel, J. (1995). *Themistius and the Imperial Court: Oratory, Civic Duty, and Paideia from Constantius to Theodosius*. Ann Arbor, Mich.

———. (1999). "Correspondence and Correspondents of Julius Julianus." *Byzantion* 69:396–478.

Varinlioglu, G. (1988). "Une inscription de Mercure aux Portes de Cilicie." *Epigraphica Anatolica* 11:59–64.

Vinson, M. (1994). "Gregory Nazianzen's Homily 15 and the Genesis of the Christian Cult of the Maccabean Martyrs." *Byzantion* 64:166–92.

Vogler, C. (1992). "L'administration impériale dans la correspondance de saint Basile et saint Grégoire de Nazianze." In *Institutions, société et vie politique dans l'empire romain au IVᵉ siècle ap. J.-C. Actes de la table ronde autour de l'oeuvre d'André Chastagnol (Paris, 20–21 janvier 1989)*, ed. M. Christol, S. Demougin, Y. Duval, C. Lepelley, and L. Pietri, pp. 447–64. Collection de l'Ecole française de Rome 159. Rome.

de Vries, W. (1981). "Die Obsorge des hl. Basilius um die Einheit der Kirche im Streit mit Papst Damasus." *Orientalia Christiana Periodica* 47:55–86.

Vryonis, S., Jr. (1957). "The Will of a Provincial Magnate, Eustathius Boilas (1059)." *Dumbarton Oaks Papers* 11: 263–77. Reprinted in S. Vryonis, Jr., *Byzantium: Its Internal History and Relations with the Muslim World. Collected Studies*, Chapter 5. London, 1971.

———. (1971). *The Decline of Medieval Hellenism in Asia Minor and the Process of Islamization from the Eleventh Through the Fifteenth Century*. Berkeley.

Weiss, P. (1985). "Argaios / Erciyas Daği—Heiliger Berg Kappadokiens, Monumente und Ikonographie." *Jahrbuch für Numismatik und Geldgeschichte* 35:21–48.

Whitby, M. (1988). *The Emperor Maurice and His Historian: Theophylact Simocatta on Persian and Balkan Warfare*. Oxford.

————. (1995). "Recruitment in Roman Armies from Justinian to Heraclius (*ca.* 565–615)." In *The Byzantine and Early Islamic Near East, III: States, Resources and Armies. Papers of the Third Workshop on Late Antiquity and Early Islam,* ed. A. Cameron, pp. 61–124. Studies in Late Antiquity and Early Islam 1. Princeton, N.J.

Wiemer, H.-U. (1995). *Libanios und Julian: Studien zum Verhältnis von Rhetorik und Politik im vierten Jahrhundert n. Chr.* Vestigia, Beitrage zur alten Geschichte 46. Munich.

Wilson, N. G., tr. (1975). *Saint Basil on the Value of Greek Literature.* London.

Witakowski, W., tr. (1996). *Pseudo-Dionysius of Tel-Mahre, Chronicle (Known Also as the Chronicle of Zuqnin) Part III.* TTH 22. Liverpool.

Wolfram, H. (1988). *History of the Goths,* tr. T. J. Dunlap. Berkeley, Calif.

Woods, D. (1992). "The Martyrdom of the Priest Basil of Ancyra." *Vigiliae Christianae* 46:31–39.

————. (2001). "Dating Basil of Caesarea's Correspondence with Arintheus and His Widow." In *Studia Patristica, Vol. XXXVII, Papers Presented at the Thirteenth International Conference on Patristic Studies Held in Oxford 1999. Cappadocian Writers, Other Greek Writers,* ed. M. F. Wiles and E. J. Yarnold, with P. M. Parvis, pp. 301–7. Leuven.

Wyss, B. (1946). "Zu Gregor von Nazianz." In *Phyllobolia für Peter Von der Mühl zum 60. Geburtstag am 1. August 1945,* pp. 153–83. Basel.

————. (1983). "Gregor II (Gregor von Nazianz)." In *Reallexikon für Antike und Christentum: Sachwörterbuch zur Auseinandersetzung des Christentums mit der antiken Welt,* ed. E. Dassmann et al., vol. 12, col. 793–863. Stuttgart.

Yourcenar, M. (1954). *Memoirs of Hadrian,* tr. G. Frick. New York.

Ziegler, R. (1996). "Civic Coins and Imperial Campaigns." In *The Roman Army in the East,* ed. D. L. Kennedy, pp. 119–134. Journal of Roman Archaeology, Supplementary Series 18. Ann Arbor, Mich.

Zilliacus, H. (1949). *Untersuchungen zu den abstrakten Anredeformen und Höflichkeitstiteln im Griechischen.* Societas Scientiarum Fennica, Commentationes Humanarum Litterarum 15.3. Helsinki.

# Index

Subentries are arranged chronologically.